To my Friend Randy

Merry Christmas 1978

Love Ray

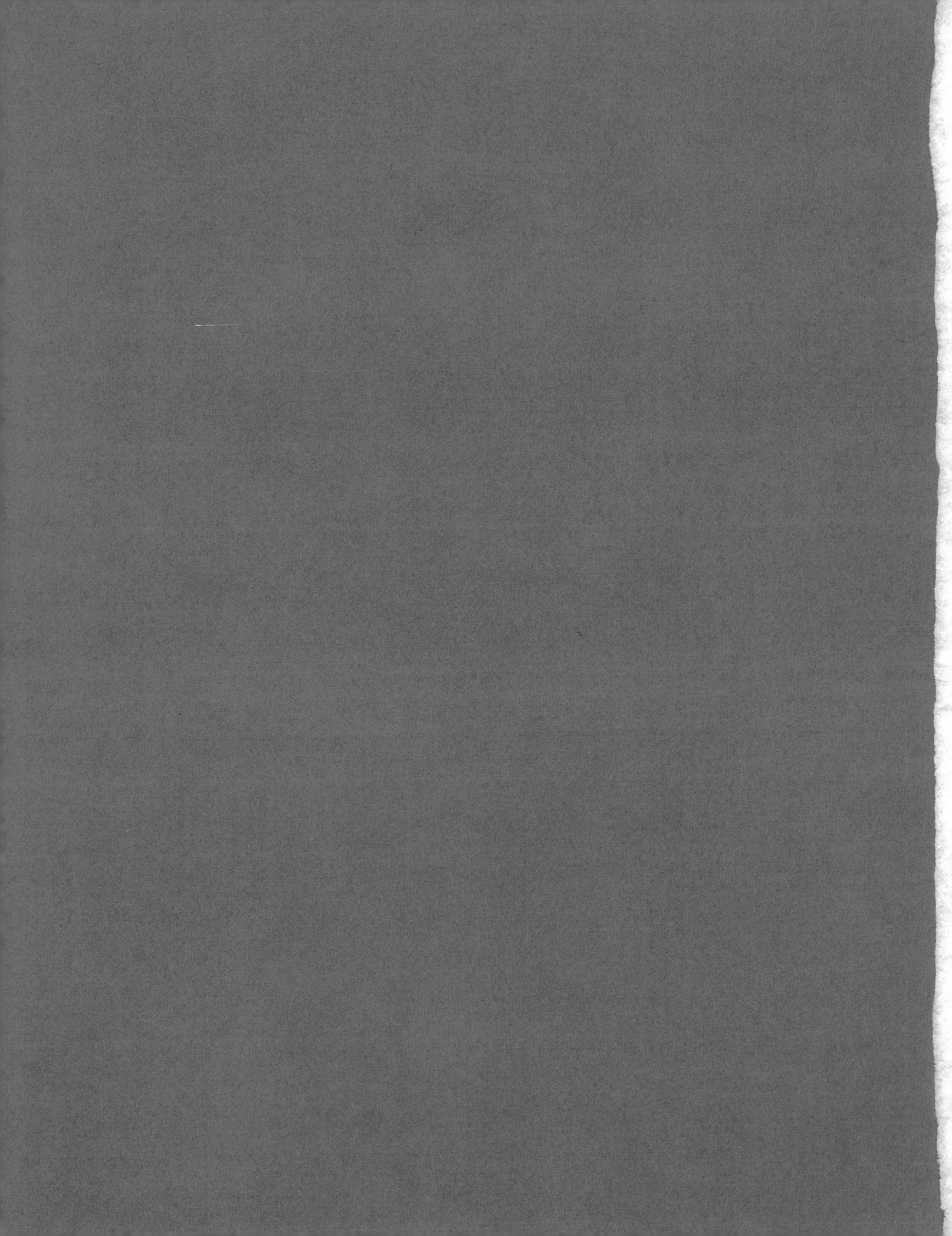

THE GUITAR BOOK

Tom Wheeler

THE GUITAR BOOK

A Handbook for Electric and Acoustic Guitarists

Revised and Enlarged Edition

HARPER & ROW, PUBLISHERS
New York, Evanston, San Francisco, London

 For information address Harper & Row, Publishers, Inc., 10 East 53rd Street, New York, N.Y. 10022. Published simultaneously in Canada by Fitzhenry & Whiteside Limited, Toronto.

Designed by C. Linda Dingler

LIBRARY OF CONGRESS CATALOG CARD NUMBER: 77-11791

ISBN: 0-06-014579-X

78 79 80 81 82 10 9 8 7 6 5 4 3 2 1

Dedicated with affection
to the heroes of my childhood:
my father and Chuck Berry

Contents

French guitar by Bernard of Paris; painting on back entitled *L'Amour Ingenieux. The Metropolitan Museum of Art, The Crosby Brown Collection of Musical Instruments, 1889*

Acknowledgments for the Original Edition

J. Richard Forbes is a West Coast sports photographer known mainly for his graphic work in aquatics, skiing, and racing of all kinds. Though he and his camera have ventured into other fields (wine-making, firefighting, fashion, and so on), this is the first time he's approached musical instruments. It was his idea to "suspend" the guitars in most of the full-length shots, and he designed the special apparatus himself. His gift for capturing the essence of uncluttered beauty befits a study of musical instruments. The book owes much to his talent.

Writers dream about editors like Peter Burling. He started working on the manuscript as soon as the project was approved, and he didn't stop until publication day. With much ability and enthusiasm, and treating me as a partner and friend, he helped me turn the mountain of papers and cassettes on my bedroom floor into a book.

Larry and Pam Smith are two friends who really came through, having somehow managed to make it all the way to the end of an extremely wordy first draft, offering many suggestions about style, phrasing and grammar.

Julius Bellson is a former officer and Walt Fuller is a chief engineer at Gibson Inc. Between them they have over seventy years experience with the company. Mr. Bellson donated a full day's interview and tour of

Gibson's plant in Kalamazoo, Michigan, and he wrote *The Gibson Story*, from which most of the information on Gibson's history is borrowed. Mr. Fuller assembled many facts about electronics and the early Les Paul guitars.

Leo Fender, a genuine living legend, opened his personal files and photo albums providing many facts and anecdotes about his career. I spent a week in Fullerton, California, rummaging through Fender's files and touring the factory. The Marketing Department's Mark Cohen conducted several interviews, and Leo Fender's right-hand man, Freddie Tavares, shed much light on Fender's early days.

James B. Lansing Sound, Inc., has a reputation for making some of the best speakers in the world. Carl Davis, Bill Cara, and Edward May (Senior Engineer) spent hours patiently explaining the finer points of speaker and cabinet operation. JBL also contributed the line drawings on which the speaker and speaker connection illustrations are based.

I am lucky to have a friend as talented as Gerry Kano, who drew the diagrams which appear throughout the book. Bernardo Rico, maker of B. C. Rich guitars, spent two afternoons explaining each step of classic-guitar construction. David Russell Young's contribution takes up a whole sub-chapter.

A few of the illustrated guitars belong to the author and other guitar players, but most were borrowed from music dealers in Los Angeles. I am much in debt to Paul Herman and his friends at The Guitar Center. Though I had not met them before, they took great interest in the book and freely lent their prized guitars —well over a dozen at a time, sometimes for several days. They contributed most of the guitars in the book and dozens of special effects for testing.

When I first met Don and Bob Griffin a few years ago, their West L.A. Music was a small shop dealing mostly in accessories. They've developed it into one of the country's larger and finer music stores, specializing in guitars and designing sound systems for televised concerts and recording artists from both America and Europe. Thanks for technical tips, for contributing guitars and many amps to be photographed, and for good times floating down the Colorado River.

Fred Walecki owner of Westwood Music, is a good friend, whom I admire for the loyalty he deserves and receives from his customers, scores of whom are rock stars, studio musicians, renowned classical guitarists, and folksingers. It's hard to find storeowners in any business who are as concerned about their clients as Fred. I appreciate his assistance and advice. His friend Mike Longworth at the Martin company contributed almost all of the material on which the company history is based. Mr. Longworth probably knows more about Martin than anybody, and his own book, tentatively titled *The Martin Guitar Story*, will be out soon.

Roy Garnaché of Expert Audio Repair in L.A. assisted in the preparation of sections of Part II. John Carruthers helped out with guitar repairs and adjustments.

Guitar Player magazine assists guitarists in all categories, assembling a talented staff to write on every facet of the instrument. Publisher-editor Jim Crockett offered to help *The Guitar Book* any way he could, and he ultimately sent pages of suggestions, many of which were followed. By reading *Guitar Player*, I learned where to look, whom to talk to and what to ask. Were it not for their work, I'd probably still be conducting interviews.

Tycobrahe Sound Co. helped arrange for me to accompany Ten Years After on their American tour of 1973, and I learned much about concert sound systems, mixers, and monitors on that tour from road manager Andy Jaworski and Tycobrahe's Jim Chase and Ralph Morris.

James Lee Reeves and Connie Bassett are friends, kind enough to help with early manuscripts. Some of the others who helped are Ed Dopera, cofounder of the Dobro company, Chet Atkins, Dan Armstrong, Hank Snow, Seth Lover, Ronald Lazar, Dave Cary, Milt Owen, Eric Gaer, Frank Garlock, Paul Floodman, Forrest White, Robb Lawrence, author of the forthcoming *The Story of American Guitars*, Ted Greene, author of *Chord Chemistry*, Sol Betnun, Bruce Bolen, Gregg Hildebrandt, Ralph Ibarra, Mick Hay, Dr. David M. Lipscomb, Paul Stull, Tito Guidotti and *Guitar Review*, and several of my guitar students.

B. B. King's generous foreword is only the visible part of his contribution to *The Guitar Book*. After our long interviews, I am much inspired by his courage and dedication. Finally, I owe an indirect but personal debt to Chuck Berry, because I've been hooked on guitars ever since I first heard the intro to *Johnny B. Goode*.

Acknowledgments for the Revised Edition

The person to whom I owe the most is Ruth Brengel, Director of Trade Promotions for Harper & Row. For three years she has helped me in every phase of the financing, preparation, distribution, and promotion of this project. Thanks again, Ruth. I am also grateful to Hal Grove and Linda Dingler, who took my manuscripts and photos and made a book out of them.

Bob Bassett taught me how to use a camera and did all of the printing for the revision—hundreds of shots. Any indications of photographic competence are as much due to his talents as mine.

In writing the revision from January to October, 1977, the work I enjoyed most was photographing collector's instruments. Many people allowed me to shoot their guitars, including Glen Quan, Roy Acuff, Forrest White, Kosta Kovachev, Dave DiMartino, Kim Johnson, and Frank Lucido. Norm Harris of Norman's Rare Guitars provided access to his huge and spectacular collection. I am most grateful to George Gruhn, perhaps America's foremost collector and all-around expert on rare instruments. My trips to his shop in Nashville were particularly enlightening, and he helped me through several stages in the preparation of materials on collectors' pieces.

Several West Coast music stores contributed instruments for photographing, including Hollywood Music,

The Eighth Note, Guitars Afire, Prune Music, Aeolian Music, and Guitar Center of L.A. Once again I am especially thankful to Fred Walecki and my other good friends at Westwood Music. I was further assisted by the Country Music Hall of Fame and Opryland Museums in Nashville, as well as the Metropolitan Museum of Art in New York. Thanks also to Jay Levin Guitars.

Decades ago, a few men of much foresight began to shape the American guitar market. I was fortunate to have interviewed several of them and their associates. Thanks to Leo Fender, Les Paul, John Huis, Wilbur Marker, Julius Bellson, Doc Kauffman, and particularly Ted McCarty, the unsung hero of American guitar design. At scores of musical instrument and accessory manufacturers I received help from executives, salesmen, designers, and others, including Ken Killman, Don Randall, Mark Cohen, Carl Spinoso, Ron Lazar, Bob Griffin, and Dave Holcomb. I am especially indebted to Travis Bean and Hartley Peavey.

Since I am not an engineer, I needed a lot of help in writing about pickups. Thanks to Chip Todd, R. T. Lowe, Bill Lawrence, Larry DiMarzio, Bill Bartolini, Arnie Lazarus, and particularly Rick Turner of Alembic and Jeff Hasselberger of Elger/Ibanez. *Guitar Player* magazine was helpful once again, and one of their columnists, Craig Anderton, provided information about special effects. Bob Easton assisted me in writing about synthesizers.

Among other friends who helped out were Mike McDonald, Jon Sievert, John Carruthers, Jol Dantzig, John Gima, Bill Sullivan, and Mike Longworth, author of *Martin Guitars: A History*.

Foreword

Tom Wheeler and I first got together in the summer of 1973, when he had been working on the first draft of a book about the guitar. We spent some time in Las Vegas, Nevada, and again in Santa Barbara, California, talking about music and guitars and guitar players. Since then, he has completed his project and he calls it *The Guitar Book*. I've been singing and playing for a long, long time, and I'd like to tell you why I think this book is a valuable thing for anybody who is interested in the guitar.

First, let me mention that I have a strong affection for the guitar. It's been with me from the very beginning, traveling around the world, working over three hundred nights each year for close to three decades now. During that time, I have always hoped that my singing and playing would help to bring people together. That has been my goal. All of us—rich or poor, no matter what color—we all have these blues from time to time, and most of us like music, and if different types of people come in to hear a singer or a guitar player, then that's an important first step in understanding one another. Once people get together, they start communicating.

My own interest in the guitar goes way back to my childhood in Mississippi, when I would go to hear the preacher play at the Sanctified Church. The music in the churches was something that a small boy, even at age forty-nine today, will never forget. Later on, in 1947, I started playing professionally. You may have heard the story about how I ran into a burning building one time to save my guitar. The fire was caused when two guys were fighting and one of them knocked the other over a big kerosene container. The building collapsed as I came running out with my guitar, and two people died in the fire. I found out later that the guys were fighting over a woman named Lucille, so I named my guitar Lucille to remind me to never again do anything so crazy.

Lucille has been by my side during my entire career of about twenty-nine years, and she's so important to me because she helps me to express what I feel at a particular moment.

I was at the Apollo Theater in New York one time and a critic wrote about it; what he said was one of the great compliments that people have given me. He said: "B. B. King sings, and then Lucille sings." That made me feel very good, because I do feel that I'm still singing when I play. People seem to like it, and they tell me that most of today's rock guitar players are influenced quite a bit by the way I've been playing.

I have owned many, many guitars. My first one was a Stella, about two and a half feet long, with the big round hole in it, and it was red—one of their little red guitars. It cost me fifteen dollars and it took me two months to pay for it, and I kept it for a long, long time. Then I had one of the first Fenders in '49 or early '50, and several Gibsons, an Epiphone, a Gretsch—many, many Lucilles. Over the years I've learned quite a bit about guitars besides how to play them, and I'm still learning. Many of these things are included in *The Guitar Book*—it's for people like me who want to find out more about the guitar. There are several reasons why I like it.

First, it's a book for *all* guitar players—acoustic and electric, beginner or professional, young or old; no matter what kind of music you like, folk, country, blues, rock, or whatever, this is a book for anyone who digs the guitar. It's about flat tops, classicals, twelve-strings, solid and hollow bodies, and there's some material on metal resophonic guitars, like the kind my cousin Bukka White plays.

You will see all the subjects that belong in a guitar encyclopedia: history, guitar designs, construction, parts, care and repair, accessories, pickups, tunings,

B. B. King

special effects, and so forth. But there are many many other fascinating and important things that you might not think of: frequencies and sound waves, dealers, discounts and trade-ins, how to select and test equipment, facts about old guitars, and so on. There is even a section on protecting your hearing. These things are talked about in great detail; for instance, there are five chapters just on amplifiers and speakers.

Another thing, you probably know that there are so many rumors and misconceptions that people have about guitars. *The Guitar Book* really helps to set the facts straight. For example, there's an explanation of tubes and transistors, and a documented chronology of the Les Paul Guitars by Gibson. There is an interview with the people who build the sound equipment for the Rolling Stones, Deep Purple, and Jethro Tull. One of the best guitar makers tells how he builds a steel-string guitar, step-by-step. In researching this book, Tom Wheeler has traveled all around, talking to craftsmen, manufacturers, repairmen, and musicians. To learn more about stage equipment, he toured with the English group Ten Years After.

I mentioned before that when I play a solo, I seem to hear me singing through the guitar. This means that my equipment has got to be right, and this is one reason why *The Guitar Book* is a big help.

I recommend this book to anyone who is interested in the guitar. I enjoyed it, and I even found out a few things about Lucille that I didn't know before.

B. B. King

B. B. KING

Introduction to the Revised Edition

The story of the American guitar is a long and involved one, and one plagued with misinformation, lost historical records, vague personal memories, and half-truths. It's also packed with colorful people, ingenious designs, masterful marketing schemes, pioneering inventions, humor, and heartache. Tom Wheeler's first edition of *The Guitar Book* did more than any prior publication to clear away the former and introduce the public to the latter.

This volume, his substantially enlarged and more detailed revision, goes even further to show what the world's most popular musical instrument is, and how it got that way.

Wheeler, a guitarist, teacher, songwriter, law student, and journalist, began *The Guitar Book* seven years ago as the proverbial labor of love. After three years of travel, research, and interviews, he produced the bestselling first edition in 1974. Today he knows more; has interviewed even greater numbers of inventors, industry executives, and artists; has probed still further into those legendary manufacturers' dusty archives; and has made his original definitive work even more valuable to musician, scholar, and fan.

This revised and updated version contains approximately 175 totally new photos, including shots of never-before-publicized prototypes and one-of-a-kind rarities. And as the technology of the instrument has expanded, so has Tom's coverage of such new subjects as mini-amps, acoustic guitar pickups, electronic tuners, synthesizers, and radically new guitar designs.

His chapters on effects devices, accessories, guitar theory, tunings, and guitar factories have all been expanded and rewritten to be even more complete, more up to date, and all the more enjoyable to the reader. There is also a new section on handmade acoustic instruments.

Tom Wheeler's first edition of *The Guitar Book* seemed impossible to top. But it wasn't. It was surpassed by the only book that could have surpassed it—this one.

Jim Crockett
Publisher
Guitar Player Magazine

February 1978

part I

The Guitar

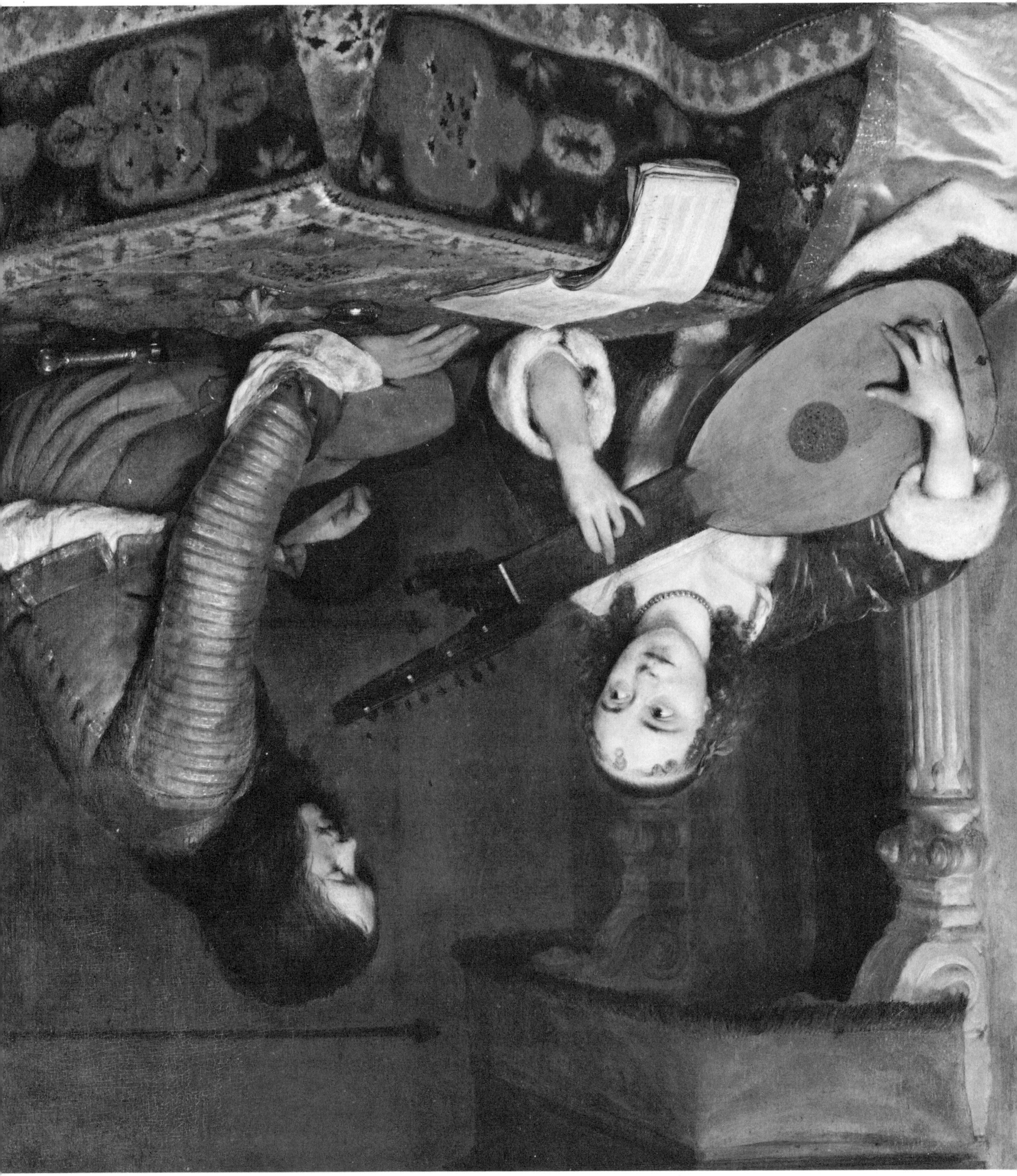

1

The Birth of the Guitar: Mythological and Historical

One of the many heroes of the ancient Greeks was Hermes—son of Zeus, guardian of travelers and the god of science and invention. A classic myth recounts the tale of how the young Hermes stole some prized cattle right from under the godly nose of Apollo. On the trip home, he invented the lyre by attaching three cow-gut strings to a bow. He stretched a piece of hide over an empty turtle shell and passed the bow through the shell. Hermes was caught with the cattle, but he began to sing, accompanying himself on his new instrument. The songs just happened to praise Apollo's countless virtues, and the god of music was impressed. In fact, he traded *all* of his livestock for Hermes' lyre, straight across.

The instrument was to remain with Apollo throughout the rest of eternity. When he was challenged to do battle with Marsyas, who was playing a mere flute, Apollo counterattacked with his lyre. He devastated his enemy, thus establishing the superiority of strings over woodwinds for all time.

Orpheus, the poet, son of Apollo, learned to play so well that he could move mountains and make the rivers stand still. He charmed the wild beasts and even the trees and rocks to get right up and follow him everywhere. Orpheus followed his dead wife, Eurydice, to Hades and begged Pluto to allow her to leave the

Apollo defeats Marsyas. Greek cast. *The Metropolitan Museum of Art, The Crosby Brown Collection of Musical Instruments, 1889*

A Woman Playing the Theorbo. Oil on wood by Gerard Terborch (1617–1681). *The Metropolitan Museum of Art, Bequest of Benjamin Altman, 1913*

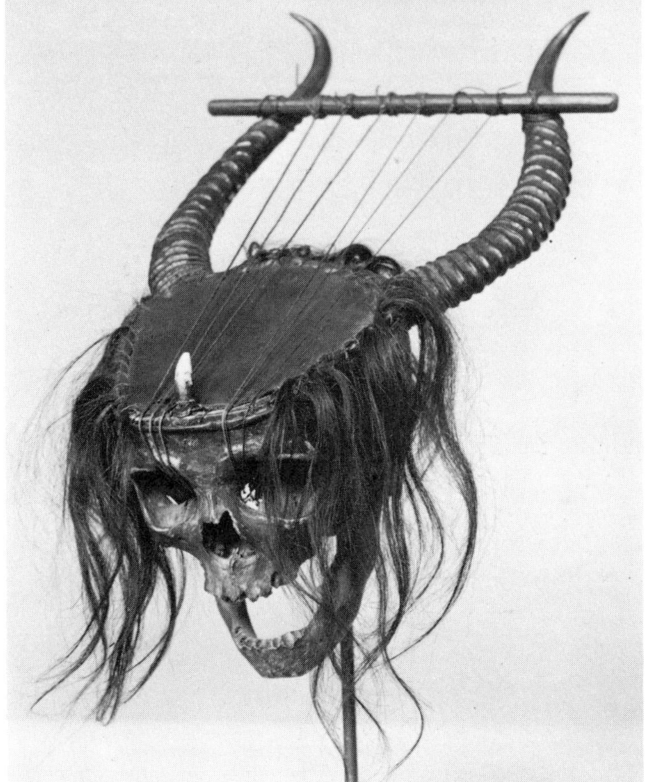

Central African kissar made from a human skull and the horns of a gazelle. *The Metropolitan Museum of Art, The Crosby Brown Collection of Musical Instruments, 1889*

Indian tamburi. *The Metropolitan Museum of Art, Gift of Alice E. Getty, 1946*

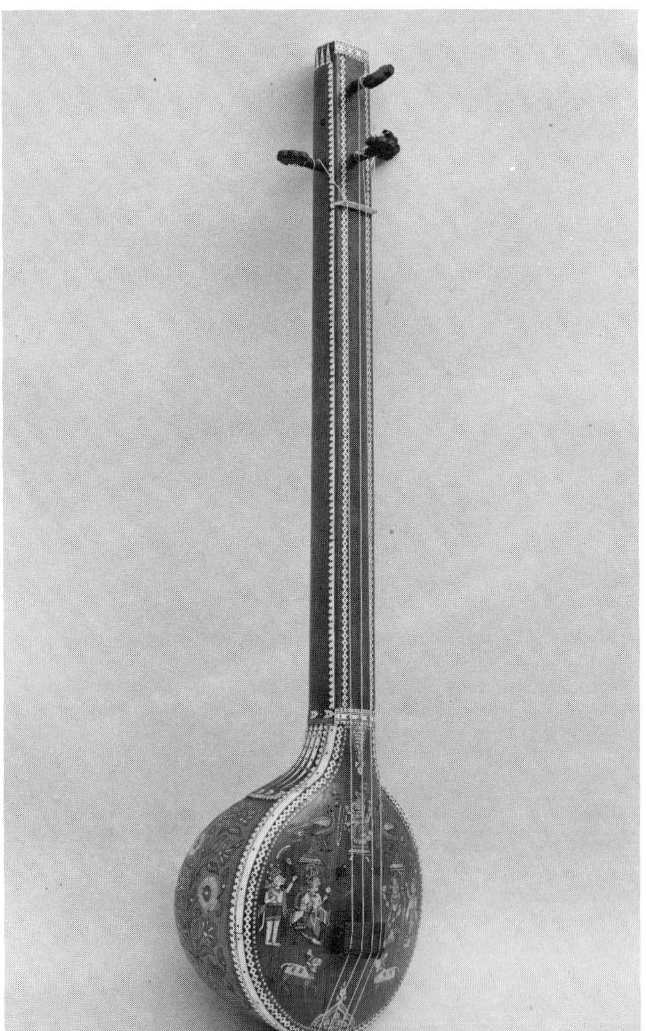

realm of the dead. Pluto was so overwhelmed by the beauty of Orpheus's singing lyre that he consented. However, Orpheus had to promise not to look at Eurydice until they had returned to earth. When he broke the vow, Eurydice was lost to him for eternity. Orpheus returned home so inconsolable that he vowed never more to associate with women. (He must have been quite a man, for the Thracian ladies, upon hearing of this pledge, were so disappointed that they ripped his body to pieces and tossed his head into the river Hebrus.)

Segovia tells the story of how the guitar was invented when the brash Apollo tried to rape the luscious river nymph Daphne. After praying to the gods for help, she was immediately transformed into a laurel tree, and from this sacred wood came the body of the first guitar.

The guitar's history resembles its tone—rich and full of passion, and subject to an immense variety of interpretations. Its background is like that of an alluring woman with a somewhat hazy past, which is carefully documented, but not without rumor.

Over the centuries, the ceaseless experimentation with instrument design has produced a number of oddities, complicating any attempt to chronicle the evolution of the guitar. We do know that percussion and wind instruments are older than strings, though the predecessors of the guitar date back several thousand years. From the very beginning, the development of the guitar has depended upon an essential human characteristic: the desire to express the inexpressible. Of course, dedication to music has its price. Frederic V. Grunfeld wrote in his witty and most informative book, *The Art and Times of the Guitar* (Macmillan):

> it is a decisive moment for civilization when man lays aside his arrows and devotes himself to plucking bowstrings for music. He can be very vulnerable at that point, as David discovered, in the Book of Kings, when he found himself suddenly the target of a tossed spear. But this very vulnerability is a precondition to all art, which reposes in fragile guitars rather than in swords. And thus the history of the guitar is essentially the story of some of man's best moments . . .

Our bow-twanging caveman ancestor knew a good thing when he heard it, because the earliest of cultures had music, and the first of the civilizations had strings. Single-stringed instruments consisted of a bow with a gourd sound chamber. Different pitches were produced by bending the bow, which changed the string's tension. In sections of Africa, instruments of this type are still found. Gourds, tortoise shells and skulls were used as resonant chambers. Early instruments of Mesopotamia and Persia are examples of this design, sometimes featuring a stick neck and an animal skin soundboard stretched over the chamber. These were given the name *tanbur* (tambura, pandore), and they appear in the guitar's direct lineage.

The Indo-European Hittites of Scripture probably migrated from the Caucasus and inhabited most of the territory between Armenia and the Aegean Sea. A carving at the stone Sphinx gate to the new Hittite Empire at Alaja Hüyük includes the first known stringed instrument with all of the general requirements of a guitar: the soft feminine curves at the waist, a flat top with an incurved arc of five sound holes on either side, and a long fretted neck that runs the entire length of the body. The guitar depicted in this stunning archeological discovery is predated in other cultures by pear-shaped tanburs having *some* of its characteristics. But the 3,300-year-old Hittite guitar represents the first time the essential features all appeared together.

The Babylonians, like the Hittites, had lyres strung with animal tendons or plant fibers, while Egyptians played a simple instrument with a neck and a resonant sound chamber, roughly approximating that of a ukulele. Ramses II, the Egyptian Pharaoh (1292–1225 B.C.), erected an obelisk which includes a representation of a guitar-shaped string instrument. On the other side of the globe, about five hundred years before Christ, the Chinese Emperor Tzi-tze gave his name to his own invention, a four-string instrument with a small, square sound box, a hole in the top, and a heavy bamboo neck.

Alexander the Great (356–323 B.C.) was a Macedonian youth of above-average ambition, having conquered most of the civilized world by the time he was twenty-five. His domain included the empires of Greece, Persia, and Egypt, with rich cultural exchange among its many peoples. For one thing, the harplike Assyrian zither was discovered and passed on to the Greeks and then to the Romans, who called it *cithara romana* or *fidicula*. Over a thousand years later, craftsmen from Provence, in southern France, would add

Ancient Chinese p'i-p'a, or balloon guitar. *The Metropolitan Museum of Art, The Crosby Brown Collection of Musical Instruments, 1889*

Japanese biwa, or lute (c. 1891); wooden bridge, four silk strings; decorated with gold, white coral, leather, and ivory. *The Metropolitan Museum of Art, Gift of the Estate of Mary Flagler Cary, 1969*

a neck and fingerboard, calling their invention a *crota* or *chrotta*. The lute appeared in Rome for a short time (about A.D. 100–200) but it disappeared for centuries after the destruction of the Empire.

Soon after the Trojan War (1193–1184 B.C.), the Greeks played both the harp and the cithara (similar to the Nubian kissar), a member of the lyre family. Asian lutes, while known to the Greeks, were usually ignored in favor of lyres and citharas with their greater number of one-note strings. Homer's *Iliad* and the *Odyssey* were sung with the accompaniment of the cithara and, centuries thereafter, Socrates played the cithara in his later years. Pythagoras, the philosopher and mathematical genius, characteristically took a scientific approach to the design of stringed instruments, enabling later guitar makers to develop a fingerboard. A large bas-relief of an Athenian tanbur player illustrates 2,200-year-old techniques of fingering that are still used today by classical and folk artists.

Vladimir Bobri, the composer and guitar historian, describes the steady migration of the guitar's predecessors to the Iberian Peninsula (now Spain and Portugal) along the northern coast of the Mediterranean Sea. In Europe, eighth-century gypsies came from the East with strange lyres and lutes of Assyrian and Persian descent. The Moorish invasion introduced the Arabian lute to Spain. Known as the *ud*, it had dozens of variations, each with a body shaped like a halved pear or melon. The ud is believed to have been derived from the Persians and influenced by the Chinese *tzi-tze*, one of several Oriental instruments which had also been exposed to Europeans by returning Crusaders.

The *gittern*, or *guiterne*, and the bowed, three-stringed *rebec* were widely used throughout Europe during the Middle Ages and thereafter. A favorite of the fun-loving Henry VIII, the rebec resembled a mandolin (pear-shaped) with a flat top, two sound holes, a bridge, and a short neck. Henry's daughter, Queen Elizabeth I, like all of his children, was an enthusiastic and accomplished player. The musicians in Shakespeare's *Romeo and Juliet* were also rebec players.

In the 1200s, a new hybrid Spanish instrument, the *laud*, began to appear in several forms, both pear-shaped and guitarlike. It spread to the rest of Europe as the German *laute*, the French *liuth*, and the English *lute*. Though the guitar's name can be traced to the cithara of the ancient lyre family, the lyre's boxy shape, twin limbs, and many strings probably had little to do with the physical development of the guitar. Rather, it is the lute which is the guitar's structural ancestor, and the earlier lute-type instruments and tanburs of the Hittites, Egyptians, Persians, and Mesopotamians suggest an evolution of the guitar fairly independent of lyres and harps.*

The design of the first guitars borrowed acoustic principles from both the Arabian ud and certain versions of the French crota, which in the thirteenth century found its way across the Pyrenees to northern Spain, where the lute was already popular. Religious wars in France had driven many crota players to Aragon and Catalonia, where cross-breeding of crotas and lutes occurred. This series of events was probably the birth of the guitar as it is known and recognized today. During this same period, Marco Polo returned home to Italy, bringing a collection of guitars and lutes from China and India.

Once belonging only to angels and gods, emperors and kings, and sorcerers and priests, relatively sophisticated stringed instruments were now coming into the streets, cottages and farmhouses. The common people adopted the rebec as perhaps their favorite instrument, ignoring the thirteenth-century Church of Spain, which had banished it from households of the faithful. Players discarded the bow and began to pluck away with their fingers and picks. Up through the sixteenth century, the rebec was slightly altered and became known as a mandola, becoming very popular, particularly in Spain.

Instrument makers experimented with tone, sound projection, various woods, and shapes. The ancient design concept of the flat back became fashionable once more, and the result was the *vihuela*, a direct ancestor of the modern guitar and a favorite of the Renaissance masters. Its name derives from the Roman term *fidula*, as do the names *violão* (Portugal), *viola*, *violin*, and *fiddle*. The vihuela coincided historically with the structural fusion of the crota and the ud. Resembling twentieth-century guitars, it was oval, with five sound holes in the top, slightly pinched at the waist, and had a short neck with ten frets and five pairs of strings, plus a single "chanter" (string). Like

*Dr. Michael Kasha, "A New Look at the History of the Classic Guitar," *Guitar Review*, GR–30, 1968.

Seventeenth-century Italian pandore. *The Metropolitan Museum of Art, The Crosby Brown Collection of Musical Instruments, 1889*

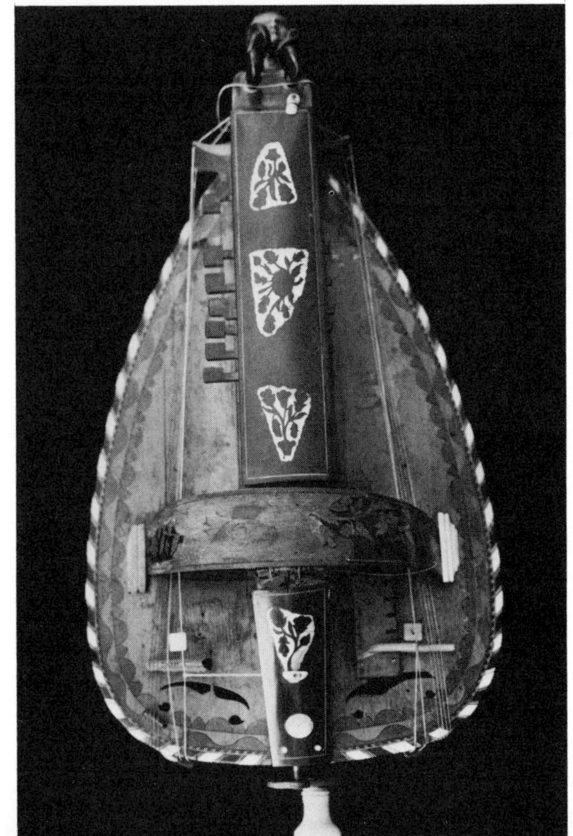

Hurdy-gurdy. *Walecki Collection*

the modern twelve-string guitar, the sets of strings were tuned either in unison or an octave apart, in an arrangement identical to the Renaissance lute: G C F A D G. Other tuning variations included four- or seven-string sets. Since the vihuela was often ornate and costly, the similar but less fancy four-string *guitarra latina* was more of a favorite among the ordinary folks. Guitarras latinas of the late thirteenth century had eight sound holes in two curved rows of four holes each, much like the Hittite instrument depicted in the carving at Alaja Hüyük. The guitarra latina had pointed tanburlike shoulders, clearly distinguishing it from its contemporary, the almond-shape *guittara morisca* of the Arabs.

Italian mandoline (c. 1768). *The Metropolitan Museum of Art, Gift of Miss Alice Getty, 1946*

In the early sixteenth century, a fifth string was added to the guitarra latina, though the invention is often ascribed to Vicente Espinel (1551–1624), the poet who popularized the new version, now generally known as the Spanish guitar. Soon it seemed to be everywhere, rapidly overshadowing the fragile and more complicated lute. Alarmed purists and lute lovers condemned the guitar, trying to give it a bad name by associating it with undignified frolicking in the streets, unrestrained body movements, and a general spirit of joyful, sensual abandon. The more the guitar was identified with such pursuits, the more it dominated folk music in Europe. Romantics loved to serenade with it, ladies loved to hear it, painters loved to paint it. Those were indeed grim days for lute makers. With a brief quote from *The Barber of Seville*, Grunfeld notes how essential a companion the guitar had come to be:

COUNT: Figaro!
FIGARO: What is it?
COUNT: Your guitar . . .
FIGARO: I have forgotten my guitar! I am losing my wits.

French and Italian guitars of the 1600s became more and more indented at the middle. The instrument played by Robert de Visée, royal guitarist to the court of Louis XIV, is remarkably similar to the modern shape, though it had five sets of strings. Louis himself reigned for seventy-two years, and was certainly the most prominent person in Europe. When he wasn't declaring war on the English, Swedish, Dutch, or Spanish, he took guitar lessons.

Supposedly around the time of the American Revolution, an extra string (bass E) was added to the existing five-string instruments, taking a crucial step in the development of today's guitar. A Dresden musician named Naumann, his associate—a luthier named August Otto—and a Spanish monk, Miguel García, have all been credited for the innovation, though the idea had been batted around for a century before them. The Carulli guitar of 1810 was one of the first to have six single strings tuned in the present arrangement: E A D G B E. The single strings eliminated the tuning problems caused by the unequal diameter of paired gut strings. Another significant contribution was the 650 mm. string length, attributed to the most influential of *guitarreros* (guitar makers), Antonio Torres Jurado (1817–1892), of Almeria, Spain. He increased the guitar's width and narrowed the fretboard to roughly two inches, permitting easier fingering. Unlike the sometimes ostentatious instruments of the day, his were strikingly functional. One of the first guitar makers to use mechanical tuning machines, he also originated the design from which existing fan-bracing patterns are taken. Except to a trained eye, his guitars are nearly identical in appearance to the classic guitar of the 1970s.

Fernando Sors, later spelled "Sor" (1778–1839), was a phenomenally talented man: composer of operas and lesser works, journalist, music teacher, army officer, and writer of a guitar-method book that remains a masterpiece of analysis and lucidity. Friend of monarchs and a renowned ladies' man, he was also the greatest guitarist of his time. His important contemporaries included his countryman, Dionisio Aguado, and the Italian Ferdinando Carulli, who was succeeded by Matteo Carcassi and Mauro Giuliani. They all wrote method books and, together, these virtuosi greatly expanded the influence of the guitar in Europe, where Rossini, Schubert, Haydn, and Berlioz all composed for it.

After a brief cultural dry spell, Francisco Tarrega, in his total commitment to the guitar, almost singlehandedly revitalized Spanish music in the late nineteenth century. His compositions still brighten the repertoire of many concert guitarists. His transcriptions of Bach, Beethoven, and Chopin are legion. Tarrega toured extensively, and the critics of his day exhausted all known superlatives in description of his performances.

German cittern by George Philip Alphenn (1749); beechwood and ebony, metal strings. *The Metropolitan Museum of Art, The Crosby Brown Collection of Musical Instruments, 1889*

The acceptance of the guitar as a modern concert instrument is largely due to the efforts of Andres Segovia, one of history's greatest musicians. Hearing this self-taught guitarist play is like listening to a handful of gifted artists blending the tones of several instruments in a suite of solos, duets, and trios. Segovia has transcribed the music of Mozart, Handel, Haydn, and many others, and he has performed for half a century on stages throughout the world, furthering the growth and the influence of his beloved instrument.

Andres Segovia

2

A Short Story of the Guitar and Its Friends in America

Whatever "American" music is, it began to develop as the influences of Europe and Western Africa intermingled through black and white people in the East and South. Tribal gourd instruments covered with hide were almost certainly the ancestors of the banjo, still a favorite in folk, mountain, and bluegrass music. Slaves occasionally substituted homemade guitars fashioned from cigar boxes, sticks, and wire, though most guitars of colonial America were crafted in Britain, such as the one belonging to Ben Franklin (who, incidentally, was regarded as being a little strange by his non-guitar playing neighbors).

In the Southwest, Mexican settlers played both the guitar and its predecessor, the sixteenth-century vihuela. Spanish missionaries took their instruments up the rich California coast, while the cowboy packed a guitar not only for entertainment, but for calming the herds at night.

In the South, what we now know as the blues was developing in the Mississippi Delta region from work songs, field hollers, and cries. Rich spirituals and harmonic, gospel melodies were often accompanied first by banjos and later by crude guitars, sometimes played with a metal slide or a glass bottleneck on one of the left-hand fingers, enabling the player to slip up the neck with that sweeping, wailing sound, so perfect for blues and still popular in modern country and rock music.

Django Reinhardt (*left*) visits Les Paul backstage in the 1940s.
Photo courtesy Les Paul

Woody Guthrie, the archetype of the ramblin' balladeer. More than anyone, he personified the legend of the minstrel who packed a guitar and hitched rides on trains. Friend of the cotton picker, oil driller, barkeep, and rail splitter, he wrote a thousand songs that comprise a substantial chunk of working-class Americana, including "This Land Is Your Land" and "This Train Is Bound for Glory." He was the chief inspiration for Bob Dylan and the others who rekindled popular interest in folk music in the 1960s. A nervous disorder called Huntington's chorea struck in the late 1950s, and Woody's condition deteriorated for more than a decade. When he died in 1967, his second wife, Marjorie, founded the Committee to Combat Huntington's Disease, now with more than thirty chapters nationwide.

In both the rural South and Midwest, music had always played a large role in religion, and religion was the center of social activity as well as the vehicle for spiritual strivings. Not surprisingly, the guitar was often seen around the farm, plantation, cattle ranch, and mining camp. After all, it was easy to transport (on foot, wagon, or horse), it was inexpensive, and practically anybody could master three or four chords without reading music, enough to play hundreds of hymns and songs about God, work, love, and life in general.

In the cities, angry poor people took their guitars to the streets, union rallies, and town halls to protest and to influence opinion. Thus, American blues, country and western, and city folk music were all guitar-oriented for much the same reasons—the guitar is an easy-to-play, easy-to-carry, good-sounding, inexpensive instrument. Though it weighs only a few pounds, its range is over half that of a grand piano. Plus, it's attractive; you feel good just getting it in your hands.

In the Chicago and New Orleans jazz bands of the early 1930s, the guitar had a rough time. No matter how hard the frustrated picker picked, he was usually drowned out by all sorts of horns and some bully on an eighty-eight-key, five-hundred-pound piano. But then, frustrated guitarists everywhere had their delicious revenge with the acceptance of the contact microphone, which could amplify the instrument's sound. Eddie Durham may have been the first jazz musician to play electric guitar.

The significance of electricity was to touch guitarists in all categories, though the new-found energy was not widely appreciated by the public. Many new melodies and inventive progressions were struck by Eddie Lang, Freddie Green, Eddie Condon, and the young genius Charlie Christian. This period was the watershed of modern guitar history. As a member of Benny Goodman's band from 1939 to 1941, Charlie Christian, more than any other man, created an identity for the electric guitar as a solo instrument, playing horn-style, single-note passages in a radical departure from the existing chord-melody approach. In less than five years, Christian caused a revolution in technique while helping to invent bebop, along with Dizzy Gillespie, Lester Young, Charlie Parker, and others. Throughout the centuries-long evolution of guitar tech-

Charlie Christian

Hank Williams

Doc Watson (*right*) with Bluegrass founder Bill Monroe

Merle Travis

Jimmy Bryant

Barney Kessel

nique, it is likely that no one contributed more than he. As Grunfeld puts it, in *The Art and Times of the Guitar*, "there is the guitar before Christian and the guitar after Christian, and they sound virtually like two different instruments." Charlie Christian died of tuberculosis at the age of twenty-three.

In the late 1940s, a Belgian-born French gypsy named Jean Baptiste "Django" Reinhardt was injecting his jazz influence into music's mainstream. At the age of eighteen he had lost the use of two left-hand fingers in a gypsy caravan fire. Still, his technique was nothing short of breathtaking. Fortunately, he cut many records with his famous Hot Club Quintet, and he came to America to play with Duke Ellington and others. Django Reinhardt's imprint overlaps whole categories of guitar styles, from the late Wes Montgomery to B. B. King.

In the last three decades, other creative jazz players have experimented with new time signatures and modes, continuing to innovate a greater variety of expression. Among these imaginative artists are Les Paul, George Van Eps, Tal Farlow, Johnny Smith, Kenny Burrell, Howard Roberts, Herb Ellis, Joe Pass, and the gifted Barney Kessel, author of *The Guitar.**

Chet Atkins

For many years, country music was the primary domain in the American guitar kingdom. Jimmie Rodgers, Hank Williams, the Carter Family, Ernest Tubb, Hank Snow, Merle Haggard, Johnny Cash—these generations of great singers, their contemporaries, and their many imitators all found the guitar to be perfectly suited to country music. A few instrumentalists, including Merle Travis, Roy Clark, Glen Campbell, Jerry Reed, Jimmy Bryant, and Joe Maphis achieved such a high level of professionalism that their admirers are found far beyond the realm of country and western. "Mr. Guitar" himself, Chet Atkins, is one of America's most versatile and respected guitarists. He began playing with crude equipment—a ukulele strung with wires from an old screen door. All during his career as a sideman, solo artist, arranger, producer, guitar designer, and record company executive, he pioneered various electronic recording techniques. In recent years, this soft-spoken Tennessean has exercised his dazzling talent in the pop and classical fields, but his trademark is still pure country at its best—a com-

*Barney Kessel, *The Guitar* (New York: Wehman), 1967.

bination of flowing melody, harmony, and a punchy, muted bass line, all played at once.

Despite the sophistication of jazz and the toe-tapping irresistibility of country and western, the post-war guitarists went unheard by the majority of Americans. Then in the mid-Fifties a new kind of music changed everything, and people started paying attention. Into the somewhat bland commercial world of polite swing and sugary ballads was born the Sun King of Rock and Roll—wriggling and quivering, choking and shaking . . . lips and hips, tight leather and disgusting sideburns and lots of beautifully greasy long and thick black hair—a hundred and eighty pounds of sex and power, a trucker from Tupelo. Quite simply, the world had never seen anything like Elvis Presley. American youth, just beginning to flex its muscles as a fairly homogeneous subculture, had found a hero, a rallying point. Best of all, the parents hated him. He was perfect.

Everyone figured out that this writhing maniac was not your ordinary musician. Among the many obvious things about the King was that he always performed with a guitar. He thumped it hard with his right hand and stroked it mean with his left—threw it around and slapped it against his body. It was absolute dynamite and, as Elvis rocketed beyond a much-deserved superstardom to near immortality, his banged-up six-string box went along for the ride.

Elvis was religious, polite, and, above all, he loved and respected his parents. According to legend, he was discovered while recording a song for his mother. Still he posed a threat, and he was bitterly condemned by the clergy and civic leaders. Young people were warned that he would corrupt their morals; they responded by buying ten million Elvis Presley records in a single year (1956). While their girl friends were sobbing and swooning over the Memphis Male, the panic-stricken local fellows may have thought: any instrument that can be molested while jerking your knees, closing your eyes and sneering, all at the same time, can't be too hard to master. Besides, back then, you could order one from Sears for about eight bucks. American youth took a look and said, "If he can, I can." And as far as the actual guitar playing goes, they were right. "Hound Dog" has just three chords. So does "Surfin' USA," "This Land Is Your Land," "Why I Sing the Blues," "I Second That Emotion," "Gimme

The King, with Scotty Moore on lead guitar

The Ventures

Shelter," "Mr. Tambourine Man," and so many other rock, blues, soul, country, and folk songs by B. B. King, the Rolling Stones, Joan Baez, and countless more. That's the beauty of it.

In those growing-pain days of rock and roll, instrumentals were a big deal. Every time you turned on the radio, someone's saxophone was honking, stuttering, and squealing, and records like "Tequila" by the Champs and "Red River Rock" by Johnny and the Hurricanes were cleaning up. The Ventures' classic "Walk Don't Run" was on the charts for nearly five months, making it up to number two. The late King Curtis was probably playing the best sax in rock and roll, adding immeasurable style to the early Coasters' classics. He later went on to grace the sessions of Delaney & Bonnie and others. Duane Eddy discovered "twang," claimed it as his very own, and turned out albums full of note-bending, rebel-yelling hits. Playing almost exclusively in the bass range, it was late in his career before his melodies ventured above the fourth string. Like other records of the time, his were unsophisticated by today's standards, but many were as catchy and raucous as their titles: "Ramrod," "Cannonball," "Rebel Rouser"—the kind of songs that sound best when played loud. Duane Eddy encouraged the growth of the electric guitar as a solo instrument by continuously proving one of the nicest things about it: It can sound good and be easy to play at the same time.

The guitar began to strongly assert itself in the Fifties as a lead instrument in the spidery fingers of Our Father, Chuck Berry, the slick, flashy-eyed guitar-slinger poet. "Oh my, but that little country boy could play." (He returned to the top of the national charts, cruising high in the rock-and-roll revival of the Seventies.) In between some of the very best of the early rock lyrics, duck-walkin' Chuck's two-string licks and syncopated rhythms were jumping out of jukeboxes at sockhops everywhere. Among those tuning in were Mick Jagger, Keith Richard, Marc Bolan, Eric Clapton, George Harrison, and other youngsters across the seas.

Still, good guitar players seemed to be scarce, though there were fortunate exceptions. Mickey Baker spiced up Mickey and Sylvia's calypso hit "Love Is Strange" with melodic guitar lines and a nice blues lick at the end of each verse. James Burton did those sassy

Duane Eddy

Chuck Berry, the father of rock and roll guitar

country-rock solos on the early cuts by Rick Nelson (he was still "Ricky" in '57), and he continued to do studio work for just about everybody. Then Elvis Presley came out of retirement in the late Sixties to unleash the magic once more. The King was no slouch —when he needed a guitar player, he looked up James Burton. You can hear some good Southern stuff on the rockabilly hits of Eddie Cochran (one of Jeff Beck's and Paul McCartney's influences), Carl Perkins, and Buddy Holly, and there's also plenty of fast picking on Bill Haley records and by Scotty Moore, Elvis' first guitarist and good friend.

First on the golden West Coast and then everywhere, surf music was doing great things for guitar sales. Anybody who saw Dick Dale leaning out of a careening

Jimmie Rodgers, the singing brakeman

woodie full of bouncing flesh—with a Sparkle-Koated Stratocaster dangling around his waist—had to be impressed. Who cared if it wasn't plugged in? If you couldn't live in Malibu and surf for a living, making out with beach bunnies and seeking the Eternal Wave, the least you could do was buy a Fender and figure out all three notes of the bass run in "Pipeline." Clarinet lessons were out, hand vibratos were in, and the Beach Boys were selling records by the ton. Untrained beginners bought crates of Ventures albums and began to sit down with the hi-fi, copying relatively intricate leads, one note at a time.

Writers and performers began to revitalize several forms of traditional American music. Right in the middle of the first wave of rock-and-roll screamers and shakers, the perfectly clean-cut, letter-sweatered, harmonizing Kingston Trio was establishing itself as one of the most successful groups in the history of show business, singing about railroads, seafaring tales, and hangings. They had short haircuts and colossal record sales. Pete Seeger, Joan Baez, and Phil Ochs sang about similar subjects, but they also had thoughts about politics, war, civil rights, and hunger. Few people outside the coffeehouse circuit knew who Bob Dylan was, but the Byrds and sweet-singing Peter, Paul, and Mary were commercial enough in the mid-Sixties to slip a few of his startling messages onto the playlists of the rigidly controlled "Top Forty" AM radio stations. Bob Dylan—right on the charts with Leslie Gore, Jan & Dean, and Freddie & the Dreamers. You know the rest. Listeners wanted to find out about the honest, gimmick-free music that had something more to offer—songs with ideas, songs that made you think, stories about real people. In uncovering the blues and country and western roots of the new folk music, the listening public began to rediscover names such as Hank Williams, Jack Elliott, Arthel "Doc" Watson, Woody Guthrie, Robert Johnson, Mississippi John Hurt, Blind Lemon Jefferson, Son House, Walter "Furry" Lewis, Leadbelly, Sam "Lightnin'" Hopkins, Josh White, Fred McDowell, and Brownie McGhee. Some were the descendants of slaves, migrant workers, and tenant farmers. Most of them did not live to enjoy this belated appreciation; a few tasted real fame for the first time in their seventies. There have been almost as many systems of classifying the styles of these singers as there have been writers on the subject. But a common bond among them was that practically all played the guitar.

The folk music of the Sixties was asking many disturbing questions about values and human relationships, and one result seemed to be that everybody wanted to tell everybody else what the answers were. Since many of the probing songs of Dylan and his heirs (like those of Presley and the early Beatles) were for the most part easy to play, many people decided to buy a guitar and join in.

When pop music had really become group-oriented in the middle 1960s, Brian Epstein cashed in on a mountain of talent, and Beatlemania conquered the world. That did it. Practically every school in the country had three guitar players standing cheek-to-cheek around a microphone, screaming "Twist and Shout"—all banging away through the same, groaning Montgomery Ward amplifier. After all—why get a job like a normal person with hassles like haircuts and life insurance when you could be a rock star just as easily, and only worry about groupies and royalty checks?

The electric guitar had done a lot for the growth of the blues, but racism of various sorts in this country confined much of it to the South—the so-called "chitlin' circuit"—and to Chicago and Detroit, where Muddy Waters and John Lee Hooker were laying the foundations of a guitar style that is still growing in popularity. In the early Sixties, while B. B. King was doing one-nighters in Twist, Arkansas, stinging and teasing his guitar, sweet Lucille, many of us were dozing by the radio, listening to Bobby Vinton and wondering whatever happened to rock and roll. B. B. King, an intelligent, thoroughly charming and fiercely proud artist, is credited with the invention of the finger-style, perpendicular-to-the-neck vibrato employed by virtually all rock and blues players. His style and phrasing are so widely copied that guitarists in pop, jazz, and country fields are also touched by him. These facts combine to make him possibly the most influential nonclassical guitarist alive today. Speaking of the vibrato, he modestly comments:

Let's put it this way: I won't say I invented it, but they wasn't doing it before I started. I *will* say that I'm still trying. My cousin, Bukka White, and quite a few other people used bottlenecks. Well, I got stupid fingers. They won't work. If I get something like that in my hand and try to use it, it just won't work. So my ears told me, when

Freddie King

Jeff Beck

I trill my hand, that I'd get a sound similar to the sound they were getting with a bottleneck. And so, for about twenty-seven or twenty-eight years, I've been trying to do it, and now they tell me that I'm doing a little better.

Most Americans ignored blues guitar players, but in Europe things were different. Eric Clapton, playing the best guitar on the continent, had very strong roots in Southern blues, as did Jeff Beck, Jimmy Page, John Mayall's bands, and Jimi Hendrix. There was much unrecognized talent in the United States, and exciting music was going to waste for a long time. The typical record buyer understandably thought that he was informed about what was going on in music. With a radio glued securely to his ear, he could recite every lyric, whistle every sax solo on all those throbbing Little Richard songs, and play every Chuck Berry lick on his imaginary guitar. He owned a reverb kit and a pair of Beatle boots; he'd seen "Ride the Wild Surf" twice. (What more could he do?) And yet later, in the midst of the neo-Beatles, English guitar rage, when Peter Green and Mick Taylor said that many of those "new" phrases and licks had come from across the Atlantic—from the rural South, our very own country—many amateur rock guitarists were surprised. Anyway, people finally woke up, and it's not just coincidence that B. B. King's first big white audience (Fillmore Auditorium, San Fran-

Lucille and Friend

Robben Ford

Eric Clapton

cisco) was also his first standing ovation. It took this recognition by grateful foreign superstars and second-generation American rock/bluesmen like Duane Allman and Mike Bloomfield to shake the public into realizing that acclaim for the likes of Muddy Waters, Freddie King, and others was long overdue.

It is unlikely that we can overestimate the impact of the musical descendants of what used to be called "race music." Blues, the literary outlet of an oppressed people, is as full of humor as it is of pain and suffering. You already know this if you've ever seen B. B. King strike a sassy pose—one hand on his hip, wagging his finger, talking to the ladies in the audience. James Brown put together a huge, power-packed band. Rufus Thomas, Booker T. & the MG's, and the incredibly soulful Otis Redding and others on the Atlantic, Stax and Volt labels were spreading the Memphis sound. Detroit's Berry Gordy turned his seven-hundred-dollar loan into the multimillion-dollar-a-month Motown record empire, and its many groups laid their vocal tracks over smooth rock orchestras, complete with horns, strings, and choruses. Across town, Reverend C. L. Franklin's little girl, Aretha, was making a name for herself by unleashing her four-octave voice on gospel-rock and blues. The rock concert struck it rich at the box office with "Monterey Pop," "Woodstock," "Bangladesh," "Rainbow Bridge," and "Gimme Shelter." The guitar was taking on new and different roles.

After 1966, with the West Coast-centered acid rock, experimentation with feedback and special effects became the rage. Steve Stills and a few other players knew how to use these electronic devices to create original rock styles and to modify existing country and blues themes. The Yardbirds' Eric Clapton was already one of the world's best rock guitarists when he joined John Mayall's blues band and later Cream, Blind Faith, and Derek and The Dominos. "White Room" is a classic example of wah-wah technique, and it's only one of Clapton's many masterpieces. The late Jimi Hendrix was a sorcerer among guitarists. Alone in his category, he made music that was wildly beautiful, terrifying, and exhilarating at the same time. In addition to his mastery of the hand vibrato, wah-wah pedal and controlled feedback, he embarked on strange and powerful melodic adventures that none of us had heard before. Mike Bloomfield, a guitar

Jimi Hendrix

Duane Allman

Mahavishnu John McLaughlin

player who knows, said of him in *Guitar Player Magazine*: "Hendrix is possibly the most innovative guitar player . . . of the last twenty years . . . there was no one near him in any way."

The horizon is full of promise. With the interaction of jazz, Indian ragas, and classical styles, and with the technical brilliance of artists such as Mahavishnu John McLaughlin and Larry Coryell, we have much to look forward to. At the same time, there is a refreshing return to the basics—knock-down, drag-'em-out, pumping rock and roll, and crying, screaming, hard-driving blues. We can choose between the refined and sophisticated on the one hand, and good-old, sensual exhibitionism on the other. Guitar music has so many personalities, so many moods. It's no wonder that millions of Americans have realized that guitars can help us to articulate our thoughts, emotions, and drives. The results are good. Guitars are everywhere.

Clarence White (June 7, 1944–July 14, 1973), one of the best flatpickers who ever lived. As a kid he formed bluegrass bands with his brothers, Eric and Roland. Then in the early 1960s he founded the Kentucky Colonels, for years a bluegrass institution. Under the influence of James Burton and others, he began to spend more time with a newly acquired Telecaster than his D-28. He rapidly gained a formidable reputation as a session guitarist, playing with Linda Ronstadt, the Flying Burrito Brothers, Joe Cocker (e.g., "Dear Landlord"), and, crucially, the Byrds, which he joined as a full-fledged member at Chris Hillman's invitation in September of 1968. His contributions permitted the Byrds to regain their commercial success while shifting their stance from folk rock to country rock. They folded in the spring of 1973, and Clarence moved on to more session work and solo projects. A couple of months later he was struck down and killed by a drunk driver. *Photo courtesy Mildred White*

Michael Bloomfield. One of the most influential electric guitarists of the late 1960s, he turned on millions of players to the blues with his work in the Paul Butterfield Blues Band and the Electric Flag. He was also Bob Dylan's first notable electric guitarist (*Highway 61 Revisited*). Michael helped initiate the supergroup concept with the classic *Super Session* album. His *If You Love These Blues, Play 'Em As You Please* album was nominated for a Grammy in 1977. Setting trends with every guitar he used, Bloomfield popularized Telecasters, gold-tops, and sunburst Les Pauls.

George Benson

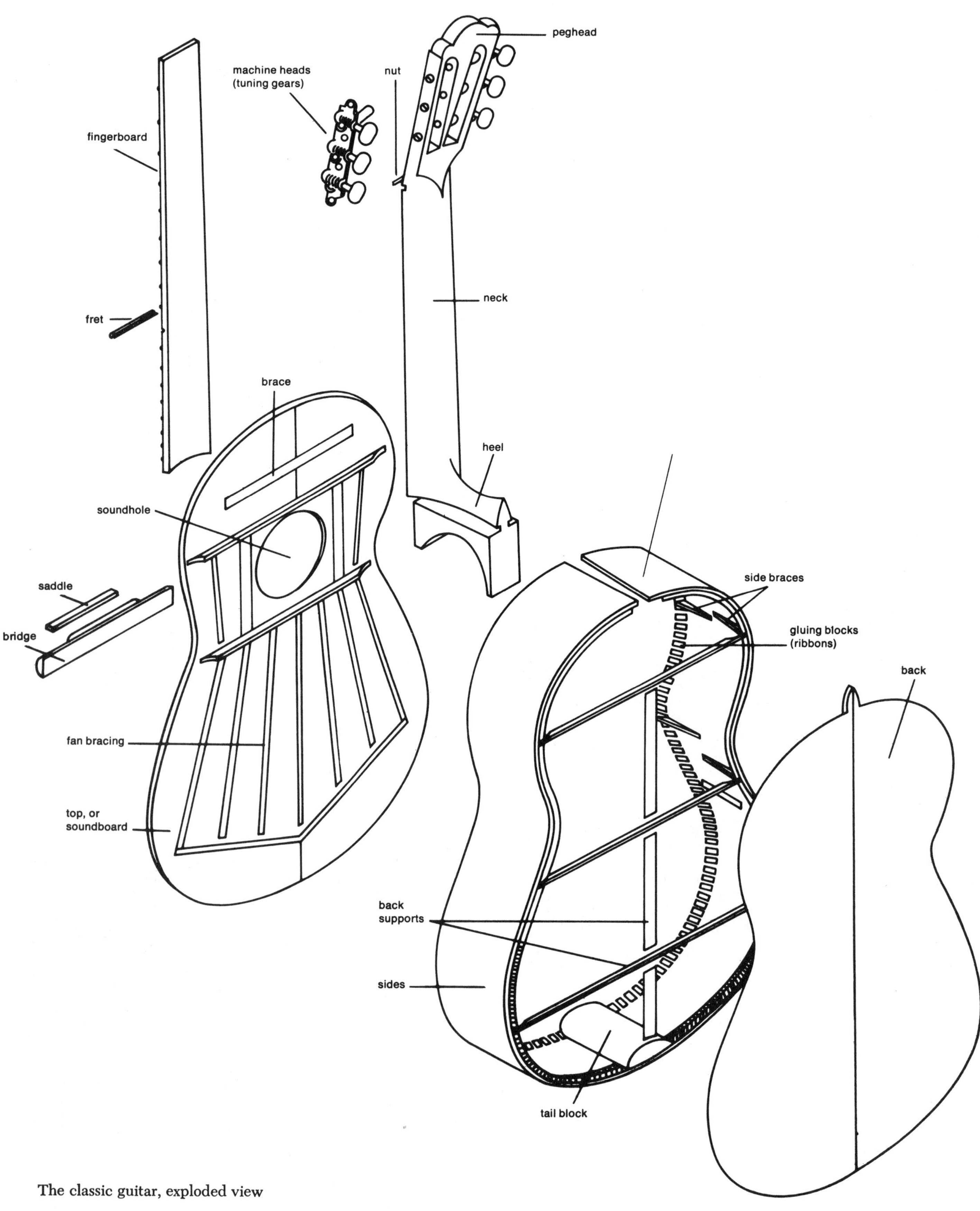

The classic guitar, exploded view

3

Acoustic Guitars

Martin D-45

TYPES AND USES

A guitar is designed to act as a resonator, an acoustic amplifier that moves a larger mass of air than the strings could move by themselves. A pure tone from a string unattached to a guitar body would be barely audible. There are four general categories of acoustic (nonelectric) guitars: flat-top steel-string, arched-top, classic, and flamenco. Even though they are all tuned and chorded the same way, each type has its own feel and tone, so try them all before deciding which one suits your tastes. These different guitars are closely related, and reading about one will increase your understanding of the others.

Flat-Top Steel-String (Folk Guitar, Western Guitar)

This is perhaps the most widely used guitar in this country; its name describes its distinguishing features. At first glance, the top is indeed flat. However, after a closer look, you may find that the top and back have a slight arch. The arched back is much more pro-

Takamine F-375

nounced in the Gibson J-55 and some models by Harptone. Typical flat-top dimensions are:

	STANDARD GUITAR	DREADNOUGHT OR JUMBO
Greatest Width	14″	15⅝″ to 16″
Body Length	19″	19⅜″ to 20″
Body Depth	4½″	4⅛″ to 4⅝″
Overall Length	38¼″	39⅜″ to 40½″

The back and sides of good flat-tops are usually constructed of East Indian or Brazilian rosewood or, occasionally, maple.* Less expensive, good quality models are frequently made from mahogany.

Most guitars have a two-piece back, though three-piece backs are not uncommon. The difference in construction entails a variation in the back bracing, a factor which may or may not affect the tone, depending upon the opinion of the particular guitar maker. In the last decade, manufacturers have experimented with synthetic materials; one successful result is Ovation's round-back guitar with its body of multilayered glass fibers.

The top is traditionally a tight-grained Alpine spruce, though cedar and redwood have been substituted in recent years with good results. Guitars constructed of plywood are generally more resistant to cracks, but their tone is not as rich. Factory-produced acoustic guitars are finished with several coats of spray lacquer or polyester.

The flat-top's neck is commonly carved from mahogany (less often from maple or cedar) and joins the body at the fourteenth or twelfth fret, usually employing a dovetail design which permits the guitar maker to construct the body before he attaches the neck. In professional guitars, ebony and rosewood are most often used for the fingerboard and bridge.

Scales range in length from 20 to 26 inches, the majority being about 25½ inches with 18 to 20 frets, giving the instrument a range of nearly four octaves.† A relatively short scale, called a three-quarter-size neck, is recommended only for players with unusually small hands. Unless you fall into that category, get a full-size neck for proper chording, picking, and the

*The percentage of East Indian rosewood used in guitar manufacture has increased, due to restrictions imposed by the Brazilian government on rosewood exports.

†There may be a difference between acoustic and electric models in the spacing of the fingerboard, so that an electric may have more frets, even though its scale is sometimes a little shorter.

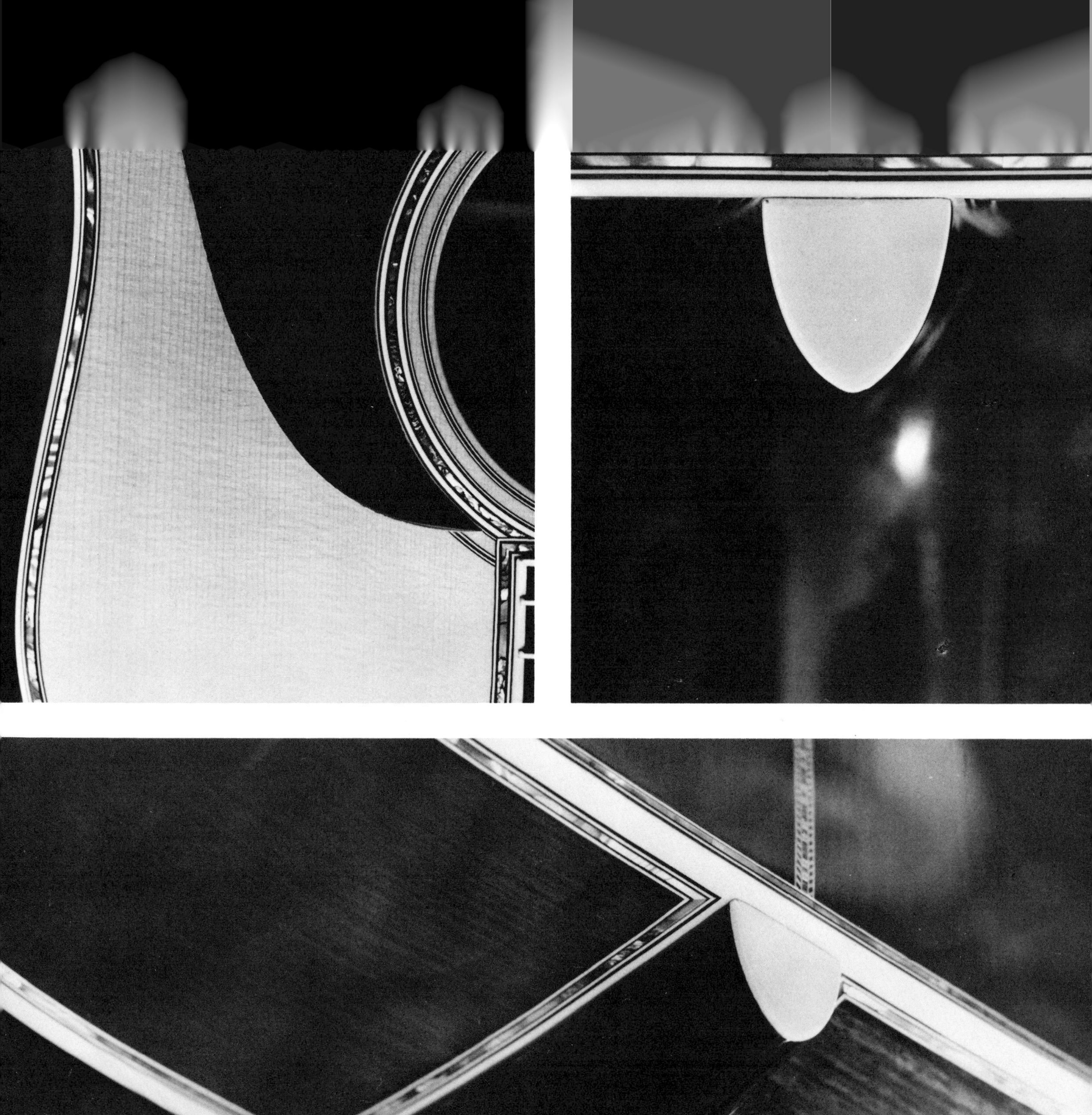

Gibson Super 400, introduced in 1934

best tone response. On a standard neck the width of the fretboard at the nut runs from 1½″ up to about 1⅞″. Fretboards are slightly rounded.

The flat-top guitar should be used only with strings made of some type of metal (steel, copper, bronze, and so forth). Using both flat pick and fingers, guitarists in folk, country and western, and folk-rock play the flat-top for rhythm and solo work. Hard rock musicians occasionally mike it for concerts or sessions, but the flat-top's tone is more often associated with such artists as Paul Simon, James Taylor, Joan Baez, Cat Stevens, Joni Mitchell, and Neil Diamond.

Some manufacturers offer electric models with a factory-equipped, magnetic pickup, and any flat-top may be converted to acoustic-electric by installing this device. Pickups are discussed in chapter 9.

Read the section on the classic guitar, since many of its topics also pertain to the steel string, including the way in which the tone is affected by the materials, sound hole, top, and bracing.

The Arched-Top Guitar

The nonelectric arched-top guitar has become rare, because of the declining popularity of the "big band" sound and the widespread use of electric guitars. It features both an arched top and back, with part of the body cut away on some models to permit the guitarist to reach the higher notes of the fingerboard (a Gibson innovation). Instead of a single, round hole, it has a sigmoid (f-shaped) hole on either side of the top, much like a violin. The purpose of any sound hole is to enhance the vibration of the top and to allow the air inside the body to escape. F-holes improve the pliability of the top, particularly near its outer edges, and they leave the center of the arched sound board undisturbed.

Unlike the flat fingerboard of the classic and flamenco guitars, the arched-top's fingerboard is slightly curved, permitting easier fretting of bar chords. The bridge is usually not glued to the top; it is held in place only by the string tension.

Strummed with a hard, flat pick and strung with medium- or heavy-gauge strings, the arched-top's bright tone and ability to project make it suitable for rhythm work in a combo or a dance band. Electric arched-tops are popular; in fact, most jazz players wouldn't think of using anything else.

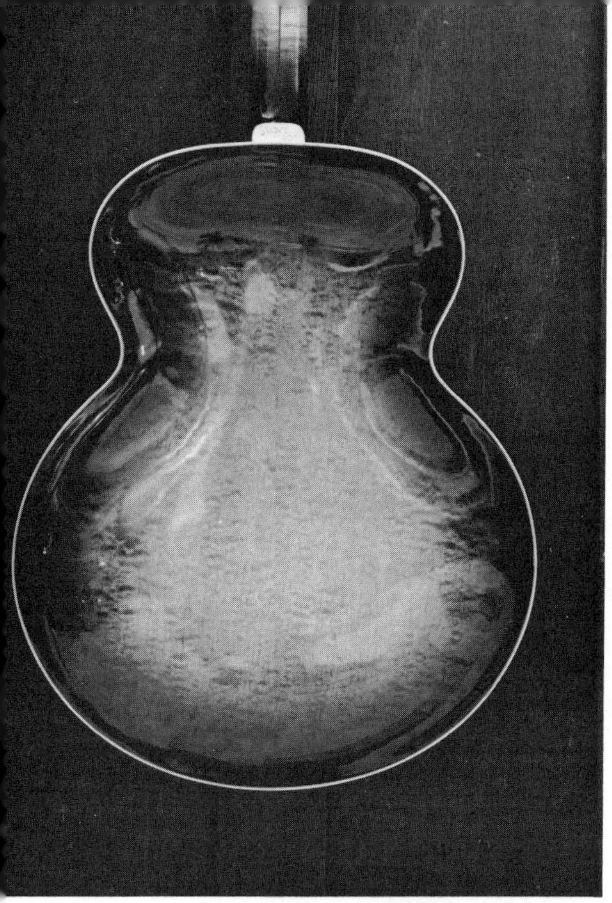

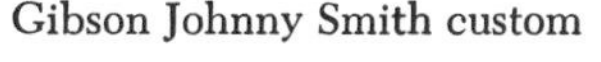

Gibson Johnny Smith custom

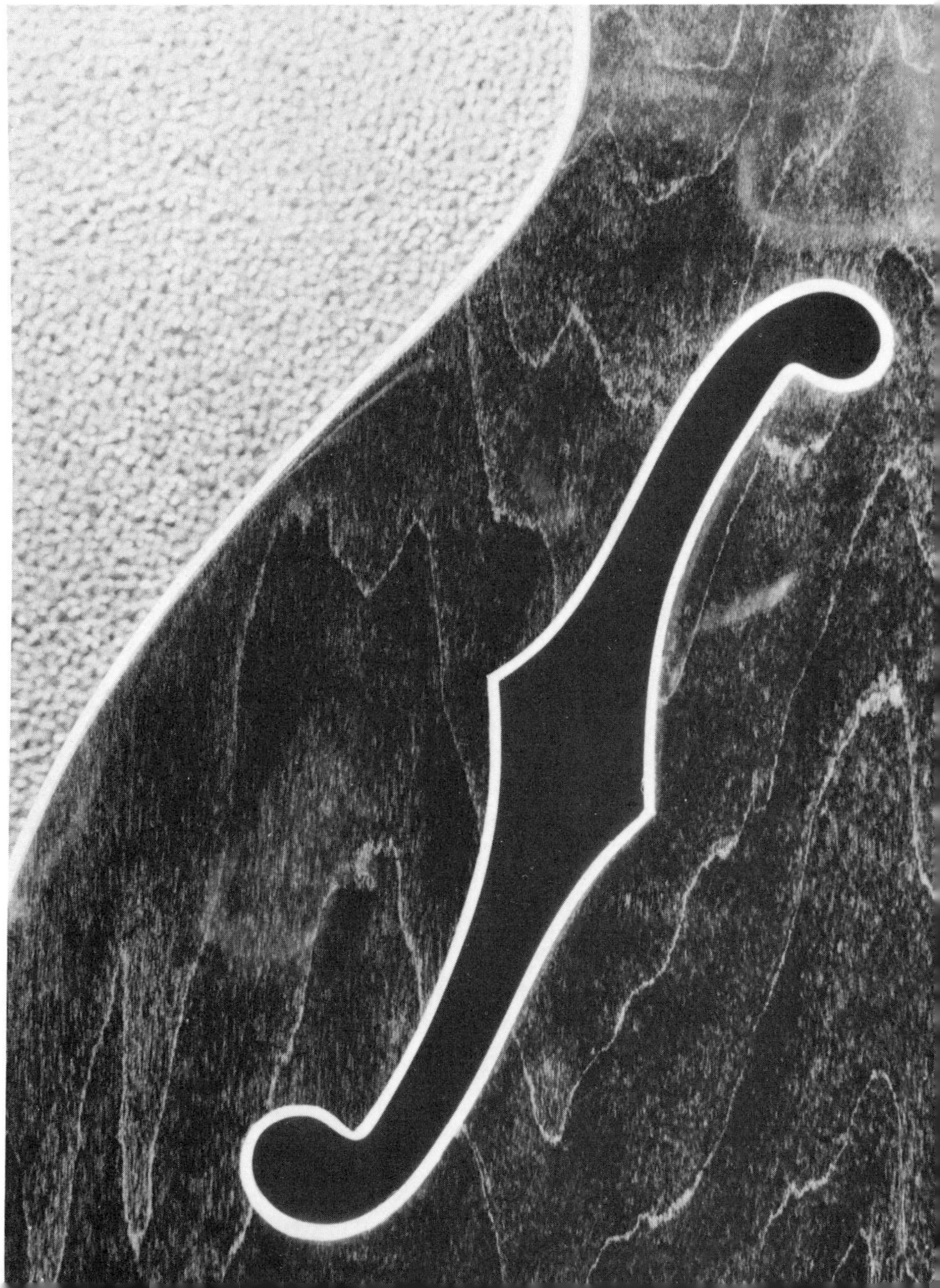

The Classic Guitar

The classic, or classical, guitar is the immediate ancestor of all other versions of the Spanish guitar, including the flamenco, flat-top steel-string, arched-top, metal resophonic, and the various electrics. Many factors affect its tone: the thickness and grain of the top, pattern of fan bracing, size, shape and location of the sound hole, composition and dimensions of the resonant chamber and, of course, the strings. Less significant tonal considerations are the manner in which the pieces are fitted and glued and the materials used for the nut and bridge saddle.

By far, the primary determinant of the tone is the top (table, soundboard). Finer tops are constructed of two "bookmatched" (see p. 46) halves of a single sheet of wood, quarter-cut, the grain widening toward the outside edges. Antique violins may have soundboards with fifty or more seasonal rings per inch, though wood of this caliber is now either rare or nonexistent. One luthier (guitar maker) recommends at least fifteen rings per inch in a handmade instrument. Gibson requires a minimum of fourteen rings.

Some makers carve the top slightly thinner on the treble side. Near the bridge, it may be only about $1/16''$ thick, so that when a small light bulb is placed inside the sound chamber, its light will shine through the top. This technique exposes the particular arrangement of the interior bracing and helps locate repairs.

A top must be strong enough to resist the tension of the strings, and it must vibrate in a manner that will produce an acceptable tone. These two considerations determine the types of wood to be used. Spruce (Alpine, Sitka, or German) and Spanish pine are excellent.

The guitar top has been compared to a speaker cone, which projects sound waves both to the front and to the rear. The vibrating top emits sound waves directly outward from its exterior surface and indirectly from the underside as well. The inside waves are deflected from the interior surfaces of the sound chamber and "focused" so that they project from the sound hole. As is the case in the design of speaker enclosures, the top and chamber must be constructed so that these direct and indirect sound waves are projected from the body simultaneously, "in phase." Oth-

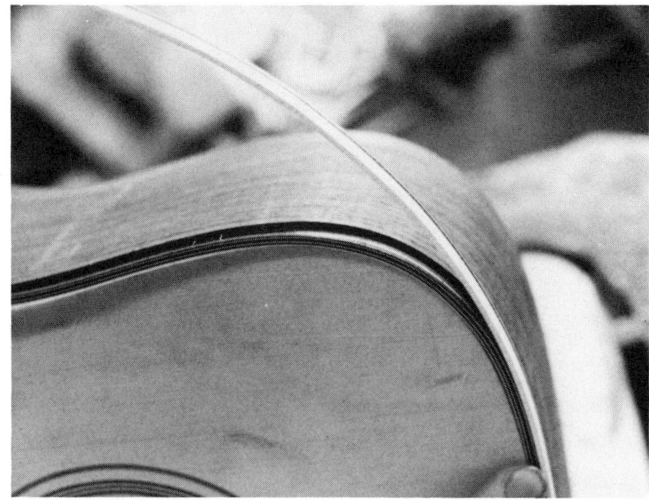

The light-colored protective edge strip is called "binding"; the decorative strips inlaid just inside the binding are known as "purfling."

Seasonal rings

erwise, they tend to cancel each other, decreasing the sound.

The sound hole balances the tone, partially regulating the amount of treble frequencies that emerge from the body. According to C. F. Martin & Co., the larger the sound hole, the greater the treble emphasis within limits. Its diameter is usually from 3¼″ to 3½″ in a classic guitar, though it varies with the size of the body. Complex inlays of colored woods, plastic, or mother-of-pearl often surround the sound hole. This pattern, or rosette, is a remnant of the Moorish influence on the guitar's evolution.

The entire body of the guitar vibrates, so the density and bracing of the sides and back, and even the materials used in the neck and fingerboard will affect the sound. Respected guitar builders disagree about the significance of the vibration of the various parts other than the top.

Rosewood is somewhat prone to splitting if exposed to changing weather conditions. However, it is still generally thought to be the finest wood for the resonant chamber. The main sources are South America, India, or, less often, Africa. South American rosewood, usually from Brazil, is known as palisander or *palo santo.* Mahogany and walnut are also good woods for guitar-making, and maple is thought to be the equal of rosewood, particularly in the northern European countries where violin makers have used it for centuries. There is a definite variation in quality among samples of any type of wood; a top grade mahogany is superior to a low grade rosewood.

The best guitars are made from aged woods. Having been stored for perhaps a decade, swelling and contracting with seasonal fluctuations in temperature and humidity, they are more stable and less likely to crack than young woods. Because of the scarcity of fine, aged woods, and for other economic reasons, inexpensive guitars may be made from plywood. The opposing grains of the various plys contribute much strength, but they greatly inhibit vibration—creating an inferior tone.

The thin top of a good classic guitar would splinter under the pressure exerted by the strings were it not reinforced by an arrangement of internal struts and braces. The size, shape, density, and distribution of these sound conductors affect the tone, and the personality of the guitar may be altered by shaving or sanding them. This strut job could severely weaken the top, unless performed by an expert.

The great luthier Antonio Torres Jurado (1817–1892), known simply as Torres, originated the fan system from which today's patterns are derived. Variations that bear the names of their designers are Córdoba and Esteso, among several others.

Usually constructed of cedar or mahogany, the neck of the classic guitar is shorter (usually nineteen frets) and wider (about two inches at the nut) than that of the folk or Western guitar, and its strings are spaced farther apart. Traditionally, the ebony or rosewood fingerboard has no dots or other position markers. Another distinguishing feature is the tuning machines, which face toward the back instead of to the sides. The nut is fashioned from ivory, plastic, bone, or, less often, ebony. The body of the classic guitar joins the neck at the twelfth fret, unlike the steel-string, which usually joins at fret 14.

Torres developed the scale length of 650 mm., just under 25$\frac{5}{7}$″. The frets are located on the fingerboard according to a mathematical formula by which the space between each two consecutive frets continues to decrease; the interval between frets 1 and 2 is just under three times the interval between frets 18 and 19. The formula states that the distance between the nut and fret 1 equals $\frac{1}{18}$ of the entire string length; the distance between frets 1 and 2 equals $\frac{1}{18}$ of the *remaining* string length. The frets proceed in this manner at decreasing intervals up the length of the fingerboard. Conveniently termed the "Rule of Eighteen," the formula's precise multiplier is actually 17.835.

Today's classic guitar may have an extra fret about

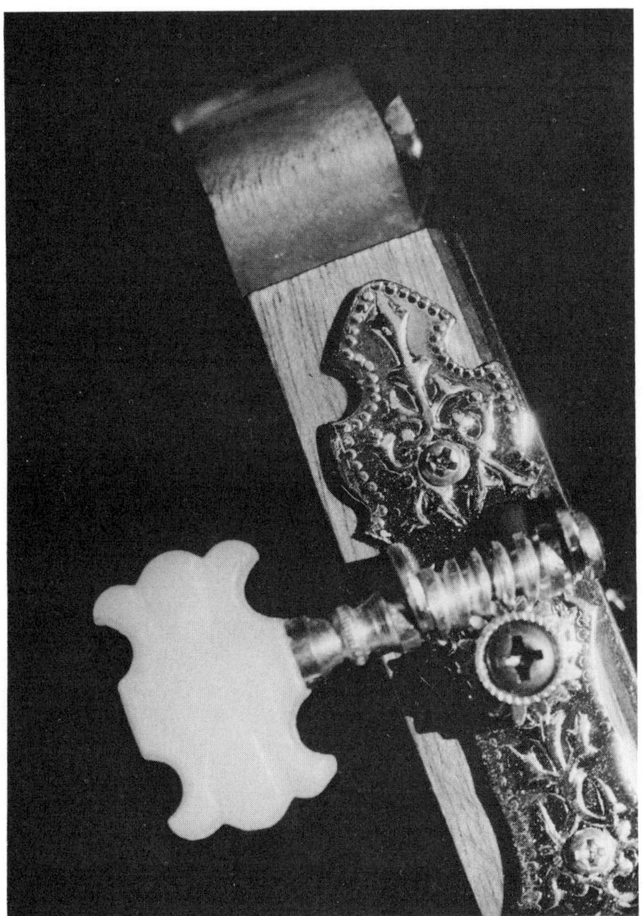

⅛″ from the nut. Intended to provide easier fretting, the design is borrowed from German luthiers, especially Hermann Hauser (1882–1952). On these guitars, the string length is measured from the extra fret to the bridge saddle.

The classic guitar is the instrument of Andres Segovia, Julian Bream, Laurindo Almeida, Oscar Ghiglia, Christopher Parkening, and a handful of other concert masters, though many folk singers also prefer its mellower, more delicate sound and gentle feel.

Unfortunately, there are relatively few great luthiers. José Ramírez III of Madrid heads one of the world's great guitar-making families. His grandfather, José Ramírez I (about 1857–1923), was an apprentice to Gonzales. Manuel Ramírez, the younger brother of José I, was so greatly influenced by Torres that he broke with José to build his own guitars. One of them was presented in 1916 to Segovia, who was enraptured with its beauty and resonance. Two of Manuel's students were Domingo Esteso and Santos Hernández, great guitarreros in their own right.

José Ramírez II was instructed by his father, José I, although his guitars more closely resembled those of his uncle, Manuel. José Ramírez II trained his own son, José III, who now builds guitars in the family workshop on Madrid's Calle Concepción Jerónima, where a fourth generation of the Ramírez family is learning the craft.

Other great names include Rodríguez, Sobrinos de Esteso (nephews of Esteso), and Ignacio Fleta, who builds about thirty-five guitars a year. Marcelo Barbero, a student of José Ramírez II, was the teacher of the great Arcangel Fernández who, in turn, is teaching Marcelo Barbero, Jr. Though still a young man, Manuel Reyes is another respected maker of both flamenco and classic guitars. In America, we are fortunate to have the brilliant luthiers, Velásquez of New York and José Oribe of Los Angeles.

The Flamenco Guitar

Flamenco is a broad art form of many variations, reflecting the history and temperament of the Andalusian gypsy. With roots entwined in rich Mediterranean cultures—Jewish, Moorish, Portuguese, Byzantine, and others—its structure is complex and its impact is dazzling. Segovia characterizes this well-named musical style (from *flama*, or flame) as "that most difficult of arts." Poignant, hypnotic and impassioned, the many

Flamenco tuning pegs

Bending sides in a body mold at the Dobro plant. The metal hoses attach to heating elements.

moods of flamenco have influenced musicians and composers from Miles Davis to Stravinsky; Ravel, Debussy, and Rimsky-Korsakov. Contemporary flamenco masters include Paco de Lucia, Juan Serrano, Manitas de Plata, Sabicas, and, of course, Carlos Montoya.

The flamenco guitar is essentially a modification of the classic guitar, nearly identical in shape, but specially designed to capture the vigor of the music. The sides and back are made of Spanish cypress, because it produces a tone more *brillante* than the various woods used in classic guitars. The cypress gives the flamenco guitar its most distinguishing visual characteristic: its color is blond instead of the dark, reddish brown of rosewood.*

The flamenco traditionally has an ebony fingerboard on a cedar neck. The top, made of straight-grained spruce or pine, often from Germany, is sometimes specially carved to be extra thin. Since the flamenco guitar weighs less than the classical, the lightweight, ebony tuning keys, which project directly through the face of the peghead, help to balance it when held in the almost upright flamenco position. Still, mechanical (worm and gear) tuners are often substituted. Another mark of the flamenco guitar is its *golpeador*, the thin celluloid plate on which the artist performs the percussive tapping characteristic of gypsy music.

The depth of the flamenco guitar's sound chamber is about 3½″ at the top and 3¾″ at the bottom; its length is 16″ and its width is 14″. In the classic guitar, all of these dimensions slightly increase.

There are other, less obvious, variations between the flamenco and the classic guitars, intended to accommodate the differences in technique between the two arts. The fingerboard of the traditional flamenco guitar is narrower than that of the classic guitar. Its bridge saddle is carved to set the strings closer to the frets, necessitating a sensitive operation in which the luthier planes the neck, so that it inclines at just the right angle. All of these modifications give the flamenco guitar a faster playing action.

The Metal Resophonic Guitar

John, Rudy, and Emil Dopera† (originally spelled Dopyera) were three Czechoslovakian brothers who were partners in a musical instrument company called

*Arcangel Fernández of Madrid sometimes makes the "black flamenco" guitar of rosewood, when ordered by the client.

† There were two other brothers in the family. Louis, now deceased, joined in the mid-Thirties to assist in the company's administration. Robert was not involved in the business.

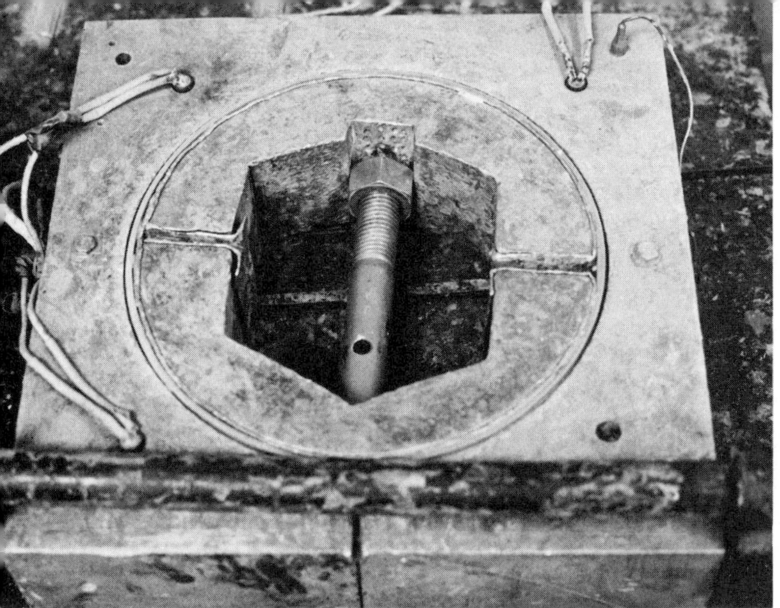

Dobro interior sound ring being shaped in a mold

Clamps hold edge strips in place while the glue dries.

Most Nationals had metal bodies, but this wooden Trojan was an exception. It cost $37.50 in 1936. The other single-resonator guitars of that period were the Triolian (simulated mahogany finish, $47.50), Duolian ("prismatic" gray/green crackle finish, $35), and the Style 0 (plated brass alloy body with etchings of a lagoon, palm trees, $65). Mid-Thirties Tri-Plates (three resonators each) included the Style 4 (heavily engraved, $195), Model 35 (silver alloy body, etching of a Renaissance musician, $135), and the Style 97 (nickel-plated brass alloy, surf rider etching, $97.50).

National. In 1926, they invented National's Tri-Plate metal resophonic guitar: this consisted of an all-metal body, with three 6″ spun cones straddled by a T-shaped bridge support. The brothers split from National in 1928, formed the Dobro (an abbreviation of Dopera Brothers) company and offered guitars with wooden bodies and metal resonators beginning in 1929. Dobro's designs so completely dominated the market that its brand name identified the instrument itself, just as Coke, Scotch Tape, and Kleenex do in their respective fields. Musicians called a metal resophonic guitar a dobro, regardless of who manufactured it.

The events of the early Thirties were sufficiently confusing to guarantee a rich folklore for the resophonic guitar, complete with legends, misconceptions, and rumors. Before that time, Nationals had metal bodies, Dobros had wooden ones. Because of vigorous competition, National began making wooden bodies, and Dobro began making metal bodies. Tired of fighting, the two companies called it quits and merged in 1934, making National Dobro guitars until America joined World War II in 1941.

During the war, National became Valco, and in about 1947 the name Dobro was dropped in favor of National and Supro. Emil (Ed) Dopera again(1961) began building metal resophonic guitars with wooden

Two types of resonators have been used over the years. The original National style (*top*) is a smooth cone of spun metal, the peak capped by the wooden bridge piece, or "biscuit." The Dobro type is bowl shaped, the bridge resting on a separate, eight-legged supporting brace, or "spider."

Dobro model 36

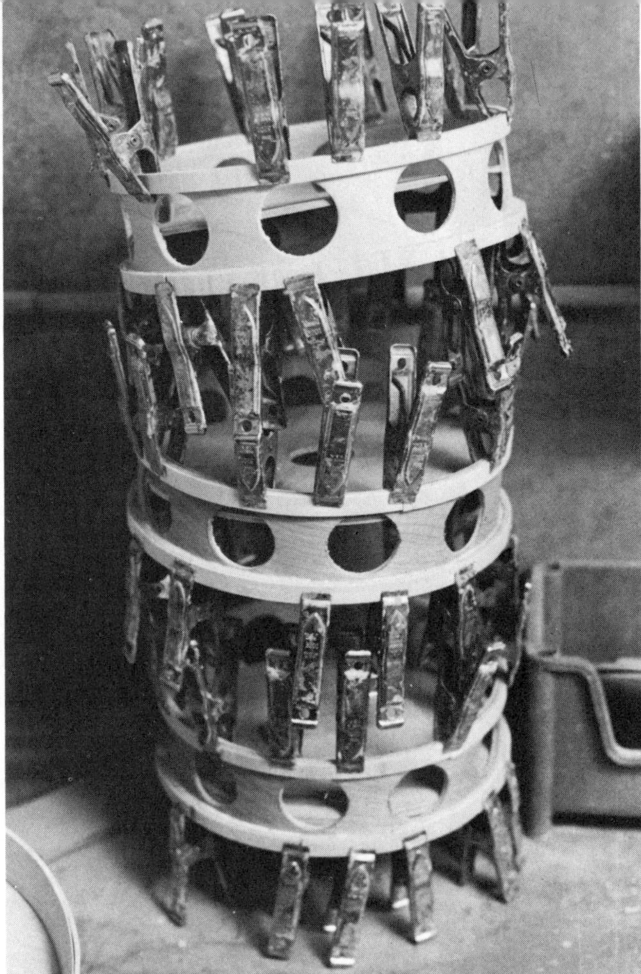

A stack of sound rings, held together with clips while the glue dries. Early Dobro sound rings had smaller holes. Some were made with parallelogram-shaped holes, but the dies were lost c. 1939.

A gluing press

bodies. The Mosrite company acquired interests in 1966 or 1967, but built few guitars. Ed's instruments were called Dopera Originals and Hound Dogs after 1968, when legal restrictions prohibited him from using the name Dobro. In 1971 the name Dobro became available again. Ed presently makes his guitars at the Original Musical Instrument factory in Long Beach, California. The body of the guitar is made from either maple, sheet steel, or chrome-plated bell brass. The instruments range from about three hundred seventy-five to twelve hundred dollars. OMI is managed by Ron Lazar, a Dopera relative.

Like its predecessor, the Hawaiian steel guitar, the dobro is played with a metal bar, though it may also be tuned and strummed conventionally. Since the bar does not press the strings to the fingerboard, the player may glide up and down in a sweeping motion, producing a wavering tone of variable pitch.

The acceptance of the resophonic guitar rose and fell in proportion to the popularity of Hawaiian and country music. It was also a favorite among Southern blues players, including Bukka White, Tampa Red, Leroy Carr, and Blind Boy Fuller. Around 1960, the instrument was reborn in the resurgence of enthusiasm for bluegrass music. The dobro shared the stage with the five-string banjo, acoustic guitar, mandolin, fiddle, and the washtub or acoustic bass.

In the late Sixties, with the influence of country and western becoming greater in rock circles, the demand for dobros could not be ignored. Until they were reissued, practically any dobro was a collector's item and sold for up to ten times its original price. The Gretsch company markets resophonic guitars with the obviously derivative name of Sho-Bro. Tut Taylor and Del Vecchio are other manufacturers.

Speedy-fingered Buck "Uncle Josh" Graves was formerly with Flatt & Scruggs, the archetype modern bluegrass band. Recently a member of the Earl Scruggs Revue, he is probably the most influential player of the dobro in its history. Shot Jackson and Tut Taylor are other masters. Their younger colleagues in rock music have included the late Duane Allman, Richard Betts (Allman Brothers), Johnny Winter, and Poco's Rusty Young. The instrument is featured in "A Child's Claim To Fame" (Buffalo Springfield, with James Burton's dobro duet), "Pony Boy" (Allman Brothers), "You Gotta Move" (Rolling Stones) and the *Nashville Skyline* album (Bob Dylan).

Attaching the bridge saddle to supporting spokes, or "spider"

Shaping the interior neck joint

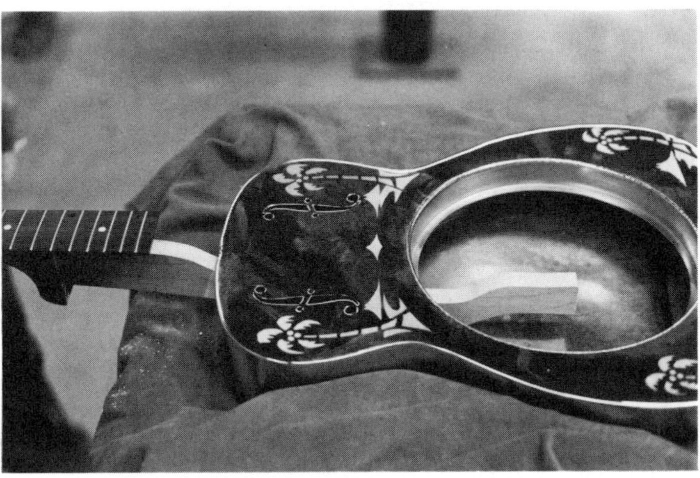

The neck and fingerboard are glued to a sturdy brace; this assembly is then bolted to the metal body.

The Twelve-String Guitar

Identical in many respects to the six-string flat-top guitar, the twelve-string is found in most forms of contemporary music, particularly folk. Huddie Ledbetter, well known to fans of acoustic blues as Leadbelly, proclaimed himself "King of the Twelve-String Guitar." Barbecue Bob, Howlin' Wolf, Charlie Lincoln, and John Lee Hooker were other early blues guitarists who sometimes played the twelve. Pete Seeger, the exceptional artist and tireless student of American music, revived the twelve among folk guitarists. Then, thanks to the Byrds, electric twelve-string guitars enjoyed short-lived though substantial popularity in the late 1960s. The vast majority of models currently produced are acoustic.

The twelve strings are arranged in six pairs, subject to a variety of tunings. Additional neck reinforcement, necessitated by the extra string tension, distinguishes the twelve from the standard flat-top. It's played in the same manner as the standard guitar, as far as chords, scales, picking, and strumming are concerned, though the neck usually joins at fret 12, instead of fret 14. However, the proper fretting of clear notes and chords entails more concentration until you can get used to the greater left-hand effort required. As Barney Kessel notes in *The Guitar*, certain dissonant chords may be inappropriate on the twelve-string because of its extra-rich but delicate sound.

Tunings *

The most common tuning system is based on the six-string guitar. The strings of either the first two or three sets are tuned in unison, while the remaining sets each consist of two strings tuned one octave apart.

Twelve-String Tuning, Standard Pitch

12th string	E:	164.8 Hz
11th string		82.4
10th string	A:	220.0
9th string		110.0
8th string	D:	293.6
7th string		146.8
6th string	G:	392.0
5th string		196.0
4th string	B:	246.9
3rd string		246.9
2nd string	E:	329.6
1st string		329.6

*Six-string tuning variations are found in chapter 7, pp. 124, 125.

Guild F-512 12-string flat top

A variation consists of these six-string notes, each lowered by one whole step (two frets) to reduce string tension: D G C F A D. To avoid damage, most twelves *must* be tuned down to this level. To accommpany other instruments without transposing the chords, a capo at the second fret provides the standard "E" pitch.

Glen Campbell was a respected studio musician long before he became a full-fledged superstar, and his twelve-string guitar albums are good examples of the instrument's capabilities. Flashy country and western twelve-string is a specialty of Larry Collins, and any jazz-guitar fan should investigate the brilliant New Yorker Pat Martino.

Bozo 12-string

ACOUSTIC GUITAR CONSTRUCTION

An Interview with David Russell Young

David Russell Young makes guitars. Those musicians who will settle only for handmade instruments consider him to be one of America's most talented luthiers. His guitars, distinguished by their balanced tone and often complex inlays of abalone and mother-of-pearl, are played by John Prine and other discriminating artists. One of his most exceptional guitars was constructed for the late Gram Parsons.

The thirty-year-old author of *The Steel String Guitar: Construction and Repair* works in his San Fernando Valley shop in Los Angeles, California. David Young builds about a dozen guitars each year, ranging in price up to two thousand dollars.

T.W.: What is the first stage in building a David Young guitar?

D.Y.: I have to buy a lot of top-grade wood, wherever I can find it. There is East Indian rosewood for the two- and three-piece backs. It's getting extremely difficult to find good wood, and the prices have increased outrageously—they've almost doubled in the past couple of years. A hardwood specialty house cuts the wood into planks, and I sift through it, finding about one piece in a hundred that's suitable. It's got to have just about a straight vertical grain, with no flaws in it. Rosewood is really prone to checks and cracks. It's also tough to get a wide enough board for a two-piece back. That's why there are a lot more three-piece backs now.

T.W.: What is bookmatching, and what are its advantages?

D.Y.: Bookmatching is a way of cutting the pieces for the top and the back. You take a single piece, and slice it into two sheets, each the same length and width as the original, but only half as thick. It's like opening a book at its center and laying out the two halves, which are now symmetrically grained. It looks very nice, and there are structural considerations as well. Most pieces of wood will "work" or shrink a tiny bit, and bookmatching assures even, symmetrical seasoning. Shrinkage isn't too much of a problem if the wood has been around the shop for several months, all spliced up and thinned down, because you can observe it and get a pretty good idea of how stable it is.

T.W.: Has the wood been cured by the time it reaches you?

D.Y.: I think most of the rosewood has been kiln-dried, though it's preferable to get it air-dried, because the wood is stronger. That's where they just stack it and cover it for a while. It takes a long time, and because of the economic factors, they want to shove the stuff through as fast as they can. So kiln-drying is common. The air-dried wood, if you can get it at all, is more expensive.

The first step is to join the pieces for the top and back. They are glued and held into place by means of clamps and wedges. The purfling strip down the middle of the back is primarily decorative.

T.W.: What kind of wood is used for the top?

D.Y.: Traditionally, spruce is used. However, I use redwood or Canadian cedar almost all of the time. One of the first things you'll notice is the reddish color; they look like they're fifty years old the day they're finished. It's getting almost impossible to get good European spruce for the tops, because the demand is outrunning the supply, but cedar and redwood are fairly easy to obtain. Also, by the time spruce gets here from Germany or Yugoslavia or wherever, it's been picked over in the original country, picked over again before it's shipped, picked over in New York . . . by the time it arrives there is maybe one pretty nice top in a hundred. Acoustically, I have just as good results with redwood or cedar as I have with spruce. If anything, I've had a little better luck with them. Though redwood and cedar tops are not quite as strong as spruce, they are less likely to change dimension from fluctuations in humidity. The pieces are bookmatched for the top, the same way as for the back, except that the top is always of two pieces, whereas the back is sometimes three pieces.

T.W.: What sort of materials are used for the rest of the instrument?

D.Y.: Rosewood or mahogany for the back and sides, ebony for the fingerboard and peghead veneer, and then it's the redwood, cedar, or spruce for the top.

T.W.: How are the top and back thinned?

D.Y.: I take them to a commercial sander, where the equipment is extremely precise. Hand sanding is tedious, and you really don't get any better results. Of course, there is a lot of hand sanding in the later stages. A redwood top should be a little thicker than a cedar top, and a cedar top should be a little thicker than one of spruce. Perhaps 100 to 125/1,000 of an inch for redwood, and maybe 5/1,000 thinner for the cedar, and another 5/1,000 thinner for spruce. The softer the wood, the thicker you want it.

T.W.: How is the rosette inlaid?

D.Y.: I rout out the circular groove, and then inlay about ten separate bands with epoxy between them, alternating strips of white holly, blue-dyed harewood, and either black ebony or fiberboard, such as they use in violin purfling. The abalone requires quite a bit more work. I buy it in small sheets, scribe it to size, and cut it with a fret saw. It usually takes about twenty separate pieces of abalone to complete the circle.

T.W.: How much of the guitar's tone depends upon the design of the top bracing?

Inside the acoustic guitar

Guitar Woods: Maple

Maple is widely found throughout Canada and in the northern and eastern United States. Usually an off-white in color, it is hard, heavy, strong, shock resistant and stiff. Often the grain is fairly straight, but exotic variations in pattern include bird's-eye and curly maple. The latter is used for the backs and sides of some of America's finest guitars (e.g., Guild F-50), and highly figured "flame" maple distinguishes Gibson's 1958–1960 Les Paul Standards. Rock maple and hard maple (common names for sugar maple) are used by Fender for fingerboards and solid necks.

Lower left: large guitar clamp, crack-repair clamp
Top row: circle cutters, flexible mirror, Deep-throat clamp
Lower right: end nippers, awls, tapered reamer, Vernier caliper

Back row: dovetail saw, fret saw, chisel, gouge, carving knives, surform file and purfling cutter
Center: violinmakers' planes
Front row: sanding drum, rotary rasp, files, violin scrapers, files, scales and straightedge

D.Y.: I'd say the tone is at least 80 percent the top and the way you brace it. That seems to be the consensus among guitar makers. Like most luthiers, I use an "X" bracing pattern for steel-string guitars. It is nonsymmetrical because of the difference in response of the treble side and the bass side. The treble side is braced stiffer to provide balanced volume. The braces should be constructed of spruce, for strength. There is one extra-sturdy brace that runs straight across the top, from left to right, above the hole, and it's made of Honduras mahogany. That part of the guitar doesn't vibrate very much to begin with, and mahogany is very rigid and stable, making it suitable for connecting the brace to the reinforcing block which joins the neck.

Another thing, any object will resonate more easily at some frequencies than at others. When you tap the top of a good acoustic guitar, you will produce a tone—not a pure tone, but it will have a recognizable pitch. The resonant pitch of the top is lowered by thinning either the braces or the top itself, making it more flexible. The guitar will respond more strongly at that particular pitch, so some makers try to "tune" the top to an A, a D, or an E, since those are common guitar keys. A top made from spruce, redwood, or cedar will resonate differently than the rosewood or mahogany back, because of the difference in the density of the wood. The result is that there is less chance of producing the dissonant overtones or buzzing that sometimes occur when the top and back are very similar in density and acoustic properties. However, there's not much consensus on this point.

The back is braced with strips of hard mahogany running parallel from left to right, plus there is a cross-grained strip running down the length of the back's glue joint, for added support.

T.W.: Is the back supposed to vibrate, as well as the top?

D.Y.: There's a division of opinion on that. Some builders say that they don't want the back to vibrate at all, that it's supposed to serve only as the rear limit of the volume of air you are enclosing. However, I remember that my first really good classic guitar projected much better if I didn't hold it against my body, damping the vibration of the back. I don't think anyone has yet measured the importance of the back's vibration to the overall tone.

T.W.: How are the sides bent?

D.Y.: The sides are from 3/32 of an inch to 1/10 of an inch thick. I generally soak the wood overnight, and then I heat up a metal tube with a torch, and bend the sides over the tube by hand to their rough shape. Then they're clamped into a mold overnight to insure symmetry. Strips of low-grain basswood are grooved to make them flexible, and they are attached to the sides to provide a gluing surface for joining the top and back. Additionally, there are blocks of Honduras mahogany placed at the front and rear ends, and about seven reinforcing strips of rosewood on each side, running perpendicular to the grain. If the guitar

Guitar Woods: Mahogany

Mahogany is a fine wood for backs and sides, though considered to be a notch below rosewood or maple. Several of the well-known companies begin their lines with a mahogany guitar (e.g., Guild F-20, Martin D-18), and many use this wood for necks in both acoustic and electric guitars (e.g., Gibson). This light-to-dark reddish brown wood is stable, durable, attractive, consistent in texture, but moderately variable in weight, hardness, and strength. It is a low-shrinkage wood, easy to work with glues and tools, and it finishes beautifully.

Mahogany grows in the West Indies and on the mainland from Mexico through all of Central America to the northern half of South America. Honduras is the major source of mahogany used in guitar construction. "African mahogany" and "Philippine mahogany," as they are known in the lumber trade, include many of the two hundred or so species of wood often substituted for true mahogany.

Bending the side

A David Russell Young Guitar

is rapped on the side, it's a lot less likely to crack, and if it does, it will probably only crack in between two consecutive strips. Some guitars will crack all the way around, because of inadequate side bracing.

T.W.: What kind of glues do you use?

D.Y.: Either epoxy, or a substance called Tite-bond. Animal glues tend to break down in time, and they're hygroscopic—if the humidity goes up, they absorb moisture. The top and back are glued on to overlap the sides, and held in place with a jig and about sixty spring-compression clamps, all the way around. Each clamp has about five pounds of pressure, so I can get a lot of tension, very evenly distributed. It's clamped up overnight, but its full strength isn't reached until the glue has been dry a week.

T.W.: How is the binding applied to the sides?

D.Y.: The sides are sanded, to smooth out the overlapping top, and then there's a groove routed out of the corner where the top and the sides join. This groove accommodates the rosewood and holly strips of binding. They are shaped on the heated metal tube, like the sides, and glued on, held tight for a day with elastic shock cord. I never use plastic, because it doesn't look as good, and more important, it's not as dimensionally stable as the wood. It may shrink, and pull away from the sides at the guitar's waists. The binding covers over the end grain of the wood, protecting against the absorption of moisture.

T.W.: What kind of wood do you use for the neck?

D.Y.: Generally, Honduras mahogany, because of its stability, and sometimes rosewood, which is beautiful and also very hard. A hard wood in the neck allows the notes to sustain longer; it'll ring longer. I splice the peghead to the neck, rather than bandsawing the neck from a single piece of wood; this keeps the pull of the strings parallel to the wood grain. I rout down the center of the neck for a ½″ × ¼″ steel reinforcing bar, which is held in place with epoxy cement. This makes the neck very stiff, improves the sound of the guitar, and absolutely prevents warping. I don't use an adjustable truss rod, because they place a tremendous compression load on the neck and eventually tend to produce an S-shaped warp.

There is a sheet of either ebony or rosewood veneer glued to the face of the peghead, and holes are drilled for the machines. The holes are a little larger at the top end to accommodate a washer, which keeps the lacquer from cracking. I often place strips of abalone and outer binding around the edge of the peghead and along the sides of the fingerboard, by the same process used in applying the binding to the guitar body.

T.W.: What kind of material is used for the fingerboard?

D.Y.: Ebony or rosewood. Ebony probably helps the sound a little, because it is so dense. Also, it's a lot more resistant to wear from fingers and strings, and it's easier to work with for inlays. A precision machine cuts the grooves for the frets, and the side markers are made from

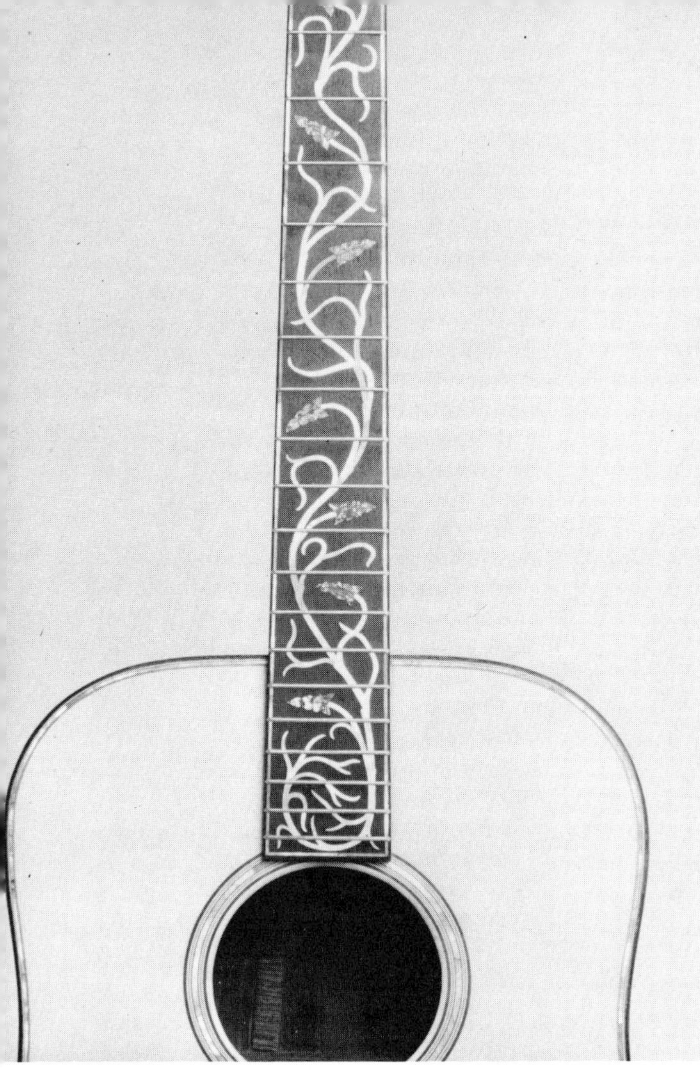

One of the world's most prized woods, Brazilian rosewood grows in many shades of brown, red, and even purple. Its large pores, wild colors, and swirling black grain are especially distinctive. It is known in its native land as "jacaranda," though some guitar makers reserve that term for their most exotic pieces. Most of the Brazilian forests are severely depleted.

Indian rosewood

Sitka spruce, also known as "yellow," "coast," or "tideland spruce," is a moderately strong, uniformly textured wood with an off-white or light yellow color, generally straight grain, high degree of resonance, and few resin ducts. These properties, plus the fact that the wood can be easily worked, make it ideal for guitar tops and piano soundboards. Almost ninety percent of America's spruce is from Alaska, though it also grows in a narrow 1,800 mile strip that extends down the Pacific coast of northern California. Incidentally, more than half of Alaska's spruce is exported to Japan.

African ebony is sometimes used in guitar building for tuning pegs and bridges, but more often for fingerboards on the finest instruments (e.g., Martin D-35, Gibson Les Paul Custom). One of the strongest, densest, and heaviest of all commercial woods, it averages over sixty pounds per cubic foot. It is so hard that metal-cutting equipment is sometimes required to work it. The best ebony is extremely fine in texture and pure black; inferior grades are streaked.

gold wire, set ⅛″ deep into holes which are cut with a drill press. Standard nickel-silver fret wire is used.

T.W.: Is the heel one piece?

D.Y.: It can be, though it's often several pieces cut from the same wood as the neck, and epoxied together. This matches the grain in the neck and the heel. The heel and the contours of the neck are smoothed with files, rasps, and sandpaper. Then the neck is set, to make sure that the bridge is at the right height and that the action is comfortable. This is critical, because a guitar with an improperly angled neck may be impossible to play and difficult to repair.

The neck and fingerboard assembly is glued to the body, and then I inlay position markers into the fingerboard. I use ivory for the nut and bridge saddle. Ivory or bone allows better sound conduction than the softer plastic. Bone tends to discolor after a while, but ivory becomes more beautiful with age.

T.W.: How are the complicated decorations inlaid into the peghead and fingerboard—the flowers, dragonflies, and other designs?

D.Y.: I take the pattern and glue it down on a sheet of pearl, and cut out the pieces with a jeweler's saw. In this bird, each feather is a separate piece fitted into its own groove. The grooves are cut out by hand with a miniature dental chisel. An inlay like this takes a few days.

T.W.: How is the finish applied?

D.Y.: I mask off the fingerboard and the area where the bridge will go, cover the sound hole and then a filler is used to fill the pores, which in rosewood or mahogany are fairly large. It varies with the piece of wood, but there are three or four thin coats of sealer, then half a dozen coats of lacquer, all of which are sanded out. I drill holes all the way through the top for the bridge pins. There is a rosewood plate underneath the bridge for support.

After the wet-sanding with 600-grade sandpaper, the guitar is rubbed out with rubbing compound and a lamb's-wool buffer. Then the bridge goes on, the frets are filed, the nut and saddle go in—put in the tuners and string it up. I use Schaller tuning gears and medium-gauge strings.

T.W.: How long does it take to build one of these instruments?

D.Y.: The mahogany guitars take around three weeks. The rosewoods take longer, perhaps a month. If there is a lot of inlaying to be done, it's almost two months' work.

T.W.: Does the resonance of a guitar improve with age?

D.Y.: Yes. It seems as though classic guitars improve strikingly during the first year, and, maybe, very slowly after that. It's also important that they are played. If they just sit, some of the tone is lost. Violins that are kept in museums must occasionally be taken out and played to keep their tone up.*

*Gibson adds that lacquer used on their guitars contains solvents that escape during the first few years after the guitar is built. Since the lacquer affects the vibration of the wood, this ageing can mellow the tone.

T.W.: Do you have a particular tone that you try to build into your guitars?

D.Y.: I try to balance the treble and bass tones, so that it's not predominantly heavy in either extreme. That way, the guitarist can pick harder on either the bass or the treble strings for emphasis. It's better to have the resources there to go one way or the other at the discretion of the musician.

One thing I've noticed is that each maker seems to build in his own tone. I used to share this workshop with a very fine guitar maker named Mark Whitebook. We put our instruments together in almost the same manner. He built one guitar exactly the way I did—same materials and bracings, but his guitars have their characteristic tone quality and mine have a different sound. Even if they're made the same way, for all intents and purposes, his still sound like his and mine sound like mine, and we really don't have any idea why. Roy Noble pioneered many of the current techniques, and as he once said, you make your own guitars, and they sound like you and nobody else.

Martin D12–45, shaded top

C. F. MARTIN & CO.

Martin: The Company

Among manufacturers of acoustic guitars, there is no finer name than C. F. Martin. From Hank Williams and Jimmie Rodgers through Bob Dylan, Judy Collins, Joan Baez, Paul Simon, Steve Stills, and thousands of amateurs as well, the list of Martin customers is a list of some of America's most discriminating guitarists.

Johann Georg Martin lived in the hillside village of

The Martin factory, 1858

C. F. Martin, Sr., designed the "X" brace, here being shaped by hand; it has since been copied by many manufacturers.

Markneukirchen, Saxony, near the Elbe River, which divides the present city of Dresden. In the early 1800s, this hamlet was the home of a guild of violin makers, and Johann Martin worked as a carpenter, sometimes constructing the wooden packing boxes that were used by guild members to ship their fine violins. Martin was so impressed with the guitar upon its arrival in Northern Europe that he constructed a few, sold them, and thus infuriated his violin-making employers. The guild was incensed at the prospect of competition from an ordinary carpenter, and its official records show that

> the violin makers, who had already complained of this state of affairs in 1807, demanded an injunction against the bunglers and asserted that they themselves belonged to the class of . . . artists, whose work not only showed finish but gave evidence of a certain understanding, a cultured taste, while the cabinet makers by contrast were nothing more than mechanics and their product consisted of all kinds of articles known as furniture . . .*

Johann's son, Christian Friedrich (or Frederick), became the shop foreman for Viennese violin and guitar maker Johann Stauffer (also spelled Staufer). The junior and senior Martins then worked together, posing a professional threat so serious to the local guild that its members harassed the father and son team through political pressure. Christian finally decided to move to New York where, in 1833, he opened a guitar shop at 196 Hudson Street and founded C. F. Martin & Co. The huge city soon proved to be an alien, impersonal place to the guitar maker from Saxony, so after much urging from his fellow immigrant Henry Shatz, Christian decided, in 1839, to move to the tiny Moravian town of Cherry Hill, located outside Nazareth in the Lehigh Valley of eastern Pennsylvania. Martin guitars have been made in the Nazareth area ever since.

The first "factory" was an addition to Christian's house. From 1839 to 1850, he sold the instruments through a New York outlet at 385 Broadway. After eighteen years in Cherry Hill, Martin purchased a lot a few miles away, in Nazareth, where shipping connections and mailing facilities were improved. In the summer of 1859, the Martin family and business moved into a two-story brick house with an adjoining workshop on the corner of Main and North streets,

*Speech by Frank Martin in 1933, quoting from "Historical Review of the Violin Makers' Guild of Markneukirchen," Saxony, 1927.

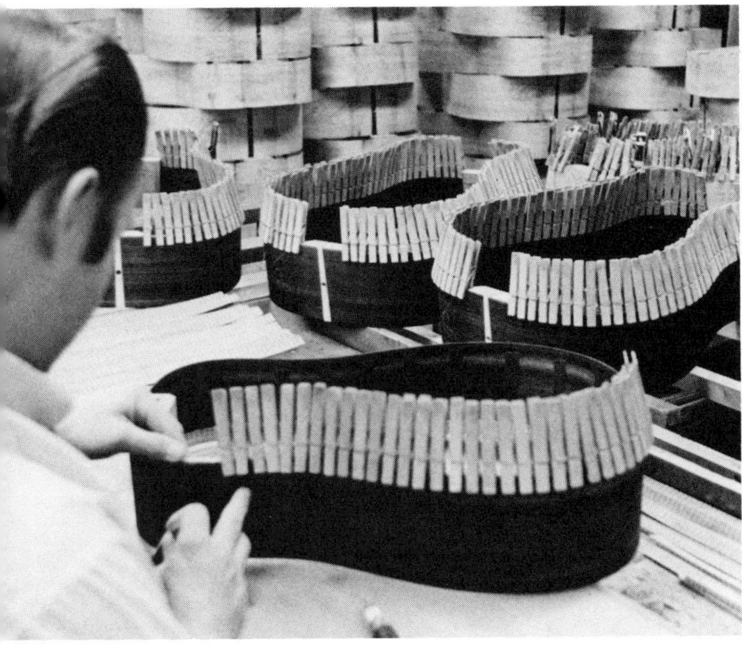

The craftsman is attaching mahogany lining strips, or "ribbons" to the inner edges of the sides to provide a gluing surface for the top and back. Once these pieces are joined, a master sprayer lacquers the guitar body with an air gun in a water wash.

where the six-member work force soon constructed two hundred guitars annually. C. F. Martin died in 1873 at the age of seventy-seven.

Nearly thirty years of success in the new plant allowed C. F. Martin, Jr. (1825–1888), to double its size in 1887 and, except for that remodeling, the 1858 North Street shop remains intact. The next generation of the family and business was headed by Frank Henry Martin (1866–1948), an astute businessman who capitalized on the booming interest in the banjo,

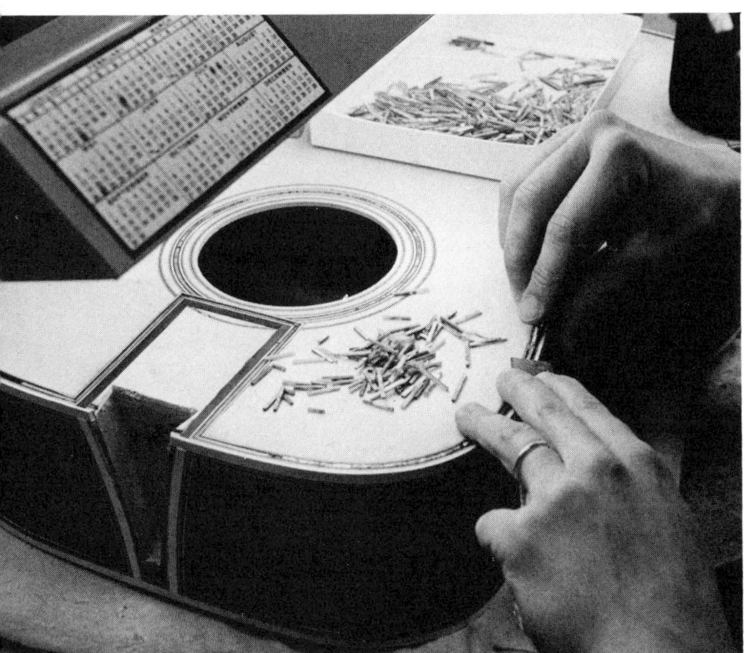

Inlaying a D-45 with abalone

Note herringbone inlay, for decades a standard feature on all Style 28 Martins.

Martin D12–20; note slotted headstock.

ukulele, and mandolin, greatly expanding his company's reputation for quality. By 1890, the number of Martin craftsmen had grown to fifteen.

To meet the consistently increasing demand for instruments, Frank enlarged the factory in 1917, 1924, and 1925. The number of employees soon jumped to seventy-five, and the yearly instrument production to three thousand. By 1960 the production of five thousand instruments a year warranted an additional facility, also in Nazareth. It was operating in 1964, though it too had to be expanded in 1970 to its present size of 62,000 square feet, which accommodates about two hundred and fifty people. The twenty thousand instruments that leave the plant each year are still built by hand with the traditional tools and methods, but modern conveniences have been added, such as the environment-monitoring equipment, which controls wood shrinkage by keeping the humidity at 35 to 45 percent and the temperature at 72° to 77°F. In only five years or so, the volume of sales has gone up more than 70 percent under the leadership of Frank Martin, current president, and his father, C. F. Martin III, chairman of the board.

Martin: The Guitars

Influenced by the work of Johann Stauffer, the earliest guitars by Johann and Christian Martin were dramatically pinched at the waist, in an almost figure-

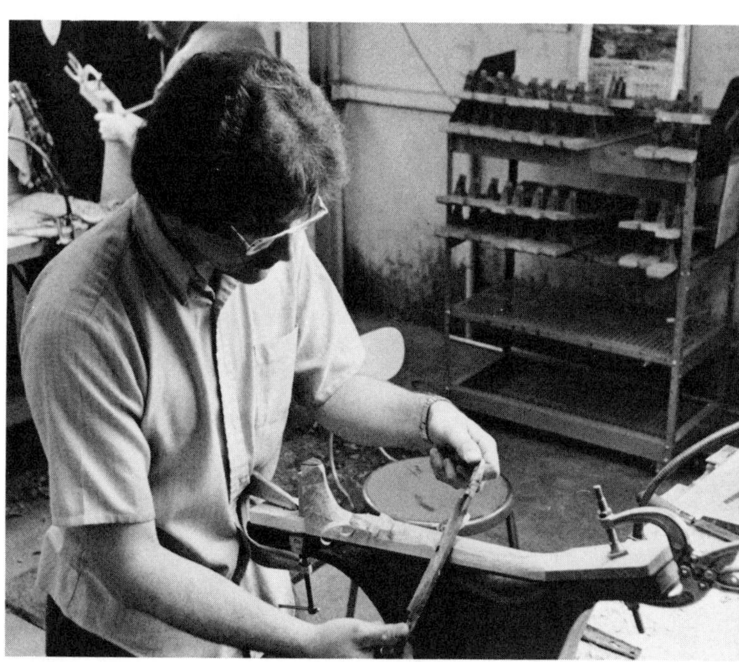

Shaping of the neck: another delicate hand operation

To permit wood-to-wood contact, this craftsman is using a toothing iron to scrape the finish from the spot where the bridge will be glued to the top.

eight shape, with all of the tuning keys on one side of the sculptured peghead. The guitars made in the 1800s were quite small, but, in 1917, Frank Henry Martin and an employee of the Ditson music publishing company collaborated in the design of a new, large-body guitar. Stamped with the words, "Oliver Ditson Co., Boston, New York," it was named Dreadnought after the pride of the British navy, an 18,000-ton battleship launched in 1906. Beginning in 1931, the Dreadnought (often spelled "Dreadnaught") was stamped with the Martin name.

The 1917 catalogue listed six styles plus a special-order auditorium model, 15 inches wide. Prices of the concert guitars ranged from $25 for the O-18 to $110 for the O-45. Martin's first fourteen-fret neck was introduced in 1929 on the OM–28. The first twelve-fret D-18 and D-28 models appeared in 1931, and the fourteen-fret D-28 came out in 1934. In that same year, the first "T-bar" neck rod was installed in guitar #57305. One of Martin's best and most handsome guitars was the D-28 Herringbone, of which 1,800 were made from 1933 to 1946. In 1931, Martin offered the unusual C-1 arched-top guitar with a round sound hole. It was re-

A general depletion of rosewood sources caused a scarcity of boards wide enough to yield two-piece backs. The D-35, introduced in 1965, features a three-piece back with a center wedge bordered by bookmatched, contrasting pieces. This particular guitar was built after Martin changed to Indian rosewood in 1969.

placed two years later by f-hole models, which were built until wartime restrictions on materials forced their discontinuation.

Martin entered the acoustic-electric field with the OO-18E, the D-28E (about 1959–1965), and the D-18E (about 1959–1961). Electric, arched-top guitars with f-holes appeared from 1962 to 1968, including the F-50, F-55, F-65, GT-70, GT-75, and GT-75-12.

The top of the Martin line is the D-45. This guitar is so beautiful that it is hard to believe it sounds even better than it looks, but it does. Martin built the first D-45 in 1933 especially for Gene Autry, and five years later it was formally added to the Martin line. Ninety-one D-45's had been made at the time they were discontinued in October of 1942. Currently priced at $1,650 (with case), they were reissued in 1968 in response to public demand.

Some of the guitars made by C. F. Martin, Sr., soon after his arrival in New York were labeled "C. F. Martin, Upstairs." Until 1867, "C. F. Martin, New York" was stamped inside the body. Then, from 1867 until 1898, the words were changed to "C. F. Martin & Co., New York." The guitars made until 1898 are known collectively as the "New York" Martins.

Since 1898, the inside of the body has been stamped with the words, "C. F. Martin & Co., Nazareth, Pa." In order to date the guitars, Martin assigned serial numbers to each instrument produced since 1898. The numbers began with the figure 8000, the best estimate of the number of guitars made prior to the serialization.

YEAR	LAST NO.	YEAR	LAST NO.	YEAR	LAST NO.	YEAR	LAST NO.
1898	8348	1917	12988	1936	65176	1955	147328
1899	8716	1918	13450	1937	68865	1956	152775
1900	9128	1919	14512	1938	71866	1957	159061
1901	9310	1920	15848	1939	74061	1958	165576
1902	9528	1921	16758	1940	76734	1959	171047
1903	9810	1922	17839	1941	80013	1960	175869
1904	9988	1923	19891	1942	83107	1961	181297
1905	10120	1924	22008	1943	86724	1962	187384
1906	10329	1925	24116	1944	90149	1963	193327
1907	10727	1926	28689	1945	93623	1964	199626
1908	10883	1927	34435	1946	98158	1965	207030
1909	11018	1928	37568	1947	103468	1966	217215
1910	11203	1929	40843	1948	108269	1967	230095
1911	11413	1930	45317	1949	112961	1968	241925
1912	11565	1931	49589	1950	117961	1969	256003
1913	11821	1932	52590	1951	122799	1970	271633
1914	12047	1933	55084	1952	128436	1971	294270
1915	12209	1934	58679	1953	134501	1972	313302
1916	12390	1935	61947	1954	141345	1973	333873

New Martins include the M-38, similar to the carved-top F-style Martins of the late Thirties and early Forties, but with a flat top, Grand Auditorium body, solid rosewood back and sides, scalloped bracing, and ebony fingerboard; also the D-19—mahogany sides and back, solid spruce top with dark stain, rosewood fingerboard.

Martin Herringbones (1933–1946) are generally the most admired steel strings ever made. This HD-28 was put into production in late 1976. It offers some of the features of the original, including herringbone trim around the top edge, zipper back strip, and scalloped bracing.

C. F. Martin III with old and new Martin guitars

MARTIN INSTRUMENT SPECIFICATIONS

	D-45	D12-45	D-41	D-35	D-28	D-18	D12-35	D12-28	D12-20	D-35S	D-28S
Type	Steel	12-String	Steel	Steel	Steel	Steel	12-String	12-String	12-String	Steel	Steel
Top	Spruce	Spruce	Spruce	Spruce	Spruce	Spruce	Spruce	Spruce	Spruce	Spruce	Spruce
Back & Sides	Rosewood	Rosewood	Rosewood	3 Piece Rosewood Back	Rosewood	Mahogany	3 Piece Rosewood Back	Rosewood	Mahogany	3 Piece Rosewood Back	Rosewood
Neck	Mahogany	Mahogany	Mahogany	Mahogany	Mahogany	Mahogany	Mahogany	Mahogany	Mahogany	Mahogany	Mahogany
Rod	Steel	Steel	Steel	Steel	Steel	Steel	Steel	Steel	Steel	Steel	Steel
Fingerboard Bridge	Ebony	Ebony	Ebony	Ebony	Ebony	Rosewood	Ebony	Ebony	Rosewood	Ebony	Ebony
Position Dots	Pearl	Pearl	Pearl	Pearl	Pearl	Pearl	Pearl	Pearl	Pearl	Pearl	Pearl
Binding	White	White	White	White	White	Dark	White	White	Dark	White	White
Pick guard	Yes	Yes	Yes	Yes	Yes	Yes	Yes	Yes	Yes	Yes	Yes
No. of Frets Clear	14	12	14	14	14	14	12	14	12	12	12
No. of Frets Total	20	19	20	20	20	20	19	20	19	20	20
Scale	25.4	24.9	25.4	25.4	25.4	25.4	24.9	24.9	24.9	25.4	25.4
Neck width at nut	1$\frac{11}{16}$	1$\frac{7}{8}$	1$\frac{11}{16}$	1$\frac{11}{16}$	1$\frac{11}{16}$	1$\frac{11}{16}$	1$\frac{7}{8}$	1$\frac{7}{8}$	1$\frac{7}{8}$	1$\frac{7}{8}$	1$\frac{7}{8}$
Finish	Natural Gloss	Natural Gloss	Natural Gloss	Natural Gloss	Natural Gloss	Stain Gloss	Natural Gloss	Natural Gloss	Stain Gloss	Natural Gloss	Natural Gloss
Strings	Med. Bronze	Compound or Lt. Bronze	Med. Bronze	Med. Bronze	Med Bronze	Med. Bronze	Compound or Lt. Bronze	Compound or Lt. Bronze	Compound or Lt. Bronze	Lt. Bronze	Lt. Bronze

Guitar sizes

	5	O	OO	OOO	D	N
TOTAL LENGTH	33	38 3/8	38 5/8	39 3/8	40 1/4	38 1/2
BODY LENGTH	16	18 3/16	18 7/8	19 3/8	20	19 1/8
BODY WIDTH	11 1/4	13 1/2	14 5/16	15	15 5/8	14 7/16
BODY DEPTH	3 7/8	4 1/4	4 1/8	4 1/8	4 7/8	4 1/8

Ukulele sizes

	Standard	Tenor	Baritone
TOTAL LENGTH	21	26 1/4	30 11/16
BODY LENGTH	9 7/16	12 1/16	14
BODY WIDTH	6 3/8	8 15/16	10
BODY DEPTH	2 5/16	2 15/16	3 3/8

D-18S	000-28	0-18 00-18 000-18	00-45	00-21	5-18	0-18T	0-16NY	N-20	N-10	00-28C	00-18C	00-16C
Steel	Steel	Steel	Steel	Steel	Steel	Steel	Folk	Classic	Classic	Classic	Classic	Classic
Spruce	Spruce	Spruce	Spruce	Spruce	Spruce	Spruce	Spruce	Spruce	Spruce	Spruce	Spruce	Spruce
Mahogany	Rosewood	Mahogany	Rosewood	Rosewood	Mahogany	Mahogany	Mahogany	Rosewood	Mahogany	Rosewood	Mahogany	Mahogany
Mahogany	Mahogany	Mahogany	Mahogany	Mahogany	Mahogany	Mahogany	Mahogany	Mahogany	Mahogany	Mahogany	Mahogany	Mahogany
Steel	Steel	Steel	Steel	Steel	None	Ebony	Steel	Steel	Steel	Steel	Steel	Steel
Rosewood	Ebony	Rosewood	Ebony	Rosewood	Rosewood	Rosewood	Rosewood	Ebony	Rosewood	Ebony	Rosewood	Rosewood
Pearl	Pearl	Pearl	Pearl	Pearl	Pearl	Pearl	None	None	None	None	None	None
Dark	White	Dark	White	Dark	Dark	Dark	Dark	Dark	Dark	White	Dark	Dark
Yes	Yes	Yes	Yes	Yes	Yes	Yes	No	No	No	No	No	No
12	14	14	12	12	12	14	12	12	12	12	12	12
20	20	20	19	19	18	20	19	19	19	19	19	19
25.4	24.9	24.9	25.4	24.9	21 3/8	23.2	24.9	26 3/8	26 3/8	26 3/8	26 3/8	26 3/8
1 7/8	1 11/16	1 11/16	1 7/8	1 7/8	1 5/8	1 1/4	1 7/8	2 1/8	2 1/8	2 1/8	2 1/8	2 1/8
Stain	Natural	Stain	Natural	Natural	Stain	Stain	Stain	Natural	Stain	Natural	Stain	Stain
Gloss	Gloss	Gloss	Gloss	Gloss	Gloss	Gloss	Semi Gloss	Gloss	Gloss	Gloss	Gloss	Semi Gloss
Lt. Bronze	Med. Bronze	Med. Bronze	Med. Bronze	Med. Bronze	Med. Bronze	Bronze	Compound	Nylon	Nylon	Nylon	Nylon	Nylon

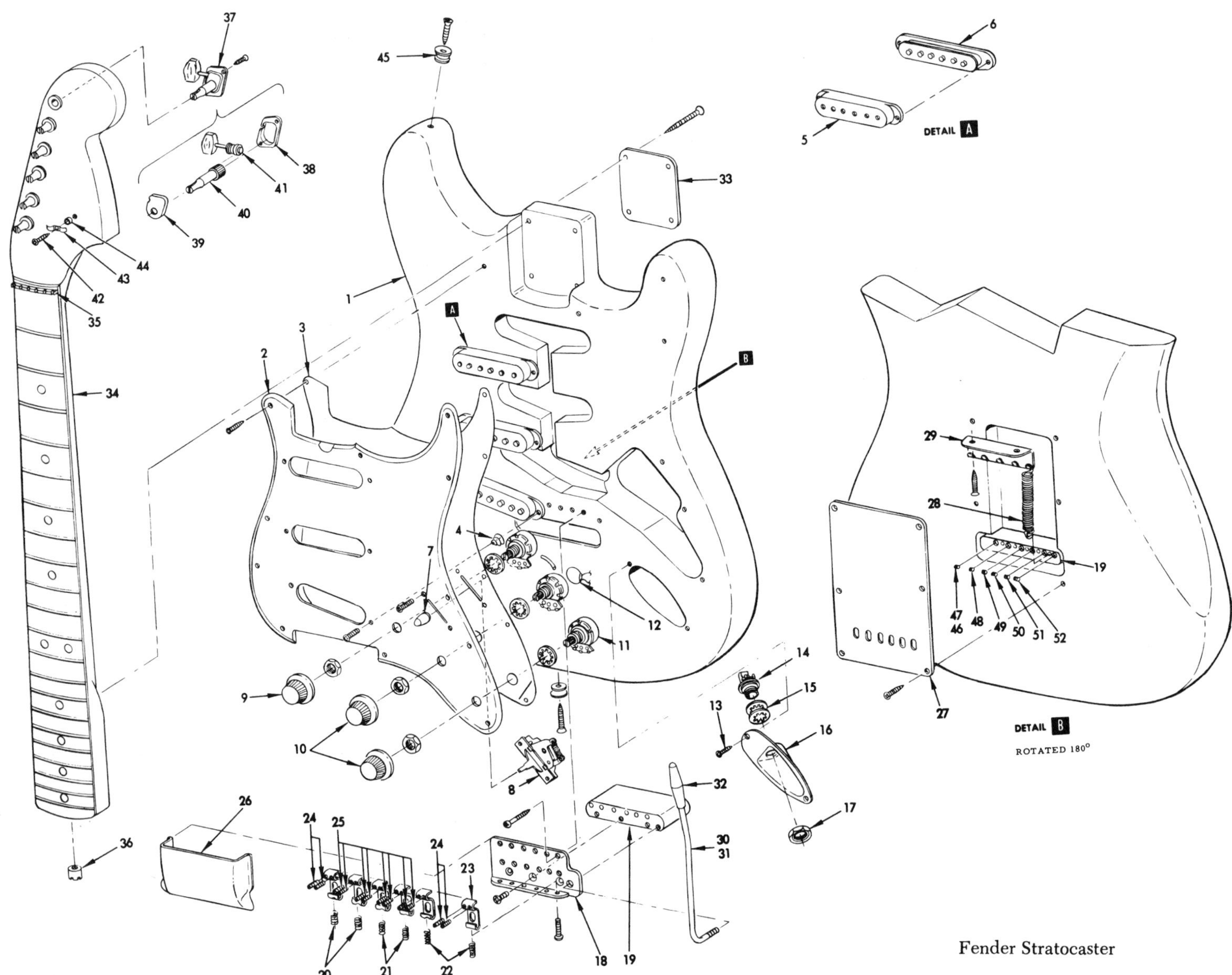

Fender Stratocaster

1 Guitar Body

PICKGUARD ASSEMBLY

2 Pickguard
3 Pickguard Shield
4 Pickup Compression Spring
5 Pickup Cover
6 Pickup Core Assembly
7 Lever Knob
8 Pickup Selector Switch
9 Volume Knob
10 Tone Knob
11 Volume & Tone Potentiometers (Controls: 250K)
12 Ceramic Capacitor

13-17 OUTPUT PLUG ASSEMBLY

BRIDGE ASSEMBLY

18 Bridge Base Plate
19 Tremolo Block*
20 ¼″ Compression Spring
21 5⁄16″ Compression Spring
22 7⁄16″ Compression Spring
23 Bridge Bar
24, 25 Set Screws
26 Bridge Cover
27 Rear Cover Plate
28 Tension Spring
29 Tremolo Tension Spring Holder
30-32 Lever Assembly

*"Tremolo" is used by Fender as a synonym for Vibrato.

NECK AND PEGHEAD ASSEMBLY

33 Neck Plate
34 Neck & Fingerboard, Frets & Position Markers
35 Nut
36 Neck Rod Adjusting Nut

TUNING KEY ASSEMBLY

37 Complete Key Assembly
38 Key Assembly Cover
39 Key Assembly Housing
40 Post and Gear
41 Head and Worm

MISCELLANEOUS

42-44 String Guide Assembly
45 Strap Button
46-52 Strings (Ball Ends)

Charles Kaman is an aerospace corporation executive who also happens to pick a little guitar. He challenged his engineers and metallurgists to build a better instrument, and after intensive analysis with the world's most sophisticated sonic equipment, they settled on a one-piece parabolic body shell of synthetic fibers. In just over a decade their roundback Ovation has become a world leader.

The Adamas is the top of the Ovation line and represents an even more radical departure from traditional guitar design theory. The top is a laminate of two .005" plies of carbon graphite with a .035" birch veneer sheet sandwiched between them. Initially developed for supersonic aircraft, carbon graphite is strong enough to permit a much thinner top than usual. The most readily apparent innovation is the use of multiple sound holes and their relocation to the upper bouts, which, in the words of Mr. Kaman, "enhances the integrity of the top as a vibrating membrane while permitting us to use our newest brace system to transmit sound rather than support the weakness of the sound hole."

Ovation's line is one of the industry's most extensive, and all of the instruments are revolutionary in that they feature the company's hallmark, the round back. Some models evidence additional influences of modern technology, such as the aluminum-necked (and moderately priced) Matrix.

This Ovation worker has just removed a one-piece parabolic body from the high-pressure mold. The exceptionally reflective interior surface and sound-focusing shape of the body produce a bright tone with good projection.

Gurian

HANDMADE ACOUSTIC GUITARS

Guitar making is an ancient craft existing in a modern world. To some, "automation" conjures up images of mile-long assembly lines attended by robots, so some advertisers would love for you to associate their instruments with a solitary, white-haired craftsman in a cottage in the glen. In fact, such luthiers do exist. Nevertheless, commercial realities demand that certain tasks once performed by hand be turned over to machines, though it is certainly possible to have a modern facility where skilled artisans are intimately involved at every stage. The foremost example is Martin, whose "still handmade" claim is justifiable.

Unfortunately, "handmade" means different things to different manufacturers; sometimes the term is misleading. Whether achieved with chisels or computers, what really matters is still the quality of the guitar. Judge an instrument by its sound and workmanship, not by the label, and keep in mind that some "handmade" guitars are a lot more handmade than others.

There are several brilliant luthiers who make outstanding guitars in strictly limited quantities. For example, David Russell Young, Phil Petillo, and Jim D'Aquisto each complete a dozen or so instruments of impeccable standards each year. Most or all of the work is done on custom order. Other guitarmakers have combined commercial ambitions and craftsmanship in order to produce guitars that are both handcrafted and more accessible. Some of them are discussed in this section.

Michael Gurian's shop is in Hinsdale, New Hampshire, where he and a couple dozen employees build about sixty to eighty guitars each month. Gurian's background as an expert with old-fashioned techniques manifests itself in his instruments, the unusually rounded bodies of which are aesthetically appealing. Their hallmark is a combination of classical appointments and modern interior construction; the tone is bright and strong. Other manufacturers, particularly some of the larger ones, could benefit from Gurian's approach to organizing options in woods and body sizes. Optional F.R.A.P.

This book has avoided listing specific artists' endorsements, since they are sometimes frivolous and always changing. Let's make an exception for Doc

B. C. Rich rosewood jumbo

Bozo

Watson, who plays and recommends the guitars of J. W. Gallagher & Son, though there is no formal agreement between them. In Wartrace, Tennessee, J. W., his family, and a tiny crew build about 150 guitars a year in a dozen models or so. Their style is traditional, the detailing and inlay exquisite.

Bernardo Rico is gaining fame for his radical B. C. Rich electrics, but for years he has been building acoustics as well. In fact, Bernardo is a second-generation luthier. He and his handful of assistants make two Brazilian rosewood steel-strings, a jumbo and a Dreadnought, each costing about $1,000.

Thanks to a national distributor, the guitars of Jean-Claude Larrivée are now available in larger quantities. The rosewood bodies are more rounded than typical Dreadnoughts, giving them a classic and romantic quality. Extra touches include wood binding and abalone peghead inlays of near breathtaking beauty.

Bozo (pronounced *bo-zho*) Podunavac builds his special-order Signature flat-tops ($1500–$4000) by himself in Escondido, California. In order to make his unique designs more available, he went to Japan and

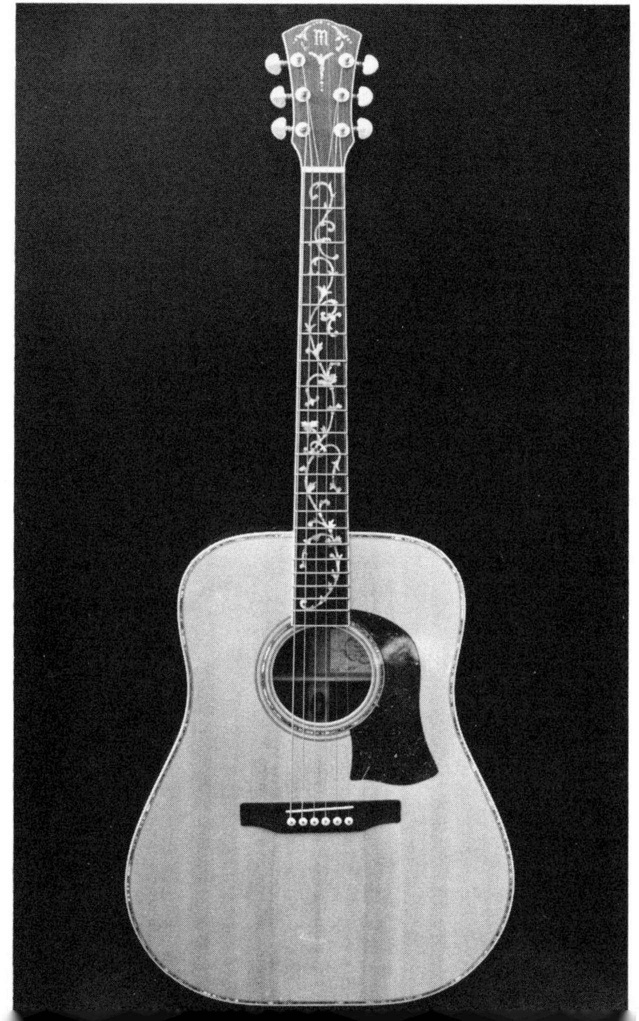

Mossman Golden Era

contacted a small guitar-making facility whose production is not nearly so limited. Each import is inspected by Bozo prior to distribution. Bozos are distinguished by their unusual Bell Western bodies, with squared upper bouts and big, round lower bouts. The carved pegheads are extra large, and the inlay and detailing are especially ornate.

A. LoPrinzi guitars are made in Plainsboro, New Jersey. There are over a dozen steel-string models from about $550 to over $1,000. Traditional appointments give them a rare beauty, unadorned with extraneous decoration.

Augustine LoPrinzi is no longer associated with A. LoPrinzi guitars; his line of six Dreadnoughts bears the Augustino name.

Bob Taylor of Lemon Grove, California, and John Greven of Nashville are among other luthiers whose nationally distributed guitars merit your consideration.

A. LoPrinzi

Augustino

4

Electric Guitars

INTRODUCTION TO THE ELECTRIC GUITAR

Andres Segovia dislikes the electric guitar so much he doesn't even like to talk about it. "An abomination," he calls it, and others share his opinion. Even Bob Dylan was booed when he walked on stage at the 1965 Newport Folk Festival and cranked up his Fender. If the guitar family has a black sheep, it is indeed the electric. So why is it so irresistible to so many? One reason is a craving for self-expression. The blend of acoustics and electronics has not been fully explored, promising that the electric guitar's already boggling variety of communicative tools will grow even larger. Another reason is power. It's true that a classic guitar, in skilled hands, can make an audience weep. But it can't vibrate their seats. The electric guitar's split personality can accomplish both. High volume and special effects are abused sometimes, but an imaginative musician can use them to add a supernatural aura to good guitar work. With its many powers, the electric guitar has proved itself to be reality's closest thing to the magic wand. Some old-fashioned purists are still hoping that it'll go away, but everybody else knows better—it's here for good.

The thing that makes a guitar electric is the pickup, a device, something like a microphone, which converts the energy from string vibrations into an electrical

Johnny Winter with 1963-style Gibson Firebird V

Ovation Breadwinner pickup

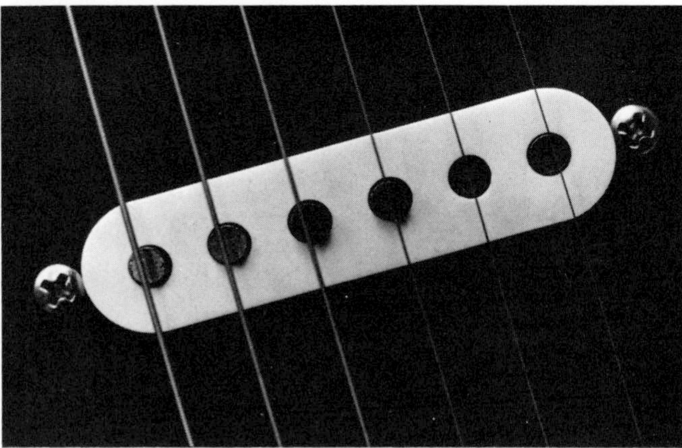

Fender Stratocaster pickup

Gibson ES-335TD (modified)

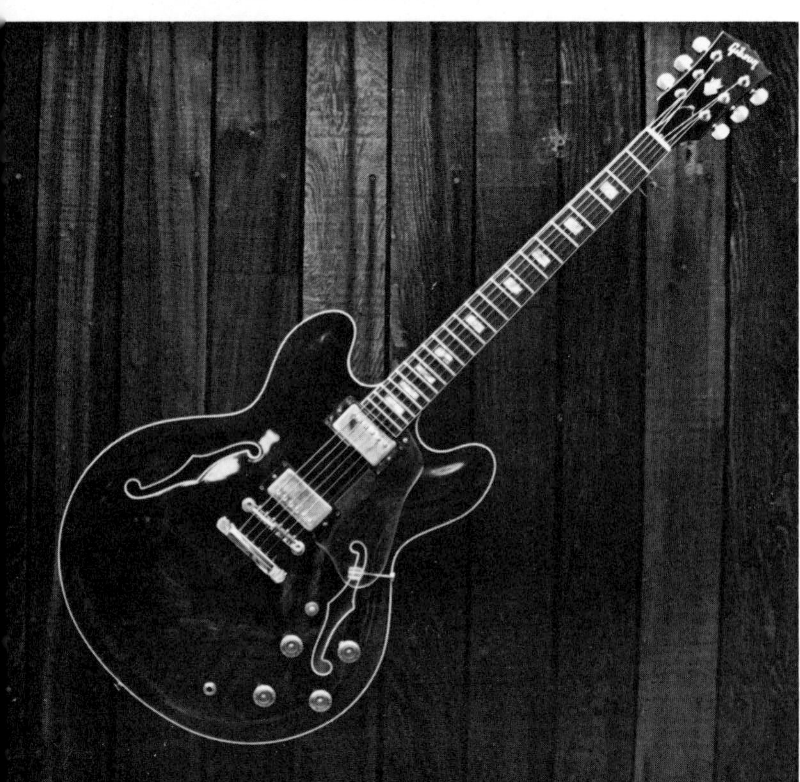

signal. This impulse is sent to the amplifier, where it is boosted thousands of times. Since separate pickups are available, any guitar may be electrified. Pickups are discussed on pp. 119 to 132

There are three general types of electric guitars: solid-body, hollow-body, and semi-solid. The solid guitar is the most radical, its body cut from a single or laminated slab of wood. It's heavier than the others, and its tone is almost purely electric in origin, with virtually none of the resonance of the hollow-body guitar. Being less susceptible to feedback, it's much better suited to high-volume playing than a hollow guitar. The density permits more treble emphasis and sustain. The more dense the body, the better the sustain.* Different woods vary in "sustainability," but beyond that, the solid body's sound is determined by the pickups and strings. It's been associated almost exclusively with rock, blues, country, and soul, but exceptions and overlaps are becoming more common.

A hollow-body electric guitar is more subdued in tone than a solid-body, though still capable of a bright, high-frequency sound. Its separate top, sides, and back are designed for acoustical reasons (see page 33), so the sound of the hollow-body is a combination of its resonant and electric qualities. Distinguished by its arched top and back, f-shaped sound holes, and deep sides, it is the choice of almost all jazz guitarists.

Gibson developed the semi-solid (or semi-acoustic) guitar in 1958, and it has since become a favorite of guitar players everywhere. It almost always consists of a thin, double-cutaway body with arched top and back, f-holes, and a solid block of wood down the center. Ideally, it is more crisp than a hollow guitar and more mellow than a solid guitar. With a stop-type tailpiece (p. 208), the center block can give it good sustain. B. B. King's various Lucilles have been semi-solids ever since that type of guitar was first built, and many other blues and rock guitar players have also chosen them for their versatility.

The terms acoustic-electric and electric-acoustic are used for flat-tops and arched-tops with built-in or added pickups. Finally, although Segovia would find

*The people at Fender's Research and Development Department report that guitars with bodies of solid marble and granite were submitted by private parties in 1973.

Fender Stratocaster

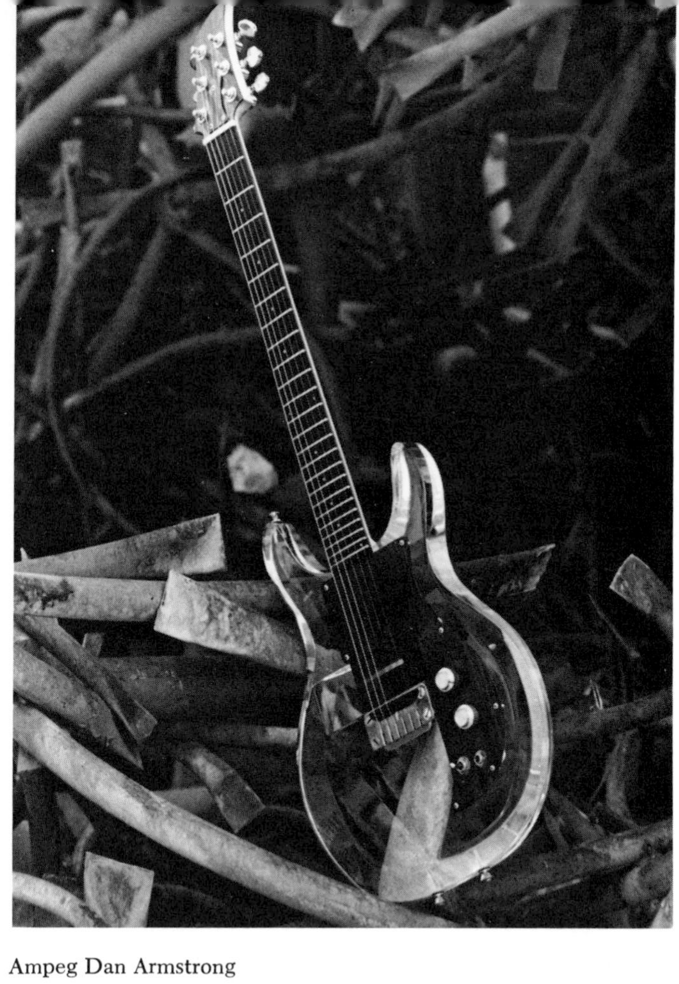

Ampeg Dan Armstrong

Gibson L-5CES

Gretsch Super Chet

An experimental lyre-mandolin, the only one of its kind, handmade by Orville Gibson between 1898 and 1902.

Orville Gibson

it hopelessly tasteless, the inevitable electric classic guitar is also with us.

GIBSON INC.

Gibson is the world's only manufacturer that offers a huge selection of professional guitars in nearly every category. Other companies successfully compete in specialized areas (Martin's acoustic guitars, Fender's solid bodies, and so forth) but, with more than two hundred models of instruments, Gibson is the giant. About a century ago, Orville H. Gibson (1856–1918) worked as a shoe-store clerk and part-time guitar player in Kalamazoo, Michigan. He was a handsome, gifted bachelor from a family of creative people. He must have had a sense of humor, for in one formal portrait, the stern-faced Gibson is shown wearing an outrageous costume of striped pants, plaid coat—they clashed horribly—a foot-wide bow tie around an oversized collar and a tiny sombrero.

In the 1870s and 1880s, Gibson made mandolins and guitars in his ten-by-twelve-foot workshop. He ripped apart fine furniture to obtain good grades of spruce, walnut, and cedar. Carving the tops and backs to give them a violinlike arch, he extended the sound chamber through the hollow, tubular neck. Orville tapped the wood as he carved, tuning the top and back to complementary resonances. The painstaking construction of one instrument took over a month.

Impressed with Gibson's work, a Boston company mailed a large order for mandolins. He wrote back that each one would cost $100, and that they would be promptly delivered in five hundred years. He was a proud man, contemptuous of his competitors. The 1903 catalogue boldly advertised his instruments as "the first serious mandolins and guitars ever manufactured."

The Gibson Mandolin-Guitar Mfg. Company began in 1902 with $12,000 capital stock, and soon became known as Gibson Inc. Working in the first plant, formerly an old bakery, the employees produced mandolas, mando-basses, harp-guitars, mando-cellos, violins, and lutes, in addition to guitars and mandolins. Popular vocalists and whole orchestras of Gibson-equipped musicians confirmed the increasing reputation for good workmanship. Consequently, the company's growth was explosive. After thirteen years, the capital stock was nearly ten times its original figure.

World War I affected practically everything, including American music tastes. In *The Gibson Story,** Julius Bellson wrote: "The swinging marching songs and the trend toward boisterous spontaneity after the war led to a decline in the popularity of the mandolin and a bandwagon rush to the banjo and orchestra-type guitar."

New hybrid instruments appeared: mandolin-banjos, cello-banjos, bass-banjos, and others. In 1920 the Gibson company had the good fortune to employ Lloyd Loar, a musician, composer, and acoustical engineer. He was responsible for the Mastertone Banjo, the F-5 Mandolin, and other innovations. The arched-top L-5 guitar replaced the ten-year-old L-4 and became a favorite in jazz orchestras. The L-7, L-10, L-12, and L-50 were soon added. Lloyd Loar and two other executives left the company in 1924 in a dispute with Gibson over amplified instruments. They founded the Vivi-Tone Company and introduced several electrics, including Loar's ingenious electric double bass. A decade or two ahead of their time, these efforts failed to arouse enough public interest to sustain the offshoot company.

Gibson first made the Super 400 and larger "Advanced" versions of the L series in the mid-Thirties, as f-hole guitars increased in popularity and variety. A few years later, electric steel guitars caught on, followed by the ES-150 (about 1934) electric Spanish guitar with its "Charlie Christian" pickup. Soon the Super Jumbo 200 flat-top and the single-cutaway arched-tops joined the catalogue.

In 1944, Chicago Musical Instrument Company (CMI) purchased Gibson. The factory was enlarged and a network of franchised dealers replaced the agency system of distribution. Gibson thrived after the end of World War II, when the demand for instruments surpassed all previous heights. The ES series—125, 150, 300 and 350—were favorite electrics. Theodore M. McCarty joined Gibson in 1948 and was elected its president two years later. His many contributions included the Flying V, the phenomenally popular ES-335TD-SV) and the Tune-O-Matic bridge (p.157). Gibson was endorsed by the major guitarists of the early Fifties: Herb Ellis, Tony Mottola, George

*Gibson, Inc., *The Gibson Story,* a pamphlet distributed to those in the industry by Gibson. Also available to the general public.

Gibson L6-S; laminated maple neck, extra-powerful ceramic magnet pickups designed for Gibson by Bill Lawrence

Gibson ES-355TD-SV

Barnes, and dozens more. Several lent their names to Gibson guitars, including Barney Kessel, Johnny Smith (both in 1961), and Tal Farlow (about 1962). More new guitars were built: the three-pickup ES-5, the Super 400 CESN (Cutaway, Electric Spanish, Natural finish), L-5 CES (1951), ES-295, and the Les Paul solid-body guitars (p. 70). The Byrdland (named for its designers, guitarists Billy Byrd and Hank Garland) and the ES-5 Switchmaster (three pickups, six knobs, four-way toggle switch) were developed in 1955 along with Gibson's thin-bodied electrics.

Two-necked instruments (six- and twelve-string necks, guitar and mandolin, guitar and bass with a built in fuzztone) became available in 1957 on special order. Also in 1957, CMI purchased the Epiphone company shortly after Epi Stathopoulo's death. Gibson manufactured guitars with the Epiphone name from 1959 through 1968. At one time Epiphones comprised 15 percent of Gibson's production.

The ES-335T (later ES-335TD) was a widely copied, thin-body, semi-solid guitar that was first manufactured in 1958. Annual sales now exceed 1,000. Companions in the semi-solid line later included the ES-355, 345, 330, 340 (1969), 325, and the ES-320. The all-mahogany LG-0 flat-top was purchased in amazing quantities; its annual sales regularly exceeded the total yearly sales of Gibson's entire line during the company's first quarter-century. The J-45, J-50, Hummingbird, and Dove were other widely accepted steel-strings.

Gibson ES-175

These decades of success warranted eight factory additions between 1917 and 1964. Gibson instruments were so in demand that year-long back orders were common. Business doubled from 1960 to 1963, the year when the Firebird guitars were introduced. After employment and production increased another 80 percent in a short time, Gibson developed still more new guitars. The Trini Lopez model was built from 1964 through 1969. The name ES-150 was revived for another new guitar in 1969. Despite its size, the company makes limited-edition guitars for a handful of ultra-fastidious musicians. The $2,515 Citation (1971) is sold in yearly quantities of about eight or nine. Gibson presented several new guitars to the 1973 convention of the National Association of Music Merchants, including the Howard Roberts jazz electric and Gospel flat-top.

Gibson began to manufacture acoustic basses in 1937, and the violin-body EB-1 (Electric Bass, number one) was unveiled in 1953 and reintroduced in 1969. Subsequent basses included the double-cutaway EB-2 (introduced in 1958–1959), EB-0 (1959–1960, redesigned at least twice), EB-6 (1959, six strings), EB-OF (1962, built in fuzztone), Thunderbird (first in 1963, and redesigned about 1965), EB-3, Les Paul Bass (1970), Les Paul Triumph (1971), EB-4, SB-450, SB-350, Les Paul Signature (1973), L9-S (1973), and the Ripper (early 1974).

During the Thirties, Gibson amps were made by Lyon and Healy. Models during the Forties included the BR series, named for designer Barnes Reinecke. The Les Paul amp and the GA line were produced during the Fifties and early Sixties. Then piggybacks and single-cabinet amps with space-age names (Titan, Mercury, Atlas, and others) appeared in 1963, and the GSS solid-state models shortly afterward. The Les Paul name was used again on a large piggyback model in 1970. In 1971 and 1972 the amps had a "G" prefix. CMI distributed transistorized Standel amps until the early Seventies, and now markets the SG series.

In early 1974, CMI became Norlin Music, Inc.

Gibson imports some of the raw materials used in guitar construction. A partial list: rosewood (Brazil, the East Indies, Burma), ebony (Nigeria), mother-of-pearl (New Zealand, Australia), mahogany (Peru, Honduras, Brazil), rosettes and purflings (Mexico),

The godfather of the electric guitar, Lester William Polsfuss, better known as Les Paul

1952 Les Paul Model, gold top

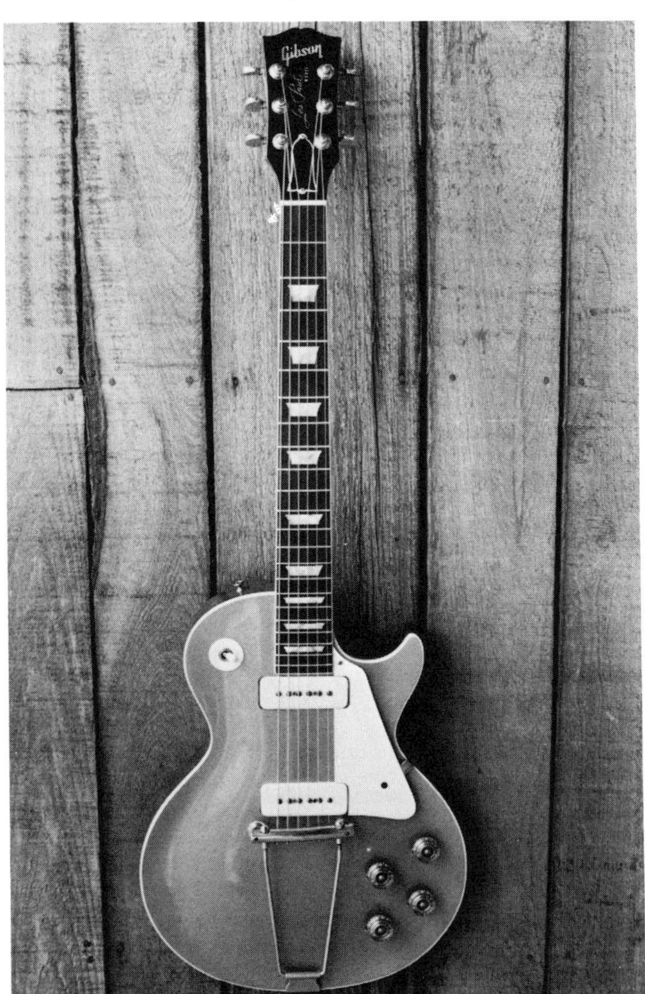

crafted parts (West Germany, Italy, France, England) and steel (Sweden). Domestic materials include spruce (Alaska), curly maple (Canada, Northwest United States) and abalone (California coast).

Nearly seven hundred craftsmen work in today's modern factory, though the atmosphere is more like that of an oversized workshop. Gibson has plans to increase in size. For each instrument, over two hundred parts must be stored (aged, in some cases) and prepared. Complete assembly and finishing takes more than three months. From the purchased spruce, less than 5 percent is considered good enough for the deluxe guitars, and 80 percent of that is sawed off or shaved away.

Gibson Solid-Body Guitars, 1952 to 1974

Les Paul is a blend of vision and courage, wisdom and determination. Born in 1916, he became known to country fans as Rhubarb Red, a cheerful kid with a guitar. Pop and jazz fans knew him by his real name as the architect of a futuristic sound that combined his artistry and knack for electronics. The first to use the now-indispensable technique of multiple recording, he is credited with developing eight-track equipment. Les Paul and his wife, Mary Ford, made hit records and had their own television show until Les's car accident in Oklahoma. The bones in his right arm were hopelessly crushed and had to be supported with grafts from his leg. Told by the doctor that he would probably never move his arm again, he requested that it be set to allow him to continue playing.

Les Paul remembers:

I started designing solid-bodies back in the Thirties. I went to see August Larson and his brother in 1937. They were instrument makers. Their plant was in this barn in downtown Chicago, if you can believe it. It was still country then. They built a guitar for me with a half-inch solid maple top, no f-holes, and two pickups. Later, when I was living in New York, I went over to the guys at Epiphone, and I said to Epi (Stathopoulo), "Is there any chance I could do some experimenting, maybe on a Sunday, and use your machinery?" Epi said, "Be our guest." They were interested to see what I was going to build.

I built the "Log" out of a 4″ × 4″ board and stuck on some wings, you know, two halves from a regular guitar body, for looks. These guys took a look and said, "Gee, this guy's *strange!*" A while later I took it over to Gibson—I was a dyed-in-the-wool Gibson man, still am—and I showed it to [CMI president] Mr. Berlin, and he called it the broomstick with a pickup on it. They said forget it. It laid around for a while. Later, around 1950, Mr. Berlin said, "Go find that kid with the broomstick and sign him up."

In 1950, Gibson's new president, Ted McCarty, met with Les and Mary at a Pennsylvania mountaintop retreat. He showed them a single cutaway, solid-body Gibson with a carved maple top. Les was excited about it and suggested his own trapeze tailpiece. They worked all night on a two-page, longhand contract that specified that Gibson would market the guitar as a Les Paul with Les's tailpiece, and that Les would play no other instrument in public in return for a royalty on each one sold. It was the beginning of perhaps the world's most esteemed electric guitar.

Les continues:

In 1928 in my small little $5-a-week room, I can remember I'd go to bed after cleaning my guitar. I'd put it across the room so that when you open your eyes in the morning, first thing, you're looking at your guitar, and that's my first love.

Group I

THE LES PAUL GUITAR. Introduced mid-1952. Hard-maple carved top. Mahogany back and neck, two non-humbucking pickups with cream-colored plastic covers, individual poles. 22 frets. 24¾″ scale. Gold top with ivory trim. Cream pickguard. Single-cutaway body measured 12¾″ × 17¼″ × 1¾″. All had long, trapeze-style, bar combination bridge/tailpiece, which extended over the rear edge of the top. On the first few, the strings were pulled under the bar; on subsequent guitars, they passed over it.

1954: The stud or "stop" tailpiece replaced the trapeze.

1955: The Tune-O-Matic bridge was added.

1957: Humbuckings were substituted, despite 1957 catalog photos depicting older models with cream covers.

1958: Cherry Sunburst, "flame maple" top replaces the gold top.

LES PAUL STANDARD. 1960. Gibson first used the name Standard in 1960, applying it to the 1958–1960-style Cherry Sunburst ($265). However, dealers and collectors sometimes use the term in referring to previous gold tops as well (technically, the Les Paul or Les

1959 Cherry Sunburst Les Paul

Late 1961 Les Paul Standard (or "SG Les Paul")

Note: The original tuning machines on some of the illustrated guitars have been replaced.

Paul Model) in order to distinguish them from Customs, Jrs., etc.

Late 1961. Double-cutaway SG style replaces original body. Now joins neck at fret 22. Gibson vibrato has swing-away arm, pulled sideways, across face of guitar (unlike usual downward motion). Solid cherry finish. $290.

1974. The single-cutaway Les Paul Standard was reintroduced. Same as the 1974 Deluxe, but full-sized Humbucking pickups.

SG STANDARD. 1964. Replaced 1962 Les Paul Standard (two Humbucking pickups). Same specs. New Gibson Vibrola with large metal base plate; arm now has curved white plastic tip. Cherry finish. Pickguard enlarged about 1969, extending over to left side as well as the right. Replaced after 1970 by the SG Deluxe, then reintroduced in late 1972 with new Tune-O-Matic bridge in an enlarged rectangular housing, 1964–1966-style pickguard (wing-shaped, flush-mounted, right-hand side only); 1958-style barrel (speed) knobs.

GOLD TOP REISSUES. According to the manufacturer, a very few leftover gold tops may have been shipped in 1957 or 1958, still with the cream pickups and either the old, 54-type bridge or the newer Tune-O-Matic. This is probably why Gibson called its early Seventies gold top reissue the "58-style," even though it was really the 54 model. The reissue may be distinguished from the original by the following features, none of which appears on the 54 version: "Gibson" in raised letters on the pickup covers, a raised ridge on the tailpiece, and the words "Made in USA" stamped on the back of the headstock. Also, the original had the serial number stamped in ink, while on the reissue it is actually impressed into the wood. The 54 reissue is easily refitted with the older parts, so beware of forgeries.

In addition to the 54 gold top reissue (no Tune-O-Matic), Gibson also reissued the 55-style gold top (*with* Tune-O-Matic). This 1968 reissue is easily distinguished from the original 55 by the binding inside the cutaway; it is exceptionally wide on the reissue, covering the edge line between the mahogany and maple pieces.

LES PAUL DELUXE. The 1968 reissue of the 55-style gold top was made for less than a year. Gibson then decided to install small Humbuckings, which would fit the holes originally routed out for the old cream pickups. This guitar was called the Les Paul Deluxe.

Group II

LES PAUL CUSTOM. Introduced 1954. Low, flat frets and ebony finish gave rise to "Fretless Wonder" and "Black Beauty" nicknames. 2 pickups with staplelike gold-plated poles. Black plastic pickup covers. Mahogany neck, bound ebony fingerboard. One-piece solid Honduras mahogany body. Separate Tune-O-Matic bridge. Same body size, scale, number of frets as 1952 Les Paul guitar. The 1954-style Custom reissued in late 1972 in a limited series.

November 1957. Now with three humbucking pickups. $375 without Bigsby vibrato. Toggle switch allows front pickup alone, center plus rear, or rear (near bridge) alone. Joins body and neck at fret 16. Same through 1960. A very few made with 2 pickups.

Late 1961. Completely restyled, now SG type double-cutaway body, $12\frac{3}{4}'' \times 16'' \times 1\frac{5}{16}''$. All-white finish with gold-plated parts. Gibson vibrato (see late 1961 Les Paul Standard). Scale and frets unchanged. Neck joins at fret 22. Three Humbuckings (the 2-pickup Custom shown with Les Paul is not stock).

Late 1968. Original single-cutaway shape reintroduced. 2 Humbucking pickups. In compliance with the public's request, Gibson built the new Custom with a carved maple top that produced a sharper tone than the one-piece mahogany body of the original Custom.

SG CUSTOM. 1964. Replaced SG style Les Paul Custom of 1962. All specs same except for restyled Deluxe Vibrola (see SG Standard of 1964). Unchanged through 1966.

1970. Walnut finish. Enlarged pickguard was white plastic, flush-mounted, covering most of the body's upper half. In 1972, it changed to elevated triangular pickguard; controls housed in semicircular plate. A Bigsby vibrato replaced the Gibson Vibrola. In 1973, the smaller wing-shaped pickguard (roughly 1966-style) returned; new Tune-O-Matic bridge in enlarged rectangular housing; cylindrical speed knobs.

Les Paul Customs now have standard, rounded frets.

Group III

LES PAUL JR. AND SG JR. Originated 1954. Les Paul Jr. had a flat, single-cutaway body. One pickup. Mahog-

1954-style Les Paul Custom; note bar polepieces on front pickup.

Late 1957 Les Paul Custom

any neck. Brazilian rosewood fingerboard. 22 frets. Combination bridge/tailpiece. Same dimensions, frets, and scale as 1952 Les Paul guitar. Sunburst top.

December 1958. Changed to double-cutaway with rounded edges, unlike the fairly sharp single-cutaway of the 1954 Jr. All 22 frets now accessible. New cherry red finish. $120. A few made in ¾ size.

Late 1961. Still Les Paul name, but now SG type body. Most other specifications unchanged. Cherry finish.

1964. Name changed to SG Jr. Added Gibson Vibrola in 1966.

The pickup of the SG Jr. of 1964 and 1966 was separated from the pickguard. The 1970 pickguard was enlarged, engulfing the pickup, covering most of both sides of the body's upper half. Discontinued after 1970.

LES PAUL TV AND SG TV. 1957. Except for its limed mahogany finish, the Les Paul TV was identical to the 1954 Les Paul Jr. Also went to double-cutaway in December 1958. (See 1958 Jr.) Name changed to SG TV in 1960, but retained the 1958 shape. Went to current SG shape (sharp instead of rounded cutaways) in 1962. White finish. Discontinued after 1964.

LES PAUL SPECIAL. Introduced September 1955. Same specifications as 1954 Jr. and TV but with 2 nonhumbucking pickups. Limed mahogany. In March 1959, it changed to double-cutaway (see 1958 Jr.). Optional ¾ size. Also available in cherry red after March 1959.

1957 Les Paul TV

Les Paul Special (c. 1957)

Les Paul Jr. (c. 1957)

SG SPECIAL. 1960. Same guitar as 1959 Les Paul Special (2 nonhumbucking pickups).

1962. Current SG shape (sharp instead of rounded cutaways). Cherry or white. Added Vibrola in 1966. Enlarged pickguard by 1970 (see 1970 SG Jr.). Discontinued in 1971 (replaced by SG Pro). Reintroduced in late 1972 with new Tune-O-Matic bridge in enlarged, rectangular housing and new plastic-covered Humbucking pickups. 1966-style wing-shaped pickguard returned.

SG DELUXE. Late 1971. Replaced the 1970 SG Standard. 2 Humbucking pickups. Elevated, triangular pickguard. Controls housed in semicircular plate. Bigsby vibrato tailpiece. Discontinued after 1972 when Standard reintroduced.

SG PRO. Late 1971. Replaced the 1970 SG Special. 2 nonhumbucking pickups. Same pickguard and control plate as SG Deluxe. Bigsby vibrato. Discontinued after 1972 when Special reintroduced.

Group IV

MELODY MAKER. 1959. Single-cutaway, flat body 12¾″ × 17¼″ × 1⅜″. Small peghead. Same scale and frets as 1952 Les Paul. Sunburst finish. Available in ¾ size. Single and double pickup models. Pickups were single coil, long and narrow, rounded at ends. Changed to double-cutaway body in 1962.

1966. The SG type contoured body replaced the flat body. Red and blue finishes replaced the sunburst of 1960–1964. New enlarged white pickguard. Vibrola added.

1970. The red and blue finishes were replaced by walnut. Toggle switch replaced by slide-type pickup selector. Peghead enlarged to standard size.

SG 100, 200, AND 250. In 1971, these guitars replaced the Melody Maker line. Narrow, single-coil pickups. Triangular pickguard. Rectangular tailpiece cover. Controls housed in a metal plate shaped like a tongue depressor. The 2-pickup models had slide switches.

SG I, II, AND III. Late 1972–1973. They replaced the short-lived 100, 200, and 250. Triangular pickguard. Semicircular control housing plate. New Humbucking pickups with rectangular plastic covers.

SG TV (1960); same body as the late 1958 Les Paul TV

1960 SG Special. Except for the name, it's the same guitar as the 1959 Les Paul Special

Group V

LES PAUL PERSONAL. 1969. Low impedence pickups, gold plated; old Tune-O-Matic bridge.

LES PAUL PROFESSIONAL. 1969. Low impedance pickups, nickel plated; old Tune-O-Matic bridge.

LES PAUL RECORDING. 1971. Replaced the Personal and Professional; low impedance pickups. New Tune-O-Matic bridge. All controls now surrounded by a large plastic plate.

LES PAUL SIGNATURE. 1973. The first semi-acoustic Les Paul. Low impedance pickups.

Other recent Gibson solid bodies include the ultra-fancy L5-S and the twenty-four-fret, all-maple L6-S.

Les Paul Personal

1977 Les Paul Artisan

The Les Paul, Gibson's $3,000 solid maple guitar, introduced in 1976. Unique detailing and wood trim rather than plastic.

In the mid-1950s, Gibson had a reputation as a respected but somewhat stodgy and perhaps old-fashioned company. Fender was cleaning up with its flashy solid-bodies. Tailfins and the space age were just around the corner. Gibson's then president, Ted McCarty, recalls how "we wanted to do something really different, something radical to knock everyone out, and show them that Gibson was more modern than all the rest." With the advice of sales manager Clarence Havenga and others, Mr. McCarty and an artist sat down and designed many new body shapes in about a hundred sketches. They had one goal: to be as radical as possible. Perhaps a dozen styles of prototypes were built. Three were selected and introduced for 1958: the Moderne, Explorer, and Flying V, all made of korina wood.* Only the latter two went into production.

FLYING V. The following features distinguish a 1958 Flying V from subsequent versions: knobs in a straight line, squared "shoulders" (neck/body joint), korina body, gold-plated hardware, patent-applied-for Humbuckings, all frets clear of the body, smaller pickguard with pickup mounting rings, and a raised plastic "Gibson" logo glued on the peghead. Additionally, on the original the strings passed through a wedge-shaped metal plate and through the body, while later Vs had stud tailpieces or vibratos. Finally, the 58 has an oval groove fitted with a black strip of pebbled rubber on the right wing to keep the guitar from sliding off the player's lap.

The original Flying Vs were not taken very seriously (dealers would hang them in the window as "signs"), and they sold poorly when introduced. Some original bodies made in 1958 and stamped with a 58 serial number were stored at the factory until 1963. Those that left in 63 are often considered originals, although they had patent-number pickups (rather than patent-applied-fors) and nickle-plated parts.

Theodore (Ted) McCarty. As president from 1950 to 1966, Gibson's modern golden age, Mr. McCarty saw the work force multiply by ten, the income by fifteen. He designed the Flying V, Explorer, ES-335, Tune-O-Matic bridge, and stud tailpiece, and he was a motivating force behind the Les Paul and Firebird designs. In 1966 he retired from Gibson and bought Bigsby, Inc.

1958 Flying V

* Korina is a copyrighted name for selected pieces of African limba wood.

The original Explorer prototype, or "Futura" (*left*). This guitar is depicted in a diagram registered with the U.S. Patent Office and represents Gibson's earliest Explorer-like design. According to shipping records, it left the Kalamazoo plant along with ten other handmade experimental guitars in 1955. Refinements of the body and headstock were made both for aesthetic reasons and to conform the design to limitations of the factory's regular production tooling. The restyled version (*right*) was christened Explorer and introduced in 1958.

Gibson engineers often adopted nicknames or "working titles" for experimental guitars prior to the selection of an official designation by Gibson's parent company, then CMI of Chicago. When this guitar was first displayed at a music industry trade show, it was called the Futura (remembered by some old timers as Futurama or Futuristic). However, that name was never used in catalogs, price lists, *Gibson Gazettes,* or other documents. The Futura is an Explorer prototype with an unofficial nickname and is not a separate model. It is probably one of a kind, though a very few of the earliest Explorers share a similar split headstock. This is the first published photo of the Futura.

Moderne. Among collector's guitars, the Moderne is the ultimate, the Maltese Falcon, a veritable Holy Grail. Unfortunately, this one's a fake, according to Nashville collector and Gibson expert George Gruhn. It has a colorful history of fraud, threatened lawsuits and intercontinental travel. Presently owned by a Japanese industrialist.

Most or all of the key executives, designers, and other personnel who worked at Gibson at the time were asked about the number of Modernes actually constructed. Unfortunately, their memories vary considerably. Two sources were certain that the number was between forty and fifty, and none suggested a higher figure. We do know that some were destroyed in the Gibson "morgue" subsequent to the industry's unanimously negative reaction to the guitar and the company's decision not to add it to the line. The twenty-two survivors listed in the shipping totals appeared on routine invoices and do not include Modernes sold at cut rate to Gibson employees or those which were kept at the plant for experimental purposes. The evidence suggests that at least two or three dozen left the factory one way or another, a surprisingly large number considering the fact that they are presently so scarce as to appear to be nearly extinct. Where are those Modernes?

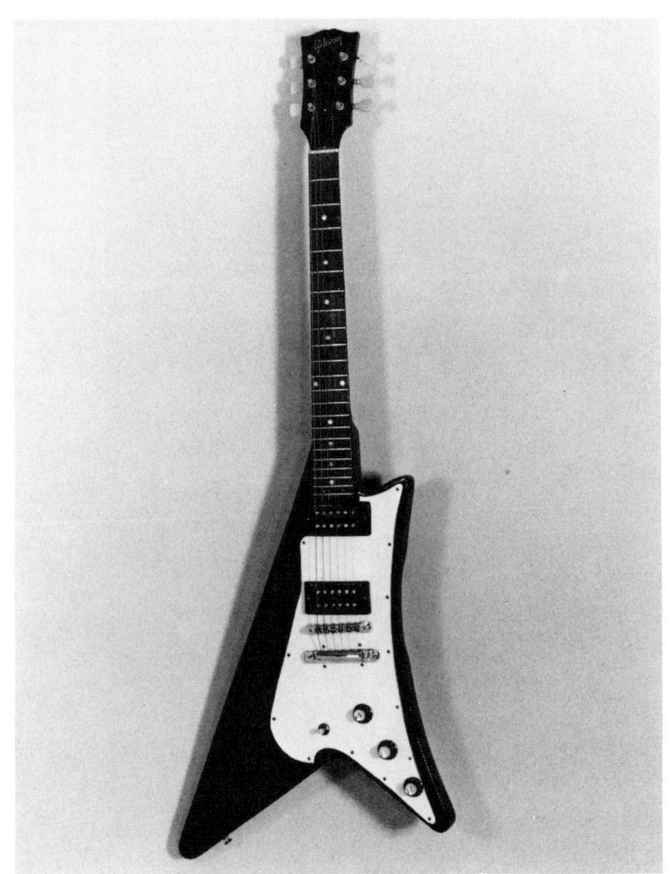

SELECTED GIBSON PRODUCTION SHIPPING TOTALS 1952–1960*

	1952	1953	1954	1955	1956	1957	1958	1959	1960
Les Paul (Gold top & sunburst)	1,716	2,245	1,504	862	920	598	434	643	635
Les Paul Custom			94	355	489	283	256	246	189
Les Paul Special				373	1,345	1,452	958	1,821	1,387
Les Paul Special ¾								12	39
Les Paul Jr.			823	2,839	3,129	2,959	2,408	4,364	2,513
Les Paul Jr. ¾					18	222	181	199	96
Les Paul TV			5	230	511	552	429	543	419
ES 335 TD (sunburst)							267	521	405
ES 335 TDN (natural, or blond)							50	73	88
ES 335 TDC (cherry)									21
ES 345 TD								446	251
ES 345 TDN								32	18
ES 345 TDC									252
ES 355 TD							10	177	128
ES 355 TD-SV (Stereo & Vari-tone)								123	189
Flying V							81	17	
Moderne							19	3	
Melody Maker								1,397	2,430
Melody Maker ¾								1,676	424
Melody Maker-D									1,196

* These production figures are complete for the guitars listed, 1952–1960; if a column is blank, none of that model was made that year. The official charts are incomplete in some places and ambiguous in others regarding the number of Explorers made in the late 50s. The lists were compiled by the secretary to the president of Gibson and are based on the number of instruments actually shipped.

Firebird I

Firebird V

Firebird VII

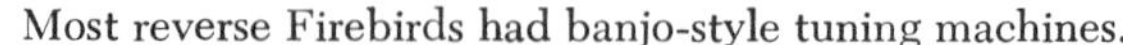

Most reverse Firebirds had banjo-style tuning machines.

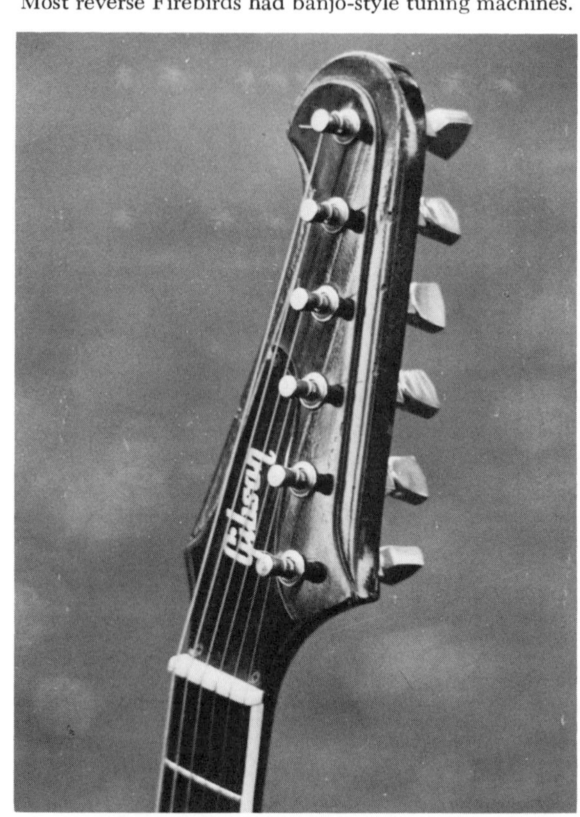

FIREBIRDS. Gibson president Ted McCarty hired noted auto designer Ray Dietrich to design a new guitar for 1963. He and an artist came up with the Firebird, a refined, less outrageous variation on the zigzag Explorer. The original "reverse-body" Firebirds were made for less than two years, from late 1963 to mid 1965. These were well-engineered instruments, with full-length neck centerpieces and unique pickups and tuners.

After an out-of-court dispute with Fender over the offset waist design, Gibson changed to the less distinctive "nonreverse" Firebirds of late 1965–1969. All had stock vibratos and conventional tuners. (The original Firebirds did look remotely like backward, or left-handed, Fenders. Ironically, the later, nonreverse guitars were, if anything, more Fender-like than ever, especially in the peghead.) The nonreverse guitars are worth substantially less as collector's items. In the early Seventies Gibson reissued a reverse-body Firebird with mixed features taken from various originals.

Firebird III

Firebird V

Firebird VII

Gibson Thunderbird II bass (c. 1964)

This unusual model was built during the transition from reverse to nonreverse guitars. It has the original body and pickups but newer vibrato. The peghead is shaped like the later versions but with banjo pegs and a sculptured ridge around the rim, like the originals.

Another transition guitar, a reverse Firebird III body and vibrato with nonreverse Firebird I pickups, all stock. Even the peghead is a hybrid: old shape, but flat and unsculptured like later models; newer tuners instead of banjo pegs.

Reverse Body	There are other differences, but the easiest way to tell one reverse-body Firebird from another is simply to check the pickups and fingerboard inlays. All reverse bodies have metal pickup covers.
Firebird I:	One pickup.
Firebird III:	Two pickups, dot inlays.
Firebird V:	Two pickups, trapezoidal inlays.
Firebird VII:	Three pickups, rectangular inlays, gold hardware.
Nonreverse Firebirds	Note that the number and type of pickups change on several models. All nonreverse Firebirds had dot inlays.
Firebird I:	Now featuring two pickups with black plastic covers.
Firebird III:	Three pickups, black covers.
Firebird V:	Two pickups, metal covers.
Firebird VII:	Three pickups, metal covers.
Basses:	The Thunderbird II bass had one pickup; the IV had two.

Gibson Serial Numbers

1950s Solid-Bodies

In late 1953, Gibson inaugurated a system of serial numbers for all solid-bodies in which the first digit indicates the year. For example, 6 2241 is a 56. This continued through very early 1961. Most 1952 and 1953 Les Pauls have no serial number and are difficult to distinguish from each other (some or all 52s have taller knobs), though the trapeze tailpiece easily distinguishes them from later Gold tops.

Other Gibsons

Unfortunately, serial numbers for other Gibsons are inconclusive when determining the year of manufacture. There are three broad numbering schemes, each covering several years. Each series contains many duplicate numbers from the other two series, and sometimes the same number could be used on, say, a classic and an electric twelve-string made a year or two apart. By using the features of your guitar to narrow down the date to a particular series and then by looking up the number, the people at the Gibson factory in Kalamazoo, Michigan, can usually date the instrument. If you write to them, be sure to send a photo of your guitar.*

Official Gibson Shipping Totals for Reverse and Non-Reverse Firebirds

Model	1963	1964	1965	1966	1967	1968	1969
I	80	497	800	1,164	200	192	34
III	272	1,254	1,020	935	463	10	27
V	62	510	353	342	83	50	17
VII	20	173	110	46	9	19	5
XII (12-string: Nonreverse only)				248	24		

* A partial list of Gibson serial numbers is available from *Mugwumps* magazine. It includes representative numbers from various instruments covering the years 1915–1923 and 1935–1958. Though far from complete, it provides some guidelines. For information, write to Mugwumps, 12704 Barbara Road, Silver Spring, Maryland 20906.

A Tour Through the Gibson Factory

The old Gibson plant

Highly figured boards with rough sketches laid out

A bin full of potentiometers

Roughing out a solid body. Notice uncut plank at right.

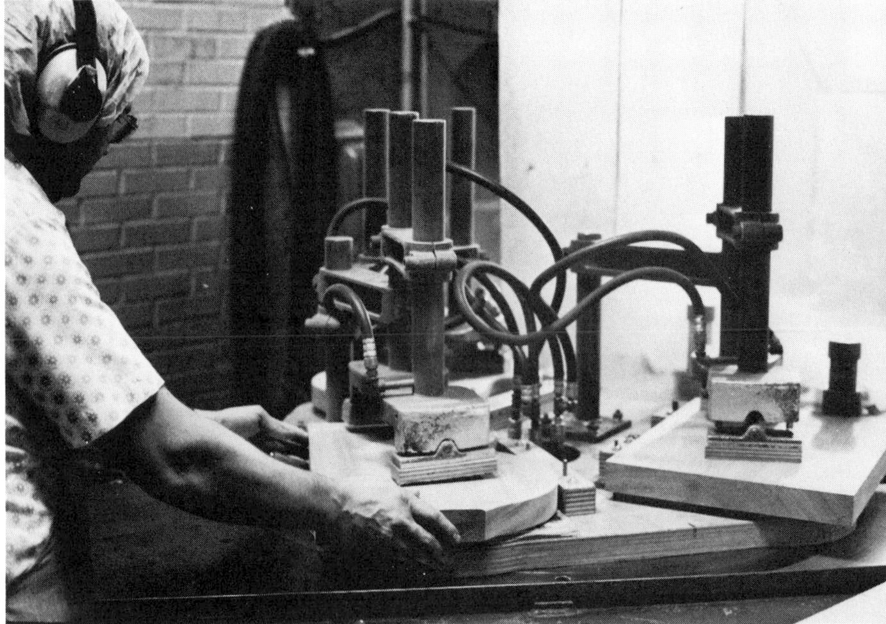

Cutting a stack of pickguards

Cutting a slot for the bridge saddle

Gluing together a three-piece headstock

Drilling a hole for neck-rod adjustment mechanism

Once the frets have been aligned in their slots, this press clamps them into the fingerboard under uniform pressure.

Routing out the slots for position markers

Inlaying position markers

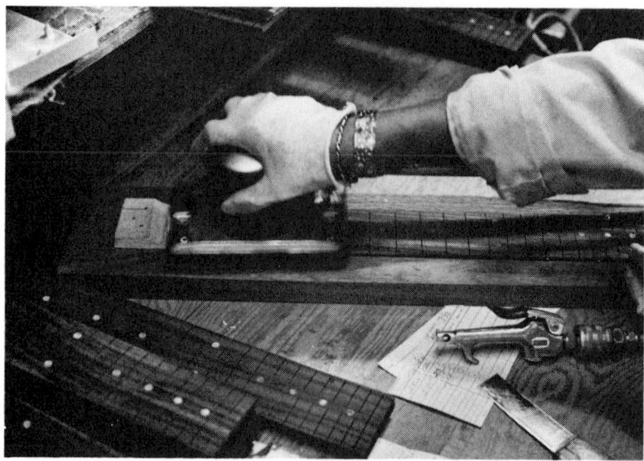

Sanding the fingerboard

Installing side dots

Shaping a Firebird headstock on a belt sander

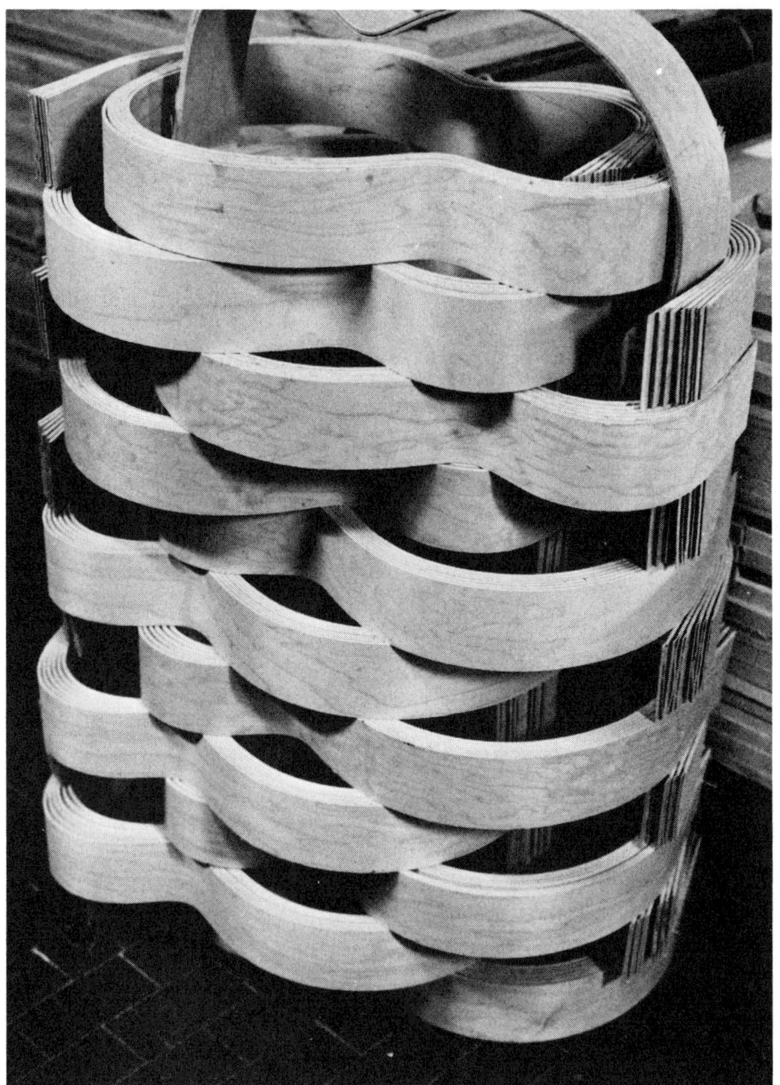

End block clamped into place while the glue dries

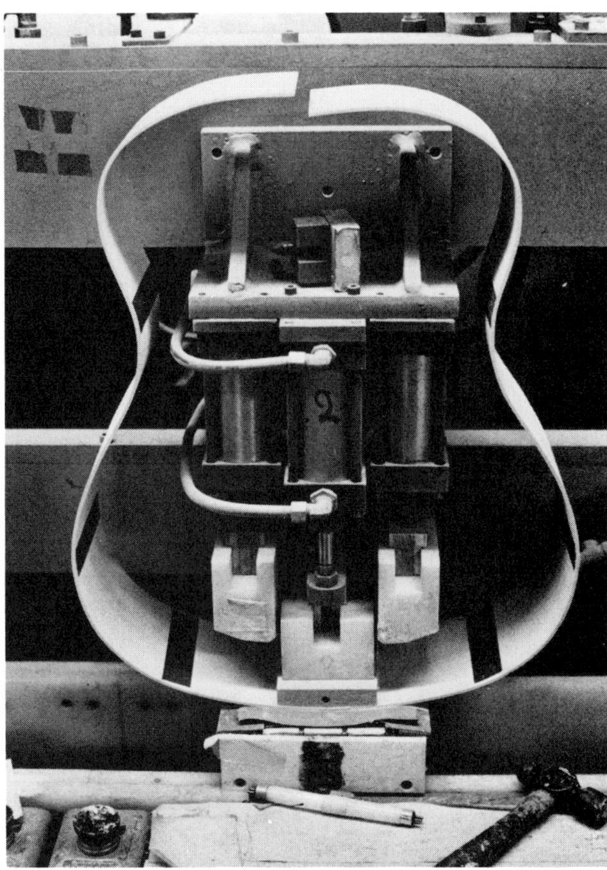

Binding is attached to these Les Paul bodies with elastic while the glue dries.

Hand sanding

FENDER MUSICAL INSTRUMENTS

Leo Fender may be the single most influential person in the history of the electric guitar manufacturing industry. An electronics engineer and compulsive experimenter, he has enormous talents for understanding how things work. He estimates that his patents number between fifty and seventy-five.

In 1932, Leo owned a small radio repair shop. Musicians would drop by to order custom-built amplifiers and public address systems. Many of them were steel-guitar players, and they often complained of defects in existing pickups. Mr. Fender had already improved such things as automatic record changers, and he turned his efforts toward designing better pickups and musical instrument amplifiers. He soon began building steel guitars, and in about 1944, he started experimenting with a solid-body electric Spanish guitar with a pickup adapted from his steel guitar. This prototype was rented to local Western bands who encouraged further production.

Leo Fender

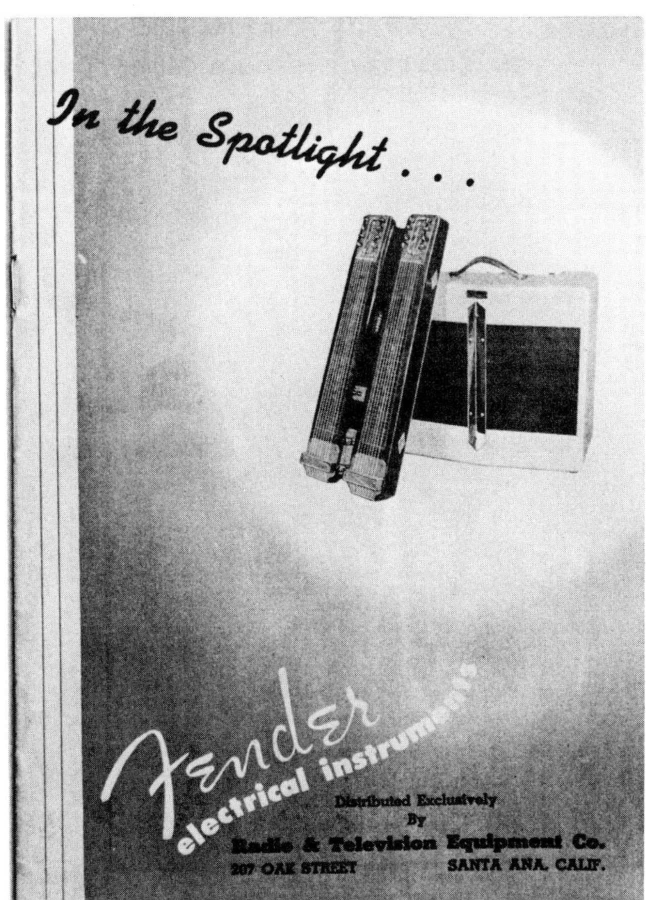

Fender's first catalog (c. 1946). There were no regular electric guitars in this brochure, only steels and amplifiers. Note the Super Amp on the cover; one of the very first twin-speaker guitar amps, it had an angled front panel, V shaped from a top view. Fender's distributor, Radio-Tel, was operated from a house in Santa Ana.

Mr. Fender formed the K & F company with Doc Kauffman, a former associate of Mr. Rickenbacker (who owned the guitar company of that name). K & F produced steel guitars and various amps. Mr. Kauffman left in January or February of 1946 as the Fender Electric Instrument Co. was formed, consisting of Leo and five or six assistants. Sales were handled by Pacific Music Supply, Francis Hall, and several nationwide organizations which established teaching studios for the steel guitar.

Fender's staff grew to fifteen employees, and the company soon moved to a 3,600-square-foot plant. It was enlarged to 5,400 square feet in 1949, and the company moved again in 1953 to a 20,000-square-foot facility. Fender formed its own distribution organization, Fender Sales, Inc., supervised by Donald D. Randall, now president of Randall Instruments, Inc. There were fifty employees in 1955, and the number more than doubled over the next five years. New buildings were added in 1959; another 6,000 square feet of floor space was leased in 1960.

The Fender plant (July 1950). *Photo by Leo Fender*

At first, Leo Fender was the chief engineer as well as the sole owner and administrator of his firm's business. One of his assistants was an affable Hawaiian named Freddie Tavares, whose skill as an engineer-musician contributed greatly to the world-wide popularity of Fender Musical Instruments. Today, the company is fortunate enough to have Mr. Tavares in the Research and Development Department of its modern plant in Fullerton, California. Fender has grown to become one of the two companies (the other is Gibson) that leads the world's professional electric guitar market. Mr. Tavares reminisces about the exciting times shortly after he joined Leo Fender in March 1953:

I had a marvelous job in those days. I would draw something on the board and Leo would come along, and he would say, "Try something like this," and he'd make a rough sketch. Then I would proceed to fancy it up. He was the owner, and his every word was the law, and it made life very simple for us. Leo and I would make a guitar and go around to musicians we knew and say, "Try this guitar; try this amp." Many's the time, the two of us, after working all day—we'd go get cleaned up and go out and promote the stuff. Most of our people were cowboys in those days, country and western players. Some *colossal* players; couldn't read a note of music, but they'd play so

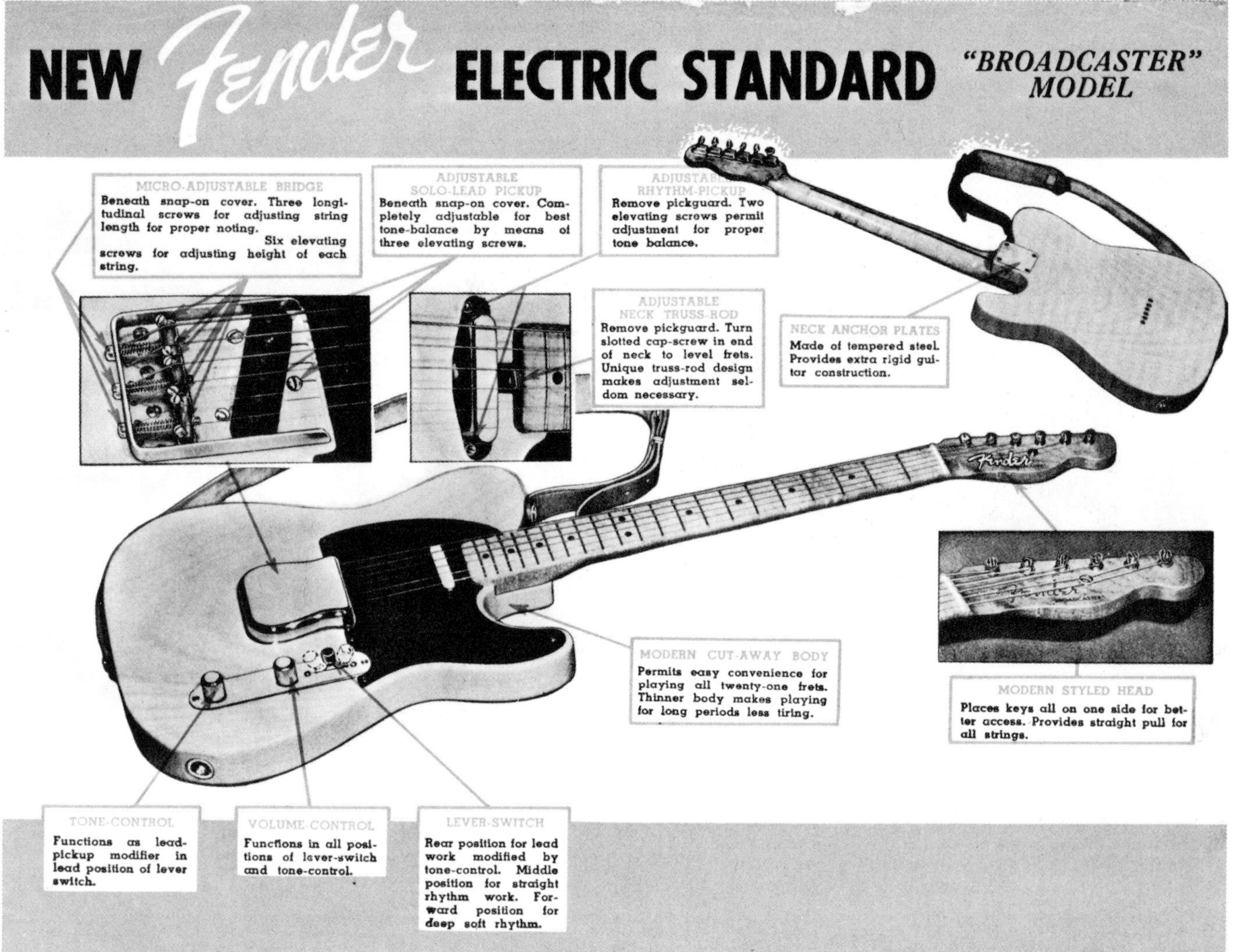

well and so fast they'd scare the daylights out of you. Anything—I did it—I welded, I'd dress up and spend all day downtown telling the patent attorney why we should have a certain patent. The next day I'd be driving the truck.

NEW Fender ELECTRIC STANDARD
"BROADCASTER" MODEL
MICRO-ADJUSTABLE BRIDGE
Beneath snap-on cover. Three longitudinal screws for adjusting string length for proper noting. Six elevating screws for adjusting height of each string.
ADJUSTABLE SOLO-LEAD PICKUP
Beneath snap-on cover. Completely adjustable for best tone-balance by means of three elevating screws.
RHYTHM-PICKUP
Remove pickguard. Two elevating screws permit adjustment for proper tone balance.
ADJUSTABLE NECK TRUSS-ROD
Remove pickguard. Turn slotted cap-screw in end of neck to level frets. Unique truss-rod design makes adjustment seldom necessary.
NECK ANCHOR PLATES
Made of tempered steel. Provides extra rigid guitar construction.
MODERN CUT-AWAY BODY
Permits easy convenience for playing all twenty-one frets. Thinner body makes playing for long periods less tiring.
MODERN STYLED HEAD
Places keys all on one side for better access. Provides straight pull for all strings.
TONE-CONTROL
Functions as lead-pickup modifier in lead position of lever switch.
VOLUME-CONTROL
Functions in all positions of lever-switch and tone-control.
LEVER-SWITCH
Rear position for lead work modified by tone-control. Middle position for straight rhythm work. Forward position for deep soft rhythm.

For reasons of health, Leo decided to sell his company. CBS purchased Fender for thirteen million dollars, and took control on January 4, 1965. Mr. Fender remained under contract to CBS for five years in an advisory capacity. Amidst a cloud of rumors, the phrase "pre-CBS" joined the vocabulary of musicians and dealers, many of whom now placed premium value on old Fenders.

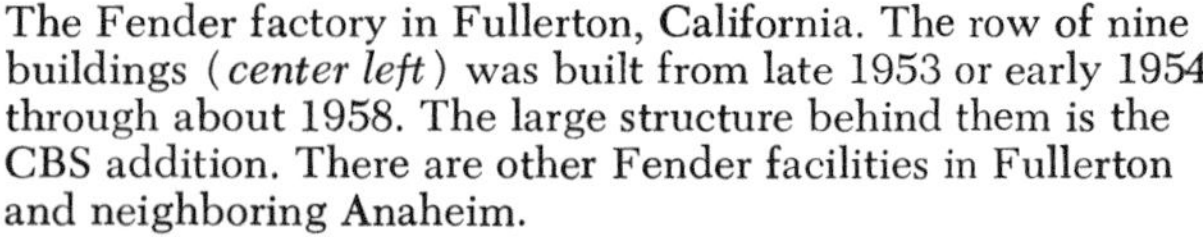

The Fender factory in Fullerton, California. The row of nine buildings (*center left*) was built from late 1953 or early 1954 through about 1958. The large structure behind them is the CBS addition. There are other Fender facilities in Fullerton and neighboring Anaheim.

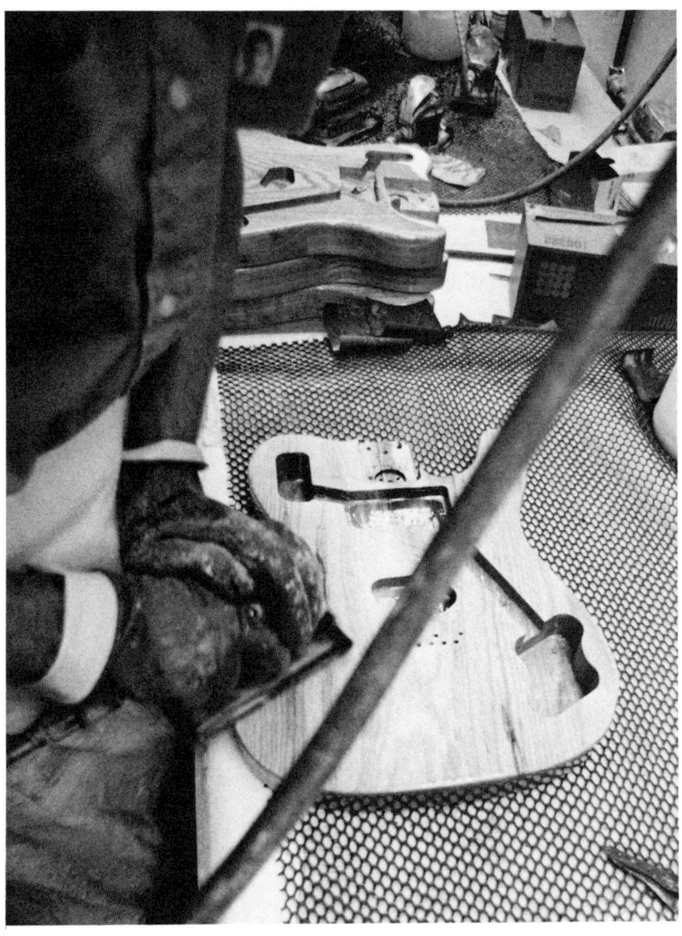

Sanding a Telecaster Deluxe body

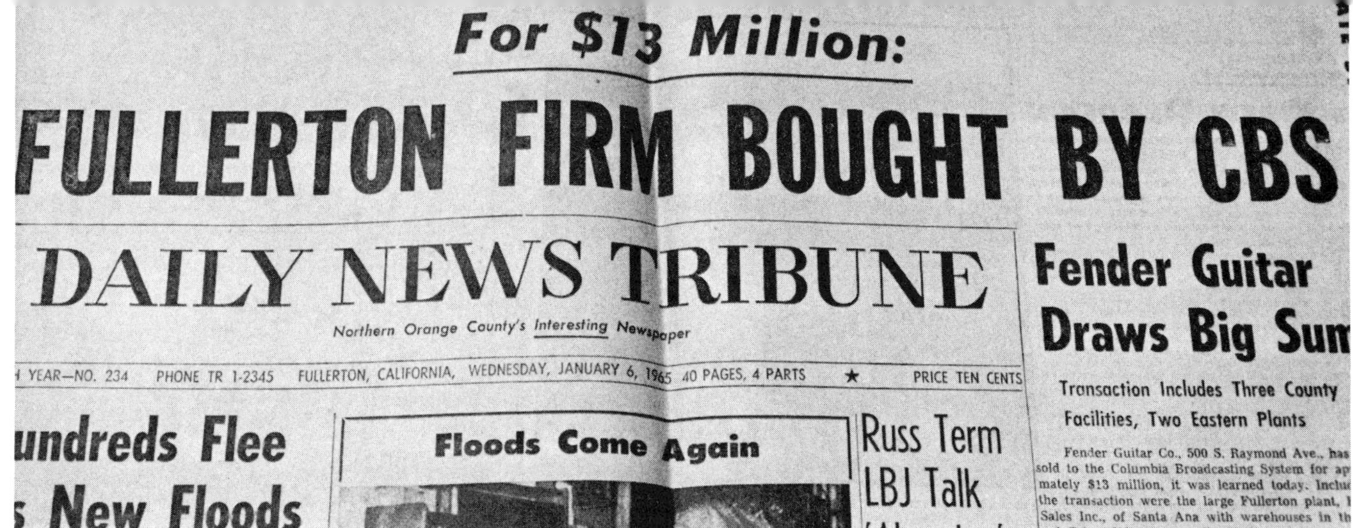

For $13 Million:

FULLERTON FIRM BOUGHT BY CBS

DAILY NEWS TRIBUNE

Northern Orange County's Interesting Newspaper

YEAR—NO. 234 PHONE TR 1-2345 FULLERTON, CALIFORNIA, WEDNESDAY, JANUARY 6, 1965 40 PAGES, 4 PARTS ★ PRICE TEN CENTS

undreds Flee
s New Floods

Floods Come Again

Russ Term
LBJ Talk

Fender Guitar
Draws Big Su

Transaction Includes Three County Facilities, Two Eastern Plants

Fender Guitar Co., 500 S. Raymond Ave., has sold to the Columbia Broadcasting System for ap mately $13 million, it was learned today. Inclu the transaction were the large Fullerton plant, Sales Inc., of Santa Ana with warehouses in th

The CBS stigma arose because of a few blunders but now seems to be fading due to improvements. Some examples: the process of dipping the Telecaster's lead pickup in wax was discontinued. When undesirable microphonics resulted, it was resumed and has continued to the present. The late Sixties transistor amplifiers were generally considered turkeys—especially compared to the world-favorite Fender tube amps—and they didn't last long. The Coronado guitars, notches below other Fenders, were dropped after only two or three years.

The people at Fender are the first to point out how time and the company have changed. Back in the old days, Leo and the folks sometimes had to dig around a bit for parts, and specifications were occasionally improvised. Two early Stratocasters made side by side may have different necks and different sounds. Today the operation is much larger, production more standardized, the guitars more consistent.

A number of points can be made in Fender's defense. The fact that it is controlled by a conglomerate is hardly unique, and all companies have introduced an occasional lemon. While the immediate post-CBS period was something of a blemish on an otherwise distinguished company history, much of the talk seems due to the sheer convenience of latching onto the CBS acquisition as some sort of comprehensive watershed. At any rate, Fender's position as a world leader is not threatened.

THE TELECASTER. The Telecaster, the guitar player's workhorse, is perhaps the world's most popular electric guitar. Relatively inexpensive and extremely durable, it has an easily recognizable twangy treble tone, a favorite in country and rock music. Even many jazz players keep a Tele in the trunk for pop recording sessions.

The Telecaster

Buffing with a lamb's-wool wheel

Installing the Telecaster pickups

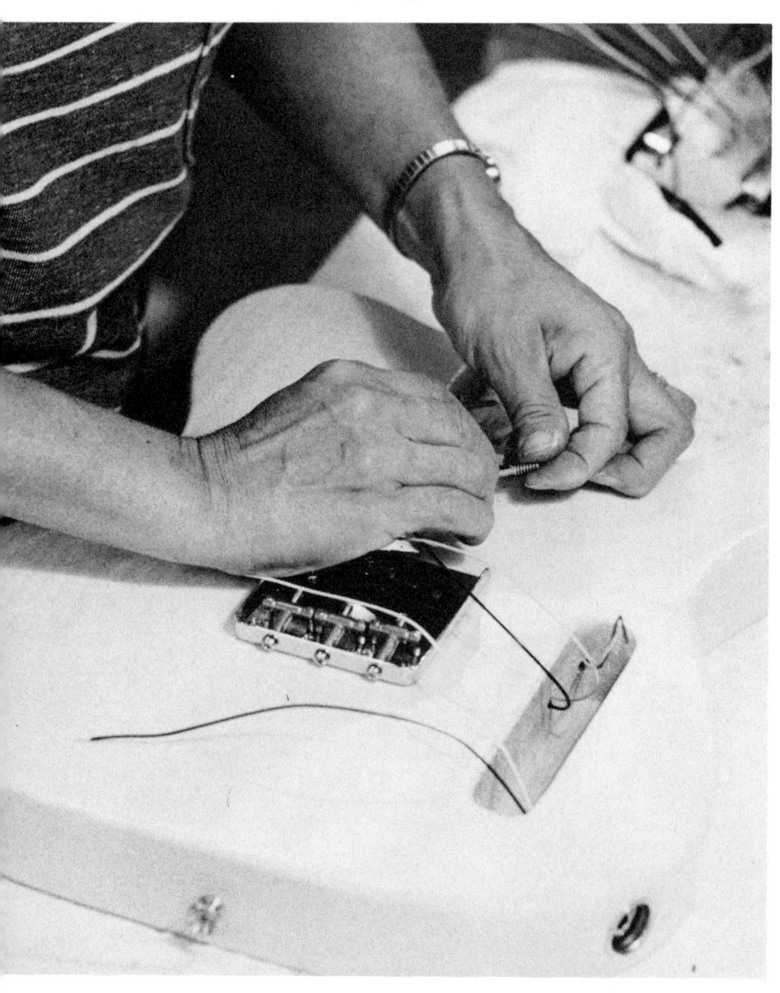

Originally called the Broadcaster, it was invented by Leo Fender and introduced in 1948. The body was ash, and the detachable neck was made from a single piece of hardrock maple. The first few Broadcasters had no truss rod and may be identified by the absence of the contrasting stripe on the back of the neck. The wooden stripe is used to fill the channel after the rod has been installed. The Fred Gretsch Company had already used the name "Broadcaster" for a set of drums, and even though Leo was fairly sure that Fender could retain the name if a conflict arose, he decided to change it to Telecaster, in anticipation of the popularity of television.

Costing $189.50, the first Telecasters were identical to the Broadcaster, and they were adopted by country and western guitar players. The tone was regulated by a three-position switch that allowed a choice between the lead pickup (rear position), the front or rhythm pickup (center position), or the front pickup with a large capacitor (front position). The last setting provided a boomy sound, good for bass lines. When moving from one position to another, the apparent loudness was changed, sometimes necessitating a compensating increase with the volume control. Furthermore, the ultra-boomy sound was no longer necessary after the introduction of the electric bass. A disadvantage was that the two pickups could not be combined. For these reasons, the Telecaster was modified during the mid-Fifties to provide a new range of choices: lead pickup alone (rear position), both pickups together (center), or front pickup alone. After the first few years of production, the Telecaster's bridges were made of plated steel instead of the original brass. In the late Sixties, the resistance load of the potentiometers (tone and volume controls) was altered from 250,000 ohms to one million ohms. Toward early 1955, several changes occurred in the Telecaster. The pickguard went from one piece of black Bake-lite to one piece of white plastic, the dome knobs were flattened on top, and the translucent finish began to get more opaque, hiding the wood grain. On guitars before this time, the serial number appears in front near the lead pickup, and the rear neck plate is blank. After late 1954, the serial number is stamped on the neck plate. At about that same time the derby-shaped cap on the pickup selector changed to the squared, top-hat shape still used.

Left - and right-handed Stratocasters

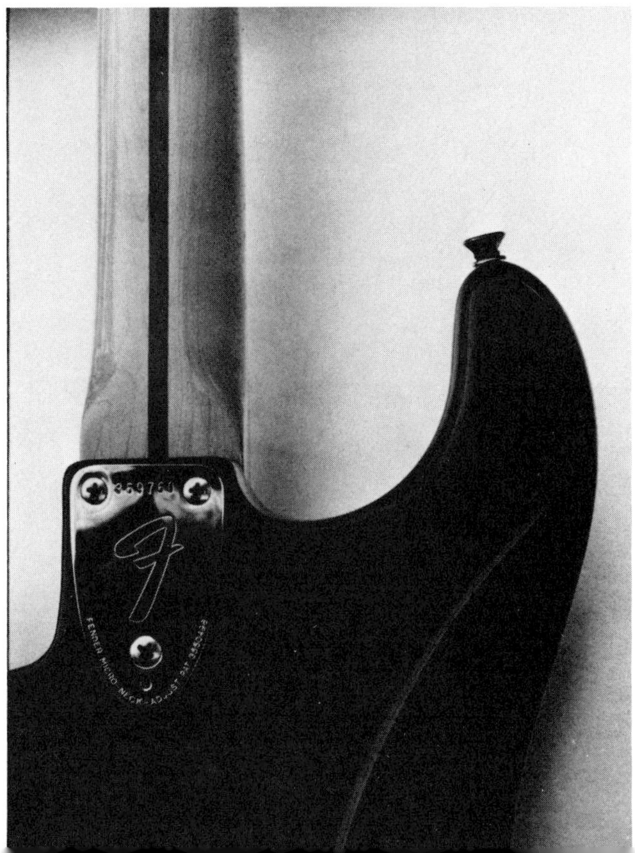

1953 Telecaster

One of the first production Stratocasters. *Photo by Leo Fender*

In addition to the always-available standard Telecaster, offshoots have included the Esquire (introduced in 1954,* discontinued after 1969; it's a Telecaster without the front pickup); the Thin Line (mid-1969, hollow on one side, with a single f-hole, two humbuckings added in February 1972); the Tele Custom (March 1970, with a front humbucking pickup); Rosewood Tele (1969, 1970, 1972); and Tele Deluxe (1973, an all-new guitar with a sculptured body, two humbuckings and new frets, string spacing and neck). The paisley and floral finish was offered in 1969 only. From 1959 to 1969, the Telecaster and Esquire were offered in an optional "Custom" finish: sunburst with white edge binding. After 1969, "Telecaster Custom" referred to the new guitar with humbucking pickup.

THE STRATOCASTER. Among rock musicians, the Stratocaster is one of the most desired of all guitars. Flashy-looking, ultra-modern in shape, it is the only existing large-scale, commercial guitar with three pickups. For hard rock, its hand vibrato (or "tremolo"), designed by Mr. Fender, is unsurpassed. Like all current Fenders, Stratocaster bodies are now made from ash. Freddie Tavares says: "Leo and I started designing it in 1953 and we worked until 1954 when it was first sold. We wanted something new, something very good, something they'd never seen before. We knew it would have three pickups from the very beginning." The first models sold for $249.50 with tremolo.

The contoured body made the Stratocaster more comfortable than the bulkier Telecaster. Solid maple necks, standard through 1959, were replaced by those with rosewood fingerboards in 1960. Maple necks became optional in early 1970. Those made prior to mid-1966 are identified by the shape of the peghead, slightly smaller than the current design. Mr. Tavares designed the head, an example of his ability to balance function and beauty. It now appears on all standard solid-body Fenders except the Telecaster. The early Stratocasters had pickguards made from a single piece of thick white plastic. Since about 1959, all Strats have had white/black/white laminated pickguards except for a very few (c. 1959) with gold-anodized pickguards. The latter type had an attractive brushed-steel look. Original Strats had bone nuts (now a type of ABS plastic) and the finishing pro-

* The actual appearance of the Esquire predated its official introduction by at least two years. Mr. Fender recalls that some one-pickup Telecasters may have been built c. 1950.

cedure has changed several times. Original tailblocks (called "inertia blocks" by Fender engineers) were steel; current ones are die-cast zinc.

The Stratocaster's three pickups may be played individually. The fact that the selector switch may also be balanced between positions one and two or between two and three, achieving a combination of pickups, is an accidental benefit unintended by Leo and Freddie. These two-pickup combinations produce something like an out-of-phase tone.

Since early 1972, Strats and humbucking Telecasters have been fitted with the "micro-tilt" adjustment on the rear metal plate, allowing for an alteration of the angle between the neck and the body, and the "bullet" truss-rod adjustment, located just above the nut on the peghead. The Stratocaster is so popular that it outsells the Telecaster during some periods.

Other Fender solid-body electrics have included the Duo-Sonic and Musicmaster (both introduced in 1956, restyled in 1964; Duo-Sonic was discontinued after 1969), Jazzmaster (late 1957; the first ones had small peghead, anodized aluminum pickguard, black pickup covers and chrome, barrel-style knobs. The next model, late 1959, also with metal pickguard, had white pickup covers and white plastic knobs. Current style pickguard by 1960,*) Bass VI six-string bass guitar (late 1961; tuned one octave lower than a standard guitar. In 1963 it received a mute, new pickups and a fourth tone selector,*) Jaguar (1961,*) Mustang (August 1964), Marauder (1965 only; never produced in large quantities, it was an abortive attempt to build a guitar with four pickups, all concealed beneath the pickguard), Electric 12-String (June 1965-1969,*) Five-String Bass (June 1965-1970,* with added high C string), Custom (mid-1969–1972, made from the 12-String body), and the Bronco (1969).

THE PRECISION BASS. The Precision Bass changed the sound of popular American music. Leo Fender recognized the need for an instrument to replace the cumbersome upright bass, and he developed an electric

*These guitars were modified in 1966: white neck binding and rectangular fretboard markers were added. In 1968 and 1969 the Electric 12- and 5-String bass appeared with earlier dot-type markers and the Jaguar appeared both ways.

1955 Precision bass

1957 Precision bass with gold-anodized pickguard

bass (often misnamed "bass guitar"), which he called the Precision. At a cost of $195.50, its advantages over the acoustic "doghouse" bass were immediately apparent: it was smaller, louder, and portable; guitarists could quickly adapt to its scale length of 34 inches, and since it was fretted, the bassist could play with "precision." The popular music industry jumped on it, and even though other manufacturers started to produce similar instruments, the name "Fender bass" was applied generally to any electric bass, regardless of brand name. The "P bass" is still the most popular bass in the world, by far.

When introduced in 1951, the body had the boxy shape of today's Telecaster bass. A few months after the Stratocaster was unveiled in 1954, with its dressed-away face, the Precision was rounded and contoured to its present shape. However, the early pickguard still remained, covering the entire body from the waist up. The knobs were housed in a separate metal piece and the peghead was still the original Telecaster type. In 1957 the current peghead was added and the split pickup replaced the single-coil unit, and the pickguard was changed to today's more graceful shape, surrounding the knobs. The pickguard was made of anodized aluminum, but it was changed to plastic by 1960. Maple necks were standard until 1959 and optional after the summer of 1969.

The Telecaster bass appeared in 1968, though it missed the 1968 catalogue. It had the shape of the earliest Precisions. In February of 1972 a humbucking pickup was added and other changes were made.

A variation of the Precision is the Fretless model (late 1970), designed for the musician trained on the acoustic bass. The curvature of the neck approaches that of the acoustic, and the attack sound of the fingers is different. Without frets, the fingering becomes more important in two ways. First, the finger must be located in just the right spot to achieve proper intonation and, second, the angle and leverage must be correct to produce a good sound. Additionally, the bassist may play microtones—notes that are in between those on the standard fretboard.

The Jazz Bass appeared in 1960, with its Jazzmaster-like offset waist, new pickups, and slim neck ($1\frac{7}{16}$″). Since 1966, it has had a bound neck and rectangular position markers.

ACOUSTIC GUITARS. Fender began to make acoustic guitars in 1962 (announced in August 1963) in an operation separate from the original factory. Roger Rossmeisl, the European luthier, supervised the plant, and in 1969 he began to build Fender's line of hollow-body jazz electrics, including the Montego and the limited-edition hand-carved LTD. Among the early Fender acoustics were the Kingman, Concert, Shenandoah, Villager, Newporter, Palomino, and Malibu. The colorful Wildwood line of late 1966–1969 featured sides and backs of dye-injected wood with swirling grain. Soon thereafter, the semi-acoustic Coronado (late 1966–1969) and Antigua (1969) guitars, basses, and twelve-strings were brought out. For several years Fender has been importing the "F-series" line of flat-top steel-string and classic guitars.

Dating Fender Guitars

The date of construction, stamped on the end of the neck, can be seen when the neck is detached. If that stamp has been rendered illegible, the date may be written on the body underneath the pickguard or in the cavity that houses the pickups. You may also discover that the neck is initialed by the person who did the final shaping, or that the area where the neck joins the body is stamped with the name of the responsible craftsman.

Serial numbers cannot be used to accurately date Fenders built before 1955. The earliest Strats and Teles apparently had independent numbering schemes, and even among Telecasters a 52 might have a higher number than a 53. Serial numbers after 1955 may be roughly consecutive.

The best way to date a Fender is simply to pop the neck and read the date. Still, serial numbers can provide some rough guides: a number preceded by a small capital L indicates an early Sixties guitar, while a large Fender "F" logo on the neck plate identifies the guitar as a post-CBS, mid-to-late Sixties.

Aside from the major design changes mentioned in the text, there are a number of minor variations: some peghead string guides are round, others are butterfly clips; some bridge screws are steel, some brass, some threaded, some plain; certain neck-rod adjustment screws have only one slot instead of the usual X; pole-pieces differ in height; some decals include patent numbers, others don't—the list goes on. However, since the great majority of Fenders will have the stamped production date still intact, and given the more obvious differences in pickguards, fingerboards, body

Telecaster bass

shapes, and finishes, reliance upon uncertain serial numbers or mechanical trivia is almost always unnecessary.

Fender Amps

Mr. Fender began building custom amplifiers on a small scale in the late 1920s. In the mid-Forties he went into production with such models as the Deluxe (in a hardwood walnut cabinet) and the Champ, sometimes marketed as the Champ 600 or the Student 600. The Champ had a single volume knob, no tone control, and three tubes. It was harmless-looking and puny in size—just under one foot square up front—but despite the appearance, the early Champs were screamers. Dual-speaker amps are now common all over the world. Mr. Fender recounts how that development came about:

> Single-speaker amps suited the requirements of a lot of musicians. I had bought quite a large quantity of 10″ speakers. The trend sort of changed to 12″ speakers, and the question was—what to do with all of these 10″ speakers? Up to that time, you found a single speaker in an amp, you see. But I thought 'Well, I'll try a pair of 10s and see how they sound.' In order to get a little better dispersion, I divided the front panel into a V shape, with the angled speakers. We called it the Super. It performed fine and was a big success. I think that the Super was about the first twin-speaker amplifier for musicians.

The Twin Amp and the Bassman appeared in about 1950. The earliest models had large grilles. Then, for several years, up through 1954, all Fender amps had wide panels above and below the grille. In 1955, they all went back to an enlarged grille with smaller borders surrounding it. These cabinets were covered with linen (see Legend) and kept the same styling until the early Sixties, when Tolex was introduced.

Leo Fender's close friend, Forrest White, was Fender's Vice President and General Manager from 1953 to 1965. The company wished to distribute a second line of amps and steel guitars solely for use in teaching studios. An amplifier covered in blue linen and a student model steel guitar were made by Fender but given the nameplate "White Musical Inst." At first, Leo did not tell Forrest that the new line was to be named after him, and it was not until the nameplates arrived that Mr. White found out. Because the company could not keep up with the demand for the regular line of Fender instruments, only a few amps and steel guitars were produced with the White nameplate. Forrest is now producing the Music Man line of amplifiers and other equipment in his Anaheim, California plant, with his partner, Tom Walker.

How to Date the Fender Amps

Beware. This table is based on the less-than-airtight evidence contained in catalogues, price lists, brochures, official and unofficial files, with a few obstacles between the researcher and total accuracy. First, an amplifier originally built in 1963 may be unchanged in the 1965–1966 catalogue, yet still characterized there as "all new." The reason is that the earliest description may be reprinted word-for-word over a period of several years. Second, a new amp may be advertised and shipped to dealers, just missing the catalogue's deadline. It is then "announced" nearly a year later as a "new" product. Third, distinguishing features (for example, the color of the knobs) may vary on two amps of the same model and year. Fourth, a catalogue description might not match the photo.* Fifth, the catalogue photos from 1960 to 1962 were tinted, causing a light grill cloth to appear dark. Finally, a company's own records may be incomplete.

Even given these variables, the few inconsistencies that did appear in official sources (other than catalogues) rarely involved a difference of more than a single year, and the author is reasonably confident that any discrepancies have been corrected through cross-referencing with other sources. Most of these amps are dated when they originally appeared in Fender's periodic announcements, sometimes earlier than their first mention in a catalogue. Some amps bear the date of construction written in grease pen on the chassis or stamped on a tube chart attached to an interior surface.

*At least once the amp's nameplate is hidden behind an instrument to conceal the difference between the model and caption.

A Tour Through the Fender Factory

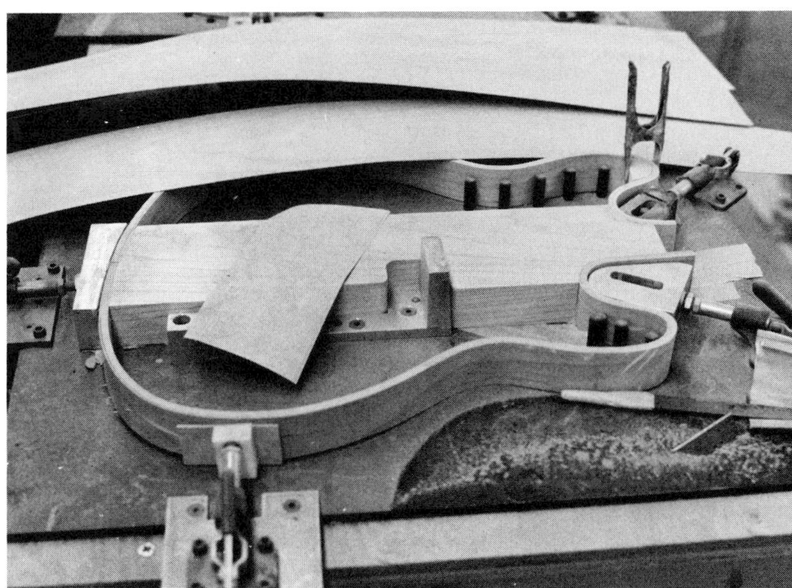

Starcaster body in a shaping jig

Starcaster bodies; glue drying

Clamping the string nut into its slot

Attaching wire to coil forms on an automatic pickup winder

Inlaying frets

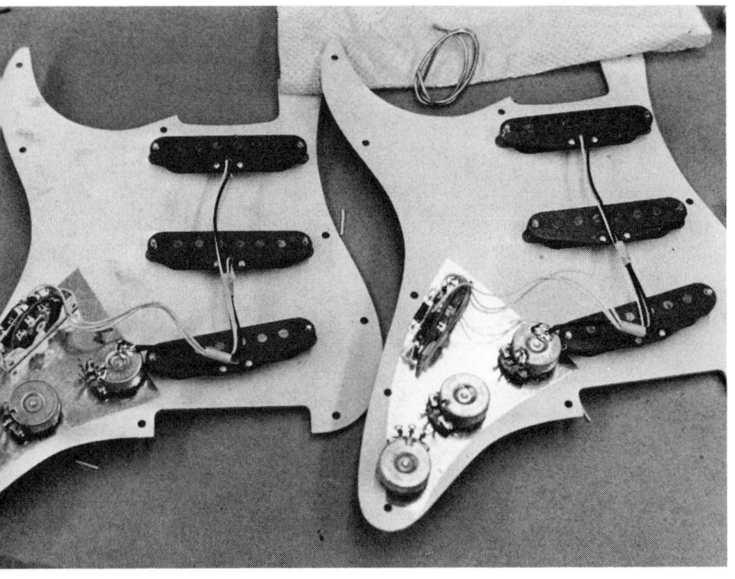

Stratocaster wiring harnesses

Attaching the neck with a powered screwdriver

Final inspection and testing

AMPLIFIERS	1954	1955	1956	1957	1958	1959	1960	1961	1962	196
CHAMP	TW STYLE 1 1-6	A STYLE 2 4 WATTS 11 X 12	B 12½ X 13½	C			TW B			
VIBRO-CHAMP										
BRONCO										
PRINCETON	TW STYLE 1 A	4½ WATTS STYLE 2 A 12½ x 13½	B 16½ X 18	C			1-8 B	TOL 1-10 M/L/D		B/S 4 BLACK KNOBS
PRINCETON-REVERB										
HARVARD			1-8 B 10 WATTS	C 1-10 (MID-1958)						
DELUXE	TW STYLE 1 A 1-12	18" WIDE STYLE 2 B 15 WATTS	20" WIDE	C			TW D	TOL M/L/D		B/S
DELUXE-REVERB										
PRO (& PRO REVERB)	TW STYLE 1 A 1-15	STYLE 2 One tone knob B 26 WATTS	SEPARATE BASS AND TREBLE	C			TOL M/L/D			B/S
VIBROVERB										FEB. 196 TOL M/L/D
SUPER (& SUPER REVERB)	TW STYLE 1 A One tone knob	STYLE 2 B 20 WATTS		C			TOL M/L/D NO REVERB 2-10S			REVERB 4-10S
CONCERT							TOL M/L/D	M/D/D	M/L/D	B/S
TREMOLUX		1-12 STYLE 2 15 WATTS 16¾ X 20	B 20 X 22	TW C 1-12			D	TOL PB L/D/W 1-10	2-10S	L/L/D
BANDMASTER	TW STYLE 1 A 1-15	STYLE 2 C 26 WATTS	3-10S				TOL M/L/D M/L/W 3-10S	PB L/D/W 1-12	2-12S	L/L/D
BANDMASTER-REVERB										
TWIN (& TWIN REVERB)	TW STYLE 1 A 2-12S	STYLE 2 Presence knob C 50 WATTS					TOL M/L/D	L/D/W		REVERB B/S S(
VIBRASONIC						LATE 1959 M/L/D L/D/W		M/L/D		
VIBROSONIC REVERB										
VIBROLUX (& VIBROLUX REVERB)			TW B 10 WATTS	C 1-10			D	TOL M/L/D 1-12		B/S
QUAD REVERB										
SUPER SIX REVERB										
SHOWMAN 12								L/D/W		L/L/D
SHOWMAN 15								L/D/W		L/L/D
DUAL SHOWMAN (DOUBLE SHOWMAN THROUGH MID-1963)									DEC. 1962 L/L/D	
DUAL SHOWMAN REVERB										
BASSMAN	TW STYLE 1 A 1-15	STYLE 2 50 WATTS C 4-10S	2 INPUTS	4 INPUTS MID-RANGE CONTROL				TOL PB L/D/W 1-12	2-12S	L/L/D

FENDER TUBE AMPLIFIER TABLE

TW "Tweed" cabinet covering, described in the early catalogues as "brown-and-white diagonal stripe airplane luggage linen." Cabinets have flat, rear-mounted chrome-plated control panels with arrowhead/pointer knobs.

TOL Tolex—the tough, pebble-grained covering still in use. Canted, front-mounted control panel; solid-color barrel-shaped knobs, later changed to black and white with numbers on the lip.

Color Schemes. These apply to the Tolex-covered amps. The initials represent the color of the cabinet, the grille cloth, and the knobs, *in that order*.

Cabinet / Grille Cloth / Knobs

Cabinet colors: L (light beige); M (medium brown); B (black)

Grille colors: L (light gold); D (dark brown); S (silver)

Knob colors: D (dark brown or black); W (white or ivory)

Examples:

M/L/D: Medium brown cabinet
Light gold grille
Dark knobs

L/D/W: Light beige cabinet
Dark brown grille
White knobs

All but a few of the black amps have the new-style black & white knobs and are abbreviat[ed] simply B/S (black cabinet w/silver grille); those with white knobs are B/S/W.

Style 1: Wide panels above and below grille
Style 2: Enlarged grille, narrow panels

Speaker sizes are given by quantity and size, 1-10 means one ten-inch speaker.

PB 1st year of piggy-back design

964 / 1965 / 1966 / 1967 / 1968 / 1969 / 1970 / 1971 / 1972 / 1973 & 74	AMPLIFIERS
1964 B/S · B/S FM SCRIPT NAMEPLATE · N2 · N3	CHAMP
AUG. 1964 · B/S SCRIPT NAMEPLATE · N2 · N3	VIBRO-CHAMP
(1968 –)	BRONCO
TE S · 5 KNOBS SCRIPT NAMEPLATE · N2 · N4 · N5	PRINCETON
AUG. 1964 · SCRIPT NAMEPLATE · N2 · N3	PRINCETON-REVERB
	HARVARD
(– 1966)	DELUXE
NAMEPLATE · N2	DELUXE-REVERB
REVERB ADDED JUNE 1965 2-12S SCRIPT NAMEPLATE · N2 40 RMS 10" DEEP · 45 RMS 10½" DEEP · N3 CASTERS ADDED	PRO (& PRO REVERB)
R B/S	VIBROVERB
24 X 24 · N1 25½ X 25½ · N2 40 RMS · 45 RMS 24½ X 25 · N3 CASTERS ADDED	SUPER (& SUPER REVERB)
	CONCERT
AUG. 1964 B/S	TREMOLUX
AUG. 1964 B/S 21 X 32 · N1 COLUMN 40 x 29½ · N3 40 RMS TOP 24" W · 45 RMS TOP 25" W · N3 CASTERS ADDED	BANDMASTER
N2 · N3 CASTERS ADDED	BANDMASTER-REVERB
PLATE 10½" D · N1 9¾" D · N2 85 RMS · 100 RMS · N3 MASTER VOLUME CASTERS ADDED	TWIN (& TWIN REVERB)
	VIBRASONIC
MID 1972	VIBROSONIC REVERB
AUG. 1964 REVERB 2-10S 18" H · N1 18½" H · N2 35 RMS · N2 40 RMS	VIBROLUX (& VIBROLUX REVERB)
EARLY 1972	QUAD REVERB
EARLY 1972	SUPER SIX REVERB
AUG. 1964 B/S	SHOWMAN 12
AUG. 1964 B/S SCRIPT NAMEPLATE · N2	SHOWMAN 15
AUG. 1964 B/S 24½ X 36 · N1 COLUMN 45½ X 30 · N2	DUAL SHOWMAN (DOUBLE SHOWMAN THROUGH MID-1963)
(1969 –) · MASTER VOLUME CASTERS ADDED	DUAL SHOWMAN REVERB
AUG. 1964 B/S · WHITE OR BLACK KNOBS · BLACK KNOBS 21 X 32 · COLUMN 40 X 29½ 2-12S · MID 1969 2-15S · MODELS 10, 50, AND 100	BASSMAN

meplate styles of early Tweed amps:

A: Single word "Fender" in block letters; "Fullerton, California" in small letters
: Single word "Fender" in script
: "Fender" plus model name (e.g. "Fender Twin Amp") in script
: Style C plus "Fullerton, California"

meplate styles of black & silver amps:

1: White script on black control panel
2: Capital letters, block-style, plus the word "AMP" (e.g., "SUPER REVERB AMP"); brushed steel control panel
3: Same as N2, without "AMP"; e.g., "SUPER REVERB"
4: Two words, one above the other
5: Two words, side by side

FM Front-mounted control panel
RM Rear-mounted control panel

Measurements refer to height and width unless specified with a D (depth).

Changes in speaker size or power rating are listed only where helpful to differentiate between years. The table is meant to pinpoint dates, not to list all specifications. For example, notice that the Bandmaster changes to piggy-back (PB) in 1961. The Showman was also a piggy-back; however, no "PB" appears in its column because it was never made any other way. Thus "PB" could not be used to distinguish one Showman from another.

Changes in 1969 from silver to blue grille cloth are not mentioned because of the various shadings and mixtures of thread.

Bass amps, other than the Bassman, are not included.

Fender 600 Amp, pre-Tweed, immediate predecessor to the Champion 600 and Champ

4-10s Bassman (c. 1955)

1956 Princeton

Vibrolux (c. 1961)

Tremolux (c. 1961)

Vibroverb (c. 1963)

1964 Princeton

A rare late-1964 black Champ with rear-mounted control panel

5

Other Electrics

Alembic standard long-scale bass. The objective of the Alembic Company is to advance guitar design to the level of development of other technological fields. Their unique guitars and basses cost far more than most electrics, but owners agree that they are worth it. Alembic bodies are characterized by exotic woods and elegant sculpturing. The electronics are exceptionally sophisticated and versatile, incorporating medium-impedance ceramic pickups (adjustable for gain), hum-canceling dummy pickups, and internal FET preamps. The tone controls are active low-pass filters that roll off at 12 dB per octave. Stock Alembics have brass bridges and string nuts, twenty-four-fret fingerboards, and full-length, five-piece laminated necks; some boast exquisite inlays. To many, Alembic is state-of-the-art.

B.C. Rich Mockingbird. Bernardo Rico has molded his family's small guitar shop into a modern manufacturer of classics, steel-strings, and electrics. His Mockingbird, like its companion, the Seagull, features one of the most versatile circuit layouts on the market, yet it is uncluttered and easy to operate: DiMarzio Dual Sound humbuckers, coil splitter, phase switch, master volume and tone controls, internal preamp and six-position varitone. Bodies available in koa, maple, and mahogany.

Travis Bean Artist 1000, a revolutionary guitar in which both ends of the strings attach to the same piece: a neck/receiver consisting of a hollowed-out billet of aircraft-grade Reynolds 6061-T6 aluminum. Hand carved body of exotic Hawaiian koa, stainless-steel pickguard, pearl inlay, aluminum nut, humbuckings, Schallers.

Spray gun and guitar body in spray booth at Travis Bean

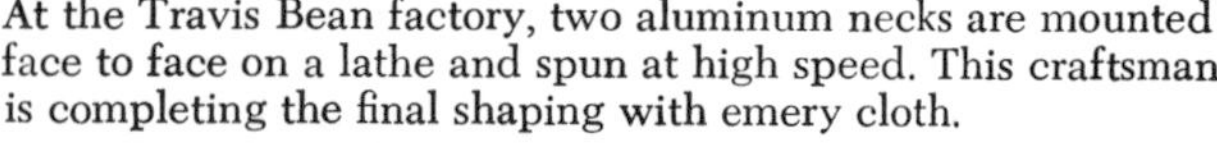

At the Travis Bean factory, two aluminum necks are mounted face to face on a lathe and spun at high speed. This craftsman is completing the final shaping with emery cloth.

Travis Bean adjusts one of his guitars.

Ibanez first gained fame in this country as the manufacturer of incredibly detailed imitations of popular Gibsons. Their guitars were exceptionally fine, particularly considering the differences in price between the copies and the originals. In recent years, this Japanese company has introduced several well-engineered models of its own, including this one, the Artist EQ Model 2623 with internal preamp. While Ibanez is a strong contender in the $400 price range, their scores of models are not merely "good guitars for the money," they are good guitars, period, having earned unqualified endorsements from several major artists.

The inspiration for Paul Hamer's $1,000 guitar was clearly the original Gibson Explorer. However, the Hamer's two-piece curly maple top is much more dazzling than the original's limed korina body. Aside from considerations of pure flash, the zigzag shape is practical, balancing the right arm in a comfortable playing position. Brass bridge and tailpiece by Schaller, ivory nut, DiMarzio pickups.

Yamaha SG 2000: gold-plated hardware, full-length neck centerpiece of laminated maple and mahogany, maple top, mahogany back, 24¾" scale, twenty-two frets, ebony fingerboard with mother-of-pearl inlays, ivory nut, high density shielding, humbuckers, and a solid brass sustain block mounted underneath the bridge. The truss rod is sheathed in a vinyl tube to eliminate sympathetic vibration. The volume and tone controls are designed to reduce the loss of highs that usually accompanies slight decreases in volume. Look for several fine Yamaha electrics in the near future.

Veillette-Citron electric twelve-string. Joe Veillette and Harvey Citron offer an especially distinctive line of solid-body instruments, including the twelve, a bass, and a standard electric guitar. Available in several choice woods, all have the long horn and deep cutaways for weight distribution and maximum fingerboard accessibility. The laminated neck runs the full length of the body; the fingerboard is ebony with mother-of-pearl edge markers. Twenty-five frets (just over two full octaves). Solid brass hardware. Standard tone and volume control layout plus master volume and phase switch. Optional "staged" pickups with a three-way switch to vary the impedance from low to high.

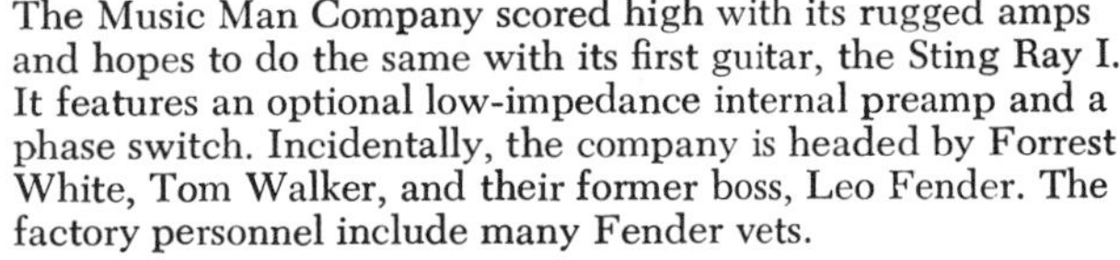

The Music Man Company scored high with its rugged amps and hopes to do the same with its first guitar, the Sting Ray I. It features an optional low-impedance internal preamp and a phase switch. Incidentally, the company is headed by Forrest White, Tom Walker, and their former boss, Leo Fender. The factory personnel include many Fender vets.

Semie Moseley was eighteen years old when he built Joe Maphis's outrageous double-neck, now in the Country Music Hall of Fame in Nashville. His Mosrite guitars had extra-thin necks, distinctive finishes, and delicate vibratos. Endorsed and distributed by the Ventures, they gained international fame during the surfing years. The New Mosrite Company of Bakersfield, California, was formed in early 1976 and offers duplicates of the original Ventures models and several others, including this one, the Brass Rail. Its most distinctive feature is a ¼″ × ¾″ brass bar running the length of the neck. Each fret is directly anchored to the bar in order to increase sustain. Alder body, maple neck, internal preamp, phase switches, bass and treble boosts, and zero fret. The fretboard and binding are laminated rosewood and maple.

The ML by Dean Guitars; mahogany body, two-piece curly maple top, DiMarzio pickups.

Kramer Artist 650G, with a forged aluminum neck that is T-shaped in cross section; full-length matching wood inlays give it a familiar feel. Other features: ebonol fingerboard, fret wire designed by Phil Petillo, aluminum and stainless-steel hardware, Schallers, 25″ scale, and zero fret. Bodies are made of various woods, including shedua, figured maple, and American black walnut.

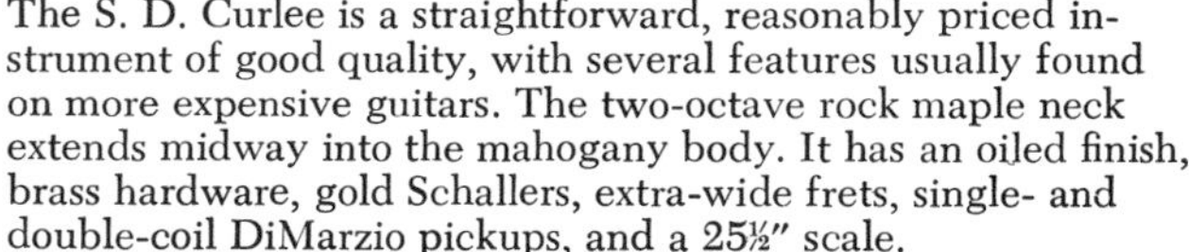

The S. D. Curlee is a straightforward, reasonably priced instrument of good quality, with several features usually found on more expensive guitars. The two-octave rock maple neck extends midway into the mahogany body. It has an oiled finish, brass hardware, gold Schallers, extra-wide frets, single- and double-coil DiMarzio pickups, and a 25½″ scale.

Carvin DC 150 Stereo, with maple body, bolt-on neck, two-octave maple fingerboard with pearl inlay, brass tailpiece, master tone, phase switch, and coil splitter. For over thirty years, this unique company has sold its guitars exclusively through mail order.

Ovation Viper, a companion to Ovation's other solid-bodies: Preacher, Breadwinner, and Deacon.

The Electra MPC (Modular Powered Circuits) guitars move tone modifiers and special effects from the floor to your fingertips. A dozen or so electronic devices may be snapped into the back. Once in place, they are controlled by the switches and knobs on the face of the guitar. Available components include phase shifter, overdrive, preamp, and automatic wah, among others.

Hartley Peavey turned the music industry around with his amplifiers, and he aims to do it again with this guitar, the moderately priced but fully professional T-60. Built in large quantities in Peavey's exceptionally modern, computer-monitored factory in Meridian, Mississippi, the guitar has unique humbucking pickups that gradually shift to a single-coil mode as the tone knobs are turned up. Other features: heavy die-cast hardware, phase switch, 25½″ scale, metal string nut, unique two-piece neck construction, neck tilt, ash body, and a molded, high-impact plastic road case.

Photo on p. 116 (bottom right), and all photos p. 117, taken at the Peavey factory, Meridian, Mississippi.

Multi-spindle gear head used to drill holes in guitar body blanks for the neck mounting screws and neck tilt

Ash body blank vacuum-locked in position on a machine that routs the outline of a bass body. The different cutting tools perform various functions. Note the holes that have been drilled for attachment of the strings and neck.

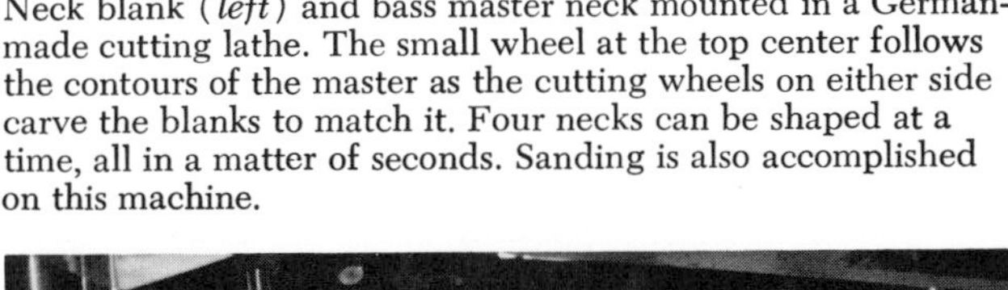

Neck blank (*left*) and bass master neck mounted in a German-made cutting lathe. The small wheel at the top center follows the contours of the master as the cutting wheels on either side carve the blanks to match it. Four necks can be shaped at a time, all in a matter of seconds. Sanding is also accomplished on this machine.

This six-spindle gear head is used to drill the tuning machine holes in the guitar peghead.

6

Pickups and Sustain

PICKUPS

A transducer is a device that converts energy from one form into another. A pickup, or electromechanical transducer, converts the tones produced by string vibrations into electrical signals. The frequency of the generated impulse theoretically corresponds to the frequency of the musical note. The typical pickup consists of a permanent magnet (or six magnetically charged polepieces) surrounded by a coil of wire. As the string vibrates in the magnetic field, it generates a variable electrical current in the coil.

The early devices were actually contact microphones of the crystal or dynamic kind, sometimes overamplifying the vibrations in the immediately surrounding area. A big disadvantage was that, in addition to receiving string vibrations, they also sensed any knocks made by the guitarist against the instrument and even nearby conversations.

Amplified instruments such as Lloyd Loar's electric double bass had appeared in the Twenties, but they were ahead of their time and commercially unsuccessful. The straight-bar pickup, which bore the nickname "Charlie Christian," was first introduced in the mid-Thirties on Gibson's EH-150 Hawaiian steel guitar. After 1945 or so, electric Spanish guitars became regular fixtures in big bands, and Gibson featured the "Christian" pickup on several models, such as the original noncutaway ES-150.

The pickup picks up string vibrations. For our purposes here, the string may be thought of as a vibrating

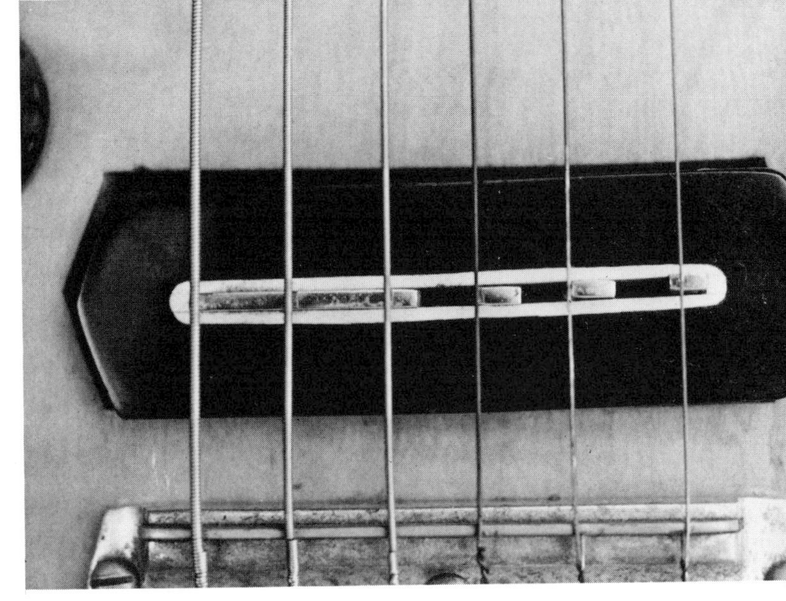

Early Gibson pickup

ellipse or loop with its widest arc at midpoint (but see Chapter 8 for qualifications and details). Near the arc the longer waves generate lower, or bass, frequencies; near either end, where the string is taut, the shorter waves produce treble frequencies. On most guitars, the only difference between the bass and treble pickups is in their location along the string length—bass pickup nearer the center, treble nearer the end.

Coils

Coils may be hand wound, but necessity requires all large-scale commercial pickups to be wound on machines. Pickups are often categorized into single- and double-coil devices. The essential single-coil pickups are found on Fender's Telecaster and Stratocaster, while the most popular double-coil pickup is Gibson's Humbucking.

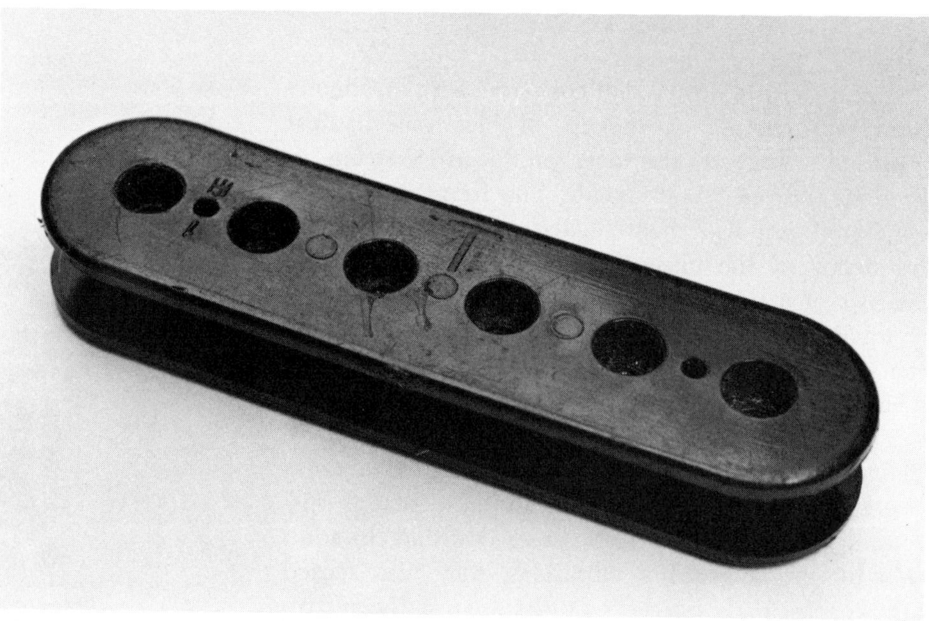

Pickup coil form

The coil of wire is usually wrapped around a bobbin; the more wraps, the stronger the pickup and, up to a point, the better the sustain. However, the more wraps, the higher the inductance, and beyond a certain level inductance noticeably impedes treble frequencies.* In a sense, too many windings turns the pickup into a big low-pass filter, gobbling highs. Therefore, the pickup designer knows that his decision concerning the number of windings will be a trade-off, a balance of several considerations: power output, sustain, frequency response, etc.

* The pickup's construction materials also affect induction.

Humbuckings; Patent-Applied-Fors

Noise is a problem in most pickups. An ingenious solution is the humbucking design. It has two coils, each with an equal or nearly equal number of turns. They are wired in series, current flowing through one, then the other, as opposed to parallel, where the current would flow through both simultaneously. The coils are connected out of phase so that an impulse of noise through one coil is offset and canceled by a corresponding impulse flowing in the opposite direction through the other. Since the coils cannot occupy the same space, hum cancellation, while substantial, is less than 100 percent. The voltages from each coil are added in phase to produce the desired musical signal.

The inductance of the many turns in a humbucking causes some loss of highs as compared to, say, a single-coil Fender with fewer turns. Another reason for the humbucker's fatter tone is that its two coils sample frequencies from a wider length of string compared to the narrow Fender pickup, and some cancellation occurs when an "up" vibration over one coil is offset by a "down" vibration over the coil next to it. Since the coils are so close together, it is the shortest wavelengths (i.e., the treble-most frequencies) that cancel, resulting in a tone with fewer highs.

A Gibson engineer named Seth Lover applied for a patent on his version of the double-coil pickup on June 22, 1955. From that time until July 28, 1959, when the patent was granted, Gibson labeled each pickup with a "Patent Applied For" sticker. Later Humbuckings have slightly smaller magnets and other minor differences in construction. A player with a good ear can distinguish the sound of a "Patent-Applied-For" from another Humbucking, but their electrical inconsistencies make generalizations difficult. In recent years, "Patent-Applied-Fors" have become popular among rock players, some of whom can perceive a difference and others who are perhaps merely status conscious. "Patent-Applied-For" coil bobbins can be cream-colored, black, or one of each. The color of the bobbin has no direct bearing upon tone.

Seth Lover's Humbucking pickup by Gibson has become the most popular and most copied pickup ever conceived. Gibson has introduced several variations over the years. Mr. Lover also designed Fender's humbucker.

Gibson humbucking, cover removed

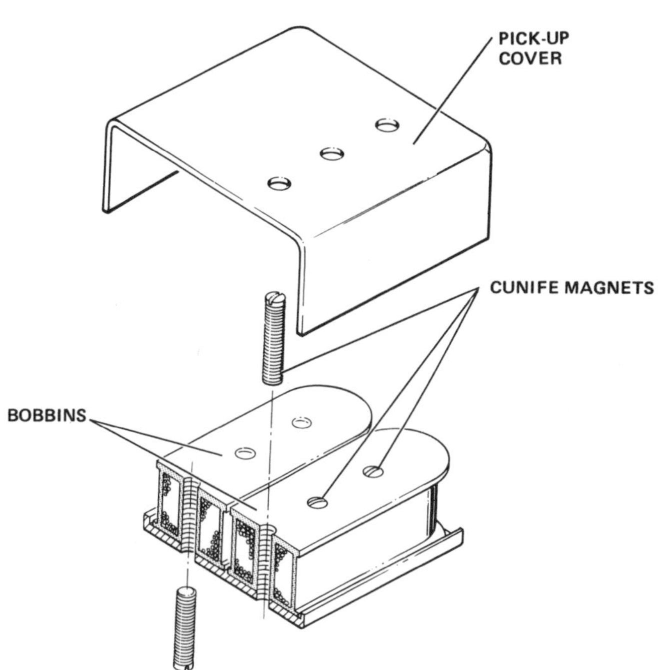

Fender humbucking pickup

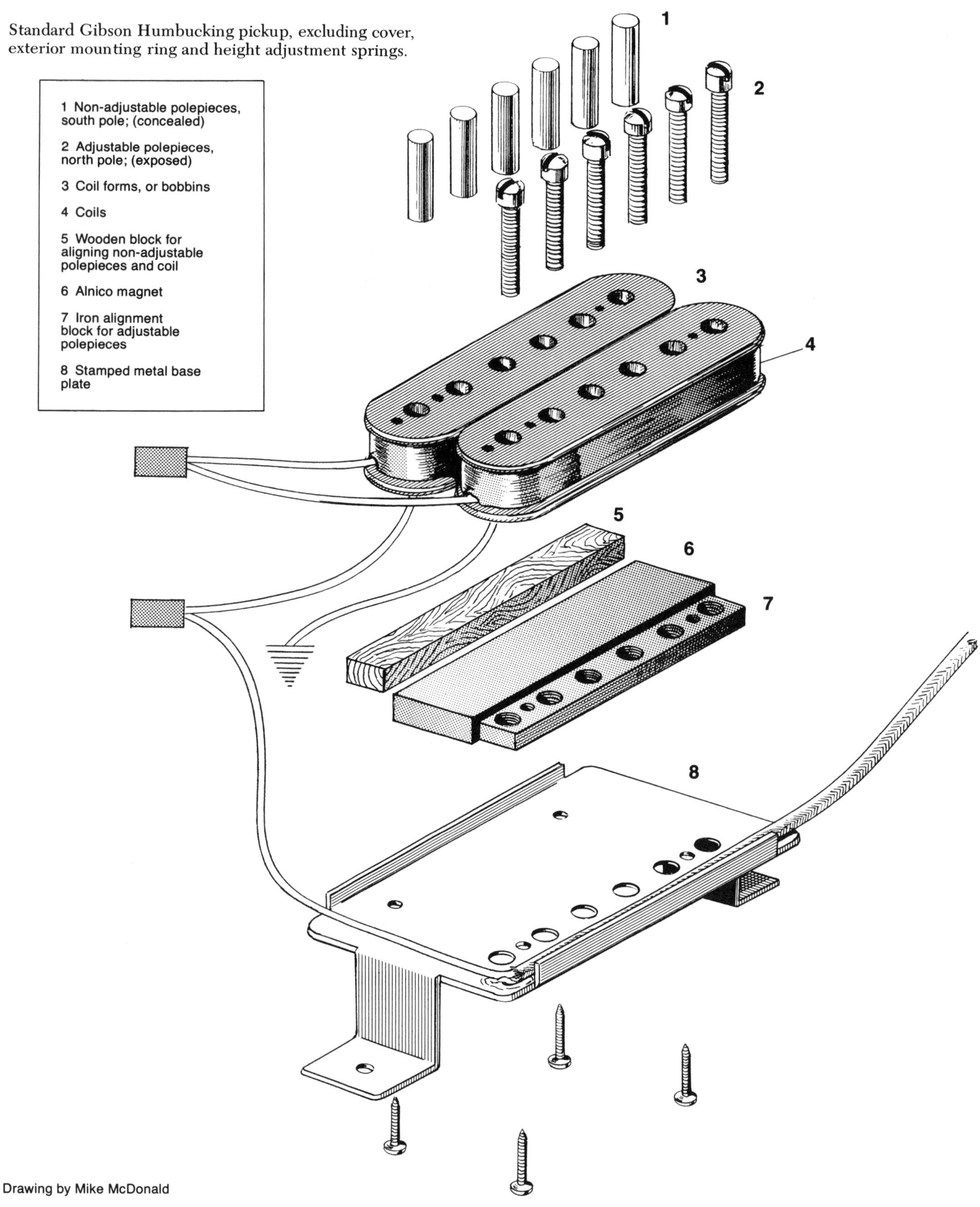

Standard Gibson Humbucking pickup, excluding cover, exterior mounting ring and height adjustment springs.

Drawing by Mike McDonald

Magnets and Polepieces

Two types of magnets are used in pickups: Alnico (iron plus *al*uminum, *ni*ckel, and *co*balt) and ceramic, each available in several grades. A very popular magnet stock for pickups is Alnico 5. Ceramic magnets (designated by "ox"—Arnox, Indox, etc.) are made from a clay impregnated with ferrous particles (e.g., barium ferrite) and put under intense heat and pressure. The particles are oriented to encourage polar alignment when later magnetized.

Other factors remaining equal, ceramic magnets are substantially cheaper and more resistant to demagnetization than Alnicos. Usually, they're stronger, too. An Alembic Hot Rod kit, for example, is simply a set of ceramic magnets that are substituted for stock Alnico magnets. The result: output is doubled (note: tone is also changed).

Another advantage claimed by some users of ceramic magnets: they are electrically nonconductive. A flow of electricity will tend to induce small swirling currents in adjacent metallic objects. These "eddy" currents may slightly offset the current in the coil. One theory is that the least amount of metal provides the least amount of distracting eddy currents and consequently provides the purest signal. Some designers contend that the eddy phenomenon may be the reason why removal of the metal pickup cover seems to cause an increase in highs. Others say that removal merely allows the pickup to be set closer to the string, which in turn increases highs. One thing is for certain—removal increases noise, since the cover is an electrical shield.

Gibson's standard Humbucking has one internal magnet underneath and between the coils. Along one edge is the north pole, which charges the polepieces of the coil nearer to it. The other long edge of the magnet and its adjacent coil and row of polepieces are south pole. The L6-S Super Humbucking has additional magnets along the outside edges of the coils for magnetic reinforcement.

On many pickups, a row of six cylinders protrudes through the cover. In some cases (e.g., Gibson Humbucking) these are polepieces that transfer the magnetism from an internal magnet to the string area. On others (e.g., Telecaster) the cylinders are actual magnets. Technically, magnets are not polepieces, but most manufacturers ignore precise terminology and call them polepieces anyway.

Iron filings reveal humbucking's magnetic fields.

A polepiece is often threaded like a screw in order to facilitate individual adjustment of the magnetic response to each string. By raising the screw, sensitivity is increased. However, if the polepiece (or entire pickup) is set too close to the strings, or if the magnet itself is too strong, the excessive magnetic force will actually exert a pull upon the string, damping its vibration and causing false harmonics, a loss of highs, or decreased sustain. The stronger the magnet (up to the point of magnetic saturation), the stronger the signal.

Exposed polepieces or magnets are considered by some designers to have a characteristic that outweighs the advantage of individual adjustment. This is the magnetic gap, or void, between the polepieces or magnets. Each cylinder is aligned directly under its respective string. However, when the string is bent, it moves away from the force field of the polepiece and some signal is lost. One solution has been the replacement of the six cylinders with a single blade or fin that spans the string without a gap. The trend in new pickups is away from individually adjustable polepieces. Examples: Travis Bean, Alembic, Dirty Works, Bill Lawrence, Peavey, Bartolini Hi-A, and Gibson's S-1 and Super Humbucking.

Pickup height-adjustment mechanism

Impedance

The number of wraps in the coil is one factor that determines its impedance, a measurement of an object's resistance to AC current flow. Abbreviated "Z" and measured in ohms, impedance is also affected by the frequency of the signal, DC resistance, and inductance. A pickup may be of low, medium, or high impedance. Most are from medium-high to high.

Low-impedance devices have some advantages, including a cleaner sound, less extraneous noise, flatter frequency response, and the ability to use long guitar cables without electrical interference or loss of highs. Requiring fewer wraps in the coil, they produce less inductance, which causes less capacitance, which in turn means more treble. Also, the loss of highs that usually accompanies a decrease in volume is minimized or eliminated in low-impedance instruments. Low-impedance pickups are made by Dirty Works and can be found on some Ovation electrics and a few Gibsons (Les Paul Recording, Professional, Personal, and Signature). Alembic pickups are medium impedance, some with about 2,000 turns, others 3,000.

Gibson low impedance pickup

Resonant Peaks

Most pickups can transduce mechanical vibrations into electrical signals with a fair amount of accuracy (i.e., with a flat frequency response) up to a point, beyond which frequency response falls off. This point is determined by the pickup's impedance, which in turn is dependent upon several of the variables discussed so far. Just *before* the fall-off point, there is a rise in output. In other words, there is a narrow band of frequencies to which the pickup responds most accurately. The location of this resonant peak, represented by a slight bump at the apex of its frequency response curve, is by far the single most important determinant of a pickup's tone. The composition, magnetic properties, and gauge of the strings are lesser but still significant considerations.

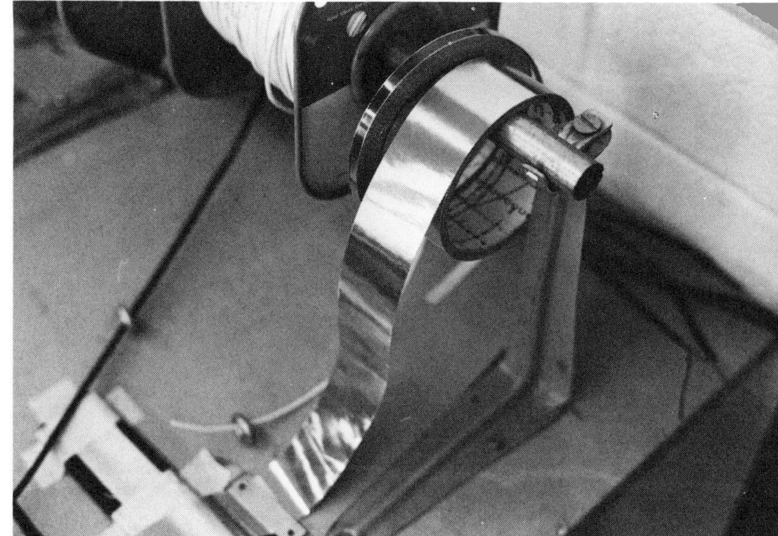

A roll of shielding at the Bill Lawrence plant, Nashville

Shielding

There are electromagnetic and electrostatic sources of unwanted noise all around us: amp transformers, household wiring, special effects devices, and fluorescent or neon lighting, to name but a few. The guitar strings can act as antennae, sensing some of these disturbances and presenting them to the pickups. (The reason that electrostatic noise is sometimes reduced by touching the strings with your hand is that your body then becomes an easier path for those weak signals to take to ground.)

The buzzing and humming can be partially or completely eliminated by proper amplifier grounding, the use of low-noise pickups, and shielding. All electrical components should be shielded—pickups, potentiometers, jacks, plugs, wires, and cords—not only to eliminate noise but to reduce the possibility of electrical shock. While inadequate shielding permits noise, excessive shielding impedes highs through increased capacitance. Still, proper shielding is not particularly difficult to provide, and it's a shame that some of America's biggest manufacturers are the most delinquent.

A few manufacturers fill their pickups with sealer in order to reduce oscillations that might cause feedback.

There are several approaches to achieving optimum shielding. One is to envelop the chamber containing electrical components with an aluminum foil sheet. Another method is to shield all internal cables, then surround the pots with cans. Some manufacturers use a pure silver conductive paint; others use a carbon conductive paint.

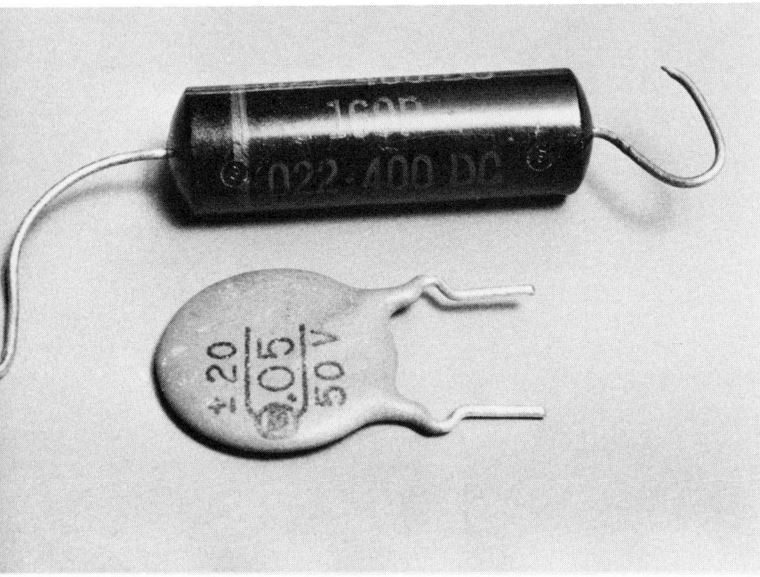

Typical capacitors, such as those used in Fender and Gibson tone circuits

Tone Controls

A standard tone control is a capacitor, an electrical component consisting of adjacent conductors with a gap between them. It provides an easy path to ground for high-frequency signals, so in a sense it drains or diverts treble frequencies. (Too much capacitance in a cheap cord or in a pickup with too many windings can seriously dampen tone.)

Most guitars are designed so that the pickup's signal is unmodified when the tone control is all the way up to full treble. By turning it down, a capacitor is gradually introduced into the circuit to roll off highs. So, the typical passive tone knob is essentially subtractive; when you twist the knob to "bass," you are not adding bass frequencies, just rolling off treble. A repairman can easily alter the tone of your guitar by substituting a capacitor of different value.

Low-impedance instruments often employ internal preamps to step up voltage in order to match the high voltage that the amp wants to "see." Such preamps are either FET (field-effect transistor) or IC (integrated circuit). Internal preamps are used with some or all

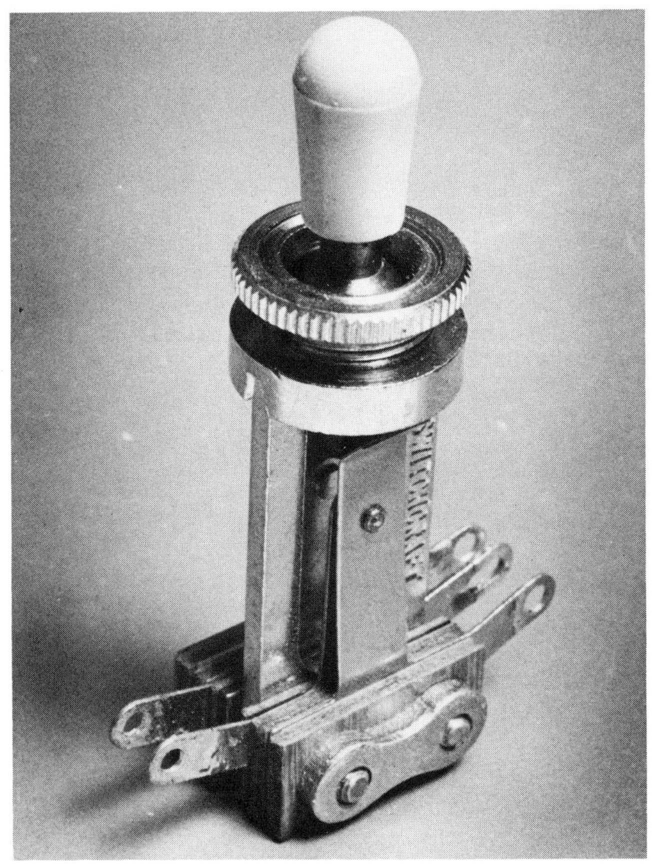

Typical pickup selector switch

Stratocaster pickup selector switch

of the pickups offered by Ovation, Dirty Works, B. C. Rich, Ibanez, and Alembic. Preamps also enable the use of active (as opposed to passive) tone circuits; one example is Alembic. Accessory preamps such as Alembic's battery-operated Stratoblaster can drastically boost output and permit distortion at low levels.

Volume Controls

A standard volume potentiometer is a variable resistor. When it is turned down, two things occur: an increase in series resistance between input and output, and a decrease in series resistance between output and ground. Turning the volume knob to zero essentially connects output to ground, shorting out the output. This short will cause most circuits to go dead, even if both pickups are on and only one of the two volume controls is turned down. Because of the interactions among resistance, impedance, and capacitance, turning down the volume pot (increasing resistance) will usually cause a loss of highs.

A standard potentiometer

Pickup Volume

Unless a preamp is involved, output is determined primarily by magnetic strength and the number of turns in the coil. (The diameter of the coil wire is less significant; most makers use from 40 to 44 gauge.) Building a loud pickup is easy. Simply by taking a magnet huge enough to slam you and your guitar into the refrigerator and wrapping it with a few miles of wire, you could conceive of a pickup powerful enough to light up Las Vegas with an E chord. The tone wouldn't be very good, however, because it is *not* so easy to build a super-loud pickup with a wide frequency response. When comparing pickups for output, be sure to note the differences in tone as well.

Out of Phase

"Phase" is defined on page 286. As noted earlier, when a string vibrates over two coils inside a single pickup, offsetting motions will cancel certain frequencies. Similarly, when both pickups are switched on, the vibrations are again slightly out of phase simply because the pickups are located at different spots along the string length. The resulting cancellations produce a sweet, thin tone.

A phase switch emphasizes this phenomenon by *electrically* reversing the two pickups' phase relationship. The hollowness of the tone is dramatically increased to a squeaky, funky snarl or honk, characterized by an attack that resembles a chicken cluck or duck quack. A typical phase switch is a simple double-throw, two-pole switch, offered as a stock item by several manufacturers or easily and inexpensively installed by a repairman.

Buying a Pickup

The domination of the pickup market by Gibson and Fender was virtually unchallenged until recent alternatives appeared. Now it seems everyone is arguing about pickups. Several companies have tooled up for major production, and the pickup wars have begun. The enthusiastic proliferation of information is a mixed blessing, educating some guitarists but confusing others with a deluge of graphs, specs, and hype.

Fender Stratocaster pickup (single coil)

Pickup design is an exercise in compromise. As noted earlier, there are advantages to having only a few turns in the coil, other advantages to having many. Most decisions involve similar trade-offs, because an emphasis upon one desirable characteristic may require the sacrifice of another, just as the car with the greatest acceleration is unlikely to be the most economical.

While all engineers are bound by the same physical laws, they clearly differ in philosophy about where to draw lines between competing considerations. A pickup's superiority in one category of electrical or magnetic performance is essential only if it delivers the sound that is most important to you. In general, ignore pickup advertisements with comparison charts *unless* all testing conditions and procedures are specified in detail. It's as easy to make a pickup "sound" good on paper as it is to make a cupcake sound nutritious on TV.

There is only one way to compare pickups: listen to them. Consider the Gibson Humbucking and the Fender Telecaster pickups. The fatter-sounding Gibson is less noisy and almost twice as strong in output, while the Fender is much brighter. Or compare a super-clean Alembic with the raunchier Di Marzio. You can make an easy choice without necessarily examining frequency response curves, so don't be intimidated by all of the technical jargon. Remember that despite the conflicting claims, the one valid criterion for choosing a pickup has not changed: What sounds good to you?

Stereo Wiring

An electric guitar may be wired so that the front and rear pickups operate independently, enabling the guitarist to separately amplify the signal of each one. The stereo input jack and the forked connecting cord allow the two signals to be run through different channels of the same amp, perhaps with different tone settings, or through two amps. One advantage is a broader dispersion of sound, which is possible when using two widely spaced amps.

Factory-equipped stereo guitars have included Gretsch's White Falcon-Stereo (introduced in 1950) and Project-O-Sonic, Gibson's ES-355 TDSV and ES-345 TD, Mosrite's 350, and certain models by Rickenbacker, Carvin, and Hoyer.

Any instrument with at least two pickups may be rewired for stereo, the cost varying with the difficulty of working with the guitar's particular body construction.

Acoustic Guitar Pickups

Microphones can satisfactorily reproduce the sound of an acoustic guitar, but they have several drawbacks. Feedback is sometimes difficult to eliminate. Onstage, the artist is restricted from moving about, and in the studio, sounds from other instruments sometimes leak into the mike. Properly engineered acoustic guitar pickups can adequately reproduce the guitar's tone while permitting the use of external sound modifiers and diminishing or eliminating the hassles associated with microphones.

Manufacturers totally disagree upon the best way to categorize pickups. Guitarists usually lump together those in which a small chip attaches with adhesive to the body or bridge, even though such pickups may be similar in appearance only. The chip is a sensor with no moving parts. These devices include the highly respected F.R.A.P. and Barcus-Berry pickups. High- or low-impedance, battery-powered preamps are sometimes incorporated as interfaces for impedance matching, EQ, volume control, and reduction of noise or distortion.

Another category encompasses pickups with diaphragms or other moving parts and may include miniature electret condensors (Buffalo) or dynamic mikes (AKG D-401). Preamps may be required, depending upon impedance. Still others are electromagnetic units

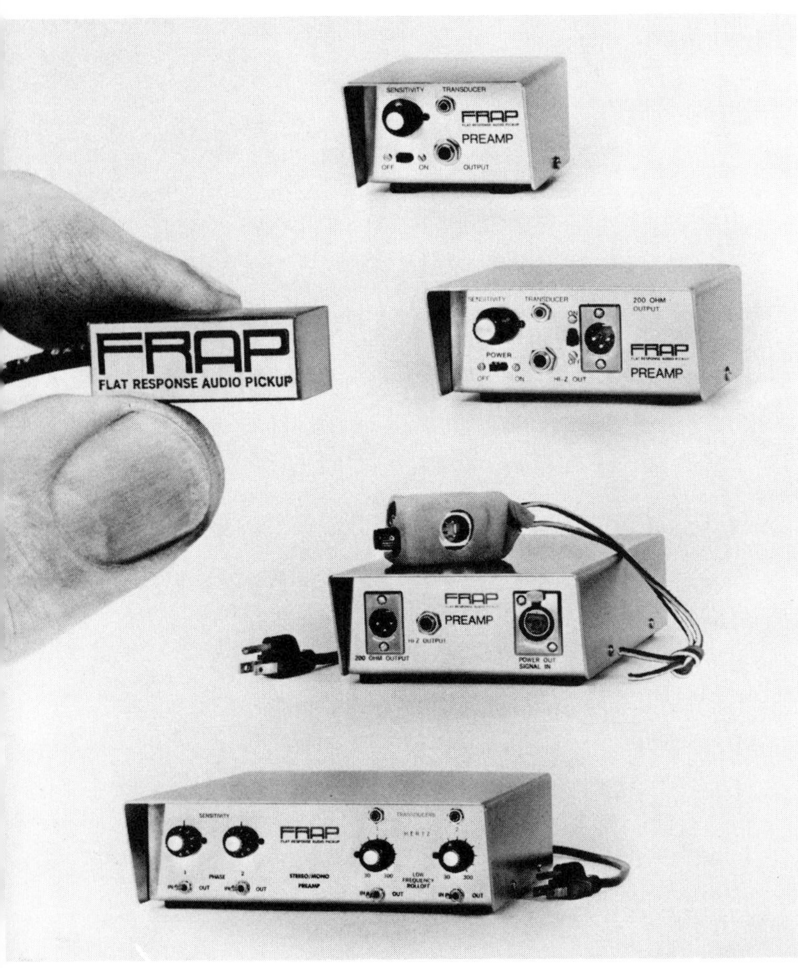

designed like electric guitar pickups except for the mounts.

Piezoelectric devices are those in which electrical polarity results from external stress or pressure upon ceramic, crystallized, or other substances. (The particular material used will partially determine capacitance and frequency response.) Piezoelectric principles are sometimes involved in pickup designs that differ in other respects. For example, Polytone, Maestro, Ibanez, Barcus-Berry and F.R.A.P. all use piezoelectric sensing elements.

Judging the sounds of competing acoustic pickups takes some time. The whole guitar vibrates, some parts obviously more than others, and the typical guitar top will produce many pockets of emphasized frequencies. Since the pickup attaches to a tiny spot, placement is critical, often requiring extensive trial and error. Even shifting one end of the sensor a fraction of an inch may alter the sound. Another consideration is that the pickup should be located where it is unlikely to be accidentally dislodged.

The patented F.R.A.P. design incorporates three piezoelectric transducers, each oriented at a right angle to the adjacent one, all mounted inside the chip. One of F.R.A.P.'s many good products is a miniaturized belt-mounted preamp that permits maximum freedom of movement onstage. Another is the MF-100 system for flat-tops, in which pickup, preamp, batteries, and wiring harness all mount inside the guitar body. The fact that Martin selected the MF-100 for its production electric-acoustic guitars is testimony to its quality. Gurian also offers optional F.R.A.P.s in its handmade acoustic guitars.

Barcus-Berry is the other giant in the field, offering an extensive array of mixers, preamps, high-impedance transducers, amps, and speakers. One popular Barcus-Berry is the subminiature Hot Dot; a newer model is the solid-state Superducer, designed to provide an acoustic sound from electric guitars.

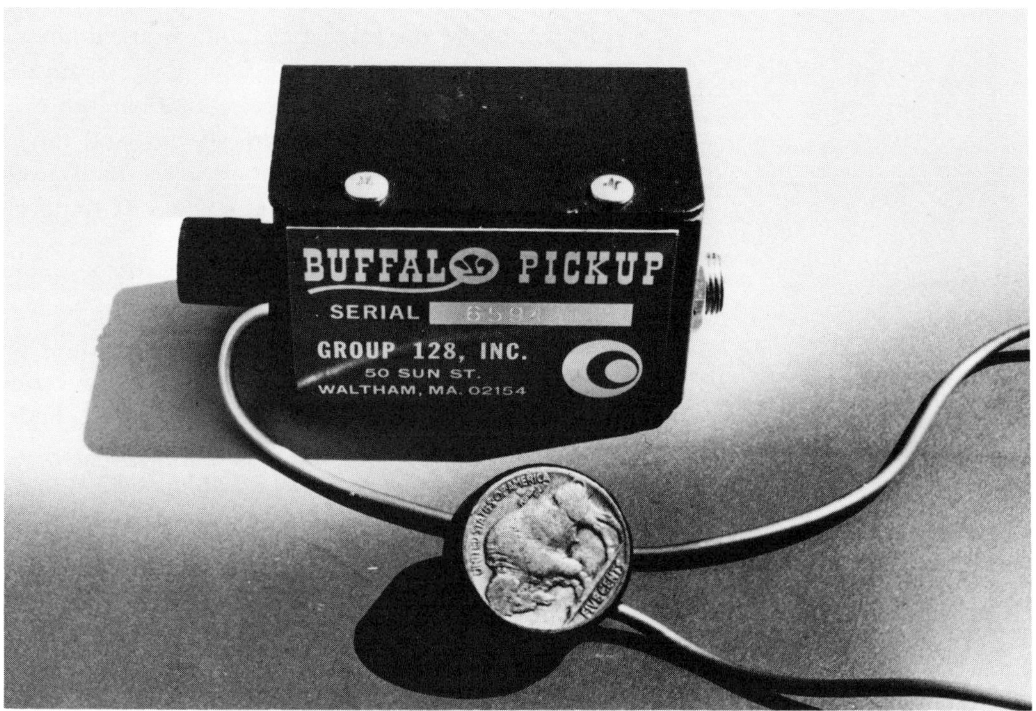

The Buffalo is a miniature electret condensor microphone with an air chamber mounted in a small cylinder and capped by a nickel. It works with a preamp; several models may be belt-mounted. Maestro offers piezoelectric, bridge-mounted, high-impedance pickups, some with preamps. Bartolini's HA-3A is a high-impedance magnetic device that mounts in the sound hole; no preamp.

Polytone's unique G-100 is a solid brass piezoelectric pickup that clamps to the body near the bottom rim. Bill Lawrence's FT-145 Silencer is a quick-mounting, medium-impedance humbucker with an Alnico-8 magnet. A high-volume variation is the FT-145 HD; the AT-170 fits arched-tops. The 100-S by PMT is a specialty item for slide players. It is a high-impedance pickup mounted into the slide itself.

DeArmond makes both dynamic pickups and ceramic-crystal transducers for many acoustic instruments. Their model 3000 includes top-mounted volume and tone controls. DiMarzio also markets an acoustic pickup.

SUSTAIN

Electrical and magnetic forces affect sustain (see pages 119–132). Feedback is covered in several discussions of amps and speakers (see also Special Effects, pages 275–292).

Sustain is a critical requirement to many guitarists, yet its causes are the subject of little empirical knowledge and much conjecture. Mechanically, sustain depends upon how efficiently string vibrations are conducted through the tailpiece, bridge, nut, and tuners to the guitar body, and upon whether the body itself maintains and encourages a continuation of those vibrations.

Conventional construction theory states that sustain is encouraged by a heavy and dense guitar body. The other general factor commonly cited is structural integrity, which encompasses solid, rattle-free glue joints and tight fittings between the neck, body, bridge, and other parts.

Super-sustaining experimental guitar bodies have been built with railroad ties and from solid marble or granite, conclusively demonstrating sustain's dependency upon body mass. However, a necessary concession to manageable weight is obviously required; the Les Paul is a good example. Gibson tried solid maple bodies, but they were too heavy. Solid mahogany didn't sustain quite well enough. Their solution: a mahogany body with a maple cap.

The significance of a bolt-on neck versus a glued-on neck is often discussed but nevertheless remains unclear. A common contention is that a glue joint provides a more permanent contact between neck and body and thus produces greater sustain. However, the guitars often used as examples of this theory are Les Pauls and Fenders, and the renowned sustain of the Les Paul is due largely to its much thicker and heavier body and comparatively high output pickups. Thorough tests that distinguish between methods of attaching the neck to the body and their relative effects upon sustain are few or nonexistent.

The attachment of both ends of the string to a single or laminated piece of wood for the improvement of sustain is the basis for the full-length or partial-length neck centerpieces in B. C. Rich, Yamaha and Alembic guitars and certain Firebirds. Extensions of this concept are the aluminum necks which characterize Travis Bean and Kramer guitars. These represent valid alternatives in instrument design rather than mere gimmicks.

Some claim that since laminations in the neck or body require glue joints, sustain is decreased. Despite this contention's apparent plausibility, properly glued pieces of wood do transfer energy with satisfactory efficiency. Most guitars have laminated necks or bodies, including several which are famous for sustain.

Solid string-to-body contact has long been recognized as an essential contributor to sustain. Some guitars (e.g., 58 Flying V) feature direct, through the body, string attachments. Gibson's stud tailpieces or similar items commonly replace trapeze units, and the improvement in sustain is noticeable. Bridge saddles and string nuts fashioned from brass, steel, or other metals were conceived for sustain improvement. Other recent attempts to improve sustain include Alembic and Yamaha bridges which mount onto a solid block of brass or other dense material. Incidentally, hand vibratos are sustain drains, since the strings attach to a spring mechanism that dissipates vibrations.

(1) Trojo, star on Keith-Albee Circuit
(2) Kane's Hawaiians, Victor Recording Artists
(3) Al Meredith and His Boys, Vitaphone, Radio and Record Artists
(4) Russell Thompson and Company, Noted Teacher and Radio Entertainer
(5) Irene and Albert Patton, Eastern Radio Stars
(6) The Silver Tone Melody Boys, Vaudeville Recording and Radio Entertainers
(7) Paul's Hawaiians, Pantages Vaudeville Artists
(8) Geo. D. Fassett of the Fassett "No Note" System of Teaching

Sam Ku West, now touring the world with Irene West's Royal Hawaiians and The Bird of Paradise, so delighted King George of England with his playing that he was titled "Kriesler of the Steel Guitar." He finds that the power and tone of NATIONAL String Instruments are not affected by extreme climatic differences. "Such rare beauty of tone, such power and volume, such dependable performance under all conditions is found only in NATIONAL String Instruments."

NATIONAL Silver Guitar Style 0

A Brand New Product

The NATIONAL Silver Guitar Style 0 is sure to win the admiration of everyone because of its beauty of design and marvelous tone quality. It has one 10-inch dynamic resonator providing amazing power and volume while retaining sweetness. May be used for both Hawaiian and Spanish playing.

PRICES

NEW STYLE 0 SILVER GUITAR.......... $ 85.00

Furnished in both Spanish & Hawaiian Styles

STYLE 1—German Silver, plain........... 125.00
STYLE 2—beautiful hand engraved....... 145.00
STYLE 3—(De Luxe) Artist's floral design.. 165.00
STYLE 4—(Artist's model) elaborately engraved, fancy pearl, etc........ 195.00

National String Instruments catalog (c. 1929)

7

Collector's Gallery

This is the very first working Dobro ever built. Most of the construction was done by John and Rudy Dopera; completed in 1928. The 1931 catalog offered three models, No. 27 G (hardwood body, $27.50), No. 37 G (mahogany body, $37.50), and No. 45 G (mahogany back and sides, spruce top, $45). By 1935 the line included the Dobro Jr. (a standard flat-top, no resonator, $12.50) and the Model 19, or Angelus (eleven small sound holes arranged in a circle around the resonator cover, $22), as well as the Model 60.

Early Thirties National Silver guitar, Style 4, Hawaiian neck. Known around the factory (and to some owners) as the Chrysanthemum, it was the top of the line. Other engraving patterns also acquired unofficial nicknames: Lily of the Valley (Style 3); and Wild Rose (Style 2). The Style 1 was plain. Known collectively as Tri-Plates, they had three six-inch resonators, arranged in a triangle and partially visible through the screens on the lower half of the body.

A number of other collector's instruments are included in previous chapters.

This early Dobro electric Hawaiian guitar sold for $67.50; a seven-string model was available for an extra $5.00.

The unusual upper sound holes gave rise to the nickname "Cyclops" for these Dobros. All were built in 1931 or 1932, the switch from the original (*top*) to the oval, twin-hole design occurring in late 1931.

Dobro Model M 14. Most Dobros had wooden bodies, but there were exceptions. The tops and backs of metal-body Dobros were fastened to the sides with a unique method that required no soldering. The resulting lip around the edges gave rise to the name Violin Edge or, as it was known around the factory, "fiddle edge."

The mid-Thirties fiddle edge came in several styles, all with the distinctive window-like sound holes in the upper bouts: the M 14 (brass alloy body, very little engraving, rosewood fingerboard, pearl-inlaid Dobro name on headstock, $67.50); M 15 (like the M 14 but with engraved German Silver body, $95); M 16 (like the M 15 but with ebony fingerboard and more elaborate engraving, including a large Dobro crest on the back, $135) and No. 62 (plated brass, etched and engraved Spanish dancer/garden scene, $62.50).

There were two budget models, No. 32 (sheet metal painted with yellowish brown sunburst, no engraving, $32.50) and No. 46, an all-aluminum guitar known as a Dobro-lite or Luma-lite, $45.

National Duolian. The elongated body of the original model (*left*) joins the neck at the twelfth fret. The fourteen-fret version was introduced c. 1933.

Dobro Model 60, early Thirties ($60). This unique carved look was achieved by first staining the body, masking off the pattern, and then sandblasting.

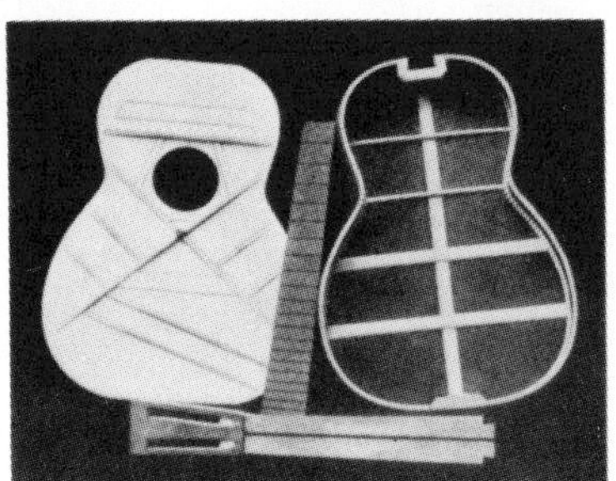

PRINCIPAL PARTS
OF A MARTIN GUITAR

RIGHT: Inside of body just before the top is glued on, showing quarter-sawn rosewood back and sides, spruce center strip, quartered spruce braces, solid mahogany end blocks, all hand fitted and smoothly finished.

LEFT: Sounding board, or top, of quarter-sawn Eastern mountain spruce, showing hard maple bridge plate and clear spruce braces graduated by hand to permit the maximum vibration for tone with enough stiffness for strength.

BOTTOM: Neck of selected Central American mahogany, showing ebony strip glued one-half inch deep in the neck for reinforcement, dovetail end to fit end-block in the body, rosewood head veneer and wide head slots.

CENTER: Fingerboard of real African ebony, slotted for solid nickel-silver frets.

⟦ 12 ⟧

Martin catalog (October 1930)

HAWAIIAN GUITAR
STYLE 18K

HAWAIIAN koawood body, bound with rosewood, bordered and inlaid with black and white wood. Mahogany neck, ebony fingerboard and bridge, pearl position marks. Ivory bridge saddle and ebony nut. Hand-rubbed lacquer finish, natural color.

Made for Hawaiian playing only, with high nut, high and level bridge, frets flush with the fingerboard; Concert size.

(This guitar is also made for Spanish playing, with low nut, beveled bridge and raised frets; but the Hawaiian model will be supplied unless the Spanish model is specified.)

No. 0-18K Concert.............. ***Price*, $45.00**

The strings used on Martin Hawaiian guitars are made of extra heavy piano wire. The treble strings are silvered and the bass strings are wound with copper wire polished to a smooth finish.

⟦ 13 ⟧

One of the earliest Martins known to exist, a Martin & Coupa. John Coupa was a New York music teacher who was apparently a salesman or distributor for Martin. The guitar was most likely made in the early 1840s, shortly after the factory moved to Nazareth, Pennsylvania.

Style 2-27 New York Martin (c. 1860)

A particularly rare 1907 Martin 0-45, with original ivory bridge

1919 koawood Martin 00-45K, the only one ever built

1929 Martin 028-K Herringbone, a koawood Hawaiian guitar. A few were made in 1917, a few more in 1921 and 1922, but most were made from 1923 to 1931.

1930 Martin 000-45

STYLE F-7

ARCHED MODEL

SPRUCE top carved and graduated like a violin, arched rosewood back with graduated spruce braces. Mahogany neck re-enforced with steel T-bar, ebony fingerboard bound with ivoroid, pearl inlaid head, six pearloid position marks. Adjustable ebony bridge, elevated pick-guard bound with ivoroid. Hand-polished lacquer finish, top shaded golden brown color, chromium-plated trimmings.

Grand Auditorium size, body 16 by 20 inches; right in tone and in appearance for professional use.

PRICE

No. F-7 Grand Auditorium.........$175.00

Martin catalog (July 1937)

Martin C-1. 449 of these unusual arched-top instruments were made from 1931 to 1933, when the round-hole design was replaced by f-holes.

1938 Martin F-9, a deluxe rosewood model with carved top, ebony fingerboard, and pearl inlays. Only seventy-two were made, from 1935 to 1942.

Martin D-76 Bicentennial model. This particular D-76 was the first one built.

Washburn (c. 1897)

GEORGE VAN EPS

HILTON "NAPPY" LAMARE
with
BOB CROSBY

ROC HILLMAN
with
KAY KYSER

KENNETH WHITE
with
CHAS. SPIVAK

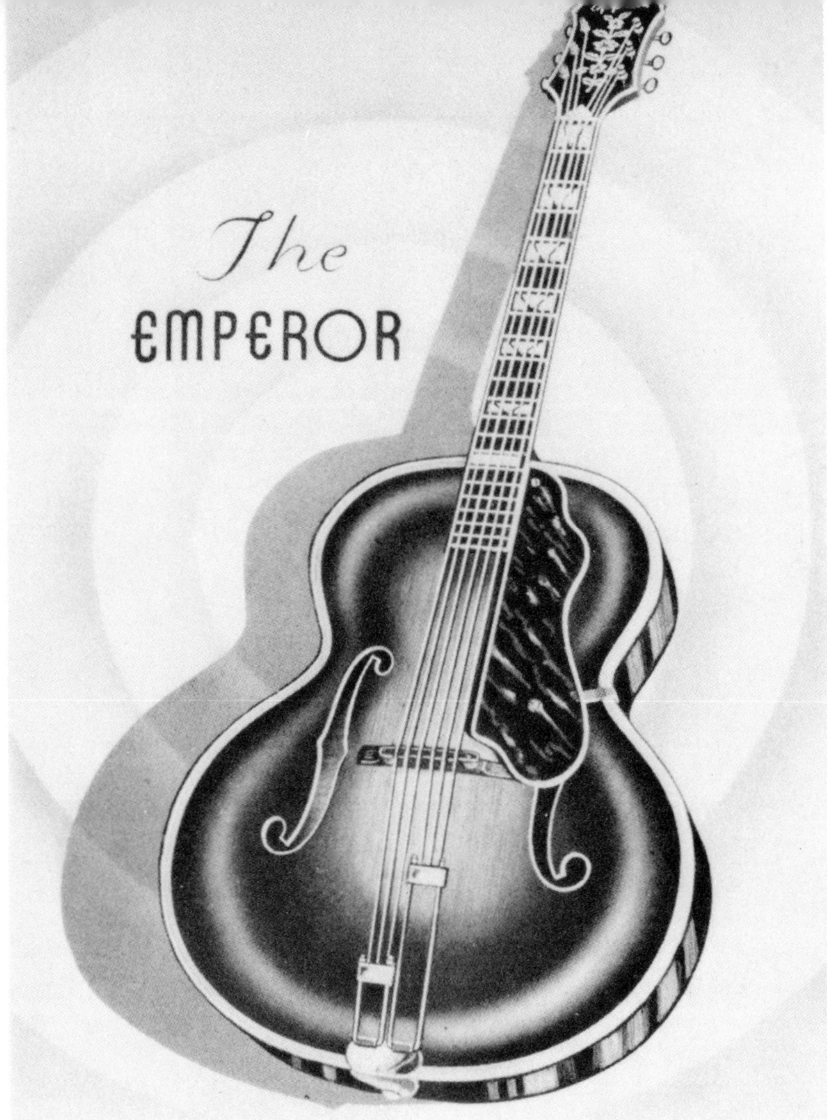

the EMPEROR

**THE ULTIMATE IN THE EVOLUTION OF THE GUITAR.
THE INSTRUMENT YOU WILL BE PROUD TO PLAY.
ITS TONE IS AN INSPIRATION.**

Undoubtedly the finest instrument ever made, the EMPEROR is custom built and **pre-tested before final finishing** assuring each artist of the uniform quality for which EPIPHONE is world famous.

The finest materials in the world such as individually selected spruce and curly maple and skilled craftsmen combine to make the EMPEROR the masterpiece it is. The workmanship in construction and finish is the result of over fifty years experience in building the best and striving for perfection.

The tone produced by the EMPEROR is in a class by itself and is characterized by a fullness and richness not obtainable in other instruments. Exacting workmanship and careful design account for its easy playing qualities and ultra responsiveness.

The EMPEROR is the largest guitar made, the body measuring 18½ inches in width and 21¾ inches in length, scientifically proportioned for extra ease in playing.

Finished in a beautifully shaded brown, highlighted, handrubbed to a very high polish. Framed in entirety by alternate white, black and white edging. The FREQUENSATOR frequency compensating tailpiece and all metal parts are heavily gold-plated and hand burnished.

EQUIPPED WITH EPIPHONE ENCLOSED TUNING UNITS

Complete with case and cover illustrated on next page

Epiphone Recording, probably made in the mid-Twenties

Epiphone Deluxe Masterbilt

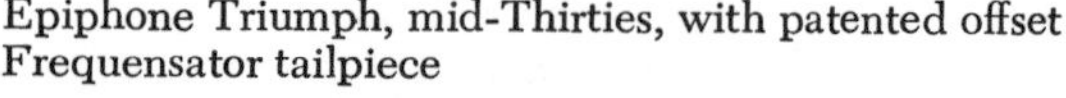

Epiphone Triumph, mid-Thirties, with patented offset Frequensator tailpiece

Epiphone Zephyr Emperor Regent (c. 1950)

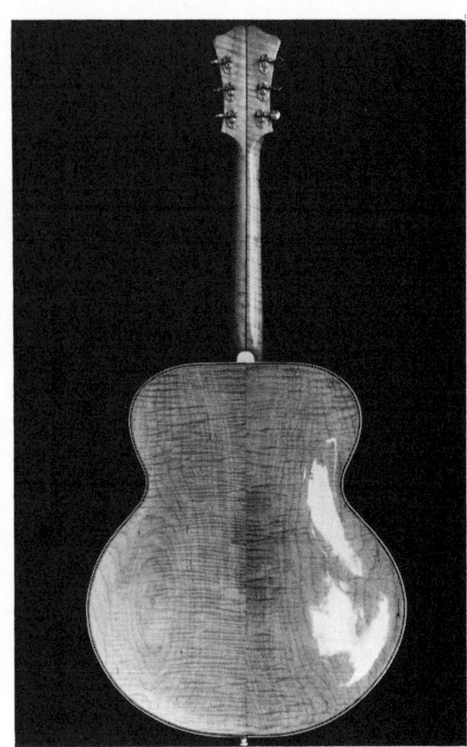

John D'Angelico of New York City built 1,164 carved-top guitars during his career, which began in 1932 and ended shortly before he died in 1964. During the big band era, the stars of the guitar world considered themselves lucky to get one, and over the years no name has earned more respect. D'Angelico was succeeded by his protege, Jimmy D'Aquisto, who built guitars in the style of the master until 1967, when he developed his own design. *Left:* 1937 D'Angelico Excel. *Center and right:* a pinnacle of orchestra-style guitar design, the D'Angelico New Yorker.

The Maccaferri guitar was invented by Mario Maccaferri in 1930 and built by the Henri Selmer Company in Paris. The original twelve-fret model was unique in that it contained a separate resonating chamber inside the body. The chamber attached to a large D-shaped sound hole. Subsequent fourteen-fret models (*above*) had no interior soundbox. From 1930 to 1940, a total of approximately 1,100 were made, including all styles and custom instruments. They were loud and bright, making them especially suitable for dance combos. The Maccaferri is best known as the guitar of Django Reinhardt.

Epiphone Caiola model, a hollow guitar with no soundholes; made by Gibson

A page from the first Gibson catalog (1903)

1923 Gibson L-3

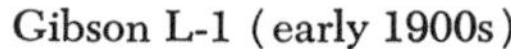

Gibson L-1 (early 1900s)

1924 Gibson Harp-Guitar, Style U

1924 Gibson L-Jr.

1924 Gibson L-5

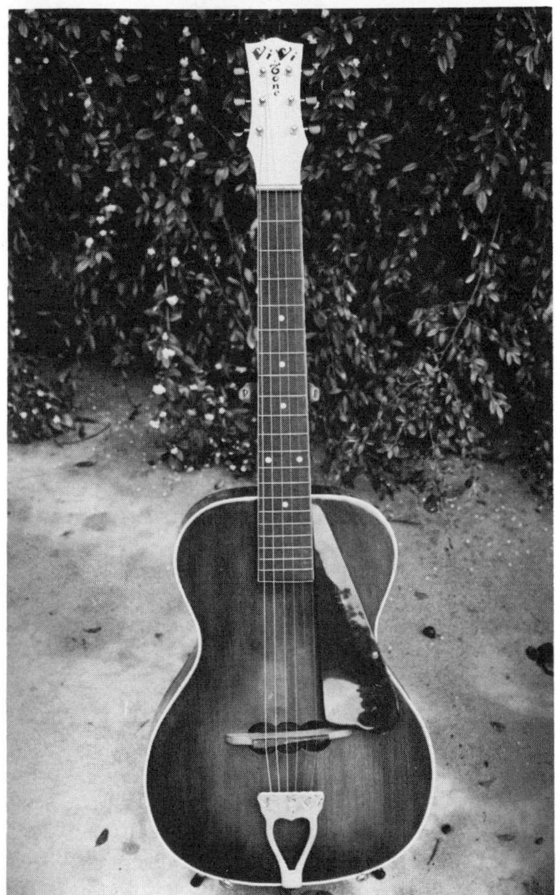

Vivi-Tone guitars were made by master designer Lloyd Loar after he left Gibson. Note the sound hole underneath the bridge; the instrument also has f-holes on its back.

1933 Gibson Century

The first Super Jumbo (SJ) 200, designed in 1938 by Gibson president Guy Hart and cowboy movie star Ray Whitley. It was intended to lure country and western singers away from Martin's popular D-28. For the first two or three years it had rosewood backs and sides like the Martin; maple was then substituted. The 17″ × 21″ × 4½″ body was the archetype of the jumbo style.

Roy Acuff with Gibson S-300

Gibson ES-150 with "Charlie Christian" pickup

Super 400C, late-Forties/ early Fifties style

Gibson ES-175, early Fifties

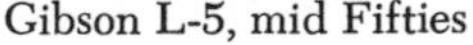

Gibson L-5, mid Fifties

1956 Gibson Byrdland. Note bar magnet pickups.

Three of Theodore M. McCarty's many design patents for Gibson. *From left:* the Moderne, the Explorer, and the Flying V. The joint patent application was submitted on June 27, 1957.

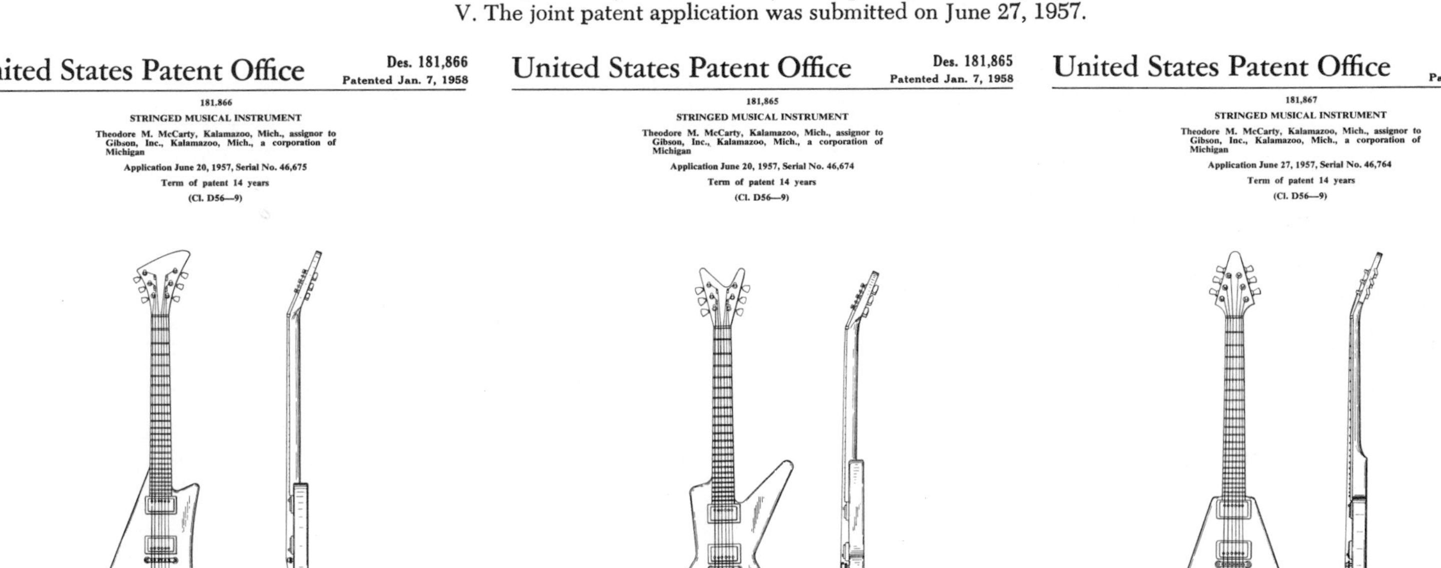

[U]nited States Patent Office — Des. 181,866 — Patented Jan. 7, 1958

181,866

STRINGED MUSICAL INSTRUMENT

Theodore M. McCarty, Kalamazoo, Mich., assignor to Gibson, Inc., Kalamazoo, Mich., a corporation of Michigan

Application June 20, 1957, Serial No. 46,675

Term of patent 14 years

(Cl. D56—9)

Fig. 1. Fig. 2.

United States Patent Office — Des. 181,865 — Patented Jan. 7, 1958

181,865

STRINGED MUSICAL INSTRUMENT

Theodore M. McCarty, Kalamazoo, Mich., assignor to Gibson, Inc., Kalamazoo, Mich., a corporation of Michigan

Application June 20, 1957, Serial No. 46,674

Term of patent 14 years

(Cl. D56—9)

Fig. 1. Fig. 2.

United States Patent Office — Des. 181,867 — Patented Jan. 7, 1958

181,867

STRINGED MUSICAL INSTRUMENT

Theodore M. McCarty, Kalamazoo, Mich., assignor to Gibson, Inc., Kalamazoo, Mich., a corporation of Michigan

Application June 27, 1957, Serial No. 46,764

Term of patent 14 years

(Cl. D56—9)

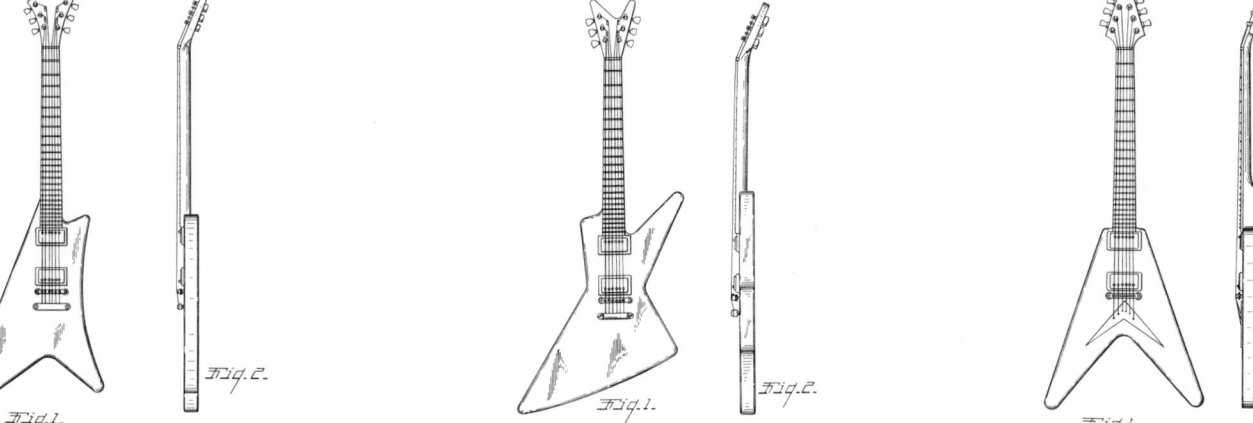

Fig. 1. Fig. 2.

1958 Gibson dot-neck ES-335.

1959 Gibson ES-345; blond, or natural finish

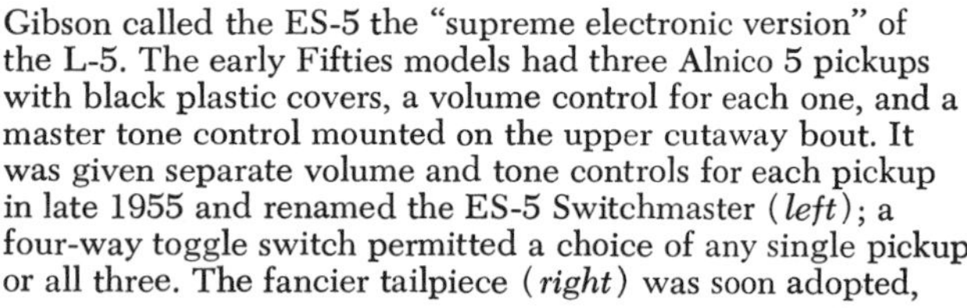

Gibson called the ES-5 the "supreme electronic version" of the L-5. The early Fifties models had three Alnico 5 pickups with black plastic covers, a volume control for each one, and a master tone control mounted on the upper cutaway bout. It was given separate volume and tone controls for each pickup in late 1955 and renamed the ES-5 Switchmaster (*left*); a four-way toggle switch permitted a choice of any single pickup or all three. The fancier tailpiece (*right*) was soon adopted, and Humbuckings were stock in 1957 and thereafter.

The 1960 catalog was the last to include the Switchmaster. Like earlier versions, that guitar had a rounded cutaway. The guitar on the right is one of the last Switchmasters made, a very rare model with a Florentine (sharp) cutaway, a feature that distinguished similar Gibsons (L-5 CES, Super 400) beginning in 1961. The Switchmaster did not appear in the 1962 catalog.

Unusual early Sixties L-5C Special electric with sharp cutaway; likely one of a kind

The Citation, the top of Gibson's line. This one was the first Citation made.

Gibson Everly Brothers (c. 1965)

Carlos Santana's Gibson Double Twelve (c. 1966)

Doc Kauffman at home, with a K & F steel guitar and amplifier set

The K & F nameplate, mounted on one of the company's first lap steels. Note the crinkle finish on the body, caused by subjecting the painted instrument to high temperatures. While Doc and Leo were building their first industrial gas oven, the guitars were baked in the Kauffman family's kitchen stove.

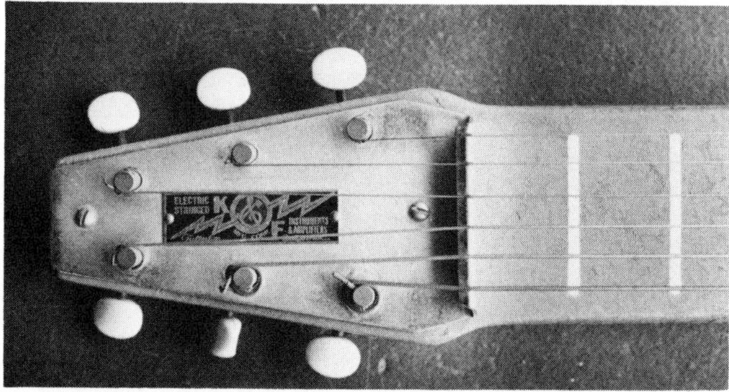

The first vibrato, patent filed August 19, 1929, by Doc Kauffman

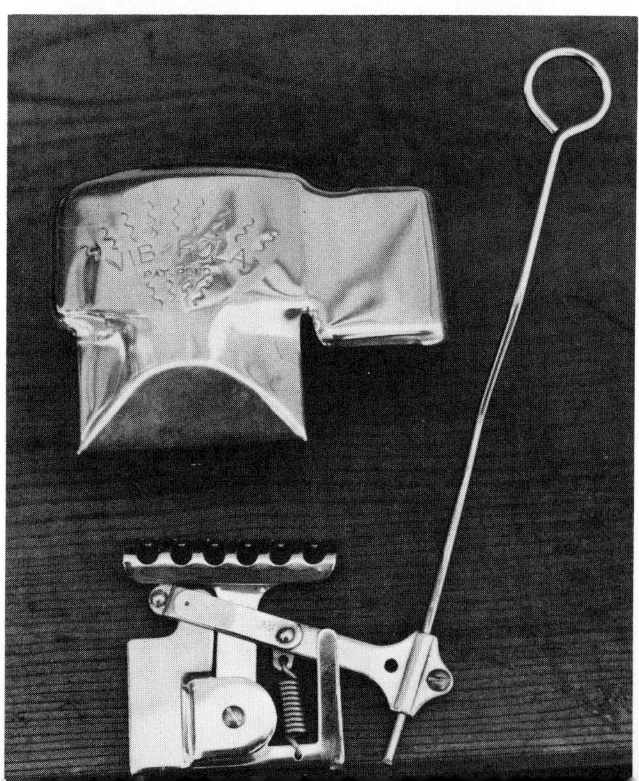

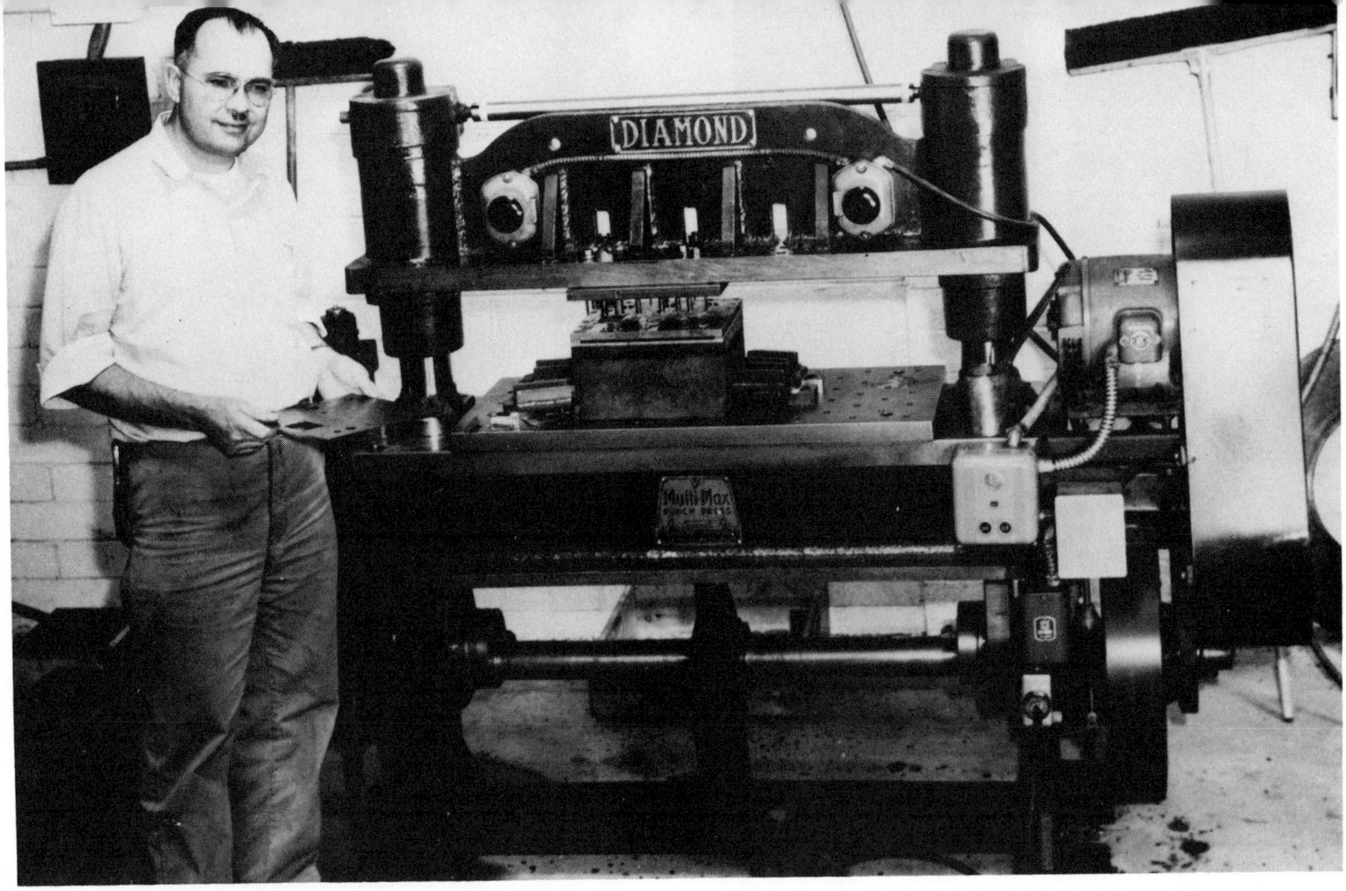

Leo Fender at the punch press in the spring of 1954

Leo Fender's first electric guitar, patent filed September 26, 1944

Fender Broadcaster, Serial No. 0022

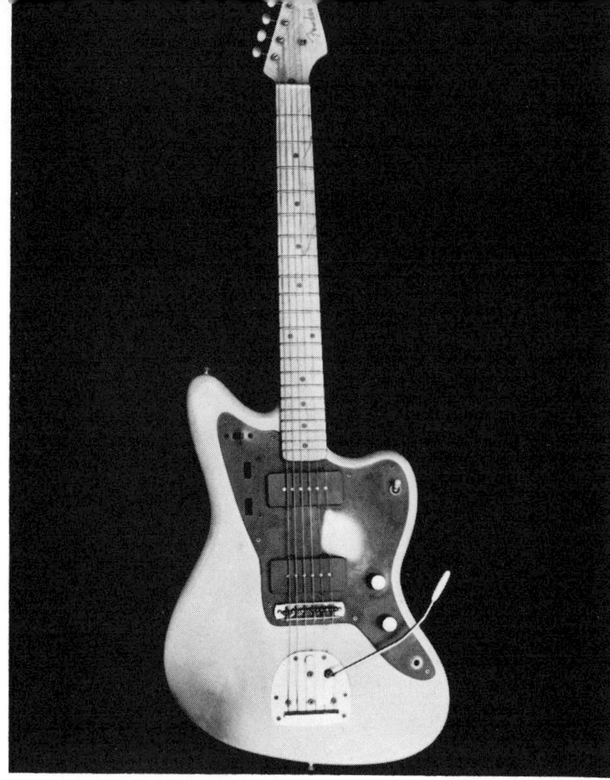

This unusual Jazzmaster, one of the first three made, has stock black pickup covers, a maple fretboard, and metal pickguard. To avoid worn spots such as the one that appears here, later versions had plastic pickguards. Designed by Leo Fender with the assistance of Freddie Tavares, the Jazzmaster featured wider pickups, a broader tone, and a unique hand vibrato. In addition to the usual three-way pickup selector, it had a circuit for choosing between two pre-set tones. This one is Mr. Tavares's personal instrument.

Rosewood Telecaster

Fender Marauder. This unique but unsuccessful guitar had four pickups concealed inside the body. Introduced in 1965, it was never mass produced.

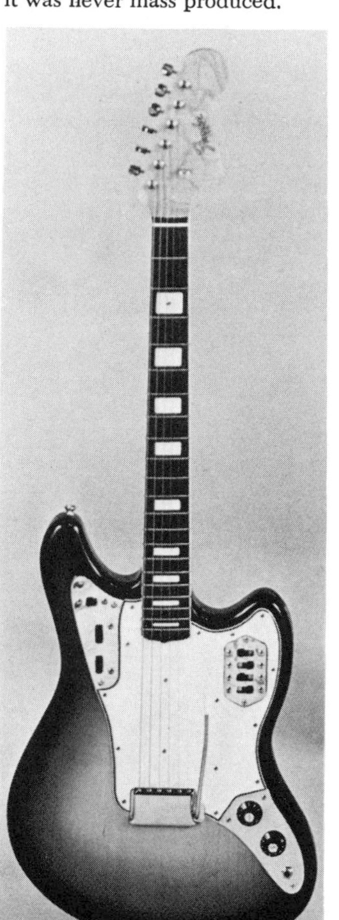

1960 Fender Jazz Bass, with tandem-mounted, or stacked, pots. Changed to three individual knobs c. 1961.

Fender Bass VI; 6-string bass guitar (c. 1962)

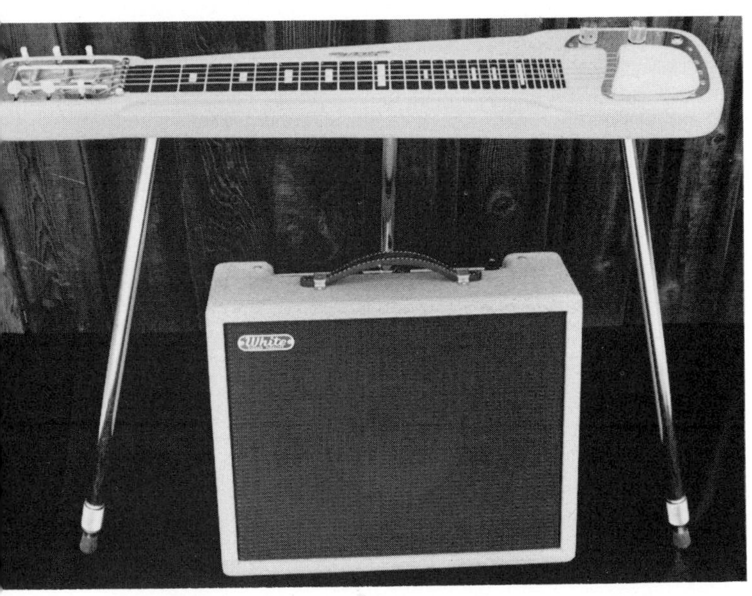

Mr. Fender inaugurated a second line of amps and steels to be sold exclusively through teaching studios. He surprised his friend, and Vice President of the company, Forrest White, by naming the line after him. The amp is light blue/gray and features a contrasting dark blue grille cloth. Very few were made, and the project was shelved when the company was unable to meet the demands for its regular Fender instruments. This immaculate pair is Mr. White's personal set.

The historic Bigsby/Travis guitar, designed by Merle Travis and built by Paul Bigsby in 1947. On the basis of this instrument, Mr. Travis claims credit for the design of the Fender guitar. Mr. Fender disagrees. On display at the Country Music Hall of Fame, Nashville.

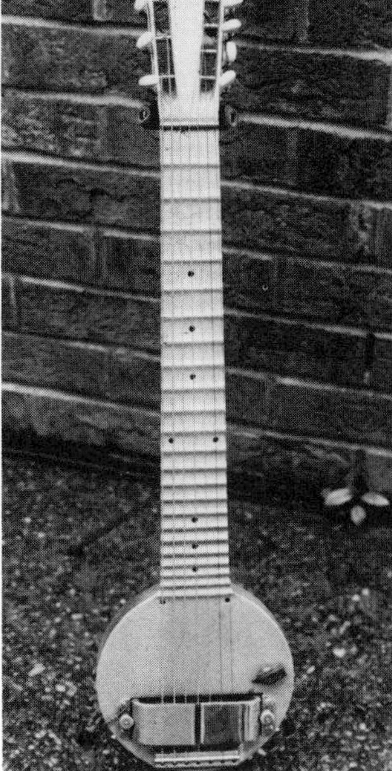

The old guitar-manufacturing community of Orange County in southern California was a remarkable group of engineers and businessmen tied to each other through a fairly complex and everchanging web of professional and personal relationships. Their considerable talents produced the National, Dobro, Rickenbacker, Fender, Randall, and Music Man companies.

A late-Twenties National catalog displays photos of the eight men who were the backbone of that company. They include Paul M. Barth, Vice President; George D. Beauchamp (pronounced Beechum), Secretary/General Manager; Harry Watson, factory superintendent; and A. Rickenbacker, engineer. This guitar is a cast-aluminum Rickenbacker Model A-22, much better known by its nickname, "the Frying Pan." It was designed by Mr. Beauchamp with the help of Mr. Barth. Mr. Watson built the maple prototype. Years ahead of Gibsons and Fenders, it is the essential forerunner of the solid-body electric guitar.

Adolph Rickenbacker owned a tool and die facility that made the metal guitar bodies for National. After seeing the Frying Pan, he decided to offer financial assistance to Beauchamp and Barth, and together they incorporated Electro String Instruments. It soon became Rickenbacher, and later the original Swiss spelling was altered to Rickenbacker to avoid confusion over pronunciation.

The Frying Pan, with six to eight strings, sold for $62.50, as did its companion, the Electro amplifier (*right*). It spawned a whole species of instrument that throughout the Thirties added the electric dimension to already-popular Hawaiian music. Country and western artists adopted it with relish; aside from the electric guitar, another direct descendant is the pedal steel.

Mr. Rickenbacker died in March of 1976.

Paul Bigsby with one of his first guitars

Early Fifties National guitar with stock, Gibson-built J-50 style body. The polepieces of the factory-installed pickup are visible near the last fret.

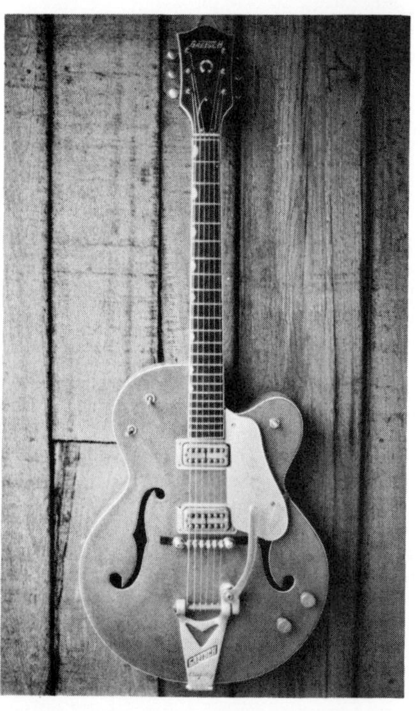
Gretsch Chet Atkins (c. 1959). Note real (not embossed) f-holes.

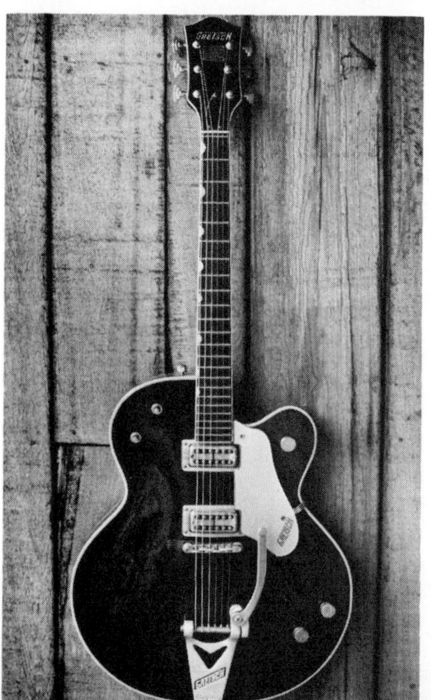
Gretsch single-cutaway Country Gentleman (c. 1960)

8

How to Choose the Right Electric or Acoustic Guitar

Most of today's popular guitars were designed since 1950. Even though the evolution of the modern guitar is a comparatively recent phenomenon, it has managed to generate much confusion. Most of the people who designed guitars were thinking of the present, not the future, and history is often blurred by manufacturers' incomplete records, inconsecutive serial numbers, or inaccurate catalogs.

The names of models are also confusing. Sometimes a company will introduce a new name for an old product; other times it might restyle the guitar and yet retain the old name. Technology is evolving more rapidly than ever, and "truly revolutionary" products seem to pop up almost weekly. It's hard to keep up. Where can you go for answers? Salesmen are too often inadequately trained, and advertisements are usually long on hype and short on information.

Manufacturers have the capability to translate technical data into lay terms and to distribute it to consumers and salesmen alike, and a few companies (particularly newer and smaller ones) have recognized a responsibility to do so, with items such as fully detailed owner's manuals. But in general, manufacturers would have you believe that each new product is the greatest thing since the chord change, and the fog thickens when they publish literature and advertisements screaming about how "mind blowing!" it sounds, rather than tell you what it does, how it works, what it's made of, or even what it is.

Gibson reissue Melody Maker

Well, when you take the poorly documented history of erratically named, rapidly changing, and relatively sophisticated electronic gear and filter it through a ragged network of communications, it's rumor city. There seem to be almost as many opinions about the guitar as there are about the music that depends upon it so heavily. Given the subjectivity of music appreciation and science's inability to fully explain the behavior of sound, facts are sometimes hard to come by, and guitar buyers routinely encounter contradictory advice from friends with rabid allegiances to certain brands. The result of all of this is that guitar lore is an exotic blend of legend, truth, confusion, and charm, only natural in a realm populated by celebrated gunslingers and wand wavers.

If you are planning to buy a guitar, the array of possibilities is boggling, but there *is* a suitable instrument somewhere between the collector's treasure and the one with the crank in Mickey's ear. Hopefully, this chapter will enable you to survey the vast guitar market, emerging with a good choice, sanity intact. Several brands are included as examples, but since the writer's preferences are as subjective as any, the emphasis is upon general criteria in judging quality, not upon whether a Stratocaster is "better" than a Les Paul.

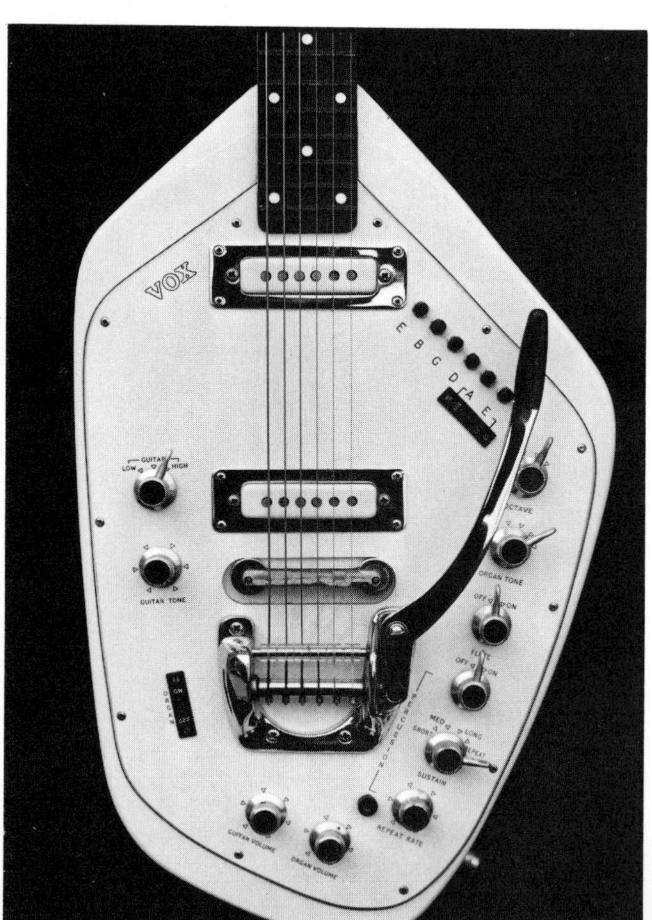

WHAT TO LOOK FOR

You walk into a giant music store, looking for your first guitar. If you are lucky, you meet a dependable salesman who's willing to take the time to see that you buy what you need at a price you can afford. If you are *un*lucky, you run up against Ralph Ripoff, who determines, after a couple of questions, that you're a beginner, a lamb. You ask what he has for one hundred and fifty bucks or so, and he shows you two guitars: one is a functional-looking used instrument with a familiar brand name, perhaps a solid-body with one pickup, a couple of knobs, a few scratches, and not much else. The other is a just-out-of-the-crate Rocketflash XF 1000—shaped like a map of Texas with eleven pickups, twenty-three neon dials, two handles, a sink and three forward gears. What do you do?

Choosing the right guitar takes plenty of time and

thought. Here are some things to look for in any good electric or acoustic guitar:

Brand Name

Buy a guitar with a recognized brand name. You can assume that a company's good reputation is based upon the reasonable-to-excellent quality of its instruments. Also, popular guitars are much easier to service and to refit with new parts, and they are likely to carry a guarantee. Off-the-wall brands are difficult to sell or to trade in, even if they are good guitars, while a well-known domestic or imported instrument in good shape will often retain substantial value for years.

Don't be fooled by a lot of gadgetry. Wires and knobs can be cheap, and good workmanship in the neck, bridge, electronics (if any), and hardware is essential if the guitar is to play in tune and have a rich sound. Whether the instrument is new or used, ask about guarantees. In addition to the factory warranty, some dealers will agree to service a new instrument and to make adjustments without cost for as long as you own it.

Neck. The neck is as important as any single feature; if it is bent or warped, the instrument cannot be played in tune. Sighting down the neck looks cool, but to an untrained eye, it can be a misleading exercise. See p. 213 for a method of checking alignment. Virtually all of the better electric models feature an adjustable neck rod for correcting warps and bends. Many of the acoustic folk models are similarly equipped, though some fine instruments such as those made by David Russell Young (pp. 46–53) and Martin (p. 56) are not adjustable.

There is a more extensive discussion of the design and function of neck rods in chapter nine.

Play a single chord in several positions up and down the fingerboard. Make sure that the notes in each position are in tune. Test each string at the open position and at the twelfth fret to see if the notes are a true octave apart. If the guitar does not play in tune at certain frets, ask the dealer to make the adjustment before money changes hands.

Bridge. Check that the intervals between the strings are evenly spaced.

An adjustable bridge allows you to set the action (the distance from the strings to the fingerboard) to

Gibson Tune-O-Matic bridge

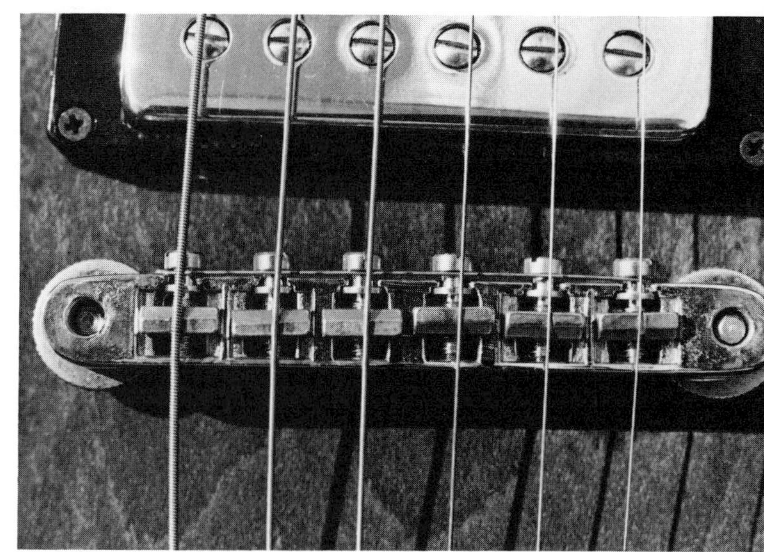

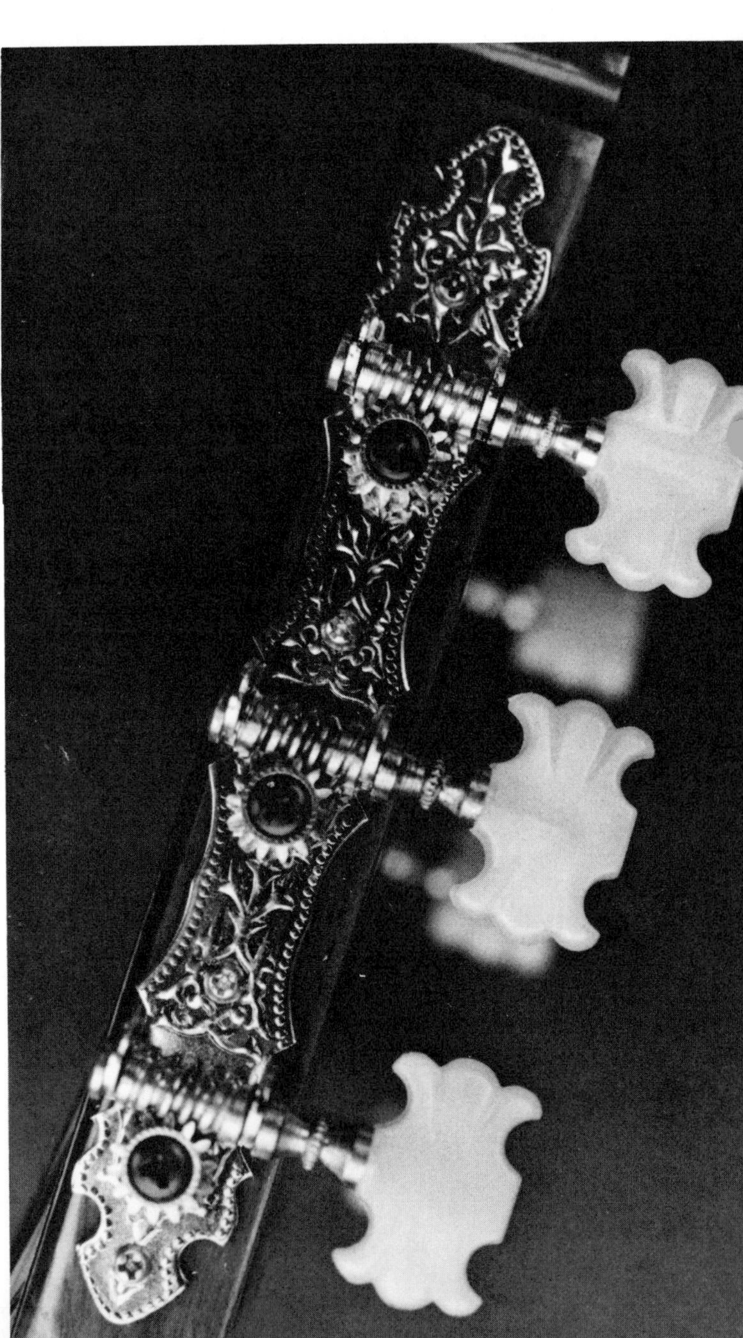

your individual preference. This is convenient on an electric, since each guitarist has his own ideas about the way an instrument should feel, and many of us change our minds about it from time to time. Some guitars are fitted with a separate mini-bridge for each string, adjustable for both height (action) and string length (the distance from the nut to the bridge). This latter feature facilitates correct intonation. On an acoustic guitar, a nonadjustable bridge may be preferred for more direct conduction of vibration from

the strings to the top. In chapter nine, bridge design, action, and intonation are explained in more detail.

Tuning Machines (keys, heads). Even if a reputable company makes the guitar, the tuning keys may present a problem. If you twist the key without any change in pitch, and then there's a sudden jump, something's wrong. It may be improperly strung. Some defects in tuning keys are easier to spot if the strings are loosened or removed. This part of the guitar is important, but don't let lousy tuning keys ruin an otherwise suitable guitar. You can substitute a set of the better, metal-encased keys (such as those by Schaller or Grover) for around thirty dollars.

More on tuning gears on pp. 221, 233.

Ibanez guitars are among the best bargains available. At first the company gained fame for its beautiful copies of American originals, such as this one. More recently, Ibanez has introduced several good models of its own. They are made at the Fuji factory in Matsumoto, Japan.

COMPARING ACOUSTIC GUITARS

Since instruments exist to make music, it is surprising how often someone buys a guitar without *really* listening to it. It may appear to be more cool to recognize the perfect guitar sound instantly, but experienced players often spend hours exploring tonal subtleties before choosing one instrument over another. Take your time.

All salesmen are aware of psychological selling techniques. Young guitar buyers are especially vulnerable, because they sometimes feel obligated to look hip, and because there are so many rumors about guitars. Trust your own judgment. Don't let a salesman hear for you. If he bangs away on a couple of guitars, saying, "See what I mean?" tell him if you *don't* see what he means. Don't be intimidated. If you cannot yet distinguish every nuance in resonance, don't worry about it. Neither can most guitar players. Neither can most salesmen, for that matter. Legitimate experts in guitar sound are not necessarily found in every music store.

Ask the salesman for his help in acquainting yourself with various guitar tones, but if you have doubts, don't be pressured by an inflection in his voice that implies that you're a dope if you don't hear it the way he hears it. You're the one who's going to live with it, not him. Maybe the El Cheapo sounds just as good to you as a more expensive model; maybe it sounds even better. If so, speak up. If you *can* tell the difference but cannot decide, come back tomorrow.

Find a quiet part of the store, perhaps an office or a storeroom if necessary. If the Deep Purple freaks

Gibson Dove

Gibson Johnny Smith

across the room are trying to see how loud the Marshall stacks can go, come back later.

When choosing a guitar, there is no substitute for meticulous, side-by-side comparison. An old man in Nashville who had been collecting guitars for fifty years once said that he had never heard two that sounded quite alike. If you want a Guild F-50, try every one you can get your hands on, new and used, all over town. You may examine two instruments of the same brand and model and be more impressed by their differences than by their similarities.

Experiment with as many techniques as you can. A guitar's best tone may not be on the surface; sometimes a certain pick attack is required to get that tone out. For example, acoustic guitars are strung more heavily than electrics. You may never discover the true potential of an acoustic guitar if you play it as you would an electric.

Test single notes, partial chords, open chords, bar chords, everything. Fingerpick it, flatpick it, sing with it, strum it. Notice how the tone changes as you move up the neck, particularly above the tenth or twelfth fret. Does it sound good in only one spot or all over? Any dead spots? Check all fret positions—any buzzes? Concentrate on the bass side and the treble side separately, and then—how do they blend? Have a friend strum the guitar while you stand a few feet in front; how does the guitar project? Too loud? Too thin? Boomy? Mushy?

You cannot fairly judge a guitar's sound if it has worn-out strings. It's that simple. Sometimes a fresh set will make a near-miraculous improvement. If you are definitely serious about buying, you are not out of line in asking the dealer to install new strings on one or two instruments in order to reveal their fullest potentials.

Guild D-40C

In addition to the things mentioned above, look at the binding and purfling; check for rough edges, dislocated joints, or crooked seams. Make sure that there are no spaces between either the bridge base, heel, or fingerboard and the top, which may be caused by a loosening of glue. Check the top at the sound hole for smoothness and uniformity of thickness. Look for irregularities in the finish. You might even borrow the dealer's long-handled mirror to inspect the interior for loose bracings or glue drippings. Inspect every inch of the guitar for cracks in the wood. Rap the guitar body with your knuckle. The chamber should resonate. A rattle in the neck may be evidence of a dislocated or broken truss rod. A buzzing sound in the body may be caused by a loose internal strut or brace. Loose tuners can cause the peghead to rattle.

ELECTRIC GUITARS

Design: Solid and Hollow Body

In choosing between solid and hollow-body guitars, it's strictly a matter of taste (see chapter four). Neither design is "better" than the other, though one may be more suited to your style of music. Generally, a guitar with a solid body has more of a bright treble sound, while hollow-bodies are deeper and more mellow. Semi-solid guitars can have some of the properties of either design. Jazz men play the hollow, arched-top, electric guitar almost exclusively. A hard-rock musician will likely choose a solid-body instrument, because its density and tailpiece design facilitate long sustain and its tone is crisp and piercing. If you're a B. B. King worshipper, who wants both subtlety and brightness, a versatile semi-solid may be your choice.

No two guitars are identical. Many are mass-assembled, but some of the component parts may be made by specialists. Just because your idol plays a Gibson Byrdland, that doesn't mean that the one hanging up there on the music-store wall is an exact duplicate. For example, the new Gibson ES-335s have different tailpieces and narrower fingerboards than those manufactured in the late Fifties. Gibson SG necks regularly change sizes. Some Fenders have rosewood fingerboards; others are made of slick, lacquered maple. In the last twenty-five years, the name "Les Paul" has been used to designate five major categories of Gibson guitar design, each one containing several models. So don't just grab the first guitar that's got the brand name you're looking for.

If you're concerned about finishes, you should know that paint jobs (particularly sunburst) and wood grains may vary greatly from guitar to guitar. If you order an instrument from the factory through a dealer, be sure to make a satisfactory purchase arrangement. Don't buy a guitar without seeing it, even though the dealer has one "just exactly like it" on display. You may find that two guitars of identical brand name, model, and color may still feel, look, and sound a little

Your first electric? The Sears Silvertone with the amp-in-the-case, a better bargain than many.

Guild M-80CS

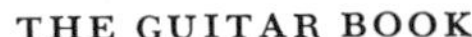

Robin Trower

different. If the dealer has several guitars of the right model, try them all before buying.

Comparing Electric Guitars; Artists' Endorsements

When comparing the sound of different guitars, try to isolate the personality of each one by playing it through different amps, including an amp like your own. Remember that the guitar is only one element in a system that includes strings, connecting cables, special effects, amp, and speakers. Try substituting various elements.

Try every possible combination of pickup and tone setting, but don't be sucked in just by the sheer number of knobs and switches. Among all guitars the few giants are simple and straightforward. A classic example is Gibson's Les Paul—one switch, two pickups, four knobs, period. On a guitar with a mission-control layout, isolate each gadget and determine its function and the range of its capabilities. If the wiring is particularly flexible (e.g., Alembic) or confusing (an old Gretsch), this may take a while. No rush. Don't allow an ego-boosting salesman to Hendrix up your sound with an arsenal of special effects until you have become acquainted with the guitar's inherent tones.

Another consideration is the manufacturer's method of joining the neck and body. (See section on Sustain.)

The customer's urge to associate with heroes is nowhere exploited more effectively than in the merchandising of guitars. Who-plays-what is a reasonable factor in choosing an instrument, but it's too bad when the beginner socks the old man for a bundle because he *knows* that a new Les Paul will have him doing Jimmy Page licks in two weeks. Many pros own a couple of guitars for versatility. Superstars may own dozens just for the hell of it. So try to find out which instruments were used for favorite tracks. *Guitar Player*'s various publications are good sources.

Most artist endorsements are at least worth considering, even if acquired in exchange for a free guitar. If the artist is successful enough to influence public tastes, he probably won't have to scrounge a free guitar in return for recommending a loser while selling out his impressionable fans. The real endorsement is in his *use* of the guitar, not in whether his name appears in an ad. Even if Honest Guitars, Inc., manufactures a Joe Flash model ("designed in close association with famed . . ."), don't be surprised if

Rory Gallagher

Peter Townshend

Jimmy Page

Richard Betts

J. Geils with customized Flying V

Albert King

Bo Diddley with his custom Gretsch

Joe is playing an old Telecaster the next time you see him in concert.

NEW, USED, AND COLLECTOR'S GUITARS

Guitar buyers, particularly beginners (or beginners' mothers, out to buy the ultimate gift), sometimes expect updates and refinements in all consumer products, and thus conclude, "The newer and flashier the guitar, the better." Not long ago, a back-to-the-roots enthusiasm for old-time values spawned a trend in the opposite direction: the older and raunchier, the better. The fact is, neither extreme offers helpful guidance to the guitar buyer. Some new Stratocasters are better than some old ones, and vice versa. It's true for Gibson and the others, so don't lock yourself into a stubborn, new-is-better or used-is-better frame of mind before you buy.

Let's dispense with an obvious point: appearance is a personal matter. If your idea of beauty is a solid chrome guitar with Christmas tree lights for position markers, great. Or if you think that twenty years of beer and barbecue sauce stains and cigarette burns lend "character" to a guitar, that's fine, too. Another subjective question involves the intangible value of pure newness or old age. Some guitarists would play the latest electronic marvel with plutonium pickups while it was still on the drawing board if they could. Others lust after relics that look like they'd been unearthed by archaeologists at the Olduvai Gorge. Why not? It doesn't matter either way.

People get into trouble, however, when they rely upon the guitar's age or looks as essential indications of quality. The fact is, both good and bad guitars run the full range of appearance and age. It's a shame when someone passes up a good but slightly worn guitar and instead chooses a piece of junk just because it glows in the dark. Of course, you should thoroughly check the instrument for defects, but don't let a few dings in the paint stand between you and an otherwise suitable choice. If you find the guitar of your dreams at a ridiculously low price, but some previous owner has painted a picture of his religious leader on the body, buy it anyway and have it refinished later, or do it yourself (p. 233). The Les Paul that looks like it's been run over by a burning tank might be a better guitar than the sparkly new competitor on the wall right next to it.

Does all of this mean that you are faced with personally inspecting every guitar on the planet before an intelligent choice is possible? Not at all. Chances are you have considerably narrowed your options long before the actual purchase anyway. After all, hollow-bodies do sound different from solid-bodies; there is a "Fender sound" and a "Humbucking sound"; Guilds do look different from Martins, and so on. You may have a mental checklist of criteria: your guitar must have that certain tone, it must glitter on stage, etc., and your absolute last-gasp maximum budget is $74 or a grand-and-a-half or whatever. So you already have some idea.

However, generalizations that go much beyond the roughest parameters are usually either untrue or have enough exceptions to render them practically useless. For example, suppose you like the fat neck on your buddy's old Fender. This does not mean that the words "old Fenders have fat necks" are chiseled on a stone tablet somewhere. Two guitars of the same model made side by side on the same day with supposedly identical parts may sound and feel slightly different. They may be *substantially* different. A 56 and a 66 are both "old," but they will likely differ in important respects. So even after you have selected a particular model, try every one you can find. You will like some D-35s better than others.

Collector's items comprise a special category of used guitars. Whole books could (and should) be written about them. All of them are rare, and most of them are "good" in the usual sense: sound, feel, etc. Some fine acoustic guitars improve with age due to seasoning and drying out over a period of years. Some electrics are especially valuable because they literally don't make certain guitars like they used to.

Whether or not you should invest the extra money in a collector's instrument depends in part on whether you want to play it or just "have" it. A collector may buy a 58 Flying V simply because it's one of the first eighty-one ever made, and he calculates an eventual increase in its value. He may never play it or even know how. On the other hand, a guitarist may choose it over a later Flying V because he prefers the original's Patent-Applied-For pickups, extra fretboard accessibility, and distinctive string-to-body contact.

Collector/columnist George Gruhn has described guitar collecting as both an art and a science. It is also a business. A 58 Explorer may be worth ten times

1954 Fender Stratocaster

SG Custom, Seventies style

The Fender look for 1977: black pickguards

The Hohner HG-370 Limited Edition Guitar

last year's model, and you can make or lose a lot of money by deciding when to trade and when to hang on. A typical guitar is priced according to the usual factors: how good it sounds, etc. The price of a collector's instrument, while related to quality, really depends upon a psychological question: How bad do you want it? If you *must* possess the only Moderne known to exist, and I have it stashed in my garage, and I want the mortgage on your home in trade for it, well, what do I care if it doesn't play or sound any better than a $500 Les Paul? A $10,000 stamp won't get your letter any farther.

Sometimes a guitar falls into a nebulous, in-between group: old, but not really a hot collector's item. Other times a noncollecting guitarist may prefer an instrument that also happens to have substantial collector's value. Prewar Martins, late-Fifties Les Pauls, dot-neck 335s, certain old Telecasters and Stratocasters are all famous for practical reasons as well as sheer scarcity. On these occasions, the shopper is faced with a decision for which he is unprepared, and salesmen have been known to overcharge the awestruck noncollector, simply because "you can't get them like this any more." While it is true that certain fine old models are unfortunately no longer made, it is also true that scores of others were discontinued because they were colossal turkeys. Unless you are willing to find out which are which, leave the collector's items to the collectors.

Don't base your decision to buy a guitar merely upon a salesman's description of its legend. If you are not a collector, the question that really matters is: Can you hear the difference? Are those rare Gibson Patent-Applied-For pickups worth more money? Yes, if they deliver the sound you want; yes, if you are a collector. Otherwise, no. (Incidentally, "identical" pickups are like "identical" guitars: they don't necessarily sound alike.)

If you are shown the "kind of guitar made back when craftsmen really cared," well, it just may be every bit as special as the salesman claims. Whether you believe his pitch about the wood for the neck coming from Noah's Ark or whatever, you should still compare the guitar's physical, mechanical, and electronic features to later, less costly versions. If you are buying the sacred oldie just to impress your friends, or to prop it up and stare at it, that's one thing. But if you are going to play it, to depend upon it, perhaps earn your living with it, then make sure it's as good as it's cracked up to be and worth the price.

MUSIC DEALERS, PRICES, AND TRADE-INS

Music dealers, for the most part, are ordinary people in business to make a profit. There are good ones and bad ones, nice guys and ripoff artists. Look for one who is interested in what you *need*, as well as what you want. Find someone who is knowledgeable and willing to take the time for all of your questions, no matter how obvious the answers may seem.

Don't hesitate to tell him that you're shopping around and comparing prices, since he'll figure it out anyway. The music dealer is a businessman, an experienced negotiator, and he will probably know if you are putting him on about where you've been and the prices you've been offered. He expects you to seek the best deal you can, and he wants your business, so if you are honest with him, he will be more inclined to be honest with you.

Find a dealer who is a guitar specialist, perhaps one who is a musician himself or is close to the entertainment business. Find out as best you can if he is fairly well versed on the more recent developments in sound equipment. If there are a couple of answers that he doesn't have, he can find them out and should be glad to do so. But if he just avoids your questions, beware. Don't buy the old routine: "I-don't-know-of-the-guitar-you-mean-but-let-me-show-you-what-we-do-have." On the other hand, the salesman is a guitar man himself (hopefully), and he should know which instrument will fit your needs and your budget. Keep an open mind and listen to what he has to say. He may bring to your attention a few important things that you hadn't previously considered.

You are much more likely to get a guarantee and good service from a reputable music dealer than from the EZ-Credit pawn shop or Honest Harry's jewelry store. However, it's sometimes possible to get a collector's item at a low price from a pawnbroker who doesn't know better or who is just anxious to unload it. If you try this approach, take along a friend who knows his guitars.

Again, don't hurry. Talk to pros. Ask your friends. In choosing a music store, consider long-range factors such as terms of the guarantee, repair facilities, and so forth. Find out if he will loan you a guitar if yours

Takamine F-450 S

Gibson S-1. Bill Lawrence, who designed the circuitry, describes it as a one-pickup guitar with three coils, rather than three pickups.

must be repaired. If you have to travel clear across the city to get to the one dealer who knows your personal needs and can fill the bill at a reasonable price, it's worth the drive every time.

Concerning your behavior in a music store, look at it from the dealer's point of view. Suppose you were closing up your shop for the day, and you noticed that the pickguard on the twelve-hundred-dollar guitar you just unpacked was covered with scratches? Suppose the careless musician who caused the damage never had any intention of buying the guitar; he just wanted to play it because it was the most expensive instrument in the store or because his girl friend thought it was flashy. What would you say the next day to the serious shopper who demands a discount, claiming that the guitar is now "used"? Those guitars are the dealer's livelihood. If you want to take one down, ask him first. If you are planning to play an amplifier at 110 dB, then you should test it at 110 dB, but first check to see if someone is trying to use the phone, and then only play at the loud volume long enough to assess the amp's capabilities.

Prices and Trade-Ins

Most buyers learn about merchandising the hard way: trial and error. If you are serious about the guitar, buy the best instrument you can afford. Get a professional guitar that you can grow into, one that will continue to serve your needs as you improve your technique. If you don't know what you want, buy an inexpensive guitar, or rent one, before obliterating your bank account on a costly model.

As far as most salesmen are concerned, there are two types of customers: those who have money in their pockets and those who don't. You will be quoted a lower price if you are ready to buy, cash in hand. Like the rest of us, the music dealer is inclined toward self-preservation, and you cannot expect him to place himself on the line regarding his rock-bottom figure if all you have to offer is plenty of questions and no budget. Remember that you and he have something in common: you want his guitar, and he wants your continued business.

Price depends upon geographical location, among other things. Since Los Angeles, San Francisco, New York, Nashville, and Memphis are music-oriented cities, the competition among dealers is keener and substantial discounts are likely. However, if there is only one dealer in your town, he may feel that there is no pressure on him to charge less than list price.

Trade-ins are tricky. Suppose you bought an instrument for $200 three years ago. It's still in good condition, and the dealer offers you $200 for it in trade, saying that, in effect, you have owned it "free of charge" for three years. A good deal? The answer depends upon these questions:

1. What can you get for your used guitar by selling it to a private party?
2. What is the dealer's lowest price for his new instrument *without* taking your guitar on trade?

Consider these two transactions, both involving a new, $650 guitar:

Trade-In: No Discount

New guitar, list price:	$650	(including tax)
Trade-in allowance:	200	
Your cost:	$450	

Discount: No Trade-In

New Guitar, list price:	$650	(including tax)
10% discount:	65	
	585	
Sell used guitar to private party:	150	
Your cost:	$435	

This comparison is *not* meant to serve as any sort of rule or general guideline. It is merely an isolated example that illustrates the importance of the two questions mentioned above. Add the dealer's no-trade discount and the amount for which you could privately sell your old guitar. If the sum is more than the trade-in allowance, then of course you'll save money by selling to a private party, all other things being equal. (Don't forget to consider the cost of advertising when deciding whether to place your guitar on sale.) In most transactions, you cannot expect to receive *both* a high trade-in and a substantial discount.

When selling or trading in your used guitar, the amount that it's worth is the amount that you can get for it, subject to prevailing trends and regardless of your initial cost. For example, a used Fender Stratocaster or Telecaster will in most cases cost more than a used Jaguar or Jazzmaster in similar condition, even

Rosewood-faced Les Paul Custom

Gibson Midnight Special, moderately priced, redesigned Humbuckings, through-the-body string attachment, bolt-on neck

though the latter two models are the company's most expensive guitars. Your year-old $500 guitar may be worth as much as you paid for it or less than $100. It's simply a matter of the demand for that particular instrument at the time you sell it or trade it in.

Franchises

A franchise is a grant of permission from a manufacturer to a dealer, enabling the dealer to sell instruments to the public. From the manufacturer's point of view, a candidate for a franchise must usually demonstrate adequate financial stability by purchasing a minimum inventory, hopefully weeding out the "quick-buck" operators from the responsible businessmen. The company in turn assists its licensee-retailer and protects his investment by refusing to grant additional franchises to competing music stores in the same immediate area. Because of the factory's cooperation with them, these authorized dealers are usually better able to service the instrument after the customer buys it.

The status of the dealer may affect the warranty. Nonfranchised retailers must "bootleg" the guitars from other stores. Since serial numbers, invoices, and other records are kept at the factory, a manufacturer may refuse to honor a guarantee if the instrument is sold through a nonfranchised dealer. Even if franchises are not mentioned in the warranty, the company might take the legal position that the franchised dealer to whom the guitar was first sent is the "original owner" and that shipment to another dealer terminates the guarantee. This argument might arise in a dispute where the manufacturer suspects that damage has occurred during shipment from the original dealer to the unauthorized dealer.

Some manufacturers will honor their guarantee without regard to where the instrument was acquired. However, repair jobs sent from authorized music stores will likely receive a priority status, while others are relegated to the shelf, perhaps for months. Whether or not the customer is charged for the shipping costs varies with the manufacturer. Rather than committing themselves to an inflexible rule, manufacturers prefer to approach each problem individually.

A franchised dealer identifies himself to his customers by prominently displaying a sticker or banner issued him by the manufacturer. The stickers are not necessarily conclusive, so call the manufacturer if in doubt. If faced with choosing between buying a guitar from a franchised store and a nonfranchised store that advertises a lower price, ask the authorized dealer if he can offer enough advantages to offset the difference in price.

Semi-Acoustic Fender Starcaster. Note the offset polepieces and conveniently positioned master volume control.

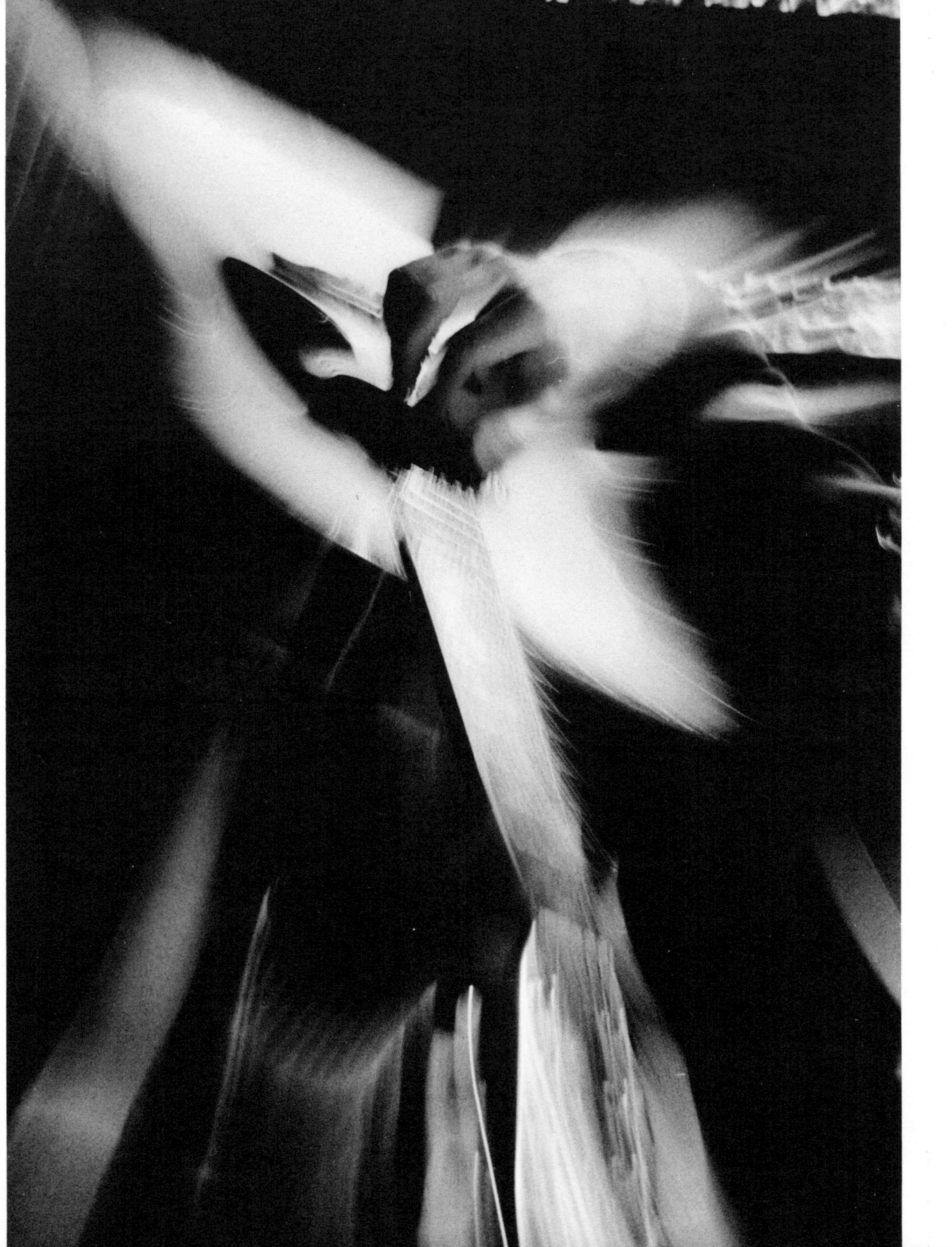

9

Six Strings–
The Voice of Your Guitar

Since the day when an imaginative cave man first twanged a musical note on his bow, people have been trying to improve the strength and sound of musical instrument strings. By experimenting with vibrations and tone properties of various metals and synthetics, manufacturers have formulated specific types of strings for different styles of playing. Though new combinations of materials and winding techniques have produced a number of variations, there are only two broad categories of strings: steel, for acoustic and electric guitars, including round wound, flat wound, and "ground-wound" strings, and nylon, for classic and flamenco guitars. There are other types of strings for more specialized purposes, including compound and nylon tape wound.

FOLK AND ROCK

Round Wound

A few nonclassical artists use nylon strings, but most prefer the brighter, more metallic sound of steel strings. The wire used in string manufacture is called "tinned mandolin wire," and it comprises both plain (unwound) strings and the core of wrapped strings. Core wire can either be round in cross-section or shaped; the most common shape is hexagonal.

A string maker can order shaped wire from the wire

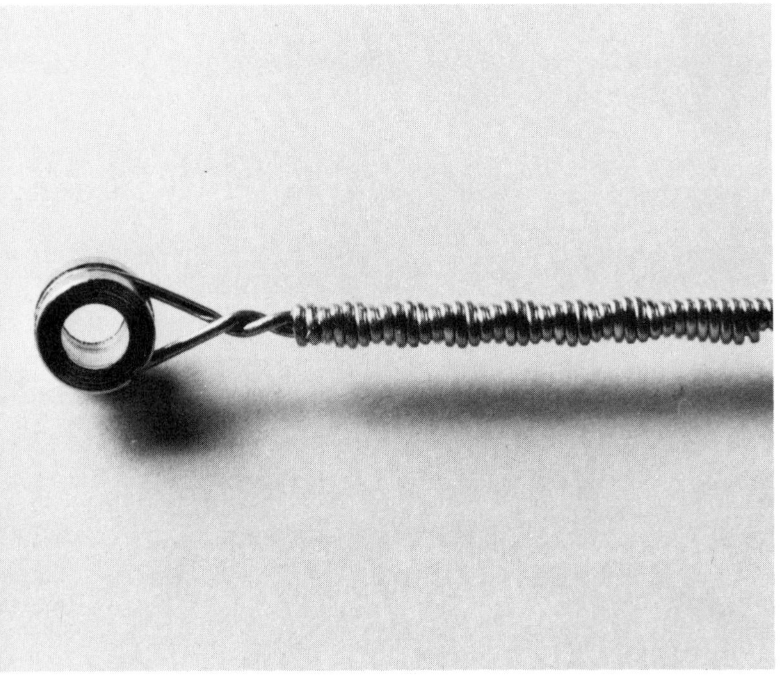

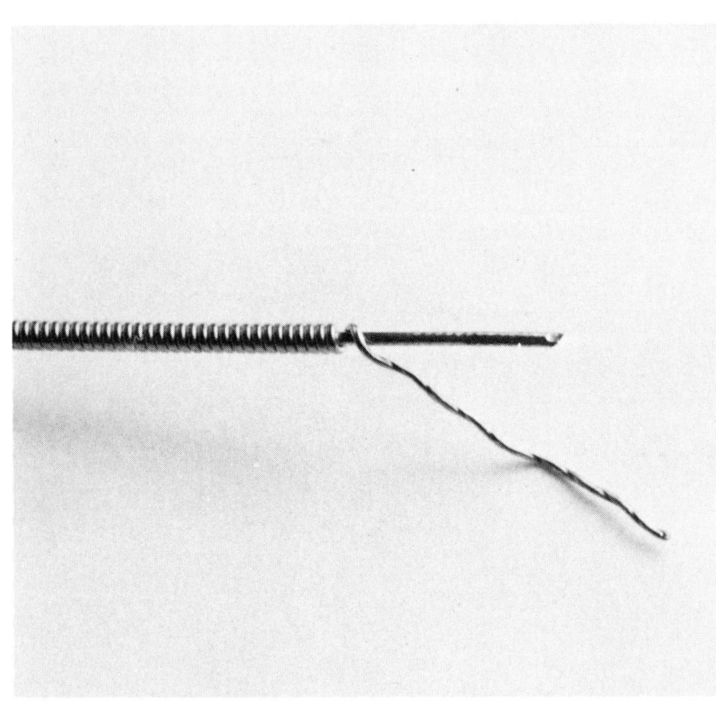

Inner core and single winding

Photos on pp. 176–181, with the exception of photo bottom p. 179, taken at the GHS factory, Battle Creek, Michigan.

mill, or he can shape it with his own equipment. Advocates of round core wire argue that the wrap is tighter, and vibration is more even and true, while users of hex core contend that its edges help to keep the wrappings from coming loose. The first and second (E and B) strings are plain, without windings or wrappings; the other four strings (G D A E) are wound. In light-gauge sets, the third string (G) is usually unwound.

The core is wound either once or twice with flat or round wire. An automatic winding machine holds the string at both ends under controlled tension; the thicker the core wire, the greater the tension. The core is rotated at high speed as the wrapping is wound over it. The tightness of the wrap affects both the tone and feel of the string.

The methods of making strings for electric guitars are similar. Magnetically responsive metals such as stainless steel, nickel, and nickel alloys are often substituted for the brass, copper, and bronze used for acoustic strings. The more magnetically responsive the material, the louder the string. Regular or "round wound" (unpolished) is the most common string in rock as well as folk because of its bright, ringing tonal quality, powerful projection, and strong sustain.

Compound Strings ("Silk and Steel")

Compound strings* are manufactured in an attempt to gain the advantages of both nylon and wound steel strings. The typical compound consists of a core of steel and nylon, rayon, or silk, which is smaller than the core used for regular strings. Wound with a silver-plated wire, it projects a slightly less metallic ring than the regular wound, and retains a smooth feel—similar to nylon and easier on the fingertips. These multi-core strings vibrate differently and thus sound different from single-core strings.

Silk-and-steels have less tension than regular steel strings and more tension than nylons. They are suited to steel-string guitars, though whether or not they may be installed on a classic guitar without damage depends upon the design of the instrument. If in doubt, consult a manufacturer's representative or a qualified dealer.

* To some manufacturers, the term "compound" designates a string with a multiple wrap.

Flatwounds (Electric Guitars)

Some wound strings of pure nickel or stainless steel are polished to give them varying degrees of smoothness, while others are wrapped with a flat band of wire. Both techniques produce a slick, light feel. While playing comfort is enhanced and finger noises are reduced, these flatwounds have several disadvantages. The tone is more subdued, they don't seem to last as long, and finally, their ability to sustain is diminished.

On the other hand, some rhythm players and jazz guitarists prefer their warmer tone and lower susceptibility to feedback. If you want a smoother touch and a more mellow electric sound, try flatwounds.

> **SEMI-FLAT**
>
> Semi-flat is used to refer either to ground wound strings or to strings with a winding that is flattened *while* it is being wrapped around the core.

Flatwounds (Acoustic Guitars)

Fender, Gibson, and other companies offer lower tension flatwounds made specifically for acoustic instruments. They are often used in the recording studio to avoid finger noises. These are the only flatwounds that should be placed on nonelectric guitars. Electric flatwounds have greater tension and could damage a guitar that is braced for normal steel strings.

Ground Wounds

Ground wounds are semi-polished strings that may provide you with both a sufficiently brilliant sound and a comfortable feel. This is a round string which has been polished to a much lesser degree than flatwounds. Any polishing will result in at least some decrease in the brightness of the tone.

Inner core with winding and outer flat wrap

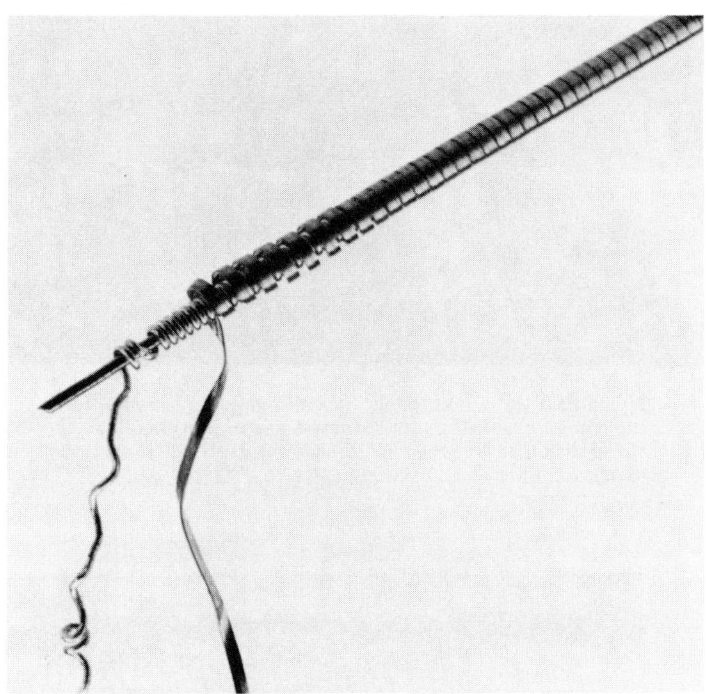

CLASSICAL

In the first few decades of this century, flamenco and classical guitars were strung with three "cat gut" strings and three silk strings wound with a silvered wire. The first three were actually made from the dried intestines of sheep, but they were understandably labeled with the euphemism "cat gut." After all, no artist wants to start thinking about sheep intestines right in the middle of a concert performance of "Malagueña." Anyway, these strings sounded rich and sweet but they weren't very dependable or strong and they lost most of their tone after a few playings.

Andres Segovia persuaded his great friend, Albert

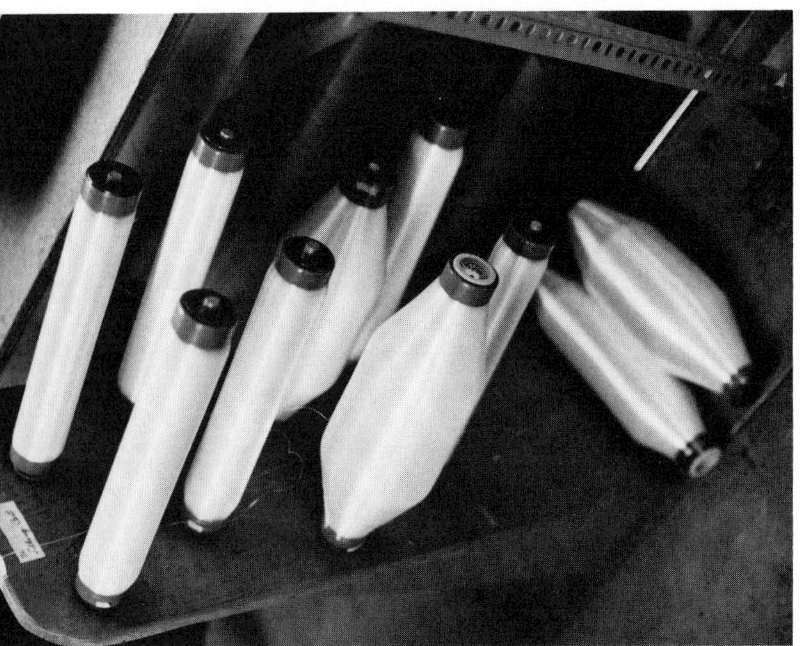

Nylon floss wound on spools. Several strands are used to form the core of classical guitar strings. A newer process allows the string maker to buy the core already multi-stranded from the manufacturer.

Augustine (1900–1967), a string-maker, to use a plain nylon developed by DuPont to replace the first three gut strings. He completed the set with nylon-cored bass strings of wound copper wire, plated with an alloy of either gold, bronze, or (most often) silver. The tone is full of color, and the new strings stay in tune much better and are more durable and precise. Because of their light polishing, they are also a little easier to play. Except for a few hard-core traditionalists, all flamenco and classical guitarists now use nylon instead of gut strings.

Today's classical strings often consist of Tynex, the synthetic material developed by DuPont. Solid nylon or monofilament (sometimes coated with a thin plastic wrap) is used for the three treble strings (E B G) and about a dozen nylon fibers form the core of each of the wrapped bass strings (D A E). Each of the metals used for plating—gold, bronze, or silver alloy—has its own sound and projection, so try all three. Pure silver strings are also available. Manufacturers now agree that there are practical differences between the materials and techniques used in producing the plain, treble strings,* so concentrate on both the treble and bass strings when comparing brands. Some nylons are equipped with a ball end that facilitates attachment to the bridge.

There are many makers of high-quality strings. To acquaint yourself with the range of available tones, you might try both the bright Savarez string and the more gentle La Bella. Keep experimenting. You may find, as a few pros have done, that the best set for you is a combination from different brands (for example, Savarez bass and La Bella treble).

JAZZ

All but a few jazz players choose an arched-top, hollow-body electric guitar, so the strings should have inherent acoustic properties in addition to the magnetic characteristics. If you are leaning toward jazz and desire a new sound, experiment with new strings. For the reasons mentioned above in the folk and rock section, you should try all three: regular or round

*Some players swear that the color of the string—black or clear—affects the tone. La Bella treble strings by E. & O. Mari, Inc., are blackened by chemical injections and a heat treatment. According to the manufacturer, X-ray microphotographs confirm that string vibration is improved.

wounds, flat wrapped or highly polished (flatwounds), and the semi-polished ground strings.

Jazz players seem to choose the round type more than any other. They have discovered that its brilliant sound can be sufficiently mellowed with the tone controls on the instrument and amplifier. However, if that scraping noise, caused by running your left hand up the wound strings, is starting to get on your nerves, flatwounds will solve that problem, and you may prefer their softened tone. In any case, give them a try. (Normal perspiration on your fingertips may be sufficient to eliminate the scraping sound.)

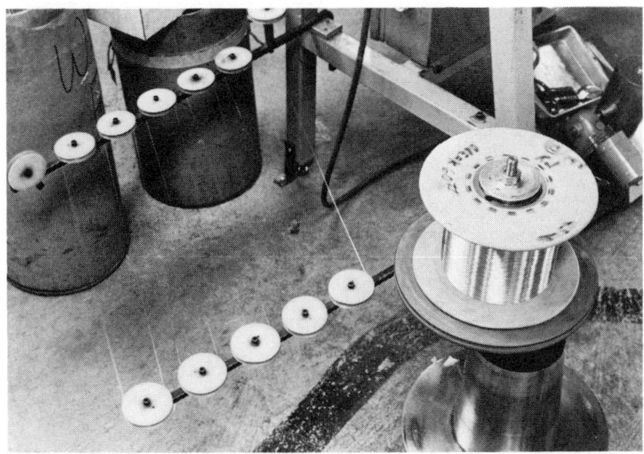

One of the more modern machines in string making, this device feeds core wire from the large spool to an automatic looping machine after passing it through a series of pulleys in order to adjust tension.

GAUGES

The gauge refers to the measured thickness of the string, a diameter which ranges from a near-microscopic, super-thin first E to a bass monster only a little smaller than the Trans-Atlantic Cable. The lighter the gauge, the easier it is to fret and to bend. Simple logic decrees, then, that those blues players who are bending notes all over the place would use the skinniest string, but it isn't necessarily true. In the first place, the heavier the string, the beefier the sound. No matter how loud you turn up your stack of Marshalls, an .008 first E won't sound as powerful or sustain as well as an .014. On the other hand, if you try to bend an .014E up a step and a half, you're liable to get blood on your new guitar. The answer, of course, is compromise. You want comfort *and* a good sound, and you can get both.

When choosing strings, pay more attention to the numbers assigned to each string than to the manufacturer's name for that particular set. The string maker may have four sets thinner than his "Light Gauge," and you're not really going to know which ones are best until you get your fingers on them. If note-bending is the crucial consideration, then get thin strings. If the tone is a little weak or too tinny, you can buy a slightly heavier set with a stronger projection and still be in the light category with easy-to-bend strings.

Thin strings are not reserved solely for electric-guitar players. Some fine acoustic guitarists choose a light gauge for fingerpicking, though thicker strings are required for really heavy, flat-pick, rhythm strumming. Rhythm players in rock groups and dance combos, who need a full, solid sound and are not worried about bending notes, often choose heavy gauge, since they stay in tune longer.

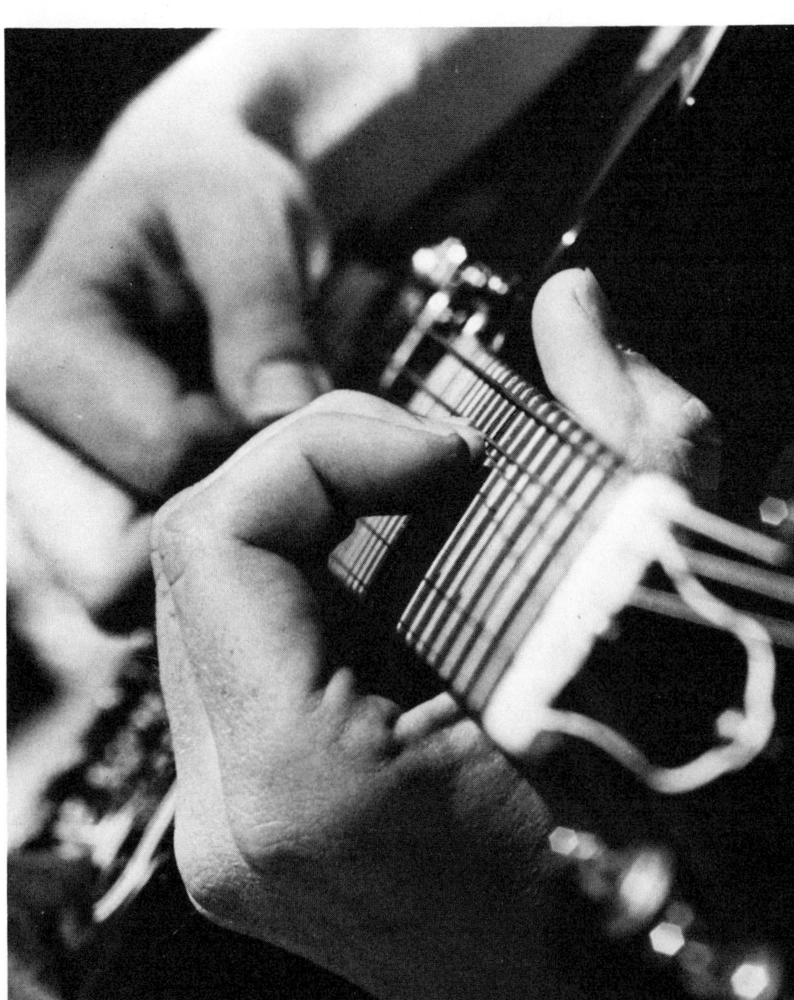

Old-style wire carriage for manual string winding machine; no longer much used in the industry

In between the light and heavy extremes are many varieties of medium-gauged strings, and there are hybrid sets, such as Ernie Ball's Skinny Top/Heavy Bottom and Fender's #150 LH set.

Fender, Ernie Ball, and others package their strings individually with the gauges printed on the envelopes, permitting the guitarist to put together a custom set. Here is a chart of some representative gauges. The "w" indicates the thinnest wound string in each set. The heavier strings are also wound; the lighter ones are plain.

A modern semiautomatic winding machine; referred to in the trade as an "automatic"

STRING #		1	2	3	4	5	6
lightest	:	.008	.011	.014	.022w	.030	.038
light	:	.011	.015	.022	.030w	.042	.052
medium	:	.013	.017	.026w	.034	.044	.054
heavy	:	.014	.018	.028w	.040	.050	.060

Several manufacturers include an extra first and second string, since these thinner ones are the first to wear out. When changing only one or two strings, make sure that the rest are not dead. Otherwise, you'll have an unbalanced set, with uneven volume and tone as you move from string to string.

Polishing necessarily reduces the diameter of the string. A "heavy gauge" sixth that has been polished to a flat texture may actually be smaller in diameter than a lighter-gauged, round-wound fifth string.

String being wound on a semiautomatic winding machine

When changing brands, you might have to experiment with gauges, since various manufacturers have their own ideas about what constitutes "light" and "heavy." When trying a lighter gauge for the first time, you might find that the new strings sit a little differently on the bridge, and since they are thinner, they will also be seated a tiny bit deeper in the grooves of the nut. Being closer to the frets, they might rattle or buzz a little. Also, the thinner the string, the more flexible it is, further increasing the possibility of a rattle. Finally, the lower tension of a lighter gauge of string may cause the neck to bend slightly backward. Each of these problems may be remedied by minor adjustments in the bridge or neck rod, and they shouldn't present any obstacle whatsoever to reasonable experimentation with the lighter gauges (see chapter nine). On acoustic guitars without adjustable neck rods, check the gauge recommended by the manufacturer. Strings of a drastically different tension could cause the neck to bend. Even if the neck is adjustable, man-

The back side of an automatic looping machine, revealing its maze of wires and compressed air hoses

ufacturers sometimes warn against strings of either extreme.

CHANGING THE STRINGS

Consider the fact that the electronic pickups, the row of knobs on the amp, or the intricate fan bracing and delicate woods all exist to capture and augment the sound produced by the vibration of six little wires. As jazz great Barney Kessel says: "The strings are the very life of the guitar."

Both nylon strings and steels eventually wear down where they are pressed against the frets, nylons a little sooner than steels. On an old set of strings, you may notice breaks in the winding over a much played position. Steel strings are subject to rust and corrosion from moisture in the air, even if the instrument is in storage. The acid in the perspiration of the guitarist's hands also contributes to deterioration. When tightening the strings, one of them may not stretch uniformly. Any changes in the diameter, including the ones mentioned above, diminish the ability of the strings to vibrate consistently throughout their length. The same will occur when the diameter is *increased* in some spots—by deposits of wax, grease, dirt, and rust.

Regardless of the cause, a string that is not uniform in diameter cannot play in tune at all locations on the fretboard. Furthermore, a string can wear out just from the strain of sitting there and vibrating all of the time; some amount of metal fatigue is certain. Worn strings are by far the most common cause of bad tone and tuning problems, such as false harmonics and poor intonation. Clean the strings often and replace them when necessary.

Keep a dry, soft, lint-free cloth in your case. After each playing session, wipe over the strings and slip the cloth between the strings and the fingerboard. Run it all the way down the length of the neck. If the cloth is damp, you might do more harm than good. Moisture corrodes the strings and may eventually contribute to a warp in the fingerboard. Players with moist hands may give the strings a quick wipe after every song, and some use a talcumlike powder to keep their fingers dry. Stay away from grease and oils, since most of them deaden the tone of the string and have been known to cause a loosening of the outer winding. Isopropyl alcohol or plain lighter fluid will remove ac-

Manual custom looper. This machine is used for making the looped ends on various kinds of musical instrument strings. A different attachment converts it into an installer of ball ends. The spinning shaft twists the string into a loop while the operator pulls the wire.

Attaching the outer wrap to the core wire on a manual string-winding machine. The chucks clamp the string and spin it at high speeds as the operator guides the outer wrap from one end of the string to the other.

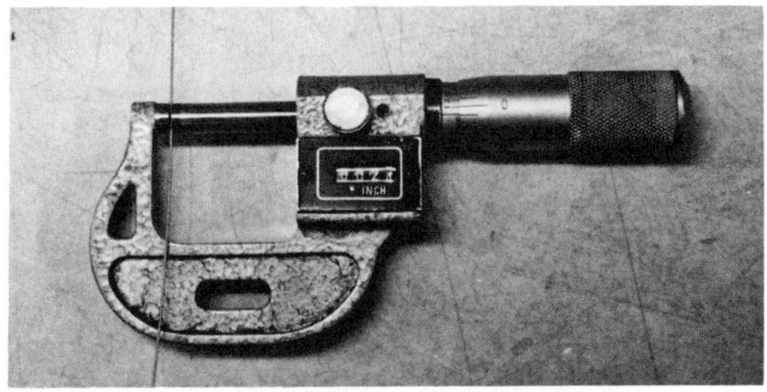

Micrometer measuring a wound string at .024 inches

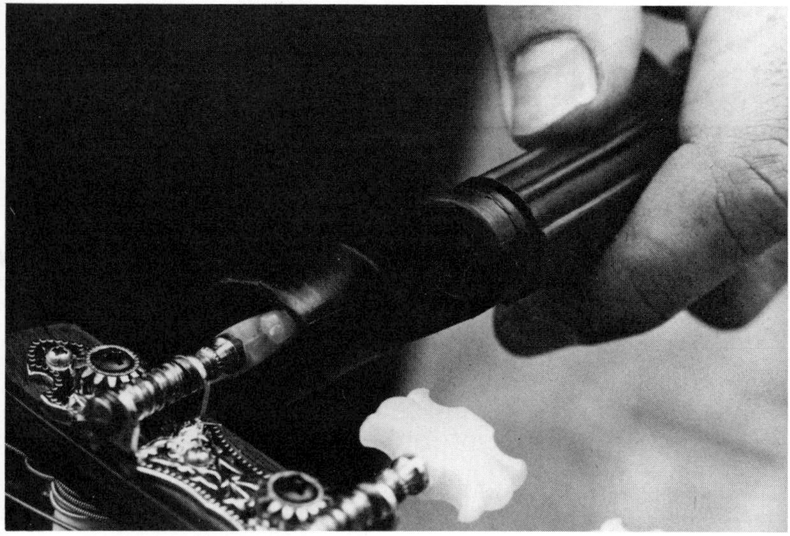

String winder

cumulations of dirt or grime. Bass players sometimes boil their expensive strings in water to clean them and preserve most of the tone. A few guitarists perform the same task, though the process is time-consuming and troublesome, considering the relatively low cost of a new set of guitar strings.

If your strings break, it is usually because you are beating on them too hard, or because they are worn in one spot. Tuning the strings higher than their capability can break them, or the bridge or nut may have a sharp edge that cuts the string. It's possible to slice through a plain, unwrapped string at the tuning-key post if it is wound over itself on the *final* twist. However, you can lock the string against the post without cutting it by wrapping it over itself on the *first* wind.

Change the strings one at a time, using the other five as tuning references. This avoids drastic changes in string tension, which might damage the neck, bridge, or top. Another advantage is that if the bridge is held in place only by the pressure of the strings, changing them one at a time will prevent its dislocation. Many repairmen have concluded that the simultaneous removal of all six strings is safe. Still, at least when working on antiques or guitars equipped with a hand vibrato or a movable bridge, the one-at-a-time method is advisable. To stabilize the string, lower it to a point below its intended pitch; then raise it.

Makers of classical guitars recommend that the strings be changed in a certain order: 1, 6, 2, 5, 3, 4. Working from the edges of the saddle toward the center avoids unbalanced stress on one side of the neck. This procedure might be followed when changing the strings on any especially delicate guitar.

You can remove the old strings and install a new set in minutes with a string winder. The cost is minimal, and it will save you hours of tedious winding in the long run.

Changing Steel Strings

Attach the bottom end first, making sure that the ball is flush with the edge of the tailpiece or hand vibrato. To keep the wrapping on a wound string from slipping, make a ninety degree bend about 2½″ beyond the proper peg. Cut the string ½″ past the bend.

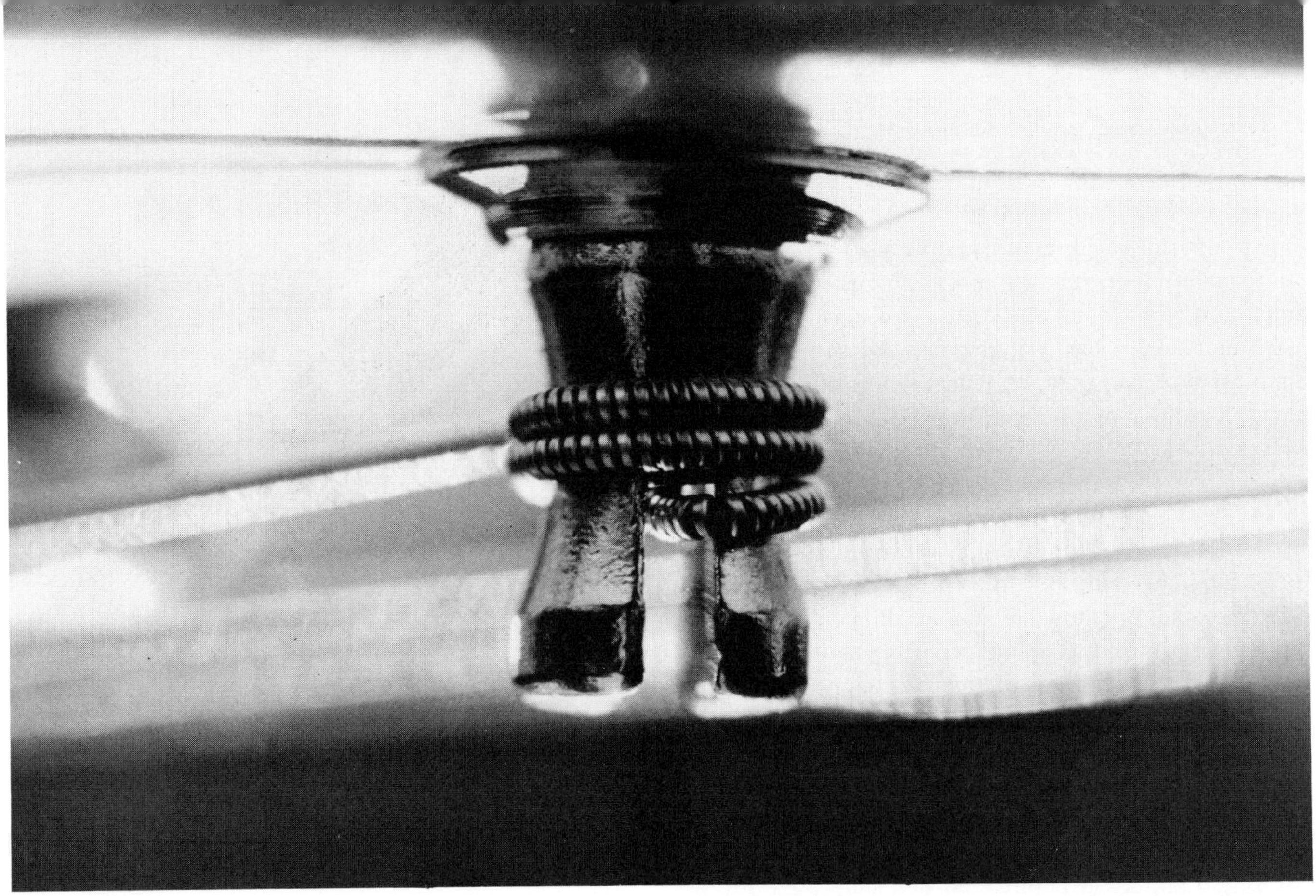

String guides

If the shaft (barrel) has a tunnel-like hole running through its center, then tune the strings to proper pitch prior to cutting. This helps to preserve the tone and avoids unraveling of the wrap. However, if the shaft is slotted, the cutting must be done first.

In the slotted shaft, insert the string into the center hole as far as it will go, and wind the string around the shaft as shown, leaving the shaft from its *inside* edge. The string is also wound in the same direction around the tunnel-type shaft. Winding in the wrong direction could conceivably disturb the balance of the neck. To avoid slippage, you might wrap the short end around the post and insert it through the hole a second time before winding. It is also common to wrap an unwound string over itself on the *first* wind to lock it firmly into place. As noted earlier, an overwrap on the *last* wind could break the string.

The final wrap should be at the bottom of the post, close to the face of the peghead. This keeps the angle of the string at the nut sufficiently sharp. If the string leaves the post at the *top* end, inadequate tension at the nut may cause a string rattle or less sustain. String guides are especially helpful in maintaining the angle if the keys are all on one side, with the uppermost keys several inches from the nut.

To avoid detuning, wind evenly with at least three winds around the post for treble strings and two winds for bass strings. As you wind, check for potential kinks in the wire; they can be avoided if spotted before the string is tightened. On a flat-top bridge, keep an eye on the bridge pin as you wind, so that it doesn't become unseated. Avoid the tendency to bring the strings to pitch too rapidly, especially if you are using a string winder. The balance of the neck may be altered by sudden changes in tension, and the core of the string may be damaged by rapid stretching. It'll hurt your feelings if you are stabbed by your own guitar, so if the short ends protrude from the shaft, trim them to ½″ or so after winding.

Changing Nylon Strings

Here are three ways to knot a plain-end nylon string to the bridge of a classical guitar. When you are making these ties for the first few times, you may wish to hold them in place with one hand while tightening the string with the other. Be sure that the knot remains on the back side of the tailpiece instead of slip-

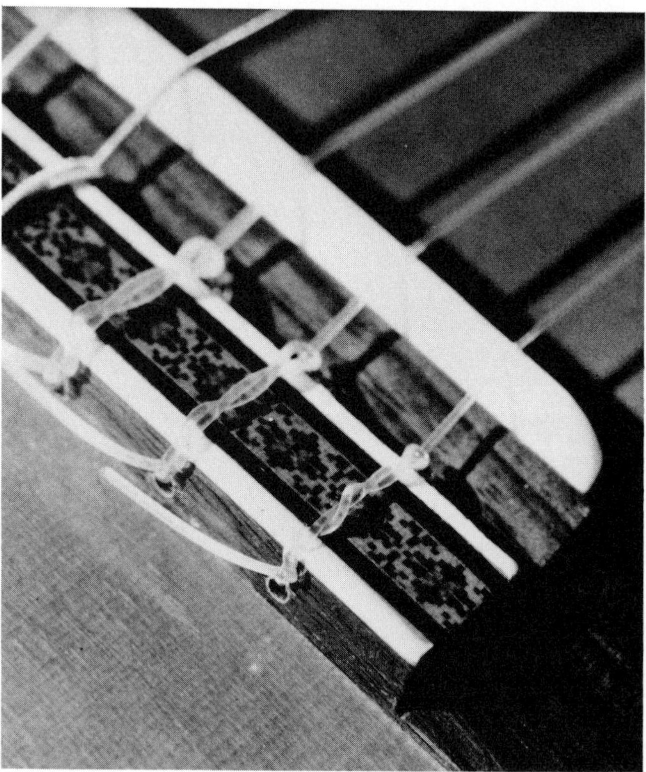

In this knot the string is wrapped around itself several times.

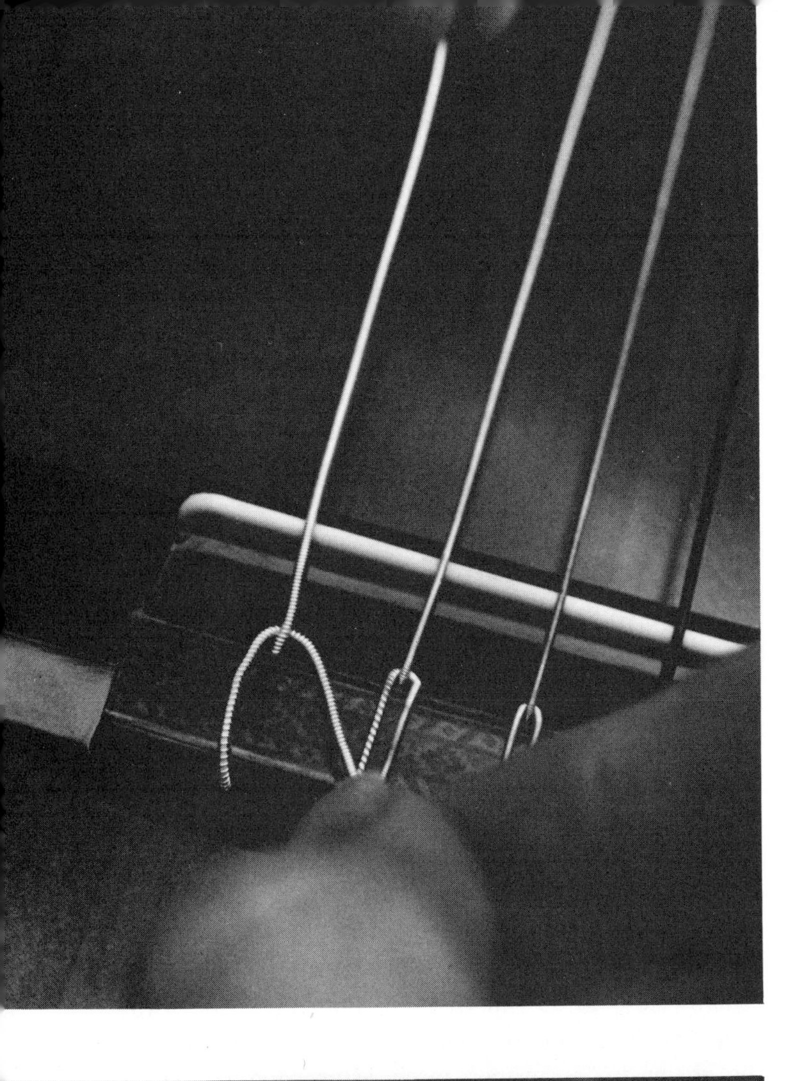
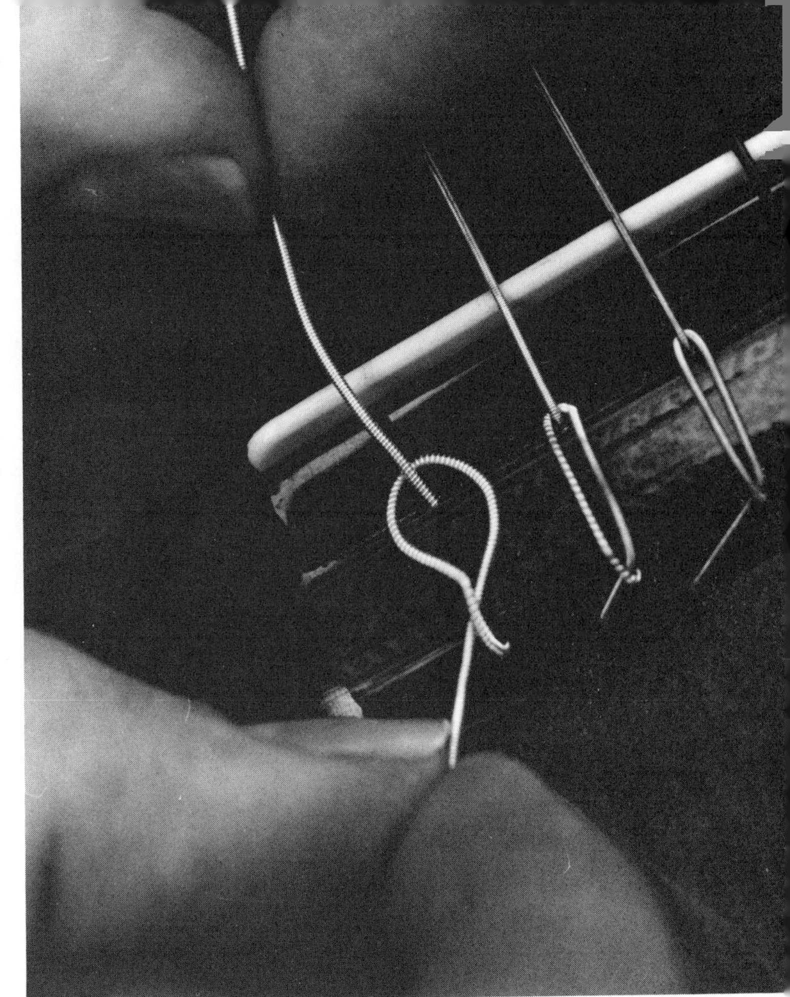
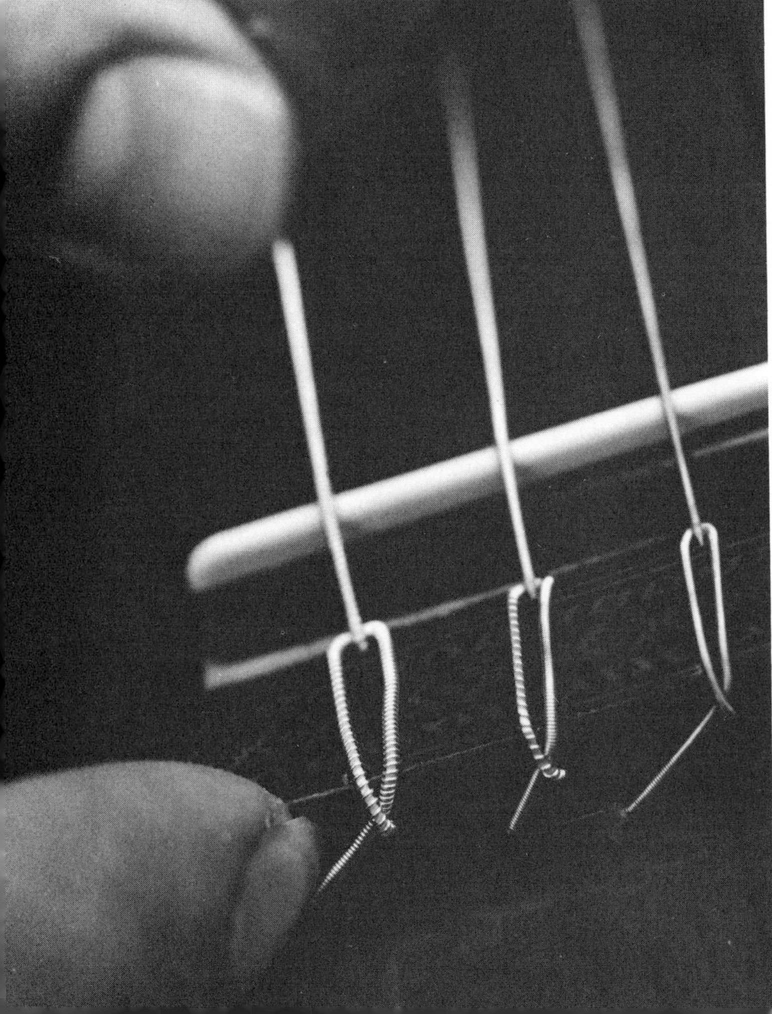

Here, the string is looped through the tailpiece an extra time.

ping over the top edge where it may unravel. Sometimes, an extra single-loop knot is tied at the very end of the string to keep the main knot from slipping. If the string is of the ball-end type, pull it through the hole in the bridge until the ball is flush.

After securing the string to the bridge, pass it along the fingerboard across the appropriate groove in the nut, and insert it through the hole in the shaft. To avoid slipping you might wind the short end back around the barrel and underneath the long end, so that the string will be locked into place when tightened.

To maintain string tension when cleaning the fretboard, remove the three treble strings and clean that half of the guitar. You can then install the new treble strings, using the old bass strings as a tuning reference. Repeat the procedure for the bass side. Don't move the saddle, since a slight shift will change the intonation.

Stretching

Most strings stretch a bit and go out of tune at first, though some are prestretched by the manufacturer. By stretching them yourself, you can help a new set remain close to its tuned pitch. Pull the string away from the fingerboard about an inch or less. Return the string to its proper pitch after each couple of stretches. This is particularly helpful if you have to change strings during a performance, since if you let them stretch naturally, it may take a day or two before they will remain in tune, depending upon the type of string. In any case, plan ahead, if you can, so that the strings will be on the guitar at least a day before a concert or a recording session.

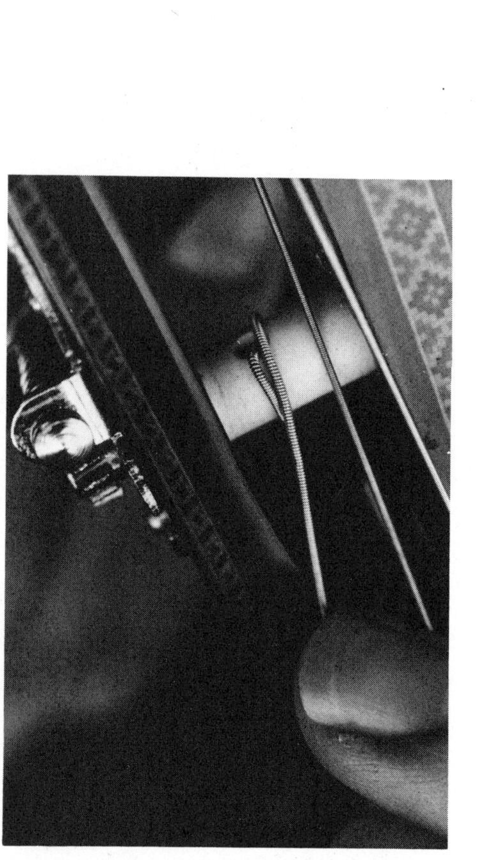

Changing Strings—General Advice

You may have worked a four-hour gig five nights a week, using light-gauge strings. Even though you wiped them several times during each set, you may have found that the first and second had to be changed almost every day. Other times, when using the guitar only for practicing, jamming with friends, and an occasional one-nighter or recording date, a set of strings may last a month or longer. A few people *prefer* dead strings. Even though they don't play in tune as well, old strings do have a nice flexible feel, if you clean them. Ry Cooder says he changes strings annually. However, most pros change steel strings at least every two weeks, though the lighter gauges—particularly the plain first and second strings (and in some sets, the third)—will lose their sound and intonation properties sooner than the medium or heavy gauges. In nylon sets, bass strings are likely to lose their sound first. As a general rule, change the strings about once a month, more often if you play a lot.

Stretching strings

Thou shalt not put steel strings on a classic or flamenco guitar. Steel strings exert about 60 pounds more tension than nylons on the head, neck, bridge, and tailpiece. The classic models are constructed with lighter materials and thinner braces to carry the vibrations of the soft nylon strings. Putting steels on a classic guitar could cause any number of catastrophes —a warped neck, a bent or split top, a ripped-off bridge, and so forth. If you want to get a more metallic sound from your classic guitar, strum the strings just in front of the bridge or try a flat pick, but *don't* use steel strings.

Thou couldst put nylons on your steel-string guitar, but it's not a great idea. The steel-string guitar is less resonant, because it is reinforced with heavy materials and sturdy braces to accommodate the increased tension of steel strings. The nylons' gentler vibrations won't project a good tone, and the volume will be diminished. The neck adjustment of a steel-string may also be disturbed by installing the lower-tension nylon strings.

A glance will usually tell you whether the instrument is a flat-top (designed for steel strings) or a classic (nylon strings). However, a few of the bargain-basement models may have characteristics of both. Traditional indications of a steel-string guitar include an arched top with "f"-holes, an unglued movable bridge, which is held in place only by the string tension, or a neck which joins the body somewhere above the twelfth fret. However, newer designs provide exceptions, such as Ovation's extended-range Country Artist 1124, a nylon-string guitar that joins the neck and body at the fourteenth fret.

There are a few fine classic guitars made by some of America's most respected manufacturers that are braced with additional support for the specific purpose of accommodating both steels and nylons. These are the only instruments that will provide good results with both types of string without risking damage to the guitar. One example is Martin's 0–16NY folk guitar.

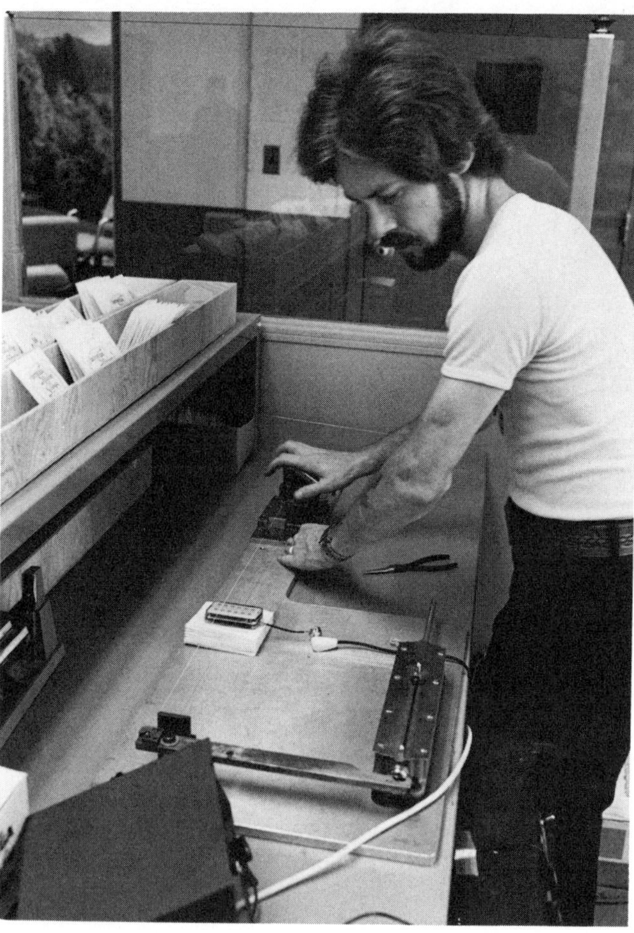

This worker at the Sterlingworth plant is testing a finished string's breaking point and consistency of vibration.

ADVERTISEMENTS AND STRING COMPANIES; CHOOSING A BRAND

Given the dozens of string labels, you might naturally turn to advertisements for some help in determining which string is best for you. Welcome to Fantasyland. Many string ads are so full of misleading information that it's easy to forget that the only way to choose a brand is simply to try several and to pick the one with the best sound. Some companies have been making strings for generations, and some employ the latest technology. With all of this experience and information, ads could be informative. However, because of the lack of uniform industry standards in measuring string performance, the string companies have concluded (perhaps correctly) that ads with gimmicks sell more strings than ads that educate the public.

Except for the manufacture of the core wire, string making is somewhat old fashioned. Most companies do not use sophisticated electronic devices for monitoring manufacture or for testing the finished product. Those who do use such equipment test the string under controlled conditions perhaps far removed from typical customer use. The validity of published "findings" depends in part upon what happens to the string *after* the test—how it is packaged, shipped, stored, installed, and played. Some ads with scientific info may be valid; others are about as relevant as the TV biochemist whose "actual laboratory analysis" clearly proves the superiority of a certain detergent.

Despite the many labels, there are only a few companies who actually manufacture strings, about a dozen at most. It is common for a manufacturer to market strings under its own label and to sell strings to several other companies as well. If you cannot tell the difference between Ultra-Wows and Phenomeno-Twangs, it may be because both were made on the same machine. Similarly, if your old faithfuls seem to sound a little different than they used to, perhaps they are now made by a different manufacturer.

Most of the companies obtain big spools of wire from the same few mills. You would never know it from the ads, however. A common promotional technique is to seize upon one aspect of the string (e.g., the shape of the core wire) and to suggest that it is somehow unique, when in fact it is practically an industry standard. Another is simply to invent a new term for an old item and to promote it as a breakthrough. The shocking "Farout Alloy," the latest metallurgical miracle, may be nothing more than the same old material that all the companies have used for years. Unfortunately for manufacturer and consumer alike, such gimmicks obscure any truly revolutionary developments.

One tradition in the string industry has been to call brass strings "bronze," not to deceive anyone but simply to avoid the connotation of a "brassy" or tinny sound. Unfortunately, some strings are in fact made from bronze, and confusion results. Another inaccuracy: there is clearly a difference between pure nickel strings and those which are nickel *plated,* yet some so-called nickel strings are in fact merely plated. Finally, terms vary among manufacturers. For example, what one calls "grinding" may be called "polishing" by another.

This is not to say that all strings are the same. On the contrary, strings vary widely in sound, feel, composition, appearance, and in how long they last. It is just that the ads are not as helpful as they might be, and it is up to you to distinguish between brands on your own.

Comparing Brands

Outside the laboratory, most string comparisons are entirely subjective. The ideal test would use only one guitar (yours) and would somehow permit you to strum back and forth, first on this set, then on that one, enabling you to concentrate on the subtlest nuances of tone, volume, and balance. The test is, of course, impossible, and all other methods have inherent problems. If you replace your old, abused strings with a new set, the new ones are bound to sound brighter, even though the old ones may have been brighter still when *they* were new.

When comparing a fresh set of Brand X on one guitar to fresh Brand Ys on another, it's hard to tell which variations in tone are caused by differences between the guitars, even if they are both, say, Martin D-28s. You could always buy several sets and try one after another on your guitar, but aside from the inconvenience, the obvious drawback is that twenty or thirty bucks is a bundle of money to spend all at once on strings, some of which you probably won't like anyway.

Perhaps the best approach is to cover the general categories with your first two or three sets. If you play an acoustic, for example, be sure to compare brass, bronze phosphor, and steel-plated strings. If you play electric, it's not really necessary to buy a trial set of flatwounds, sight unseen. Just go to a music store and play any guitar with flatwounds. If the comfortable feel knocks you out, buy a set and compare the tone to your regular round wound. Once you have selected a particular category, you can begin to narrow down brands and gauges. But keep an open mind—you may choose steel over bronze and begin to compare brands of steels only to later discover a previously untried bronze that gives you what you'd been looking for all along. With all of the difficulties of comparing strings, you really will be able to find your favorite only through experience.

10

Systems and Methods of Tuning

SYSTEMS: RELATIVE AND STANDARDIZED

Tuning the guitar places the pitches of the strings in a certain relationship to each other (relative tuning), and it may also adjust them to universally accepted standard frequencies. The correct frequencies of the six open (unfretted) guitar strings,* measured in cycles per second (Hz), are:

E(6) 82.41 A 110 D 146.82 G 196
B 246.94 E(1) 329.63

The high E (1st string) is tuned to the E above middle C on a piano.

Suppose you raised (or lowered) each of these standard frequencies by exactly the same amount. The differences *between* the pitches would still be the same, and when a chord was played, its various notes would still harmonize; however, the entire chord would now be a little higher (or lower) than the standard frequencies. Any method that accomplishes such a relative tuning places the instrument in tune only "with itself," so that the notes and chords are properly related to each other, even though all of them may be uniformly higher or lower than the universal pitches listed above.

*It might be helpful to read the discussions of frequencies on pages 199 and 247.

METHODS: FRETTED NOTES AND HARMONICS

Regardless of the method you use, quickly tune the open strings or other notes to their approximate pitch; then go back and refine the adjustments, obtaining the exact pitch for each string. By first adjusting the strings to their approximate pitch, the tension is fixed and will remain stable as the fine tuning is completed. This avoids wasting a couple of painstaking minutes insuring that one string is accurate, only to have it slip out of tune because of changes in the tension caused by tuning up the *other* strings.

Don't confine yourself to one method of tuning. You may get the best results through a combination of several methods.

Tuning by Fretted Notes

To place the guitar in either the relative or the standard tuning, a single note is usually employed as a reference point for tuning the other notes. If that reference note matches the appropriate standardized frequency, then the other notes will also correspond to their respective standardized frequencies. If it does not, the guitar may still be placed in relative tuning, "with itself."

To adjust the reference note to its standard pitch, a tuning fork or pitch pipe can produce the A/440 or "concert pitch," equal to string 1, fret 5 on the guitar, or the A above middle C on a piano keyboard. The open A string (5th), two octaves lower, is a common reference point, as are the open E strings (1st and 6th).

To tune without a piano, tuning fork, pitch pipe, or other such device (e.g. vibrating reed device and electronic pitch generator), use the open E (6th) as your first reference to tune the 5th string; the 5th is then used to tune the 4th, and so on.

1. Play an A note on the 6th string, fret 5, and tune the open 5th string (also A) to this *same* pitch, a process called tuning in unison.
2. Play a D note on the 5th string at fret 5 and tune the open 4th string (D) in unison.
3. Play a G note on the 4th string at fret 5 and tune the open 3rd string (G) in unison.
4. Play a B note on the 3rd string at fret *4* (note the exception) and tune the open 2nd string (B) in unison.

5. Play an E on the 2nd string at fret 5 and tune the open 1st string (E) in unison.

Tuning either the third (G) or the second (B) strings may be especially difficult because the interval between them is a harmonically imperfect major third. The other strings are tuned in intervals of perfect fourths; these complementary vibrations make tuning easier.

To avoid breaking a string, it is better to tune a little low than too high, in case of doubt as to the 6th string reference point.

Tuning by Harmonics

Harmonics (see chapter eight) provide several advantages in tuning: fine variations in pitch are more noticeable, and the left hand is freed to make adjustments without interrupting the vibration of the string that is being tuned. Starting with string 6 as a reference point, use it to tune string 5; use string 5 as the reference to tune string 4; use 4 to tune 3, and so on.

1. Sound the harmonic on string 6,* fret 5 (E), and tune the harmonic on string 5, fret 7 (also E), in unison.

Following the same procedure, tune the following pairs of harmonics in unison; first sound the reference note (listed on the left) and then tune the other harmonic to that same pitch.

2. 5th string, fret 5; 4th string, fret 7.
3. 4th string, fret 5; 3rd string, fret 7.
4. Since there is no G harmonic that may be produced on the open 2nd string, use the harmonic on the 3rd string, fret 5 as the reference, and tune the actual fretted *note* on the 2nd string, fret 8, to that same pitch.
5. 2nd string, fret 5; 1st string, fret 7.

Variations of the harmonic tuning method include the matching of harmonics and open string notes, such as tuning the open 2nd string (B) to the harmonic on the 6th string, fret 7 (also B), or tuning the open 1st string (E) to the harmonic on the 6th string, fret 5 (E).

One advantage to the harmonic method is that if two harmonic tones are almost, but not quite, in tune, the different frequencies (which are alternately combining and canceling, in and out of step) will produce an audible pulse. The pulse, or beat, occurs when the

*The technique for sounding a harmonic is explained on page 200.

Upper Register Notes

Lead players should confirm the correct pitch of high register notes. One method: after tuning the 6th string (E), use the note in the left column as a reference to check the tuning of the corresponding note on the right.

D; 6th string, 10th fret	Open 4th, D
G; 5th string, 10th fret	Open 3rd, G
B; 4th string, 9th fret	Open 2nd, B
E; 3rd string, 9th fret	Open 1st, E

short sound waves of the higher note "catch up" to the longer waves of the lower note. Try this experiment: tune string 4 so that it is just higher (sharp) than string 5. Sound the harmonic at string 5, fret 5, loudly. You will hear no pulse. Repeat; then, without touching the vibrating fifth string, sound the harmonic at string 4, fret 7. The combination of the two frequencies vibrating simultaneously will produce the pulse. With string 4 still a little sharp, sound both harmonics, then touch string 5, completely canceling its note. The harmonic on string 4 will continue to sustain, but the pulse will disappear, because it takes *both* vibrations to cause it.

Applying this knowledge, two different strings may be placed in tune with each other by striking a common harmonic tone on each one and adjusting the faulty string (either by raising or lowering its pitch) until the pulse disappears. For example, with the 4th string slightly sharp to the 5th string, strike the same two harmonics. The pulse will gradually disappear (placing the strings in tune with each other) *either* by raising the 5th or by lowering the 4th by the required amount.

When tuning an acoustic instrument by harmonics, place part of the right hand on the top. You will be able to feel the shifting pulse as it vibrates the wood.

Tuning by harmonics requires good strings, since worn strings may produce false harmonics.

No method can keep your guitar in tune for prolonged periods. Even a good instrument with top-caliber machines and bridge will slip a little out of tune due to string wear. Also, cold temperatures will raise the tension of the strings, causing them to go slightly sharp, while warm temperatures will have the opposite effect. If the strings are worn and cannot be adjusted in tune over the entire range of the fingerboard, try placing the guitar in tune at a central location (for example, barred A at fret 5) as a compromise measure to evenly distribute the shortcoming until the strings can be replaced. (Intonation and string-length adjustments are examined on pp. 209–210.

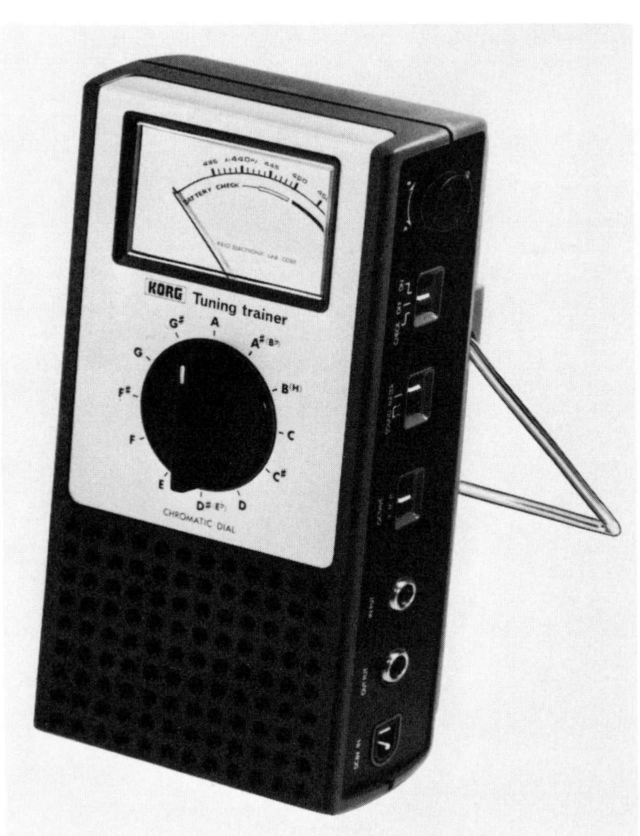

OPEN TUNINGS

There are many ways to tune the guitar. You may try a certain tuning simply for convenience or for its particular personality. Some are good for slide, others for achieving a mid-Eastern or Oriental sound and others for fingerpicking. Altering the standard tuning permits greater emphasis on the open strings, resulting in the lush sounds of the sitar, harp, zither, and other instruments.

Open tunings were favored by early Southern bluesmen—Son House, Nehemiah "Skip" James, Mississippi John Hurt, and Fred McDowell. Contemporary guitarists who often use them are Bert Jansch, David Bromberg, Leo Kottke, Ry Cooder, John Fahey, Richie Havens, and many others.

These are a few of the popular modified and open-chord tunings.

STRING	6	5	4	3	2	1
STANDARD TUNING	E	A	D	G	B	E
Open G (slack key, Hawaiian):	D	G	D	G	B	D
				or		
	G	B	D	G	B	D
Open D:	D	A	D	F♯	A	D
Open E:	E	B	E	G♯	B	E
Open A:	E	A	E	A	C♯	E
Open C:	E	G	C	G	C	E
Dropped D:	D	A	D	G	B	E
Cross-note (Open Em):	E	B	E	G	B	E
Cross-note (Open Dm):	D	A	D	F	A	D

Leo Kottke

TEMPERED TUNING

Most instruments have fixed intervals, including keyboards, valve horns (for example, trumpet) and fretted strings (guitars, mandolins, lutes, banjos, and others). Unlike the trombone, the bowed strings, and the human voice, instruments of fixed intervals are incapable of being in absolutely perfect tune in all keys. The guitar, if perfectly tuned in any one key, will be out of tune in most other keys. Since the guitarist must move freely from one key to another, the fretboard is calculated to "temper" the guitar, setting it just barely out of tune in every key. Thus divided equally among the keys, the discrepancies are imperceptible.

This problem and its solution may be illustrated by applying a set of simple mathematical equations to determine the frequencies of the notes in an A major (diatonic) scale:

A	B	C#	D	E	F#	G#	A
doh	re	mi	fa	so	la	ti	doh

These A scale notes are all found among the notes that comprise the three major chords in the key of A: the A, D, and E chords. Each major chord consists of

Ry Cooder

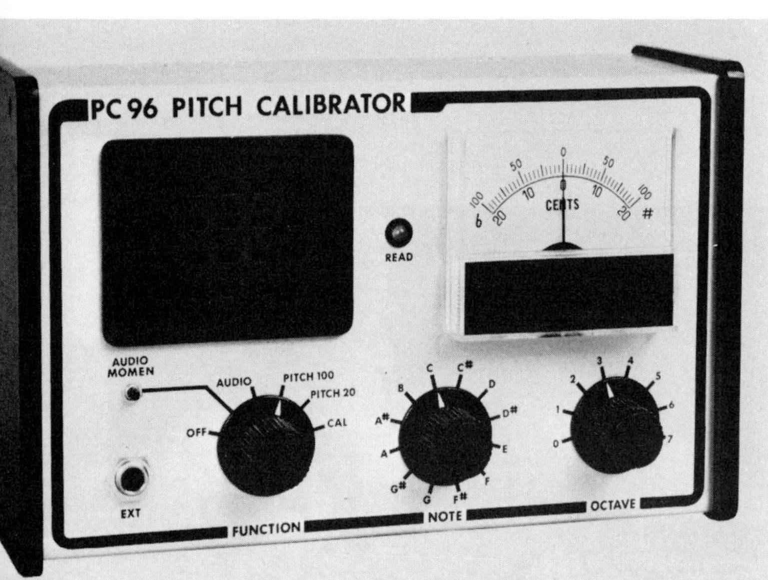

Michel Electronics PC-96 Pitch Calibrator

the first (doh), third (mi), and fifth (so) tones of the matching scale. In other words, the A chord is based on the A scale, the D chord on the D scale, and the E chord on the E scale. The frequencies of the various notes are listed in cycles per second (Hz).

A chord

A chord = A(220); C#(275); E(330).
doh mi so

From these relationships, we may derive three formulas:

Formula 1A: doh × 1.5 = so
Formula 1B: so ÷ 1.5 = doh
Formula 2 : doh × 1.25 = mi

D chord

The A note (above) also serves as the fifth (so) in the D scale. For convenience, we shall raise it an octave to 440 before applying the formulas to calculate the other notes (first and third) in the D major chord.

Formula 1B: 440 ÷ 1.5 = 293.333 = doh (D)

(Remember, the doh, mi, and so here refer to the D *scale* on which the D chord is based, not to the A scale.)

Formula 2: 293.333 × 1.25 = 366.666 = mi (F#)

E chord

The E note, taken from its original calculation back in the A scale, is 330 Hz. We may use it here in the formulas, since it is also a member of the E scale, from which the E chord is derived.

Formula 1A: 330 × 1.5 = 495 = so (B)

This B note of 495 Hz is divided in half, lowering it by one octave to 247.50, for convenience in the discussion below.

Formula 2 : 330 × 1.25 = 412.50 = mi (G#)

In order to calculate the frequencies of the notes in an A *scale*, we have applied formulas to the notes that make up the A, D, and E *chords*. The results show the A scale notes to have the following frequencies:

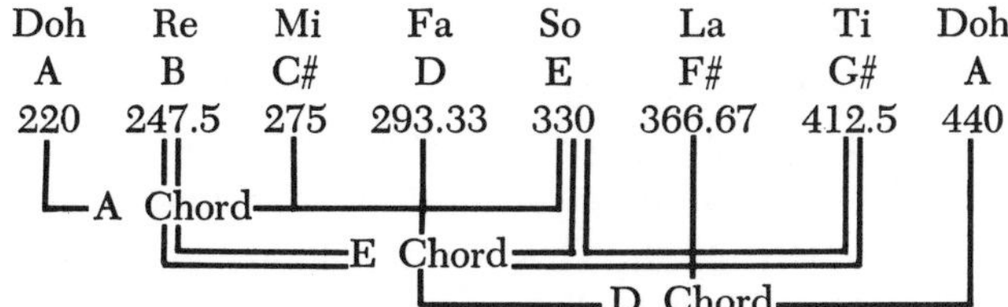

Now, to illustrate the tuning discrepancy of the guitar's fixed intervals, try moving *outside* the key of A. Apply the formulas to the three notes of a B chord, then check the results against the frequencies listed above. The B chord consists of the first (B), third (D#), and fifth (F#) tones of the B scale. According to our A scale, B = 247.5.

Apply Formula 1: 247.5 × 1.5 = 371.25 = so (F#). Here, the F# in the *B scale* is calculated to be 371.25. However, in the *A scale*, the F# was determined to be 366.67, nearly 5 cycles per second flat. In other words, the mathematical relationships between the notes in one scale do not seem to apply in another scale.

This is only one example. Applying the formulas to notes in other scales will reveal more discrepancies. The solution is known as tempered tuning, a system in which the 1.5 multiplier is reduced, or "tempered," to 1.49831. Probably the most sophisticated listener will not notice the difference, and the guitarist has the freedom to change from one key to another.

ELECTRONIC TUNERS

A number of devices can measure pitch much more accurately than the ear and can do so without the element of human fatigue. Stroboscopes and tuning meters are often accurate to 1/100 of a half-step interval (e.g., F to F#). Some employ microphones; others are connected to the guitar by a standard patch cord.

On a typical meter, a needle will point straight up when the pitch is accurately fixed and to the left when flat, right when sharp. Strobes often use illuminated spinning discs that resemble roulette wheels. Each one may have concentric rings, one for each of several octaves. As the note nears correct adjustment, the wheel slows down, and the blurry light focuses into a pattern of solid spokes. Counterclockwise movement indicates a flat note; clockwise motion indicates a sharp one. The faster the motion, the sharper or flatter

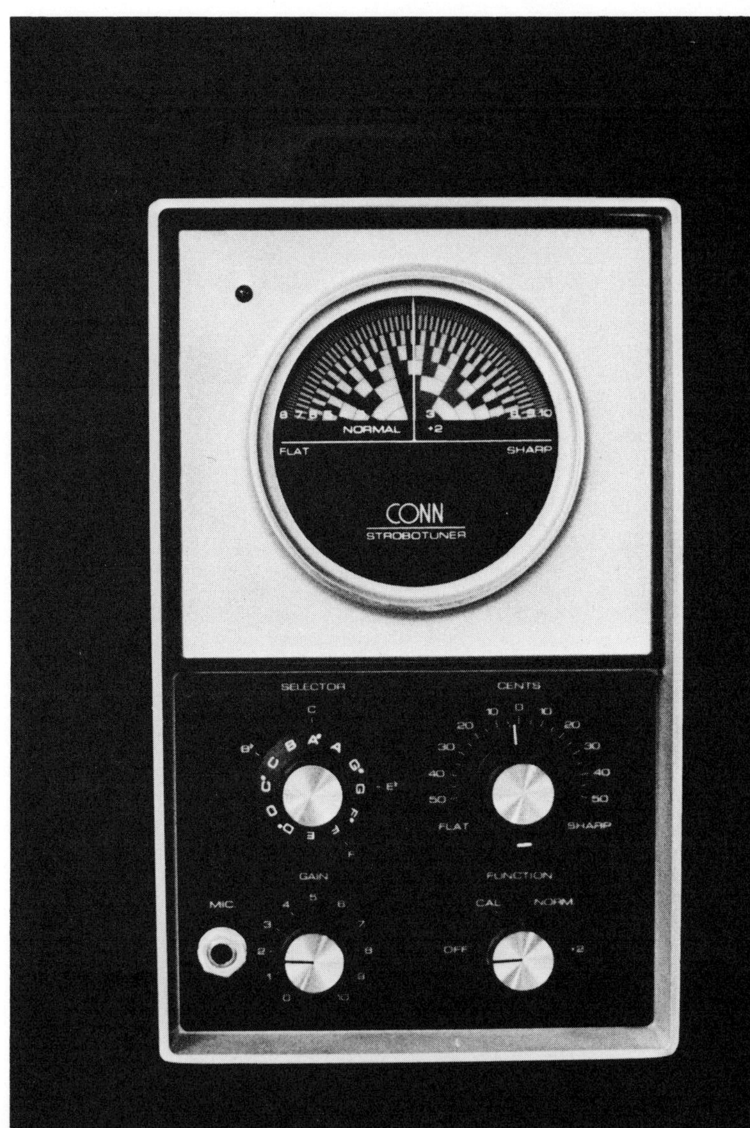

the note. When the wheel stops (or when slight motions are equidistant from center), pitch is true.

When using an electronic device for tuning or measuring intonation, quickly pre-tune the guitar to a rough standard pitch. This will preclude the possibility of the tuner responding to a harmonic overtone of the selected note as if it were the fundamental note itself. It will also fix the proper string tensions. Otherwise, a subsequent change in string tension, if extreme, might detune a previously adjusted string.

On an electric guitar, turn the volume and tone controls all the way up and see which pickup provides the clearest readings on the tuner. *Guitar Player* columnist John Carruthers suggests always using the 12th fret harmonic as a tuning reference rather than the open string. It vibrates at a higher frequency, providing a purer signal and a more readable response. Since electronic tuners are ultra-sensitive to fluctuations in string tension, be sure you use adequate but not excessive pressure when fretting notes, and keep the string aligned on center.

11

String Vibration and Harmonics

Sounds are vibrations. All musical instruments, even percussive devices such as claves, triangles, and drums, are tuned to generate sound waves which travel at certain frequencies. When a guitar string vibrates, it forces the surrounding air to move, creating a musical tone. The pitch of that tone, measured in Hertz (Hz) or cycles per second (cps), corresponds directly to the frequency of the vibration.

There are four important physical principles, formulated in 1636 by Père Mersenne in his *Harmonie Universelle,* which apply to the relationship between musical instrument strings and frequency.*

1. A long string vibrates at a lower frequency than a short one, all other things (tension, diameter, and density) being equal. Doubling the length lowers the pitch by one octave.

2. The frequency, and therefore the pitch, increases as the tension increases. Specifically, frequency rises in proportion to the square root of the tension; quadrupling the tension raises the pitch by one octave.

3. Frequency varies inversely with the diameter of the string; the thinner the string, the higher the pitch, other variables remaining constant.

*The correct frequency for each string is listed in the tuning section, p. 191.

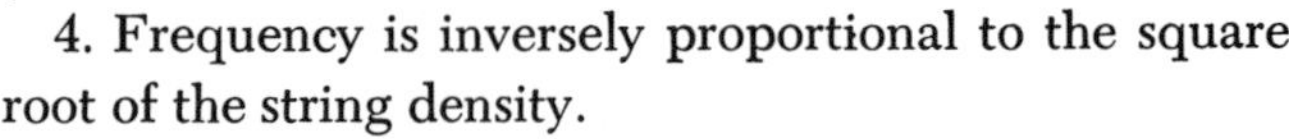

4. Frequency is inversely proportional to the square root of the string density.

THE FUNDAMENTAL

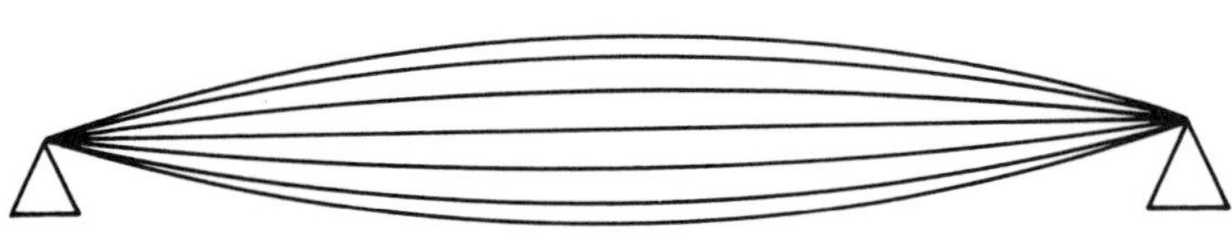

The fundamental

Theoretically, when a "perfect" open (unfretted) string is plucked under ideal circumstances, it is anchored at the ends (the nut and the bridge). These motionless anchors are called *nodes*. The string vibrates between the nodes in a single loop (Fig. 1). The result is the lowest possible tone that the string is capable of producing, called the *fundamental.*

HARMONICS

A string may also vibrate in several loops, producing frequencies that are simple multiples of the fundamental. These added tones are called *harmonics.* Harmonics may be separated from the fundamental by adding new nodes to the string at various locations along its length, changing the single loop into multiple loops, each of which is a fraction (½, ¼, and so on) of the original open string length.

To isolate a harmonic, lightly touch the string with a left-hand finger *directly over* the desired fret (not in between the frets as you do when playing a fretted note); do not depress the string. Pick the string with the right hand positioned close to the bridge and immediately remove the left-hand finger.

Second Harmonic*

In theory, the 12th fret of any guitar is exactly halfway between the nodes (the nut and bridge) of the open string length, though in actuality the position of the bridge is slightly altered (pp. 210). When the node is positioned at this 12th-fret midway point on any string, the vibrations are split into two equal loops, each of which is one half the original string length (Fig. 2). Vibrating at twice the frequency of the single-loop open string, they produce a harmonic one octave higher, called the second harmonic of the fundamental. The string is now motionless at the 12th-fret node, in addition to its original nodes at the nut and the bridge.

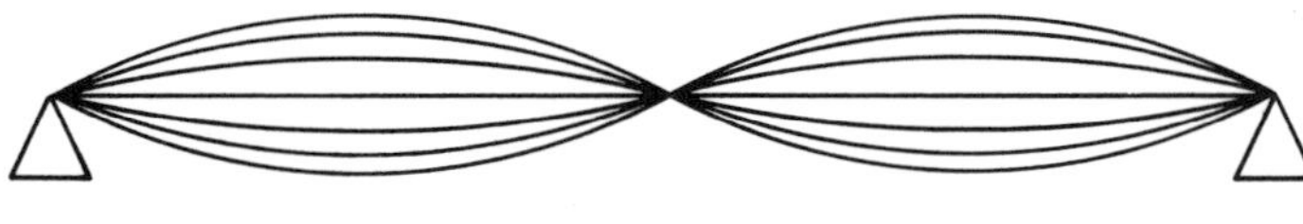

Second harmonic

*In our terminology, the first harmonic equals the fundamental. In another common system, the term "first harmonic" designates what we are here calling the second harmonic, and the other names are likewise shifted by one number. The principles are identical, and the difference is only in the terminology.

Third Harmonic

A harmonic struck one third of the string length from either end (frets 7 or 19) sets up three loops. At these points the overtones of the six open guitar strings equal the pitch of the notes at fret 19, an octave and a fifth above the open strings. These third harmonics vibrate at three times the frequency of their respective open-string fundamentals.

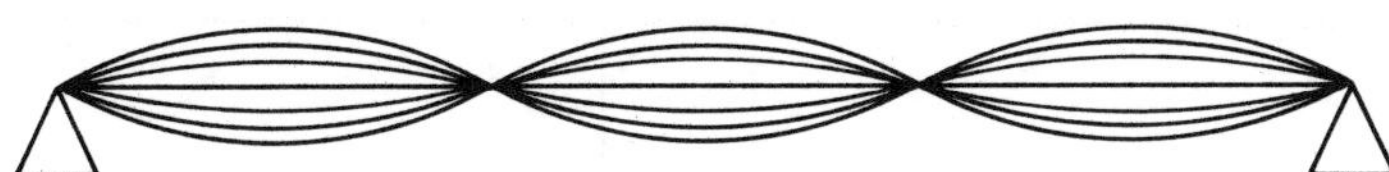

Third harmonic

Fourth Harmonic

If the harmonic is struck one fourth of the distance from either end of the string (fret 5 or the hypothetical 24th fret, located shortly beyond the end of most fretboards), four equal loops result, producing the harmonic two octaves higher than the open-string fundamental and one octave higher than the two-loop second harmonic.

Fourth harmonic

Delicate eighth harmonics of the open-string notes (an octave higher than the fourth harmonics) may be carefully struck at frets 17, just above fret 2, and the hypothetical fret 36, located a couple of inches ahead of the bridge.

Fifth Harmonic

A one fifth-length harmonic may be struck at frets 4, 9, 16, and the hypothetical 28th, producing overtones of the open strings one octave higher than the notes at fret 16. The distance from the ends of the string to frets 9 and 16 is equal to two fifths the open string length.

Composite Vibrations

These calculations are based upon the vibration of a "perfect" string. Actually, the vigorous pluck of a typical musical instrument string produces a *composite* tone resulting from the simultaneous interaction of the fundamental and one or more *overtones.* (Overtones or *upper partials* are any component tones that are higher than the fundamental. Since harmonics are exact multiples of the fundamental, they constitute a special class of overtones. The terms are often interchanged.) As the string vibrates in a single loop at the fundamental frequency, it also vibrates in two loops at twice the fundamental. The result is the combination of the fundamental and its second harmonic.

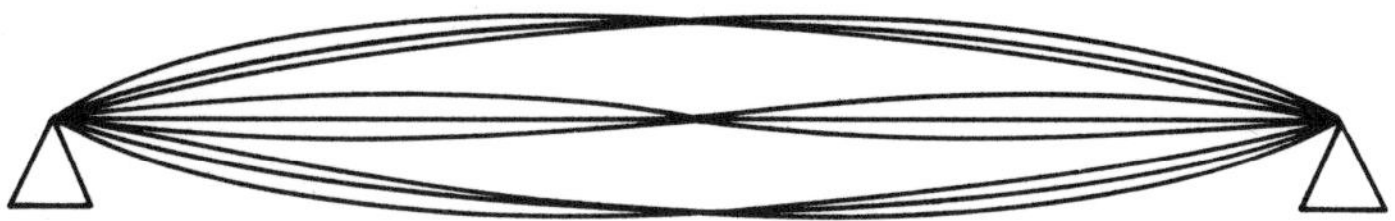

Composite vibrations

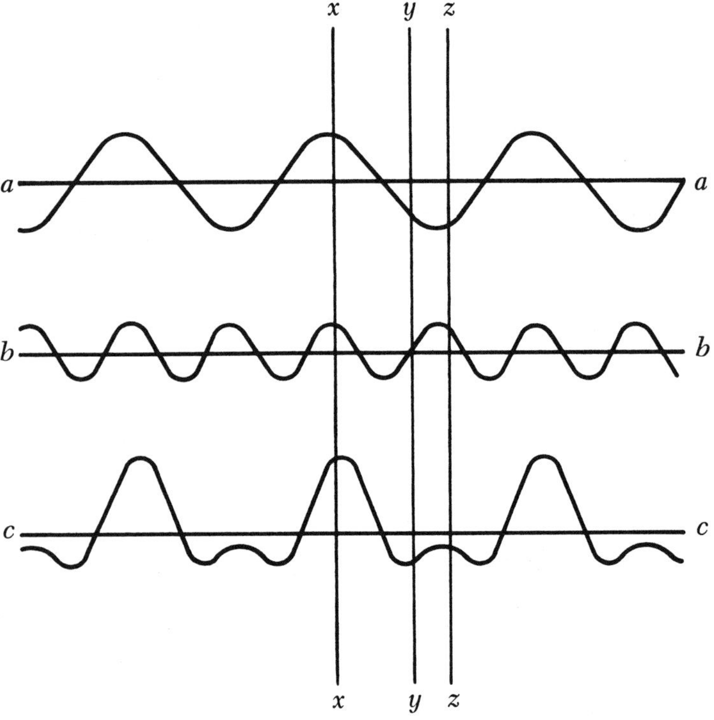

Figures *a*, *b*, and *c* illustrate the wave forms of the fundamental, the second harmonic, and the combination of both. Since the maximum peak in wave form *a* occurs simultaneously with a maximum peak in wave form *b*, the maximum peak in the composite wave form *c* equals the sum of the two. (See vertical line *x*.) The rest of wave form *c* also results from the sum of *a* and *b* (vertical lines *y* and *z*).

When a string is gently picked toward its center, an even wave form results with emphasis on the fundamental. When picked vigorously near the bridge, a more complex wave form is produced, consisting of both the fundamental and various overtones. This phenomenon has been a source of confusion, even among respected guitar manufacturers.

Thick strings tend to produce fewer high overtones than thin strings. This is why flexible nylon strings are mellow, as compared to the bright sound of higher-tension steel strings. Playing with a pick will emphasize harmonics more than playing with the fingers.

Fundamental wave form

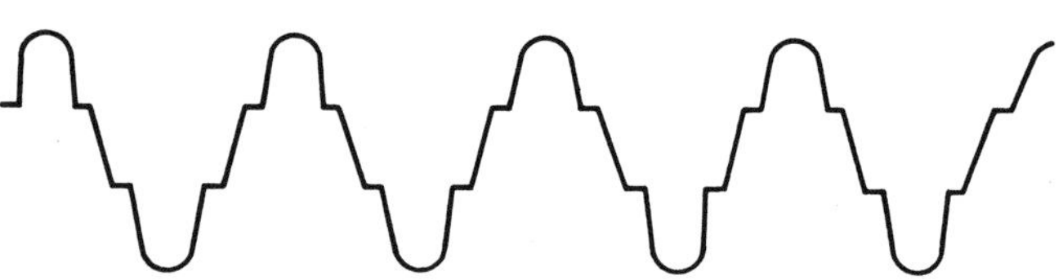

Complex wave with harmonics

Multiple Harmonics

Harmonics may be sounded in groups, up to six at a time, by touching the desired number of strings with a single left-hand finger and plucking them simultaneously with the pick or the fingers of the right hand. The harmonics on strings 2, 3, and 4 comprise a G chord at frets 12 (one octave higher than the open notes) and 5 (two octaves higher than the open notes), and a D chord at frets 19 or 7. Since the G and D chords are found together in both the keys of G (G, C, and D) and D (D, G, and A), there are many possibilities of substituting harmonics for the notes and chords in those keys. The same three strings at frets 4, 9, and 16 produce harmonics of the notes in a B major chord.

Sometimes the best effects are gained through the use of random, dissonant overtones, which are not part of the rhythm chord, and by retuning the guitar in various ways, even more possibilities arise. Try experimenting with different combinations of string, fret, and tuning. Listen to the effect produced when you strike the open string and touch a finger to a harmonic node a moment later; the note will jump from its fundamental up to the harmonic.

The following chart lists the harmonic overtones

produced at various frets on each of the open strings. At far right, the chord mentioned is the product of simultaneously sounding all six harmonics at the specified fret.

STRING # :	6	5	4	3	2	1	
Open String Fundamental	E	A	D	G	B	E	
2d Harmonic: (1 Octave)	E	A	D	G	B	E	Fret 12 (Em 11)
3d Harmonic:	B	E	A	D	F#	B	Frets 7 or 19 (Bm 11)
4th Harmonic: (2 Octaves)	E	A	D	G	B	E	Frets 5 or 24* (Em 11)
5th Harmonic:	G#	C#	F#	B	D#	G#	Frets 4, 9, 16, or 28 (G#m11)
6th Harmonic: (One octave above 3rd harmonic)	B	E	A	D	F#	B	Fret 3 1/3, 31 (Bm 11)
8th Harmonic: (One octave above 4th harmonic)	E	A	D	G	B	E	Fret 36, and just above Fret 2 (Em 11)

Harmonics can add emotional dimensions to music: serene, introspective, and melancholy (Bobby Whitlock's "Thorn Tree in the Garden," on *Layla*, Derek and The Dominos); light and frolicsome ("You Don't Have To Cry," *Crosby, Stills & Nash*); or eerie, floating, lost-in-space (introduction to Canned Heat's "On The Road Again"). Another example of the ethereal but powerful character of harmonics is found in Steve Howe's striking intro to "Roundabout" (*Fragile*, by Yes). Folk and classical artists also use harmonics.

Harmonics of Fretted Notes

Any fundamental has harmonics, and the overtones of fretted notes may be produced through the same principles used with open strings. When an F note is played on the first string, the shorter string length now runs from the new anchor at fret 1 to the bridge. The new halfway point is moved from fret 12 to fret 13, and a second harmonic may be struck in this manner:

*Most fretboards have no more than 22 frets, though a few have twenty-four. Some fret locations mentioned here (24, 28, 31, 36) are hypothetical, based on an imaginary fretboard running the entire length of the string. Harmonics may be produced at all of these positions, since actual frets aren't required.

1. Fret the F note in the usual fashion, fret 1.

2. Touch the first finger of the right hand to the string (do not depress it) at the position one octave higher than the fretted F (directly over the new halfway point, fret 13). This creates the new node.

3. With either a pick or another right-hand finger, or thumb, strike the string behind the first finger, between the node and the bridge.

Additional harmonics may be isolated by dividing the new string length (or *any* string length) into thirds, fourths, and so on. For example, fret the F note and repeat steps (2) and (3) with the new node at fret 6 (one fourth of the new string length) to produce a harmonic *two* octaves higher than the 1st-fret fundamental F note. Try it with F# at fret 2, and sound harmonics at fret 14 (one octave) and fret 7 (two octaves), and so on.

Harmonics may also be produced by a certain picking technique. See page 217.

Parts and Adjustments

ACTION

"Action" is resistance offered by the strings when they are depressed. It depends upon both the distance from the strings to the fingerboard and the string tension. Studies at C. F. Martin & Company's acoustic-research lab found that the tension exerted by bronze strings varies from 170 pounds (light gauge) to 190 pounds (medium), up to just over 200 pounds (heavy gauge).* As far as bridge height is concerned, there is no "correct" action. It's up to you; experiment with several settings. The lower the action, the less effort is required to depress the strings. As the action is lowered, it becomes more important for the neck adjustment to be accurate. If the action is *too* low or if the neck is out of line, the strings will vibrate against the frets, causing a tinny buzz. This noise can be aggravated by the use of light-gauge strings because of their increased flexibility.

*Courtesy of *Guitar Player Magazine.*

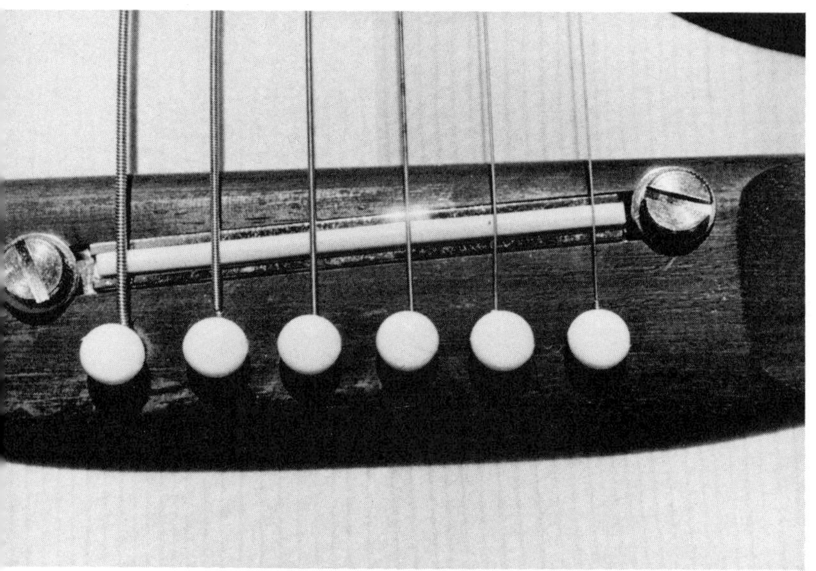

Adjustable bridges (above and below)

The Bridge

Nonadjustable Bridge

Flat-top nylon and steel-string guitars usually have a wooden tailpiece and a stationary bridge saddle of bone, ivory, or plastic. The two pieces are fitted together and glued to the top. If the strings are too high for comfortable playing, have your dealer remove the saddle and file it or sand it down a bit along the bottom edge. If they are too low, a fixed bridge can be raised by inserting a shim (a narrow, flat sliver) of wood or plastic in the slot between the saddle and bridge base. Homemade shims may be fashioned from matchbook covers, a couple of guitar picks, a paperback book cover, and so forth.* Many saddles are held in place only by the tension of the strings and readily lift out of the slot once the strings are loosened. Others may be glued, requiring a couple of light taps on each end with a mallet. To keep the saddle from leaning forward, at least half of it should be sunk into the bridge slot.

Adjustable Bridge

Virtually all electric guitars, arched-top models, and some steel-stringed flat-tops have bridges that are adjustable for height. Flat-top bridges have two spring-tension screw assemblies. One common type has the bridge saddle supported on two narrow bolts by a thin wheel at each end. By turning the wheel the bridge is raised or lowered on either the bass or treble side.

Some models, including many Fenders, enable the guitarist to adjust the height of each individual string. These bridges consist of a single master saddle, adjustable at both ends, with six separate bridges, each having two tiny screws for raising or lowering that string.

On acoustic guitars, an adjustable bridge is not necessarily better than a nonadjustable one. The world's finest flat tops are nonadjustable, the theory being that the adjusting mechanism is an obstacle to the transfer of vibrations from the strings to the top, deadening the tone. You can still modify the height of a nonadjustable bridge either by sanding or with shims.

*Acoustic guitars by Ovation feature precut removable shims, each of which changes the action $^1/_{64}$"

Rocker Bridge

A rocker bridge or "floating" device accompanies a hand vibrato (p. 217). When the lever is depressed and the strings are loosened, the master bridge moves with them, eliminating friction between the string and saddle. Gibson's Tune-O-Matic bridges on vibrato-equipped guitars have special adjusting wheels which are beveled on top to permit the bridge to rock. If they're flat, the bridge may become dislocated, disturbing the intonation. Fender's Jazzmaster-type floating bridge rocks on two pointed screws, one at the bottom of each master bridge post. Guitarists who frequently use the hand vibrato may have persistent tuning problems, since the rocking feature may cause the base of the bridge to shift, requiring a resetting.

Testing the Action

Rhythm players sometimes prefer a relatively high action for hard, clean strumming. On the other hand, if you want the lowest possible action for playing lead, without the annoying rattle, set it a little high to start with, then strike a few single notes at various fret locations, bending each one up to the pitch of the note two frets higher, sustaining it for a few moments with a finger vibrato. (You'll rarely need to bend a note much higher than a pitch-distance of two frets.) Keep doing this while lowering the bridge in very small increments. As soon as that bent note starts to buzz or fade out early, the action is set too low for a clean sound.

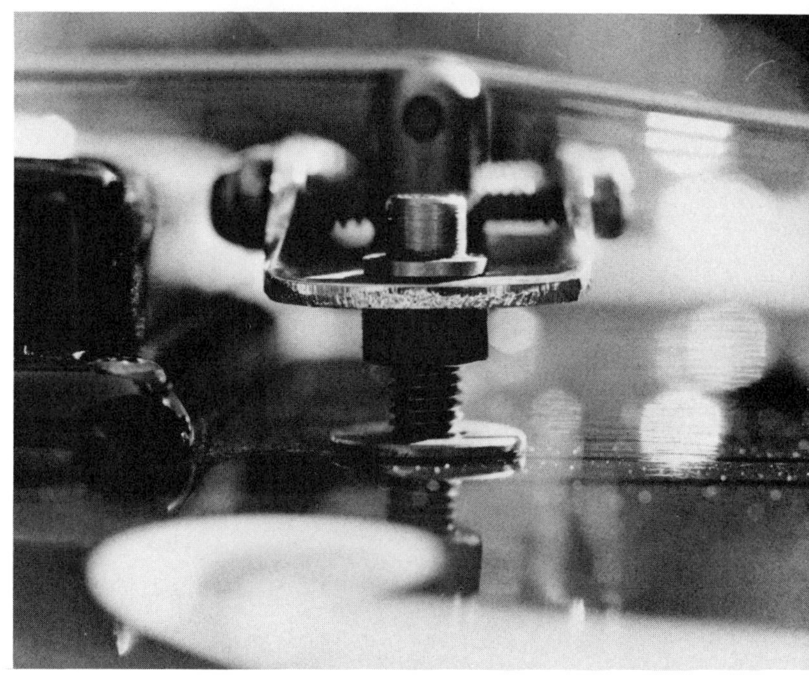

Manufacturers have standards for adjusting the distance from the underside of the string to the crest of the fret (measured at the point where the neck and body are joined): $\frac{7}{64}''$ to $\frac{8}{64}''$ on the bass side and $\frac{5}{64}''$ to $\frac{6}{64}''$ on the treble side for a flat-top steel-string guitar with an average action. Each measurement is increased $\frac{2}{64}''$ or more for classic, nylon-string guitars. It takes a shift of only $\frac{1}{64}''$ to change an "average" action to "low" or "high."*

Great players such as Freddie King, Mike Bloomfield, and Peter Townshend prefer strings that are heavier than the super-lights and a not-so-low action. If the setting on your bridge is presently ultra-low, you may find that note-bending becomes easier by raising your action, enabling you to get underneath the string with more surface area of your finger.

*Gibson sets the action of the Les Paul Custom "Fretless Wonder" down to $\frac{4}{64}''$ (bass) and $\frac{3}{64}''$ (treble) at the 12th fret.

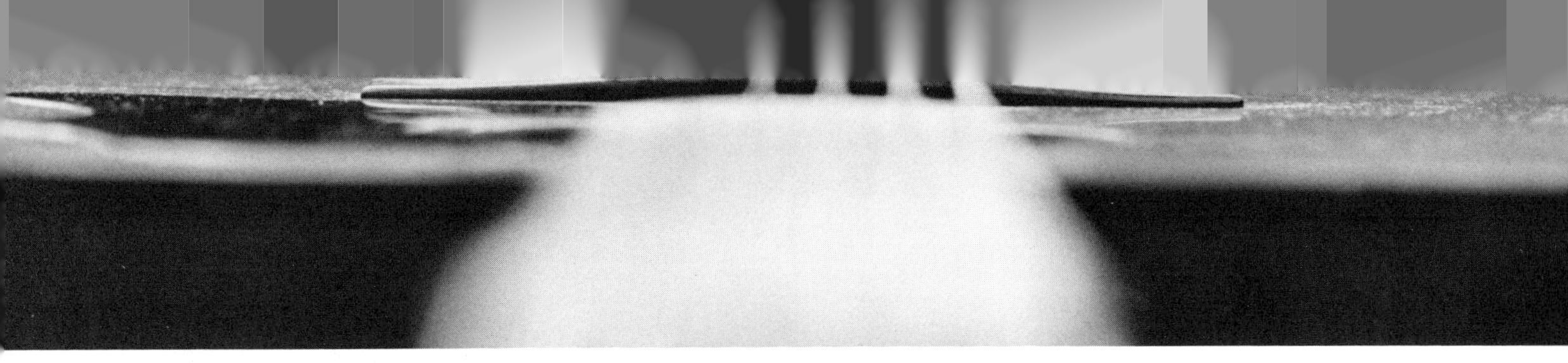

Note how the bass side of the saddle is set higher than the treble.

If you play with a low bridge setting, a lighter pick stroke will help to eliminate rattling. Also, make sure that none of the strings vibrate against the pickups. Another point: if the bridge is set too low, a bent string may buzz or die out when pushed against the fingerboard's center arch.

Bridge Saddle: Slot Depth

Sometimes a string may be seated too deeply in its bridge saddle groove, resulting in a lifeless tone. If the string sinks to a depth greater than its diameter, file down the saddle, barely reducing the depth of the slot. The filing is easy, and alleviating this deep-slot problem will increase your sustain, in addition to improving the tone. A common mistake is to file the notch parallel to the base of the bridge, producing a flat slot in which the string literally bounces and rattles. The slot should be angled, so that it slopes down, away from the fretboard, toward the tailpiece. The string then breaks over a single point, producing a clear tone.

The bass strings are both greater in diameter and more flexible than the treble strings, causing them to vibrate over a larger area. To keep the bass strings from rattling against the frets, the top of the saddle may be slanted to keep them higher off the fingerboard.

The Tailpiece

The design of the tailpiece affects the ability of the strings to sustain a note. If the distance from the bridge to the tailpiece is short, and if the "breakover" angle is sharp, then the body receives the string vibrations more directly than it otherwise would. Examples of this type of sustain-improving tailpiece are found on many solid-body guitars, not including most with a hand vibrato.*

Many semi-solid guitars including Gibson's ES-335 and others, which have a long, trapeze-style tailpiece may be refitted with a Les Paul-type "stop" tailpiece.†

Gibson Stud (or stop) tailpiece

* The Badass, designed by Glen Quan, is considered by many to be the best combination bridge/tailpiece available. It is especially recommended for Les Paul Jrs., Specials, and other solid-bodies that do not provide individual adjustments for string length.

† The 335 was fitted with the stop tailpiece when introduced in early 1958. Some repairmen caution against setting the tailpiece too low, since the sharp angle may cause string breakage.

Holes are drilled through the top, and the tailpiece is anchored in the interior block of wood. The amount of sustain improvement varies from barely noticeable to substantial, depending upon the density of the wood as well as the tailpiece design.

The Angle of the Neck

On guitars with detachable necks, you can lower the action by inserting a shim or two between the body and the neck at the point where they meet, placing the fingerboard closer to the strings. However, neck adjustments are usually performed only to correct buzzing or improper intonation.

Guitars by Earthwood, Fender's Stratocasters, and some Telecaster models since 1972 feature an adjustment system that allows for making slight changes in the angle of the neck, eliminating the necessity of shims.

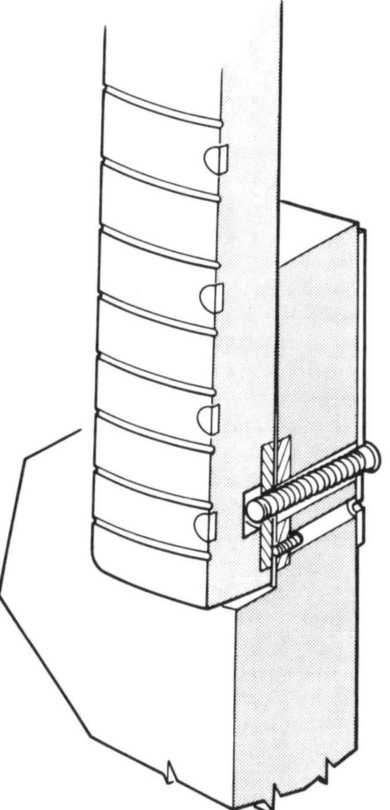

Fender Micro-Tilt neck adjustment

Adjusting the Nut

If the notches in the nut are too deep, the strings will vibrate against the first fret, causing an infuriating buzz. If they are too shallow, the strings will be hard to fret. Deepen the grooves with a rat-tail nut file. After every few strokes, tune up the string to its proper pitch and play the note at the first fret to see that it doesn't rattle. If you do file the notch too deeply, replace the nut. Like the notches in the bridge saddle, the slots in the nut must be angled down, away from the fingerboard to prevent rattling.

A temporary shim (a chip from a pick, a bit of cardboard) may be glued into the groove to raise the notch until the new nut is installed. If all of the notches are too deep to start with, the action may be raised by inserting a shim or two between the nut and its slot in the neck.

Mosrites, Gretsches, Dan Armstrongs, some Dobros, and a few Gibson classics have an extra "zero" fret (pp. 35–36), next to the nut, which presents special problems in changing the depth of the slots. Leave the task for an expert.

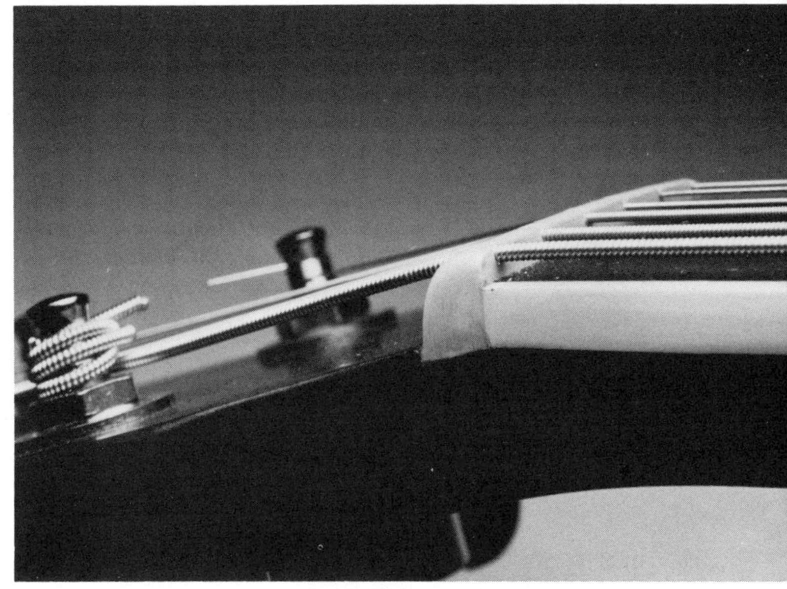

Note the angle of string breakover at the nut.

STRING LENGTH AND INTONATION

"Intonation" refers to the ability of the guitar to be played in tune at all fret locations. It depends upon

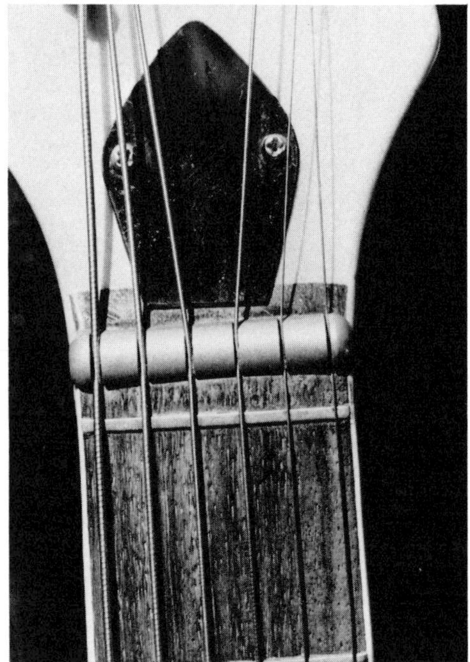
Metal nut and zero fret

Compensating bridge

string length, among other things. Manufacturers' length adjustments are usually correct, though exceptions occur. If an intonation problem is caused by worn-out or corroded strings, replace the faulty string or the entire set. Until you do, a string length adjustment can usually improve the intonation temporarily. Sometimes a bridge can become dislocated when loosening the strings. If you set the tuning machines so that an open E chord sounds perfect, but a barred chord farther up the neck is hopelessly out of tune, then you need to adjust the bridge for string length (assuming that the neck is straight and that the strings are in good shape).

Many electric guitars are fitted with six screws or movable slides that run through the individual bridges in a direction parallel to the neck. By turning one of these screws, the corresponding bridge is moved closer to, or further away from, the nut. This adjustment for string length facilitates accurate intonation. There are two available guides in checking a length adjustment: simple measurement and pitch.

If the tension of the string remained constant, then the distance from the nut to the 12th fret would be exactly the same as the distance from the 12th fret to the bridge. However, the bridge is actually moved back a distance of about 2 mm., or less, toward the tailpiece. This slight increase in the string length compensates for the fact that depressing the string to the fingerboard stretches it, increases its tension, and thus raises its pitch.

When fretting steel strings, some are sharped (raised) more than others, varying the amount of compensation required. The different patterns of string vibration dictate that the treble strings may be set closer to the fingerboard than the bass strings (see p. 208), and so they are not stretched as much when fretted. This means that their pitch is not raised as much, and they don't require as much compensation as the bass strings. Therefore, the bass side of the bridge is moved back a little farther than the treble side, resulting in the common angled bridge. A *compensating* bridge sets the 3rd string (G) to have the shortest length.

There are several variables mentioned in these pages: string gauge, vibration patterns, tension, and so on. Together they cause an interdependence between string length and string height. In summary, depressing the string causes it to stretch, *raising* its pitch. Setting the bridge to increase the string length *lowers* the pitch. The bridge is designed to balance these principles.

To use the pitch method of length adjustment, sound a harmonic directly over the 12th fret (not just behind it as you do when fretting a regular note). This is done by barely touching a left-hand finger to the string at the proper location, without depressing the string at all, and lightly picking it near the bridge with the right hand. The left-hand finger should be removed a split second after striking the string with the pick. (More on harmonics on pp. 199–204.) Compare the pitch of this harmonic tone to the pitch of the actual note played at fret 12. If the fretted note is lower than the harmonic (flat), then the string length is too long and should be shortened by moving the bridge forward, toward the nut. If the fretted note is higher than the harmonic (sharp), move the bridge back toward the tailpiece, increasing the string length.

You may find a thin indentation or scratch in the finish of an arched-top instrument at the point where the edge of the bridge is positioned. Provided you have it in the right place to start with, this guideline will be all you need in the future. A strip of double-faced masking tape in between the bridge base and guitar top will hold the bridge in place.

Flat-top acoustic guitars are generally not adjustable for string length. If an intonation difficulty arises, attempt to remedy it with a new set of strings or (if warranted) a neck adjustment. If the factory installed the bridge incorrectly, contact your dealer about a bridge replacement or regluing.

See the comments on electronic tuners and stroboscopes in Chapter 10. Such devices can be most helpful in measuring intonation.

SPACING ADJUSTMENT

Each individual bridge may be slotted to accommodate the string in several places, allowing the guitarist to set them closer together or farther apart from each other. The same advantage is found with roller-wheel bridges which traverse a master bridge bolt. A small file may be used on most types of saddles to fashion new notches, changing the distance between the strings.

Gibson Tune-O-Matic bridge insert

FENDER

NECK-ROD ADJUSTMENTS

When a steel-string guitar is tuned to the standard A-440 pitch,* the strings exert about 165 to 200 pounds of pressure on the neck. To keep the neck from bowing under the strain, most steel-string guitars are fitted with a counterbalancing steel alloy rod, which runs inside the length of the neck. Martin's 0-18T and guitars by Ramírez of Madrid have an ebony cross-grained rod for reinforcement. Some manufacturers install two parallel truss rods in twelve-string necks because of the extreme difference in tension between the bass side and treble side.

The added strength permits narrower necks, and since the tension is often adjustable, most bows, bends, and warps below the 12th fret (caused by changes in stress or sudden variations in humidity) may be repaired without removing the fingerboard. A neck with a warp or a twist between the 12th fret and the guitar body must sometimes be returned to the factory for repair. Even a change in string gauge may require a slight neck adjustment because of the differences in tension among various gauges.

The neck rod or "truss rod" was invented in the 1920s by Ted McHugh, one of Orville Gibson's jamming partners and employees. It exerts approximately 20 in./lbs. of torque on a mahogany neck and a slightly greater amount on the more dense maple necks. This torsion can be modified with the use of a screwdriver, an Allen wrench, or a special tool. Many guitars have a small plate, on the face of the peghead, which covers a slot where the rod protrudes from inside the neck. Removal of the plate exposes the rod for adjustment. In other models (many Fenders), the opposite end of the rod is fitted with the adjusting mechanism at the point where the neck is joined to the guitar body. Most nylon-string instruments do not feature adjustable necks, though Ovation is one exception.

Sighting down the length of the fingerboard from the peghead to the tailpiece looks spiffy, but unless you're an expert, or unless the neck is a real roller-coaster, it's difficult to assess neck alignment using this method alone. Let your repairman check for either a convex (arched in the middle) or a concave bend. Manufacturers' designs vary, but in most cases a clockwise twist of the neck-rod adjustment screw will tighten the rod, correcting a concave bow, and a counterclockwise turning will remedy a convex arch by loosening the torque. At all times standard tuning

*Standardized tuning systems are explained in Chapter 10.

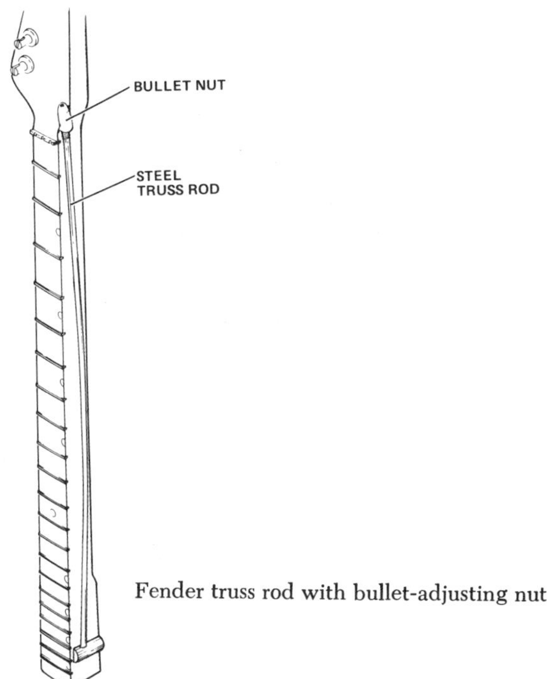

Fender truss rod with bullet-adjusting nut

Truss rod, cutaway view

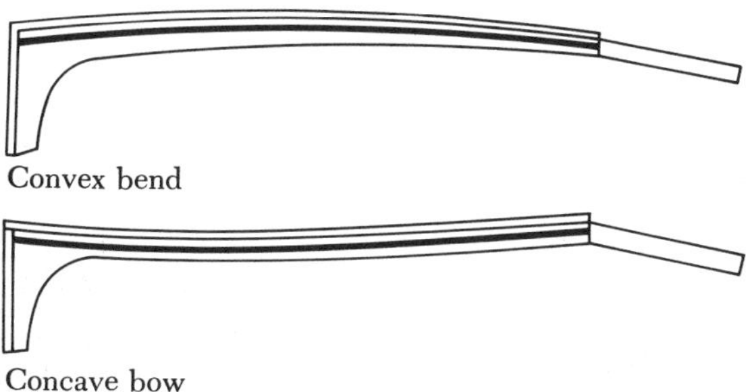

Convex bend

Concave bow

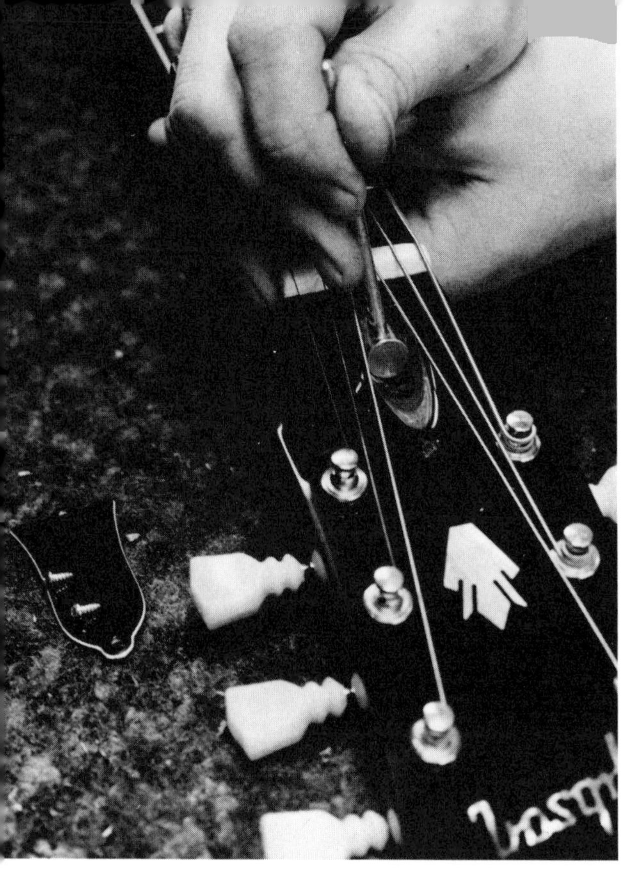

Adjusting the neck rod

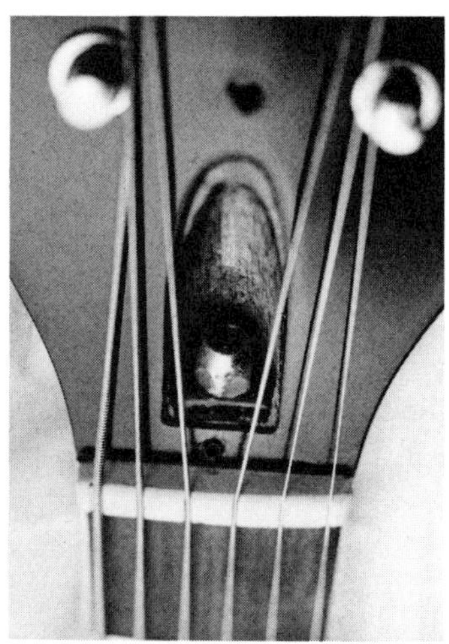

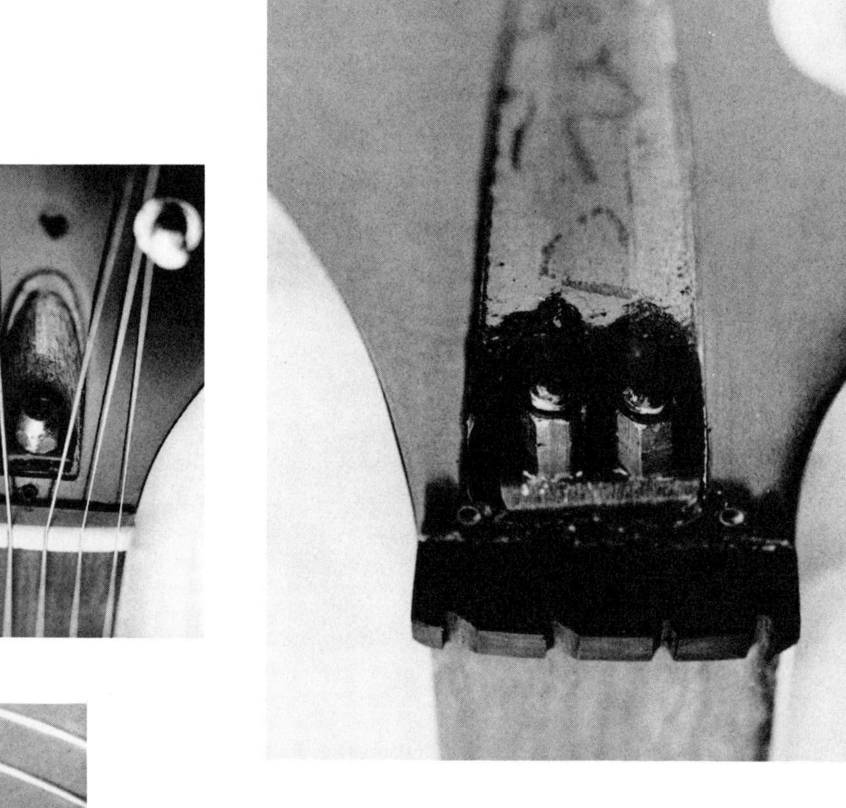

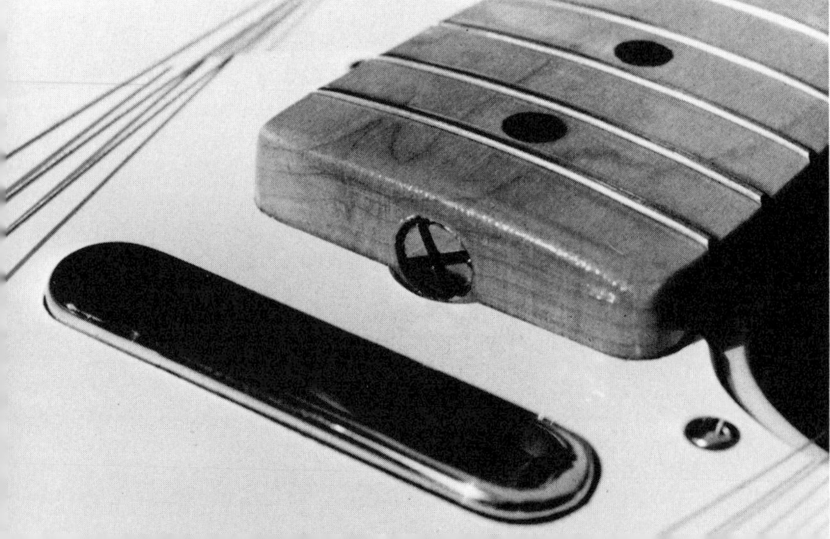

should be maintained, a precaution that may require several slight modifications of pitch. Whether tightening or loosening the rod, adjustments should be made in very small increments—quarter turns—with careful visual inspection along every step.

A popular misconception is that the neck must be perfectly straight to avoid buzzing. In fact, the guitar will fret true if the neck has a .005″ to .015″ concave curve (dipped in the middle). This barely detectable bow compensates for the fact that the string vibrates over a greater distance at its flexible center than at the ends. To check the neck, depress either the 1st or 6th string at fret 1 and at the fret where the neck joins the body. The string will form a straight line, and if there is a concave curve in the neck, there will be a space between the string and frets near the center of the fretboard.*

If the string touches all of the frets the neck may have a convex counterwarp (arched in the middle). If it touches one fret but not the immediately surrounding ones, then that fret is too high. If the space between the string and the frets is too great, then the concave bend is too extreme.

A number of repairmen use a ruler or other straightedge to gauge the uniformity of the height of the frets. This guide depends upon the shape of the neck.

Gibson warns that, in regard to its instruments: "Guitar necks are not identical with violin necks. If neck adjustments are made with a truss rod to set all frets touching against a straightedge, playing action will be greatly hampered by back lashes and buzzing, especially when higher fret positions are used."

A torque wrench may be used to measure the tension. All companies urge that the work be performed by an experienced professional repairman. Unless you are knowledgeable about the mechanics of neck rods, do *not* try the adjustment yourself. Overtightening can snap the rod, and repair involves the expensive job of removing the fingerboard.

*Los Angeles guitar builder John Carruthers specifies .005 to .015. Ovation allows a little leeway: the clearance should be a minimum of .005 to .020 on their instruments. They state: " . . . it should not be more than .032 (1/32″) or the neck is warped [concave] . . . if either E touches the 5th fret, the neck [has a convex bend] . . . a little extra clearance will help, if the strings are buzzing when played."

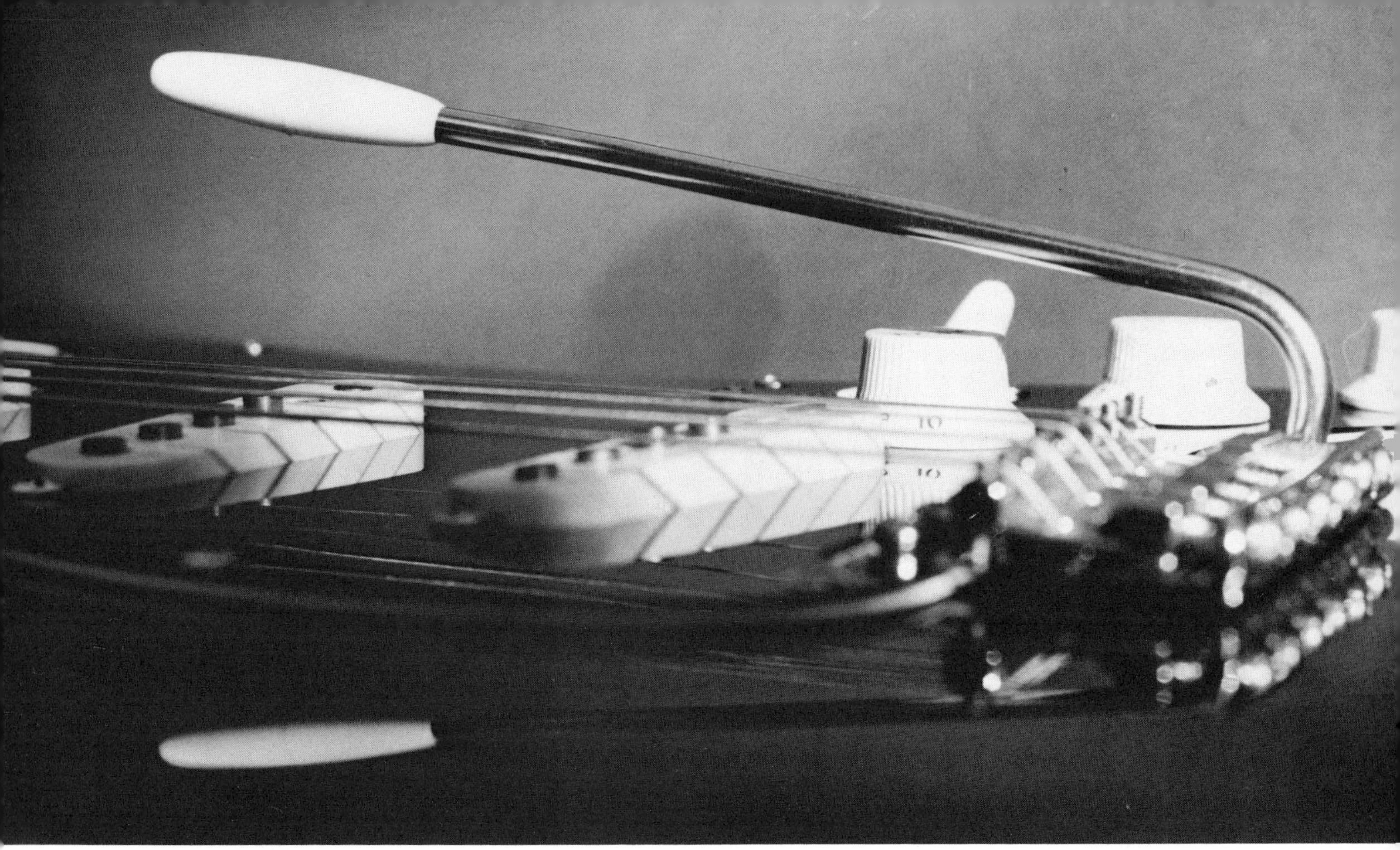

Stratocaster, hand tremolo

Bigsby, solid body

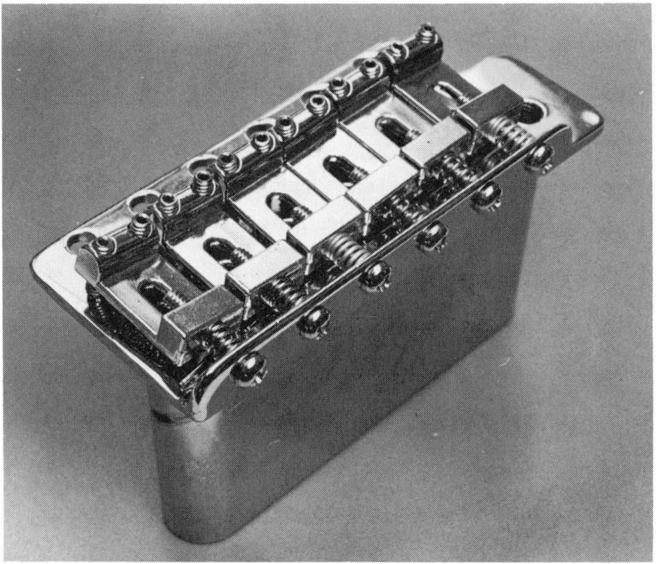

Stratocaster combination bridge/vibrato block

HAND VIBRATOS

One of the first special effects, the still-popular hand vibrato consists of a lever that attaches to the tailpiece at the bottom of the guitar body. When this handle is depressed, the tension of the strings is loosened a bit, causing them to lower in pitch. When the lever is released, a spring returns it to its original position and (hopefully) normal pitch is restored. With a light touch on the lever, you can get a note or chord to waver gently, and with a steady application and release, the result is a rippling effect. Chet Atkins is one artist who uses this technique with delicate, expressive results. With a heavy touch, you can create effects that sound like the twanging of a heavy spring. Feedback can be used to generate sounds like high-pitched screams or the drone of a jet airplane, and the vibrato handle can make these tones soar up and down like an air-raid siren. Classic examples by the late wizard of special effects, Jimi Hendrix, include: "Red House" (live version—*Hendrix in the West* album) and "Star Spangled Banner" (*Woodstock*).

Sometimes the unit is named a "hand tremolo," but this terminology is incorrect, since a tremolo is an electronic circuit which produces minute changes in loudness, and a true vibrato causes variations of pitch. The confusion of terms arises from the fact that the *electronic* vibrato (mounted in the amp) is practically indistinguishable from the tremolo effect (see p. 277).

Bigsby, hollow body

Care and Adjustments

A hand vibrato is a fairly simple mechanical assembly, and an occasional drop of oil at the points of friction is all you will need to keep it in working order. On an instrument equipped with a vibrato, change the strings one at a time. This way, you will stabilize the tension of the strings, and the bridge and tailpiece adjustments won't be disturbed.

Since the hand vibrato employs a single heavy spring, or a set of lighter springs, to counterbalance the tension of the strings, the strings are, in effect, floating or suspended. The tension is not set as securely as when the strings are anchored to a regular tailpiece, so the guitarist may spend more time retuning, especially if the strings are worn or if his vibrato technique is particularly vigorous. (Read the discussion of tailpiece designs and string tension, p. 208). You can alter the action or response of the hand vibrato by substituting a heavier or a lighter spring.

Stratocaster, back plate removed

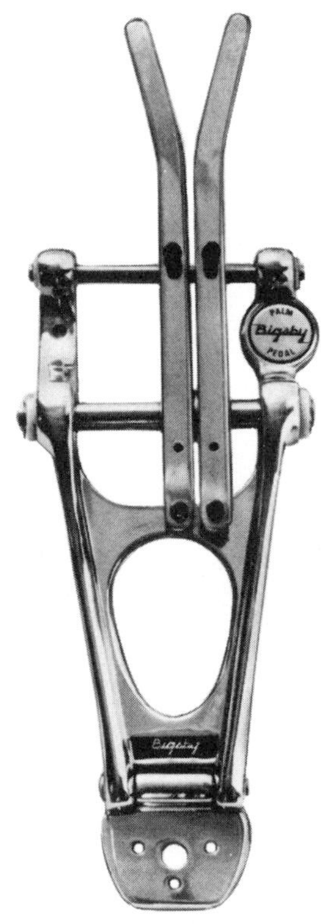

The easily installed Bigsby Palm Pedal allows a change of one or two notes in a chord without affecting the others. A small set screw in each lever permits adjustment of the interval. Skilled players can use the unit to approximate the liquid glissando effects of a pedal steel.

Among the most famous hand vibratos are the single-spring aluminum alloy and stainless steel devices designed by Bigsby, featuring a needle-bearing roller bar. Fender introduced its multi-spring "hand tremolo" in the mid-1950s, and its stiffer action makes it especially good for aggressive rock styles. The plate on the back of the Stratocaster* allows for the removal or addition of a spring to vary the action. It now comes with three springs installed and a pair of extras. If switching to a heavier gauge of string, add one or both extra springs to counterbalance the increased tension.

* In 1974, the Strat-type vibrato became available as an optional accessory on the Telecaster Deluxe. Very few of these guitars were made—perhaps only fifty and no more than one hundred.

The Parsons/White String Bender or pull-string permits the guitarist to enjoy one of the advantages of a pedal steel: the ability to raise or lower a note by a preset interval without altering the position of either hand. It incorporates a bell-crank linkage, which fits into a large rout in the back of the guitar, plus a small button installed just behind the bridge and a tuning screw for interval presets. The linkage connects to the strap button, and the bender is engaged when the guitar is pressed downward against the pull of the strap. The unit fits best into a Telecaster, Esquire, or Broadcaster.

The String Bender was designed by former Byrd Gene Parsons and the legendary Clarence White. After much experimentation, they concluded that the B string was the most practical for connection to the linkage. It is particularly effective in the resolution of suspended chords. In the hands of a good player who has mastered it, the Bender can give a guitar some of the emotional and vocal qualities of a pedal steel. Examples: "Dark End of the Street," Linda Ronstadt; "Comin' into Los Angeles," Arlo Guthrie, Clarence White on pull-string; "Peaceful Easy Feeling" and "Tequila Sunrise," Eagles, Bernie Leadon on pull-string.

13

General Care

Try a little tenderness. If you treat your guitar the same as you'd treat any other friend, it will perform well for many years. There are a few details that you should know about the care of musical instruments, but many of these suggestions are common sense.

THE GUITAR

Moderate fluctuations in the weather are harmless, but severe changes in either the temperature or humidity can damage any delicate piece of wood. Rosewood, maple, spruce, mahogany, cedar, and other woods used in guitar building are chosen for several reasons—resonance, beauty, strength, and so forth. However, these woods are hygroscopic—they both absorb and retain moisture from the air. Different woods vary in density and have pores of different sizes. Consequently, they vary in their degree of moisture absorption. Since the guitar is a unity of counterbalanced tension, problems arise when its woods react unevenly to changes in the weather, expanding and shrinking at different rates. Excessive moisture can expand the wood and loosen the adhesives, while sudden and extreme dryness or high temperatures can cause the wood to contract and split. Most factory-produced instruments are quite dry when they leave the plant, having been made in climate-controlled conditions.

Martin D-35

Still, no matter how well the woods of your guitar have been seasoned and coated, some moisture will be absorbed.

A manufacturer's recommendation of safe maximum relative humidity is from 60 percent to 85 percent for both steel-and nylon-string instruments. Maintaining this comfortable environment for your guitar requires only a little attention. In moderate to dry climates, put a slightly damp cloth or one of the inexpensive guitar humidifiers in the string compartment of the case to avoid drying out the guitar. In a wet climate, small packets of a super-absorbent sand-like material called silica gel, available at camera stores, will keep the guitar from absorbing too much moisture. Owners of the most delicate instruments may have a hygrometer (humidity indicator) installed in the case for accurate monitoring. Keep the guitar away from damp environments if possible.

Don't ignore the obvious safeguards such as keeping the guitar away from heaters. If you live in a cold climate, avoid exposing it to rapid temperature changes. For example, having survived the winter snows to trudge to a friend's party with your guitar, don't sit down by the fireplace immediately upon arriving to strum a few tunes. Instead, leave the guitar in the case awhile, so that it can gradually adjust to the warm house. This helps to prevent finish cracks or "checking." Checking happens when the finish doesn't warm up as fast as the wood. The wood swells, the finish can't keep up, and it's split into hundreds of hairline fractures on the surface. Gibson recommends that before exposing a cold instrument to warm air, you "fan" it with the case lid while in the case. "If a bright bluish fog appears on the instrument, close the lid immediately for a minute or so. When the chill has been removed from the top . . . remove the instrument, slightly, to allow the air to circulate around the rims and back, allowing these components to adjust to the new environment."

Most electric and acoustic guitars are lacquered and may be polished with ordinary products found in music stores or even household polishes such as Johnson's Pledge. Self-leveling polish removes previous coats when applied, avoiding the damping of an acoustic guitar's tone, which can result from thick layers of wax or polish.

For rare, varnished guitars, a clean, soft cloth

should be used instead of wax-based products. The thick polyurethane finishes (for example, Fender's solid-bodies) are practically indestructible and may be polished with regular guitar products. On all guitars, simple wiping between polishings will remove fingerprints and restore the luster.

Vinyl-coated guitar straps should not be left in contact with the guitar when it is in the case. The straps can bleed, discoloring the guitar's finish.

When carrying the guitar in its case, keep the lid toward you, so that if a latch should slip and the top opens, the guitar will be less likely to fall out. When you are in the car, get into the habit of keeping your guitar propped in a place where it won't fall if the car stops suddenly. Most on-stage disasters can be avoided by keeping the guitar on a stand during breaks.

Sadly, guitars are often stolen, and sometimes never recovered. Record your serial number, and make a permanent identifying mark in a hidden spot (inside the body, underneath the truss-rod adjustment cover), just in case the guitar is stolen and the serial number is filed or sanded away.

Neck and Fingerboard

Read "Dressing the Fingerboard" in the following chapter.

Tuning Machines

If the gear slips, check to see that your guitar is properly strung (p. 181). An occasional drop of general-purpose oil such as "3-in-one" on the gear teeth should keep them turning smoothly. Many gears are housed in a metal or plastic casing to keep them clean. Oil may be squirted through a small hole that was drilled for that purpose. If the gear is completely sealed, it is most likely filled with a greaselike substance and requires no further lubrication. Examples are the excellent high-ratio (about 12 to 1) machines by Schaller and Grover.

Gold Plating

Gold-plated parts must be constantly wiped to maintain their luster. Exposure to perspiration will eventually wear off some of the plating, and the pieces that are touched most frequently, such as the vibrato handle, are the first to fade. If you decide that

Roadrunner case

Anvil road cases for guitars, amps, and PAs

Heavy-duty road case with metal edges and corner protectors

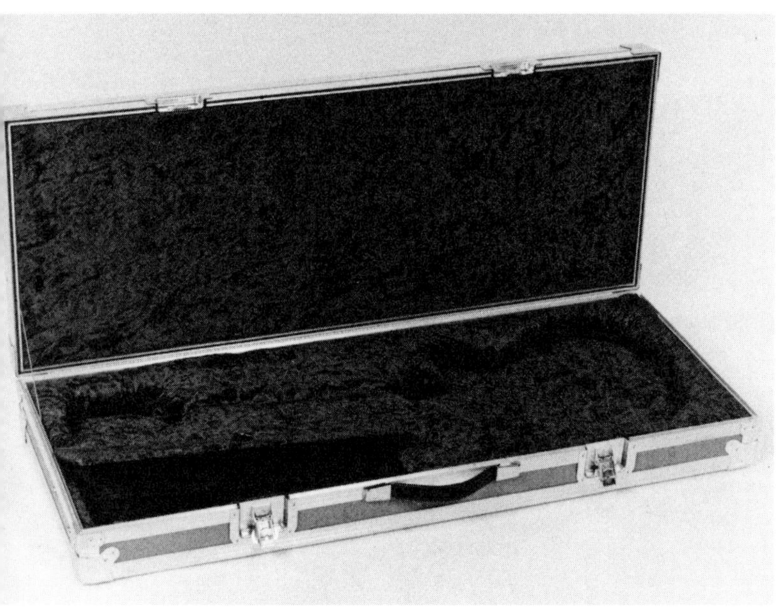

gold hardware will improve the appearance of your guitar, you can have the nickel or chromed hardware plated with gold by a jeweler. Shop around among different platers, since the costs may vary significantly. The price may depend upon the wide variety of metals sometimes involved—copper, aluminum, zinc, and others.

CASES

If you have made any sort of investment at all in your guitar, get a strong case and keep the guitar in it when it's not being played. There are four general types of cases on the market: flexible bags, softshell cardboard, hardshell veneer, and fiberglass.

Plastic carrying bags

The plastic, canvas, or simulated leather exterior and the padded lining of these low-priced bags will help guard the guitar's finish against nicks, but that's about all. Some unlined plastic covers are designed to protect hardshell cases from scratches or moisture, so be sure to buy a bag that is fitted to the instrument itself and is at least lightly padded. Ovation's heavily lined Gig Bag is one of the best available bags, much stronger than the unlined, budget kind. Harsh detergents should not be used to wash the flexible bags, but lukewarm water and plain soap will clean canvas cases, and there are several commercial products for cleaning plastic and vinyl.

Chipboard

Chipboard is pressed cardboard covered with plastic or a stitched, simulated leather. These lightweight cases come in sizes to fit all guitars, and afford much more protection against bumps and jolts than do the flexible bags. Coating with a liquid fiberglass resin and then with three coats of shellac will increase their strength. However, since it is much less durable than the hard plywood type, the chipboard case may be crushed, if subjected to substantial weight. The lack of sufficient reinforcement makes it unfit for valuable guitars.

Hardshell plywood cases

The sturdy hardshell case is made of reinforced plywood, often molded to support the neck and to fit the instrument snugly. Providing much protection, it is one of only two types of cases (the other is fiberglass or a similar synthetic) that are appropriate for expensive instruments.* The hardshell case is covered with plastic or imitation leather which is laminated to the wooden shell. Use soap and warm water or mild chemical products, formulated for plastics, to clean the exterior. If the outer covering is torn, it can be readily mended with a plastic adhesive. The exterior hardware (handle fittings, latches, locks, bump protectors) consists of solid brass, or steel with a brass or nickel plating that is resistant to rust. If a screw or rivet should be pulled loose from the case because of stripped threads or wear, simply fix the hole with a fast-drying wood filler, then sand and reinsert the screw or rivet. Should the interior lining be torn, the manufacturer can supply a replacement strip of material, which can be affixed to the plywood shell with ordinary household glue. You might send him a piece of the torn fabric so he can match the color.

Hardshell cases should be kept shut with the latches closed, because the relatively heavy lid can cause stress on the lower half of the case if left open for long periods, weakening the hinges. Furthermore, if the case is left closed, it's less subject to moisture absorption and less likely to warp. The least expensive plywood cases cost only a few dollars more than the fancier chipboard cases, and they're the best value in the low-to-moderate price range.

Fiberglass cases

Martin, Ovation, Dan Armstrong, and other companies distribute extremely tough, deluxe, molded cases made from a rigid synthetic material, such as Ovation's Boltaron. These cases are superior to the regular, hardshell, plywood cases. The interior is sculptured to fit the instrument very snugly, padded with polyurethane foam and lined with plush velour. Caution: Keep away from heaters and prolonged exposure to direct sunlight.

Custom Cases

Fragile, expensive guitars are sometimes housed in handmade, airtight cases of a strong wood or fiberglass shell with a thick foam lining. The interior provides a tight fit and is often equipped with a hygrometer. Shaped like a rounded triangle, these cases usually cost $175 and up.

* Improved products introduced in the last few years include rugged cases of high-impact plastic and metal.

In terms of strength, features, weight, and price, the rectangular ABS plastic cases by Choice Product Development are among the best bargains available. Well braced and plush lined, they fit most Gibsons and Fenders.

Anvil cases are extremely heavy duty, made with plywood panels and fitted with protective aluminum edge strips and steel corner caps.

Also investigate Gibson's rugged Protector case, made from hard Azdel, a fiberglass compound used for auto bumpers.

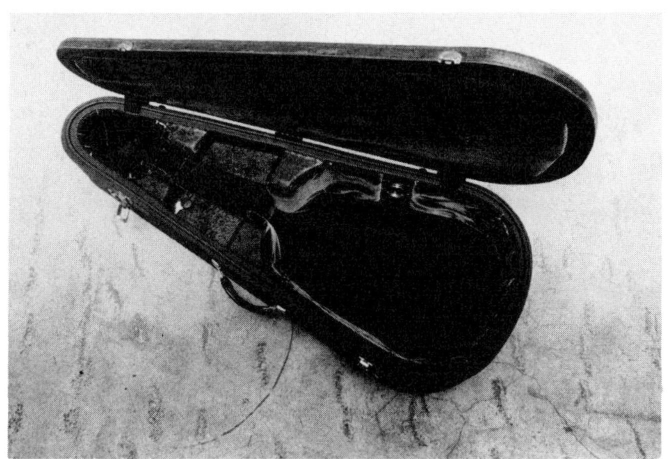

Cases—Miscellaneous Advice

The more snugly the instrument fits, the more secure it is against damage from being knocked against the walls of the case. If the case is too big, you can get a closer fit and extra protection by adding a dry towel or other pad. If the case is dropped, the guitar neck may snap at the point where it meets the peghead if not sufficiently braced by the case. This whiplash effect may be avoided by adding extra support under the base of the peghead.

When you're not playing the guitar, leave it in the case, standing on its edge or (preferably) lying down, face up. If the instrument is face down, it may press against the case, disturbing the bridge or other settings. If your guitar has a vibrato tailpiece, move the handle all the way to the rear when the guitar is in the case. Otherwise, the top may depress the handle and release it every time the case is closed or opened, causing prolonged loosening and sudden tightening of the string tension.

Guitar Lockers

The traveling musician frequently encounters the infuriating hassle of unsuccessfully attempting to carry his instrument into the passenger compartment of an airplane. (B. B. King has been known to buy a seat for Lucille.) The guitar is often tossed with regular baggage in a storage area, and no matter how much you plead (or threaten), and no matter how many "*Fragile*" stickers you put on the case, damage is common.

The guitar locker has been introduced to solve this type of problem. It is essentially a strong footlocker constructed of plywood and fiberglass and fitted with heavy-duty corners, latches, locks, and metal studs. The interior is thickly padded with dense, plush foam, cut to fit your particular instrument. They are recommended for any hard-traveling musician who owns an expensive guitar.

TRAVELING ON A COMMERCIAL AIRLINE

When taking your guitar on a plane trip, follow these steps to protect it or to guarantee an adequate settlement should damage occur:

1. Keep it in a hardshell veneer or fiberglass case. A chipboard case or plastic bag invites damage.

2. Loosen the strings. Fluctuations in pressure, caused by altitude changes, could be harmful, even if the cabin is pressurized. Should the guitar be damaged, stress caused by the string tension could make it worse.

3. Line the case interior with extra padding; wrap the head and neck of your guitar in dry towels, foam rubber, or a similar material, for a snug fit.

4. Before boarding the plane, have the guitar inspected by a clerk or other airline representative, and ask him to sign a certificate stating that it is undamaged.

5. Insure the guitar for the amount of money it would cost to replace it. If you are not sure of the worth, call a couple of music dealers before traveling and have it appraised.

6. Ask if you can take the guitar with you into the passenger compartment. If space is available, permission will probably be granted.

If the instrument is damaged and the airline does not come through with a prompt, adequate settlement, or if the company has reimbursed you for a substandard repair job, write a serious but polite letter of complaint to the president of the airline. Send copies to the representative who handled your claim, the airline's director of public relations, the Better Business Bureau, and the Civil Aeronautics Board (the address for the last is: Civil Aeronautics Board, Bureau of Enforcement, Chief/Consumer Complaint Section, Washington, D.C. 20428).

Storage

The guitar is built to resist the constant tension of the strings, and concert pitch should be maintained under normal conditions, including storage for periods of moderate length. If the guitar is going to be put away for a long time, loosen the strings. When restringing, check the straightness of the neck and have your dealer make any necessary truss rod adjustments.

14

Minor Repairs and Refinishing

Most guitar repairmen spend much of their time trying to correct problems that were caused by inexperienced owners' attempts to fix their own instruments. Be cautious about repairing your own guitar. If there's any doubt about correct procedures, take it to a pro.

INTONATION CHECKLIST

As mentioned earlier, "intonation" refers to the instrument's ability to be played in tune at various positions on the fingerboard. If your guitar is consistently playing out of tune at some frets, follow these steps to discover and remedy the problem:

1. If necessary, change the complete set of strings. Probably 90 percent or more of intonation difficulties are caused by strings that are worn, rusty, corroded, or dead. Normally, you might need to change only one or two worn strings, but when correcting a serious intonation problem, replace all six to get a balance of tone and feel.

2. Test the tuning gears to see if they are slipping. If adjustable, tighten or loosen them as needed. If they are stiff, apply a drop of oil and work it in as you twist the key. If the gear is accessible, a semi-solid lubricant is preferred (for example, Vaseline, beeswax, cork grease; Chapstick is good too). Oil might leak

A nonadjustable acoustic guitar bridge is glued to the top and held in place with "C" clamps until the glue dries.

into the wood, interfering with later attempts to refinish the guitar. (See "Tuning Machines," p. 221).

3. Test the bridge adjustment for correct string length (p. 211).

4. Check for any bends, bows, warps, or twists in the neck. Correct the defect either by having the neck rod adjusted (the usual remedy, see p. 213), or by returning the guitar to the factory (a last resort).

5. If the fingerboard is grooved, pitted, or covered with accumulations of dirt, wax, or grime, remove the strings and rub it down with woodwind bore oil or a similar liquid (p. 229).

6. Check for uneven frets. The remedy for a high fret appears below. Worn down frets should be dressed (see p. 229) or be replaced.

If you have patiently followed all of these steps and the damn thing *still* plays out of tune, give up. Take it to a local, authorized, repair station. If they can't fix it, it may have to go back to the manufacturer for repair or replacement of parts.

Using nippers to remove frets

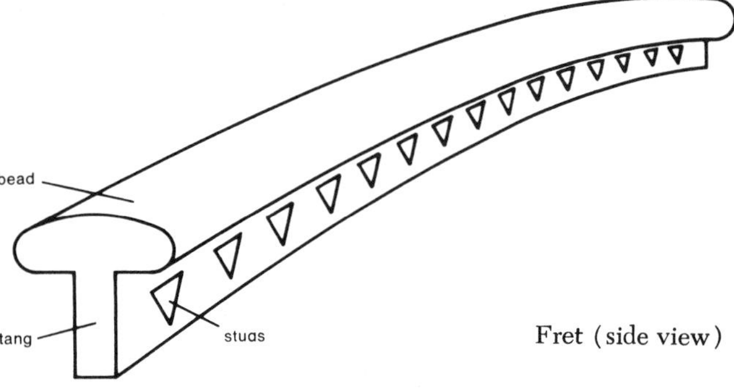

Fret (side view)

BUZZING STRINGS AND FALSE TONES

More than nine times out of ten, buzzing strings are caused either by a low action or worn strings. Some guitarists prefer a slight buzz for a raunchy sound, but if it rattles too much, or if you like a pure, clean sound, raise the bridge a little.

A convex hump in the fingerboard will cause a fret to stick up, and a string that vibrates against it will rattle. Have your dealer loosen the torque in the neck rod (see p. 215).

A fret can be too high, even though the neck is aligned. It may have been jolted out of its slot or gradually worn loose, or perhaps it was incorrectly installed at the factory in the first place. A change in the weather could shrink the wood, jarring the fret loose. Whatever the cause, the high fret can cause either a string rattle, a false tone, or both. It may protrude only slightly beyond its intended height, causing the string to vibrate against it, producing the buzz. If the dislocated fret is high enough, it may actually be substituted for the note played at a lower position, causing the false tone.

To fix the high fret, loosen the strings and move

them to the outside edges of the bridge and nut to expose the entire fingerboard. Check to see that the high fret is still seated in its slot. Then, with a folded soft cloth over the fret for protection, gently tap it back into place with light strokes of a broad-faced hammer or mallet. Support the underside of the neck. Note the position of the fret after each couple of taps.

If the fret has worked itself completely free of its slot, apply Elmer's white glue, or a similar product, to the anchor fin on the under side of the fret, before reseating it. If the slot has widened, substitute a fret with a larger tang. Bound fingerboards present special problems best left to a repairman.

Buzzing strings may also be caused by an insufficient angle in either the bridge slot (p. 208), nut slot (p. 209), or by strings that are too light (p. 179).

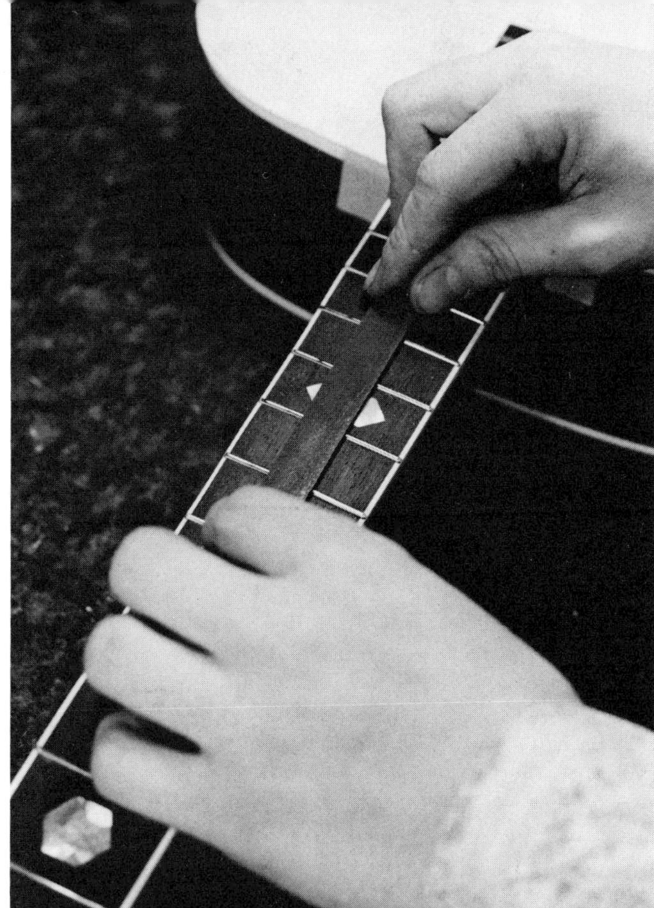

Filing the frets with mill-smooth file

DRESSING THE FINGERBOARD

Look for a fret that has been worn down lower than the others, a problem which can have the same effects as a high fret. If a fret is nicked, grooved, or excessively worn, replace it. A few drops of bore oil or linseed oil rubbed into the fingerboard every couple of months or so will keep it smooth and clean. Use 0000 steel wool, the finest grade. Xylene is a general cleaner, good for fingerboards. However, don't allow it to touch any plastic surfaces. Extremely dirty boards may be cleaned with a mild solution of carbon tetrachloride (do it outdoors, don't inhale it, and wear rubber gloves).

The fingerboard may be dressed with a mill-smooth file or a carborundum sharpening stone, evenly rubbing all of the frets in a direction parallel to the neck. This flattens the frets, smoothing out the rough spots or nicks, but it also leaves sharp edges. These can be smoothed with a fret file, a curved tool designed for this purpose. The final step is a three-stage cleaning and buffing, first with #320 sandpaper, then with #600 sandpaper, and finally with 0000-grade steel wool.

Don't try to radically alter the profile of frets that are both high and wide. They are designed to play in tune at their original height, and any increase in the area of contact (between the string and the flattened fret) may cause buzzing and intonation problems.

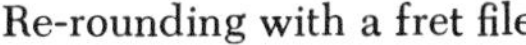

Re-rounding with a fret file

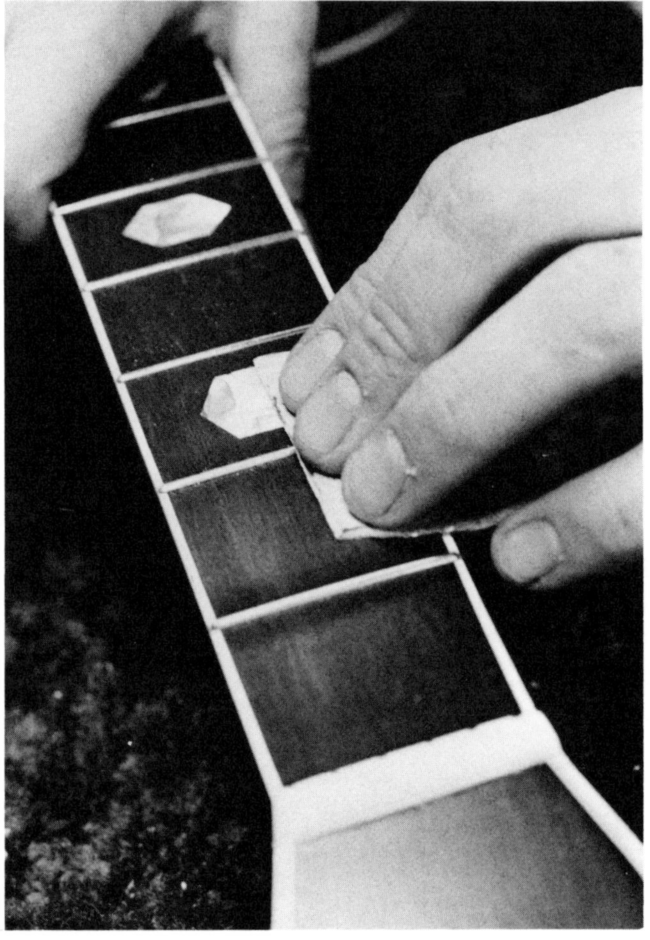

Final sanding

ROUGH-EDGED FRETS

Changes in the weather may shrink the fingerboard very slightly, leaving frets which protrude from the edge. The rough edges may be smoothed with light strokes of a fine-grain flat file at a forty-five degree angle. To insure uniformity, sand the fingerboard and all of the frets for a minute or two, first with #220, then #320, and then #600 sandpaper, using a light rubbing motion parallel to the neck. More smoothing may be done with #400 sandpaper, using brisk but gentle rubbing *perpendicular* to the length of the neck. This helps to eliminate any edges produced by the previous sanding and filing. (Excessive sanding is hazardous; it makes grooves in the fingerboard, noticeably changing the relative height of the frets.) Finally, clean the board with a few drops of a light oil and wipe completely dry with a clean, lint-free cloth.

ELECTRICAL PROBLEMS

If a part of your guitar system is not functioning properly, isolate the difficulty by using other connecting cords, amplifiers, and guitars that are known to be O.K.

Connecting Cords*

Problems in the cord are likely caused by a break in the connection inside one or both of the phone plugs, often attributable to rough handling. (Remove plugs from the jacks by gripping the plug housing, not by tugging on the cord.)

Connect one plug to a live amp and leave the other plug free. Test each end of the cord by gently bending it to both sides where it joins the plug. Lightly tap the free plug. A loud buzz or popping sound is normal, but if the grounding shield is broken, the amp will hum loudly. When the central conductor itself is severed, the guitar will produce no amplified signal at all. If the loose end of the cord causes a moderate hum when tested, and if the metal parts of the connected guitar buzz and hum when touched, the grounding has probably been disturbed at the instrument end of the cable. Resoldering can remedy the

* Low-quality cables are not worth the slight savings in purchase price. Substandard cords, especially the cheaper coil cords, cause a significant loss of treble frequencies.

break, if the housing is the removable metal or plastic type. However, if it is encased in molded-rubber insulation, replace the cord.

Most cable repairs are made in the first few inches from either end, where the cord receives the most abuse. However, it may break elsewhere along its length. Test for this by connecting the guitar to a live amp and gently bending the cord into a loop every two or three inches, listening for a disturbing hum. Internal cable defects are not really worth repairing because of the difficulty in pinpointing the break and the substantial risk of later failure. If you can locate the trouble, cut the cable and reconnect the plug at that point, or better yet, replace the entire cord.

If your guitar cord doesn't work, a dealer can check for poor grounding or a short circuit with a multimeter (volt/ohm meter). Low-quality braided shielding in cheap cords can make an annoying rushing sound when bent.

Cords are frequently broken, even if the musician takes reasonable care of his equipment. Keep a spare.

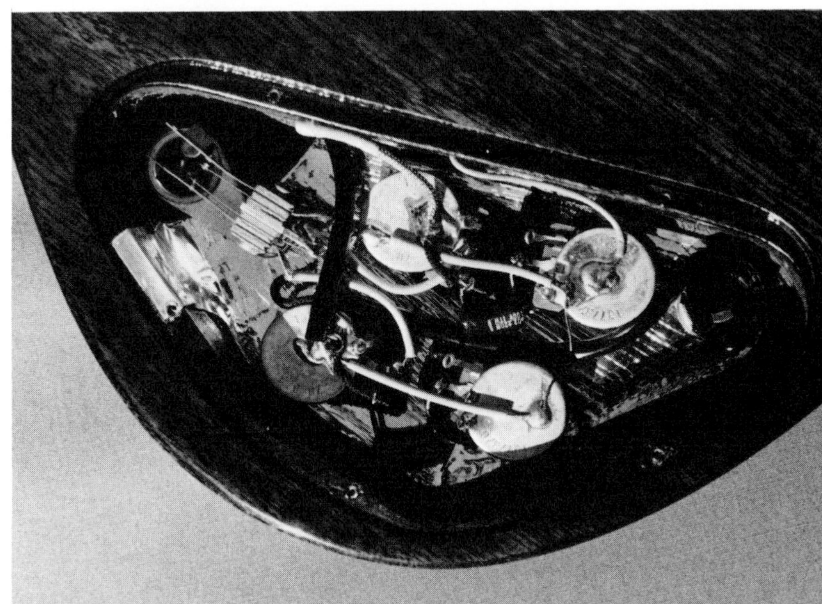

Tone and volume potentiometers

Electrical System Malfunctions

The guitarist generally needs to be concerned with only a few kinds of electrical troubles: tone or volume control defects, loose connections in the wiring, or dead pickups.

Tone and volume knobs (potentiometers, "pots")

Old control posts may become smoothed and worn down. A blast of electrical lubricant (available in hardware stores) will take care of it. Some containers are fitted with a long tube on the nozzle, facilitating application. Shoot a few drops on the base of the control shaft and rotate it to allow the lubricant to slip inside the control post.

Controls that pop or produce static may have become a little stiff and scratchy from sitting unused on a dealer's shelf for months. Normal operation or a few seconds of twisting back and forth can often remove any dust or other troublesome particles that have collected on the shaft. Contact cleaner will clear up static that is caused by deposits of dirt on the pot's internal carbon track.

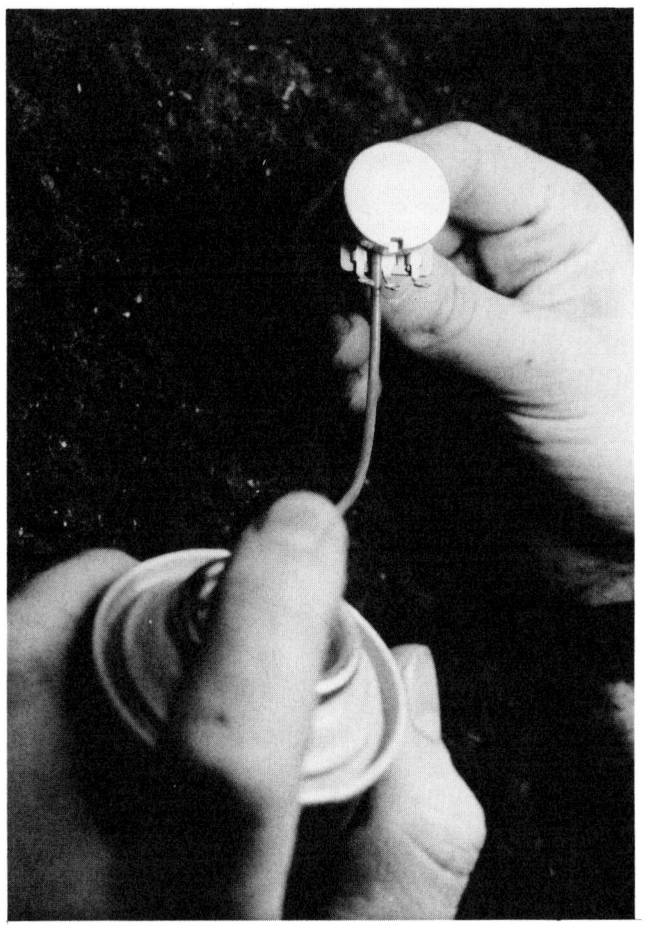

Applying electrical lubricant to control pot

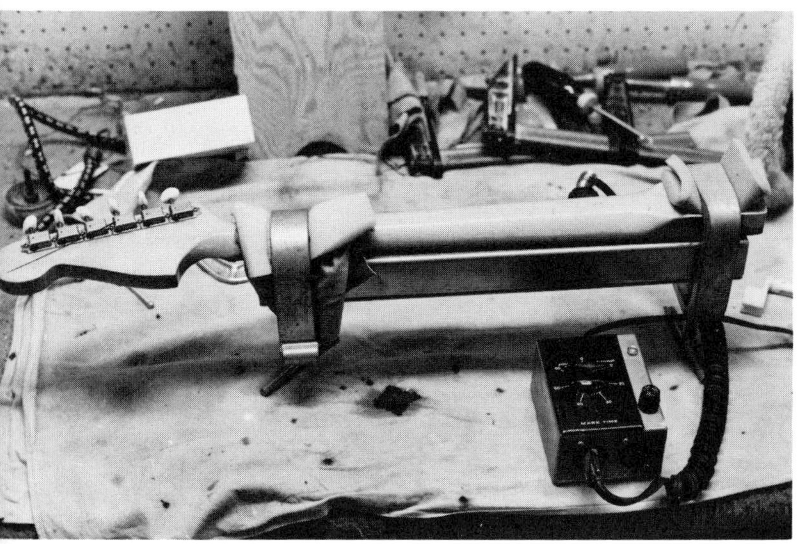

Neck being straightened on a heating element

Internal connections

A loose or broken wire within the guitar's circuitry should be repaired in the same manner as you would fix any damaged electrical connection. Soldering is best.

On most solid-body guitars, the pots are readily accessible. Rattles caused by loose wires or controls inside a hollow-body guitar should be handled by a repairman, since removal of these parts may require long-nosed tools, special techniques, and extraordinary patience.

Pickup Failure

Pickups continue to work until damaged; they don't "wear out," though slight distortion or a drastic decrease in output could be caused by a broken or defective wrap in the coil. There are two remedies for a broken coil: replacement of the whole pickup or rewinding by a repairman who has the necessary machinery. Whether rewinding is worth the effort depends upon the design of the pickup. Humbuckings are more difficult to rewind than single-coil pickups.

Trying to replace individual polepieces (other than the screw type) is almost certain to prove fruitless, and probably wouldn't help anyway. If the electrical responses of the strings are uneven, see that the polepieces are properly set for height. Mixing strings from unmatched sets may cause an imbalanced projection, since different manufacturers treat their strings to have varying electrical properties.

RATTLES IN THE GUITAR BODY

Look for loose screws on the strap buttons, tuning machines, pickguard, and so forth. Rattling necks are rare in well-made guitars, but if it happens, consult your repairman.

Sometimes a retainer nut on either the output jack or the volume and tone controls may work itself loose. Remove the knobs and tighten the nut with a wrench or pliers. To protect the controls, hold the post in the "zero" position (all the way counterclockwise) with one hand, while tightening the nut with the other. If an internal wire vibrates against the top, use any small tool to gently push it away. Rattles inside the tuning gear are best treated with a semi-solid lubricant. If the noise persists, replacement of the gear is convenient and inexpensive.

A loose individual string-length screw can be silenced with a drop of clear glue or nail polish. When readjusting the screw, the dried substance will readily split and fall off. Protect the guitar top with a cloth when applying the glue or polish.

Other buzzes might be traced to polepiece screws, unraveled strings, or a string vibrating in a nut slot or saddle slot that is either too large or insufficiently angled.

If an acoustic guitar buzzes only at certain pitches, it could be due to a loose fan brace. Your dealer should have the required probes and mirrors to pinpoint the trouble, and repairs can usually be done without removing the top.

Peavey bodies on the spray rack

NATURAL REFINISHING

A professional refinisher should tackle jobs involving hollow-body guitars or the complicated application of colored finishes. However, if you are handy with simple tools, you can turn a beat-up solid-body guitar into an attractive instrument by applying a wood finish to highlight the natural grain. The job requires stain, sealer, and lacquer. Buy all three at the same place, and ask the store owner to check their compatibility. If not properly matched, one substance could interfere with another.

Freshly sprayed bodies on the drying rack at Travis Bean

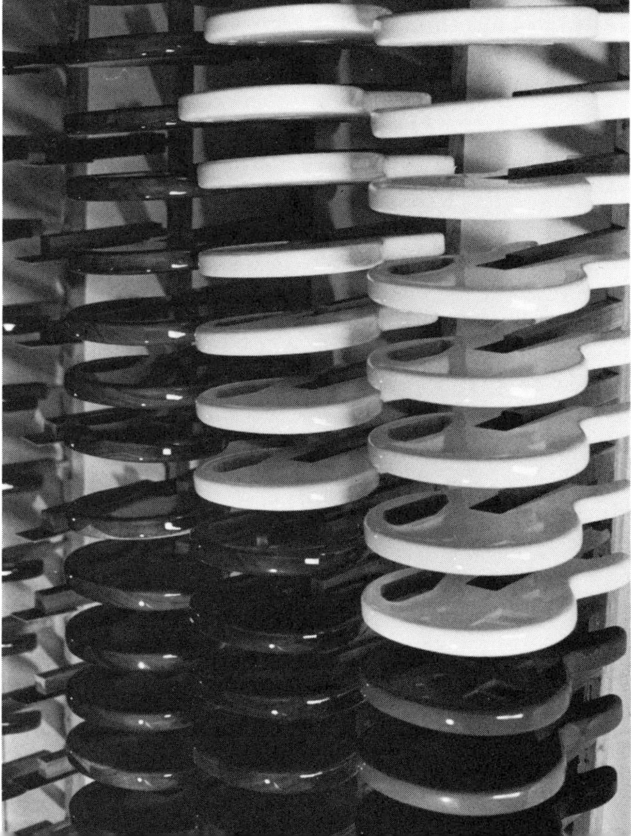

1. Remove all strings, hardware, knobs, controls, pickups, and so forth from the guitar body. This is usually accomplished easily with wirecutters, a socket screwdriver, needlenose pliers, a small, standard screwdriver and a Phillips-head screwdriver. Disconnect the pickups and wires by desoldering the connections. Tag the wires with tape to help get them back in the right place. If the neck is detachable, remove it.

2. Loosen the old paint with a thin, not too pasty paint stripper. Don't use the kind of stripper that requires washing off in water, since it could swell the grain and warp the wood of your guitar. Heavy coats of paint may require several applications, but over 90 percent of the paint may be removed by the strip-

per prior to sanding. To protect the grain, gently wipe off (don't scrape) the stripper with paper towels or rags. Paint stripper is evil stuff; do the job outdoors or in a well-ventilated place. Don't inhale it, and keep it away from your eyes and skin. Inexpensive, disposable spray masks are available at most paint stores.

3. Rub the guitar body with fine sandpaper in a direction parallel to the grain. Deep nicks may be leveled with wood filler, then sanded. After sanding, clean the wood meticulously with benzine or turpentine, to remove all particles and dust.

4. Many stains are available—mahogany, ash, birch, maple, and others. Spend time testing a couple of your favorite ones on a spare piece of the same wood used in the guitar. The color will change as the stain dries, so experiment before staining the guitar and determine the number of coats you will need to produce a color you like. Apply the stain with a brush or rag, one light coat at a time, according to the particular instructions. Spray stains are convenient. Let each coat dry before applying the next one.

5. After the final coat of stain has dried, apply one or more coats of sealer, as suggested by the paint salesman.

6. When the sealer has completely dried, apply clear lacquer to protect the new finish.

Two light coats of spray lacquer safeguard the wood without changing its soft, woodsy appearance, though it may make the stain look a little darker. You can get a bright glossy look (like Fender's natural finishes) with additional coats of clear lacquer. One method is to apply four coats, sand with fine grade wet-or-dry sandpaper, then apply four more coats. A coat hanger may be fashioned into a hook for suspending the guitar as you spray, conveniently exposing the entire surface.

Scratches and Nicks

Refinishing even a minor scratch may be a complicated job. Some of the more involved procedures require burning-in tools, alcohol lamps, pumice stones, patch lubes, and other specialized apparatus. Until you can take the guitar to a repairman, avoid touching the scratch. Dirt or oil from your skin can contaminate the wood, preventing the best possible refinishing job.

If the body or neck of your guitar is cracked, even slightly, loosen the strings and have the guitar examined right away. The defect may be structurally and acoustically harmless at present, but a crack is easier to repair in its early, hairline stages. Take care of it before the split widens.

part II

Amplifiers, Speakers and Cabinets, Special Effects, and Sound Systems

15

Amplifiers

The piggyback Fender Bandmaster of the early Sixties was considered a giant amplifier loaded with extras: two monstrous 12″ speakers, volume, bass *and* treble controls, and a vibrato circuit.* It was big and flashy, and everybody wanted one. In those days, the typical beginning guitarist knew the difference between the "speed" and "intensity" controls of his vibrato channel and that was about it. If he had a rough idea of how reverb works, he was looked upon by his peers as an eminent sage. Things have changed. Today's amp market resembles a bizarre Disneyland of dials, meters, pedals, and blinking lights. Power outputs have rocketed to levels that weren't even imagined until recently. If you have been to a Grateful Dead concert, you have witnessed the fury of over twenty tons of sound equipment. The energy consumed would be sufficient to power all of the homes in a residential area of several blocks. Over four hundred transducers (speaker devices) are loaded onto towering scaffolds, which cause the stage to resemble a metropolitan skyline.

Most of us used to get excited about volume and tone controls, but today we study graphic equalizers, oscilloscopes, and frequency curves. Since amps are so much bigger and more complicated, the guitar player should spend some time investigating a few simple electronic principles, so that he can select and use his equipment to his best advantage.

*For a short history and model chart of Fender amps see p. 104.

Jerry Garcia with Alembic gear

The Gibson EH-150 amp (c. 1939), 15 watts, one 12″ speaker.

Fortunately for some amplifier manufacturers, many buyers are still lost in a thick haze when it comes to electronics, and they enthusiastically spend tons of money for equipment, often without adequate inquiry or comparison of models. This book does not cover all of the technical details, but it should help you make an intelligent decision in choosing the best amp for your particular needs and to keep it operating without trouble.

OUTLINE OF AMPLIFIER OPERATION

The principles of guitar amplification are generally similar to those applied in stereo or hi-fi record players and public-address systems. The amp's function is to receive and increase the relatively weak signal from the guitar's pickup, preparing that electrical energy for conversion into acoustical energy through the speakers. During this process, various supplementary circuits enable the musician to modify that signal, perhaps changing its tone and volume or causing it to distort, to reverberate, or to repeat itself over and over at a controlled rate.

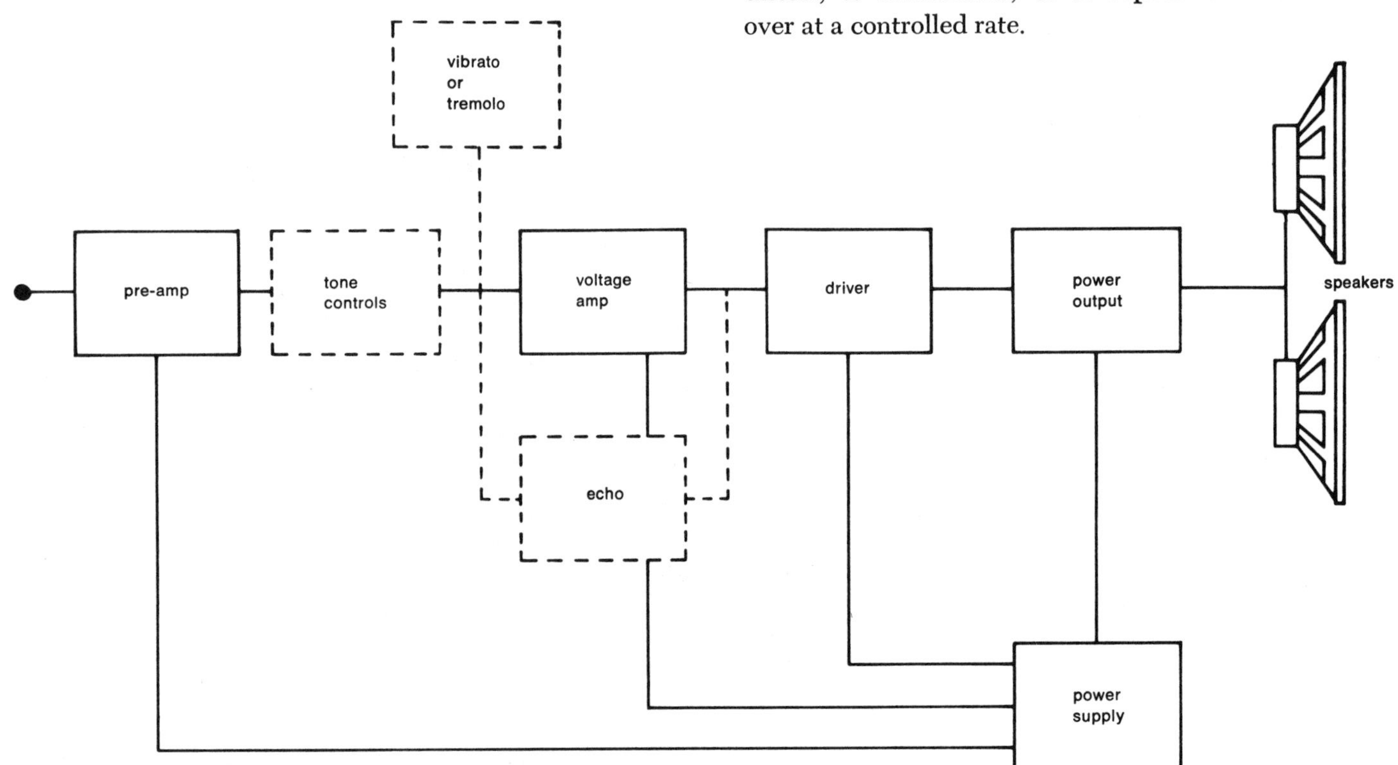

A typical guitar amplifier's various stages; optional circuits in dotted boxes.

Various stages of amplification

Stages

Much of the work is performed by the pre-amp. For example, a 12 AX7 tube can amplify a signal many thousand times. The better pre-amps include several stages, minimizing the amplification of extraneous noise. After the pre-amp, the signal enters a driver stage, which takes the increased voltage and "drives" it into the input of the power amp.

POWER RATINGS

Many shoppers are totally power-oriented, seeking an amp that will make them the first on the block with a nuclear deterrent capability. But power is only one of several considerations. Would you rather have 40 watts of clear tonal reproduction or 60 watts that sound like World War II even at low volumes? It's easy to build an amp with a voltage gain of many thousand times; the trick is to do it without amplifying unwanted noises. Of course, the maximum loudness depends upon the amount of power, but it's also affected by the quality of components, degree of craftsmanship, efficiency of the speakers, and design of the cabinet.

Did you know that a 50-watt amp may be more powerful than a 100-watt amp, or that the same one may be rated at both 200 and 600 watts? One reason for the confusion is that there is a tremendous difference between the amount of output and the draw* —if the "400 w" on the back panel refers to the energy that the amp draws, the actual output may be only 90 watts or so. A more important reason is that there are at least five different systems for measuring power output: RMS (Root Mean Square), peak, music power, peak music, and IPP or Instantaneous Peak Power. The amp makers cannot agree on which method is best, though the first two ratings are the ones most often applied.

RMS is the average watt output during one complete cycle. Accordingly, it is the most useful and dependable scale, since it describes a power load that can be handled *regularly* and consistently, telling how much actual work can be performed. RMS is originally

*The draw refers to the amount of wattage drawn from a wall socket.

measured in a controlled laboratory environment, so repairmen sometimes use .9 × RMS as a working average rating.

The terms "music power" and "peak" mean different things to various manufacturers. Music power, unlike the constant RMS rating, represents a succession of rapid energy spurts. Some amplifiers may hold a reserve of power, enabling these music power bursts to exceed the RMS rating by 15 percent or so. The peak signal is the maximum output at intervals of down to only a fraction of a second. Since the amp rests during the gaps between the notes and chords, the peak rating is usually double or more (in most tube amps) to triple (in many transistor models) the RMS standard, depending upon the particular conditions in which the manufacturer conducts his testing. In making a well-informed choice of the proper amp, the peak scale is practically useless.

There is an occasionally-used scale known as peak music power. Twice the music power rating, it measures only the maximum level of each cycle during a series of high-energy spurts. Instantaneous Peak Power or IPP is still another standard. It may be over four times the RMS rating.

Knowing how much power you can put out for a quarter of a second doesn't really help, so use the RMS rating when comparing models.

Any amplifier may produce distorted signals that are much greater than the undistorted measurement. A 200 watt RMS amp may produce 450 watts of distorted sound in an overload situation. The safest method of comparison is the side-by-side approach, since a few manufacturers specify a power rating which has been measured with a distortion level as high as 15 percent, others at 1 percent. (Read chapter 17, p. 263, on the relationship between power output and amplifier volume.

SELECTING AN AMPLIFIER

With the endless combinations of size, speakers, features, and price on today's market, how does a person shop for an amp without losing his sanity? How can you tell which brand is best, when everybody seems to play through different kinds—Led Zeppelin prefers Univox; the Rolling Stones, Faces, and Johnny Winter use Ampeg; Hendrix and Duane Allman played through Marshalls; Sly & The Family Stone and Albert King are confirmed Acoustic enthusiasts; The Who prefers Sunn or HiWatt; Carlos Santana has a Mesa; and practically everyone has used a Fender at one time or another. And people change their minds so often—your favorite guitarist may be playing through a different amp each time you see him. When you ask your friends for advice, expect a bombardment of rumors: "There's only *one* amp to buy, man, and that's the Megaton model by Concussion Electronics . . . all other amps are turkeys." Naturally, the rumors change weekly.

Selecting a brand is only part of the problem. Most companies produce a broad range of models, since musicians' requirements vary greatly. A versatile, busy pro may own several amps: one for large concerts, one for clubs and smaller rooms, another for a specific recording tone, and still another for home use and practice. Of course, that sort of variety is rarely necessary, and if you choose the right amp in the first place, it will serve many purposes and perform for a long time.

You already know that the three most significant factors in the selection of any amp are proper size, the right tone, and good quality. A model that is too small or too low in power to take the beating you give it will break down or blow up, no matter how well it's constructed, and an amp that is a product of poor workmanship or assembled with sub-standard components may fall apart in weeks, even if it weighs a quarter ton and costs a fortune.

You will not find a new amp that is big, top-quality, and inexpensive. The amplification of electrical musical instruments is a specialized field, and those high-powered amps which are the result of advanced design, engineering, and production will cost a lot of money. Should the amp prove defective, you want to have confidence in both the integrity of the manufacturer and his ability to stand behind his reputation and guarantee. So, brand names are important. If you cannot afford to buy both the biggest and the best, get a fully guaranteed, high quality, mid-sized amp rather than some titanic monster of questionable dependability.

Before making that down payment, ask yourself all

Peavey is one company that uses lock-jointed corner construction.

of these questions: What size rooms will you be trying to fill? How often and how long will you have to play at high volumes? How many instruments will be plugged in simultaneously? Will the amp ever be used with a microphone, bass, electronic keyboard, or any other additional equipment? How much money can you afford to spend without starving?

WHAT TO LOOK FOR

Size and Power

If you need an amp just for practice or use around the home, a small model with an 8″ speaker and 10 watts RMS* will do the job. In fact, the 3-watt portable amps by Pignose and comparable models are surprisingly loud. So are the 6-watt Fender Champs. As soon as you decide to make a demo record or to play a few school parties or a quiet nightclub, it may be necessary to move up to around 15 to 25 watts. (Eric Clapton and Peter Frampton like the Champ in the studio.) Popular speaker combinations for this sort of work are two 10″ speakers or one 12″. For school

*All power ratings noted here are RMS.

auditoriums, gyms, or larger clubs, you will naturally have to increase the power output. At any rate, a 100-watt amp with heavy-duty speakers will handle all but the very biggest jobs, though extension speakers for extra power and/or sound distribution are available from the manufacturer, if needed. If you run your amplifier through an adequate public-address system, then the power requirements for the amp are much smaller.

The most popular amp and speaker combinations are found in the moderate range. Good models with four 10s or two 12s and about 45 watts RMS or more are sufficient for larger parties and medium-size halls, but if you play at extreme volumes, then even a party might require 100 watts. Ultra-high-powered models are available for the largest arenas and out-door concerts, including Fender's PS 400 bass amp (440 watts RMS), Peavey's F 800 (410 watts), Sunn's Coliseum Lead (320 watts), Hiwatt's DR 450 (400 watts), Ampeg's SVT (300 watts), and Acoustic's model 270 (375 watts).

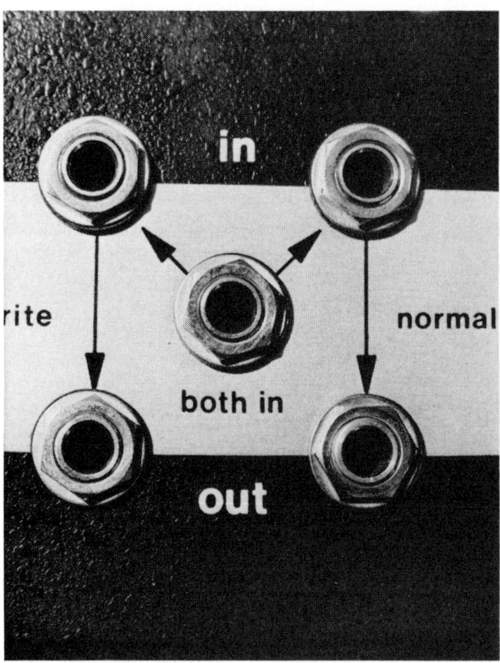

Two areas of the same size may have entirely different amplification requirements. The perceived loudness and projection of any amp will vary with the shape of the room, the height of the ceiling and the location of balconies, rugs, the materials used in the construction of the walls, the number of people in the room, the height and position of the stage, and so on. Because of all of these variables, try to test each room before you play. Outdoor gigs are the most demanding of all. Do not expect your old faithful 20-watt amp with two 10s to be heard in a large outdoor area, no matter how loud you thought it was inside.

Most amplifiers have several inputs, though the sound quality suffers unless each musician has a separate amp. Those inputs marked "microphone" have a slightly higher gain, to compensate for the mike's relatively weak output signal.

Piggyback Amps

"Piggyback" refers to a design that has separate cabinets for the amp and speakers. Among the advantages: the controls may be at the fingertips of the musician, while the speakers are positioned elsewhere for maximum dispersion; the components may be separated so that the speaker cabinet will not vibrate the amp's tubes or circuits; amps (tops, or brains) and

SOUND CITY
SMF TOUR SERIES
SOUND CITY
SOUND CITY

Marshall
Marshall
Marshall

speaker cabinets (bottoms) may be mixed and matched.

Piggybacks are usually high-powered. Designed for larger concerts, they often have an infinite baffle cabinet (a closed, sealed box), as opposed to the open-back of many self-contained ("compact," or nonpiggyback) amps. The open back permits a wider dispersion, from back as well as front, and is considered by some to produce a more "live" sound, particularly in small environments such as clubs.

Experiment with both types: piggybacks and compacts. Should you decide to buy a piggyback, get one powerful enough to drive your speakers *and* any additional cabinets you plan to buy in the future. Getting an amp with power to spare has at least two advantages: first, you can drive the speakers to maximum performance without straining the amp; second, you can get more volume later, through an additional cabinet, without having to buy a new amplifier.

Tone Controls and Graphic Equalizers

Sounds are vibrations, measured in cycles per second (Hertz, Hz, cps). The lower frequencies are bass notes and the higher frequencies are treble, and are often illustrated in chart form over a total frequency range of perhaps 20 to 20,000 Hz.

If the chart is humped in a certain area, then the tones in that range are relatively louder than the others.

If a signal is run through the amplification system with no tonal colorings added by the amp, then the frequency response is said to be "flat." A flat response is accomplished when the system amplifies equally all of the frequencies within its range. Tone controls alter the frequency balance of the signal, accenting either the lower end of the spectrum (bass control), the higher end (treble), or the mid-range. As explained in chapter eight, a single tone consists of the fundamental note and its various overtones. The tone controls alter the balance between these two elements, flavoring the sound. The simplest tone control is a capacitor that filters out certain frequencies, employing a variable potentiometer to regulate the amount of filtering. There are several types of tone controls, some with independent circuits in which each control affects a single range. Others are interlocked, so that each control overlaps into neighboring ranges. The electronic

Roland Studio Bass-100 with 6-band graphic equalizer and combined rear-loaded horn and bass reflex cabinet.

operation varies among manufacturers. On some, the response is flat when the knob is centered at 12 o'clock, providing either a boost or cut. On others the response is flat at "0" or "10."

The treble control flavors the upper harmonics of all fundamentals (bass or treble) and it may also extend down to the highest fundamentals. Those frequencies in between the lower and higher ranges may be affected by an overlap of the bass and treble controls, though more sophisticated systems feature a separate mid-range knob. The potency of each control may vary with the settings of the other controls.

A graphic equalizer is a device with separate controls for boosting or cutting several frequency ranges. Each control is designed to affect only its particular range. The controls may be slide levers centered on the various octaves within the band width. One of the industry's popular graphic equalizers is found on several of Acoustic's amps. It divides the band width into five sections: 50 to 110 Hz, 110 to 220 Hz, 220 to 460 Hz, 700 to 1500 Hz, and 1500 to 2800 Hz. (460 to 700 Hz is covered by the mid-range tone knob.) Since the electric guitar's range of fundamentals is about 82 to 1,100 Hz, the first three bands cover both fundamentals and harmonics; the fourth may cover both or harmonics only. Each of the five slide potentiometers

Acoustic's graphic equalizer

provides up to a 16 dB (decibel) cut or boost (±16 dB) of a frequency within its range. When all are centered at "0," the response is ideally flat.

Previously used in the concert and recording fields, equalizers are now available to any musician or singer. Unfortunately, some so-called graphic equalizers are nothing more than flashy-looking, overlapping tone controls. If the model that you are considering does not substantially increase your ability to narrow down specific tones, look elsewhere.

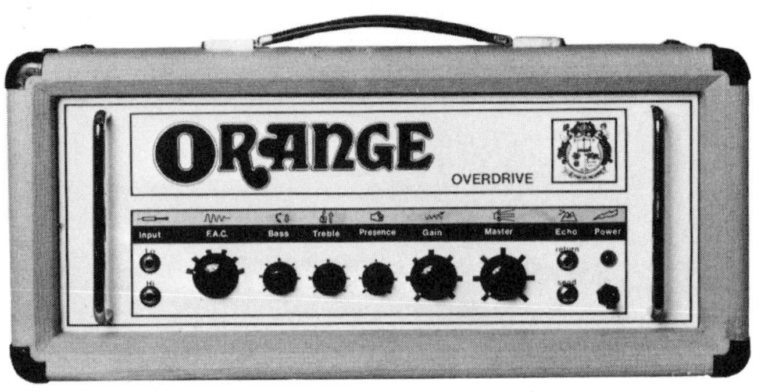

Price

Unless you're a superstar, you're limited to some degree by finances. A plain, small amp of adequate quality, but very limited application, usually costs at least $90, while the biggest professional models cost several grand. You could easily spend $300 to $600 for a medium-sized amp suitable for clubs, and $800 to $1,200 for a professional-quality concert model. Several companies, including Sunn, Acoustic, Marshall, HiWatt, and Ampeg, offer super high-powered amplifiers for arenas and large outdoor areas; list prices for the top-of-the-line models range from about $1,600 to over $5,000. Whether you can get a substantial discount depends upon those considerations discussed in chapter five: trade-in, geographical location, current trends, relations with dealers, and so forth.

A cheap, low-quality amplifier is not an economic advantage in the long run. Replacement costs for worn-out or defective parts can be high. Repairwork is also sometimes expensive. Since dependability is essential, a top-caliber amp will prove to be a good investment and should provide you with years of service. Remember, a good small amp may be inexpensive and still have a fantastic sound.

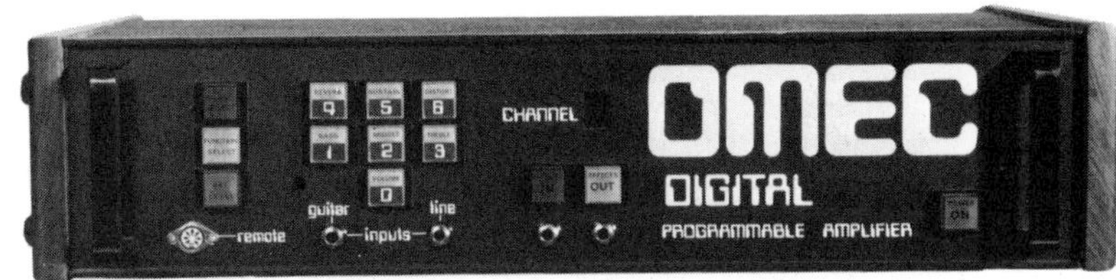

OMEC Digital Programmable Amplifier by Orange. This unique amp allows the musician to punch up any of thousands of combinations of volume, tone, and effects on each of four channels. The information is stored in the amp's binary computer network. Having programmed each channel, the guitarist can switch from one to another with either a button or footswitch. Since each button has several functions, the front panel does not require an intimidating number of switches. Despite the complexity of the internal circuits, actual operation is simple and only takes a few minutes to learn.

CHOOSING UP SIDES: TUBES OR TRANSISTORS?

In the beginning, all commercial amplifiers had vacuum tubes. Then, several years ago, transistorized solid-state models invaded the market and a great eternal controversy arose as to which design is better. Plenty of advocates on either side of the fence proclaim the total superiority of one type over the other,

but actually, neither is "better" in every way. Both have distinctive characteristics; it's up to you.

A tube amp is a voltage device, whereas the transistor is a current device, two completely different operations. The electronics of early transistor amps were relatively simple, so they rarely malfunctioned. However, many of today's transistor amps are very complicated. With developments in integrated circuitry, a delicate chip of material only ½″ long and ¼″ wide may house dozens of transistors, resistors, and capacitors. Thus, transistor amps as well as tube models should be handled carefully.

Compared to the glass tubes, solid-state systems are more resistant to two types of damage: vibration and heat. Transistors can get warm during a lengthy session, but tubes get much hotter—about 90° C. (nearly 200° F.). Still, both types are subject to damage from feedback, excessive heat, clipping (see p. 269) or vibration. For example, the amplification ability of an overheated transistor circuit may be either drastically increased or decreased. Even though a transistor is designed to operate comfortably at a higher voltage than a tube, the tube may be driven far beyond its intended limits before damage occurs, while a transistor designed to operate at 10 volts may disintegrate at 15 volts. In other words, a transistor will fail much quicker under overload conditions. Most of the better transistor amps have special protection circuits to guard the power stages from overload. (These comparisons do not take into account the possibility of speaker damage. No matter how tough your amp may be, it won't be of any use if you melt a voice coil or blow out the cone by forcing too much power through it. Any amp or speaker should be operated as suggested in the manufacturer's specifications.)

In a tube-type amp the elements within the power tubes may loosen, causing a slight noise called "afterfuzz," after the note dies out. Depending upon the design of the amp, this noise and/or the failure rate of the *power* amp tubes will necessitate their replacement (at about $25 to $50) every four to twelve months. The hard-working pro, who's really picky about his sound, will change more often, and tubes that are used infrequently will obviously last much longer.

The alternating heat and cold caused by turning the amp on and off creates fatigue. Standby switches are designed and should be used during breaks (with the power switch left on) to alleviate the strain. Pre-amp tubes have a much longer life than power-amp tubes. Replacement costs are nominal. One of the advantages of transistors is that, unlike tubes, they can operate indefinitely, reducing or eliminating maintenance costs. Also, they don't become microphonic, as tubes sometimes do.

A solid-state pre-amp may use either field-effect transistors (FETs) or bipolar transistors, each with its own distortion characteristics. Solid-state power amps are invariably bipolar. Overdriven FETs sound a little like an overdriven tube pre-amp, and they can usually be driven a bit higher than bipolar devices before entering the extreme distortion caused by overload. Other differences are that transistor amplifiers are often lighter than tube models, require no warmup, and they are more sensitive to a mismatch of impedance. Both transistor and tube amps usually operate in a "push-pull" system, where each of two components is responsible for amplifying half of each cycle. When one tube or transistor is operating, the other is resting.

Apart from these electronic considerations, the obvious factor is sound. Despite the advantages of solid state, many guitarists stick to the tubes, claiming that the sound of the transistor amps is not sufficiently "live." Some musicians feel that transistor amps are

Solid-state amp

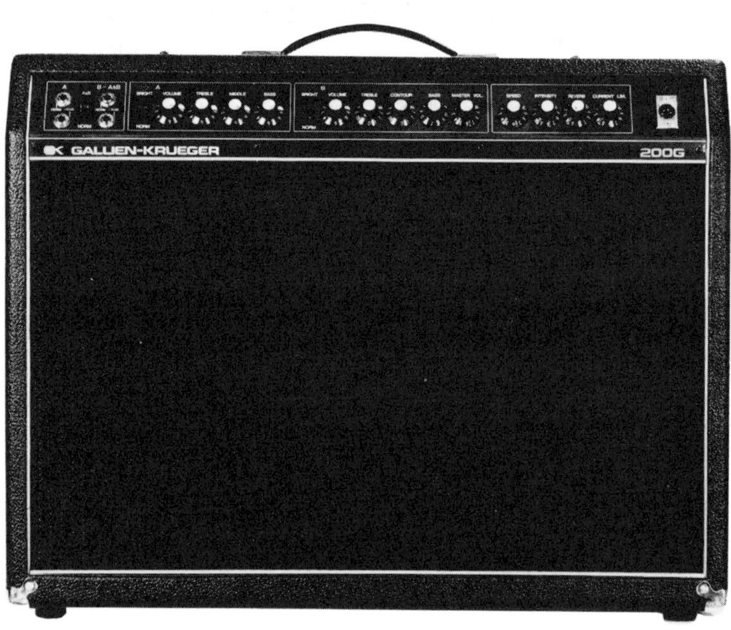

too clean; too bright and crisp. Tube amps require output transformers to match the impedance of the signal to the impedance of the speakers (see p. 265). Most of these transformers produce the harmonic distortion desired by many rock and blues players. Transistors reduce distortion by responding more efficiently to the guitar's signal. Another reason for the transistor amp's clarity is that its speaker has a higher damping factor, meaning that the speaker comes to rest quickly after its reception of the amp's signal. A fast-fingered jazz musician frequently chooses solid state for precisely the same reason that a blues player may avoid it—distortion-free purity of sound, particularly in the bass region.

Solid-state amplifier manufacturers are well aware of the popularity of competing tube products, and they have attempted—sometimes successfully—to install an optional tubelike sound in some models, perhaps a modified pre-amp, master volume control, overdrive circuit or regulator, fuzz or related distortion devices. In an effort to gain the advantages of both designs, the Peavey, Randall, Music Man, and other companies offer hybrid systems with a solid-state pre-amp and tube power supply.

It's a confusing issue. Both sides claim a broader reproduction of high and low frequencies. The manufacturers themselves, like many musicians, have changed their minds about the tube/transistor arguments. One of America's largest and best-known companies used to make only tube amps, then added a complete line of solid-state models—everything from the tiny practice amp to the concert monsters—and now they are back to producing only tubes, saying that the sound of the transistor amps isn't "warm." Another company that makes both transistor and tube amps claims that transistors have more important advantages—efficiency, maintenance, and so forth.

Both tube and transistor amplifiers are available in a broad range of quality. Test both types. Purchase the best amp you can afford, and let your personal taste in sound determine your choice.

TESTING AND COMPARING AMPLIFIERS

A music dealer will give you his opinion on the merits of each type of amplifier, but ask other musicians too, and do some concentrated comparison. For each model you try, gradually increase the volume level and note the point where the speaker begins to distort. Go ahead and turn up the amp and blast away. Do not think that the volume at "10" will be ten times louder than the setting at "1." It won't. An amp may be producing almost all of its total output at a setting of only "3."* Test for sound projection as well as sheer volume. Get a 20-foot guitar cord and stand on the other side of the room; have the salesman or a friend modify the controls at your direction as you play. Aside from the many technical factors, and regardless of what anybody says, the primary consideration is simply: which amp can be depended upon to consistently deliver the sound you are looking for?

*See chapter 17.

acoustic

16

Speakers and Cabinets

SPEAKER OPERATION

The fine details of speaker performance are somewhat complex, so here is a simplified explanation of what's going on: the speaker's function is opposite that of the pickup. The pickup (transducer) converts *acoustical* energy (vibration of the string) into an *electrical* signal which is then augmented by the amp. The speaker (also a type of transducer) converts that electrical energy *back* into audible acoustical energy (vibration of the speaker cone).

The voice coil consists of a thin wire surrounding a heavy cylindrical magnet. When it receives the alternating electrical current, the coil is temporarily magnetized. Attracted to the permanent magnet structure, or pot, the coil begins to move, vibrating the cone at a frequency corresponding to the musical note. The flexible corrugated-paper cone is stretched across a supporting circular frame or "basket," its suspension regulated by devices known as spider and compliance. The coil transfers its vibrations to the cone, and the moving cone exerts pressure on the surrounding air, producing sound waves.

Much of the strain on any guitar speaker comes from the attack (the pluck of the string), causing pressures several times the intensity of the actual note which follows. To meet the demands of long playing at loud volumes, the higher efficiency guitar speakers

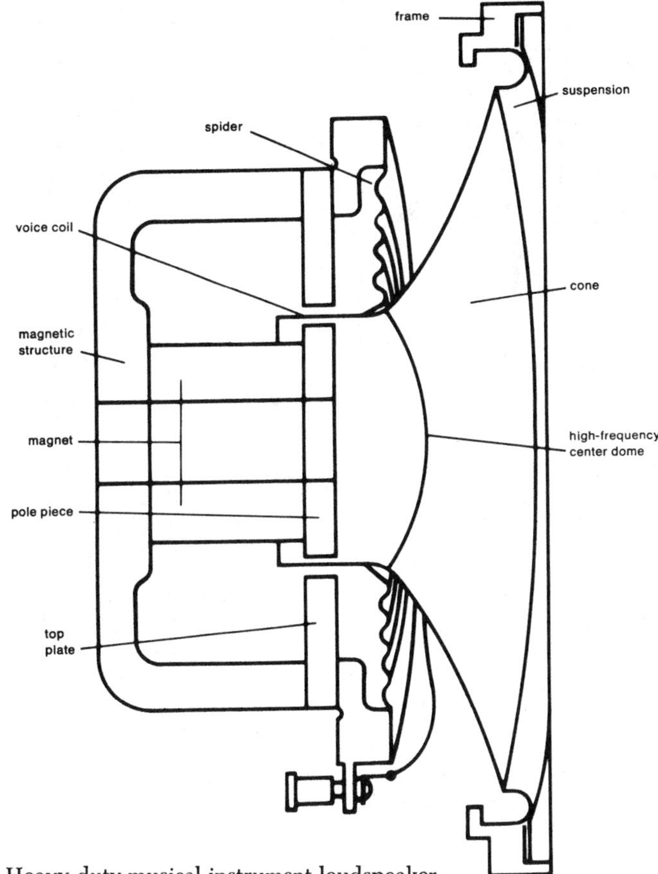

Heavy-duty musical instrument loudspeaker

are often distinguished from normal hi-fi speakers by stiffer, lower-mass cones, an aluminum (rather than copper) coil of a relatively large diameter, a heavier magnet, and a cast-aluminum basket instead of the press-punched type.

One company markets two versions of a large reverb amp. The only differences between them are the speakers and a mere $400 in price. The reason for the extra cost is that the quality of guitar speakers ranges from lousy to excellent, and the best ones can multiply the power output in addition to improving the purity and variety of tones. In the related field of hi-fi, the speaker's function is purely mechanical: to faithfully reproduce the recorded sound without affecting it. But in guitar amps, the loudspeaker assumes a musical role, contributing tone colorings of its own.

When shopping, you're way ahead of many buyers if you realize that high quality speakers are as important as any element in your amplification system, and that the price of the amp should not necessarily increase in direct proportion to the number of dials on the control panel or the sheer size of the cabinet.

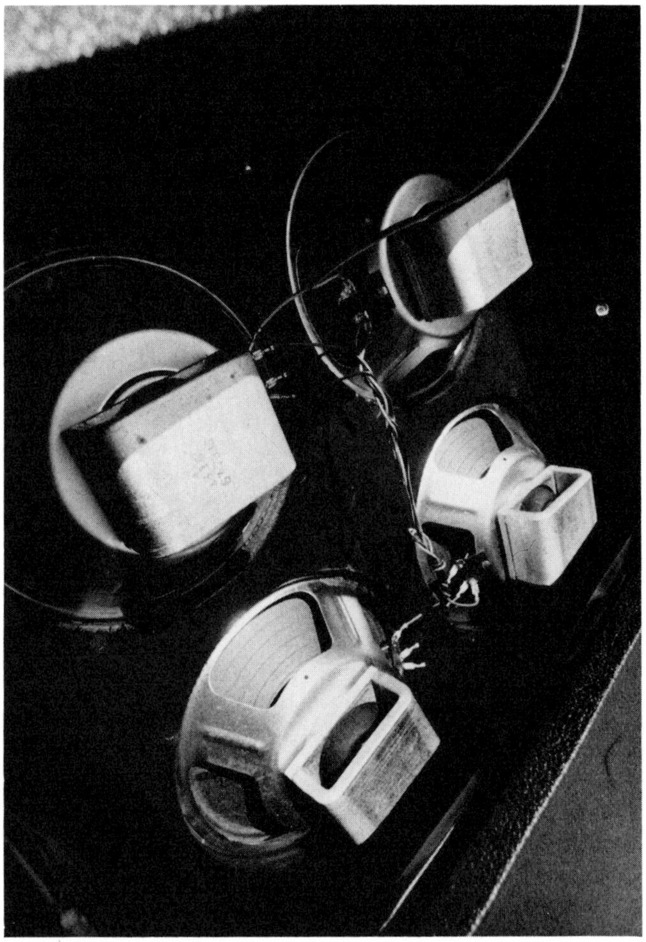

Four 10's

SPEAKER EFFICIENCY

Efficiency is the ratio of electrical input to auditory output: the percentage of energy that is actually converted to sound compared to the amount that is lost. This figure is usually measured under a standard of the Electrical Industry of America.

Hi-fi speakers may be rated extremely low (down to ½ percent or lower), while the best guitar speakers are perhaps 8 percent to 12 percent efficient, conservatively rated. Driver/horn systems range up to about 20 percent. Higher efficiency speakers are louder since they *use* a greater percentage of the available power.

SPEAKER SIZE AND COMBINATION

In addition to efficiency, consider the combination and size of the speakers. For example, two 12s (two 12″ speakers) will produce a fuller tone than the popular four 10s combination. However, four 10s have good response in the higher frequency ranges, and it's a favorite arrangement.

The reproduction of bass tones requires a larger mass of air to be moved. As a rule of thumb, the larger the cone, the bassier the sound, all other things being equal. The laws of physics state that a set of speakers will disperse a tone which is characteristic of a single speaker of that size and design. For example, four identical 10s may be played louder than one 10, but the tone will be basically the same.

Larger-coned 15″ speakers sacrifice some of the midrange and high frequencies and are too bass-heavy for most rock or blues guitar players, though some jazz musicians like the tone of a single 15. Bass speakers have greater limits of excursion (forward and backward cone motion) to handle the extremely low frequency bass signals. Running a four-string electric bass through most guitar speakers at moderate or high volumes could blow the cones.

Amps normally have more power than the speakers can handle. If an amp top is designed to drive two bottoms whose total wattage exceeds that of the amp, each cabinet alone may be rated lower than the amp. If so, playing with only one bottom at full power could blow the speakers.

SPEAKER CONNECTIONS

Speakers exert resistance (impedance) on the flow of electrons from the amplifier. All amps are designed to "look at" a certain optimum impedance; this burden or "load" is measured in ohms.* To prolong tube life and produce maximum distortion-free power, matching the output to the total impedance of the speakers is always desirable. However, it may or may not be absolutely necessary, depending upon the circuit design. Solid-state amps are especially sensitive to changes in impedance, and a mismatch can overload the system. In a tube amp, the tubes will wear out sooner if the impedance is mismatched. If the speaker's impedance is too high, power will be cut. If it is too low, power may again be cut and overheating is possible. In a multi-speaker amplifier the manner in which the speakers are connected can affect the output, frequency response, and the damping factor (p. 252).

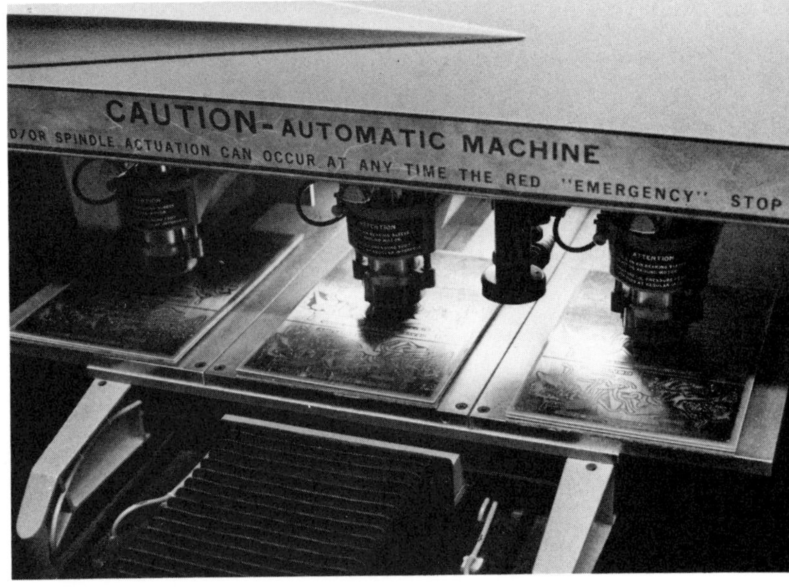

This is Peavey's computer-monitored machine for drilling holes in amplifier circuit boards. One of the most modern pieces of equipment in amplifier manufacture, it incorporates a TV camera (*center right, facing down*) that programs its computer. The printed circuit boards are mounted on a holder that floats on air cushions as the solid carbide drills move up and down. The machine "reads" computer tape and stores the information in its electronic memory for accuracy to .0002 inch.

Series Connection

Think of your amp as a water faucet connected to a hose. In this analogy, the speakers carry the amp's

*"Resistance" refers to a direct current, while "impedance" is the apparent corresponding resistance to a flow of alternating current.

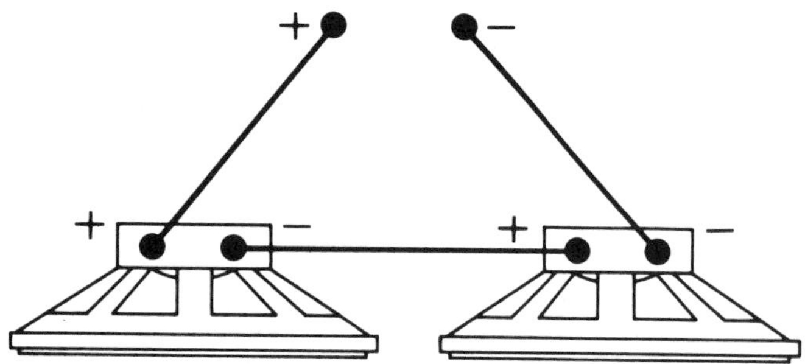

Series connection

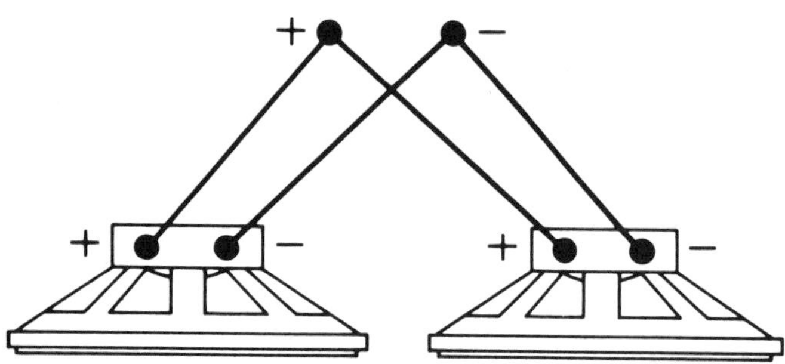

Parallel connection

signal just as the hose carries water from the faucet.

In a series system speakers are connected to *each other*—like doubling the length of the hose. The resistance of a series system equals the total resistance of all speakers combined, so if two 8-ohm speakers are connected in series, the load is *doubled* to 16 ohms. The greater cone area increases the mass of air that is being moved, and the extra speakers provide for greater distribution of the sound; both factors permit a volume increase.

Parallel Connection

Turning again to the faucet/hose analogy, a parallel connection resembles the effect of a forked "Y" attachment on the faucet; two separate hoses may be used. In the parallel system, the two speakers are *not* connected to each other as they are in the series connection. Rather, each speaker is wired *directly* to the source. Just as twice the water may be run through the two-hose "Y" set-up, the resistance to the electron flow is cut in *half* by the parallel connection of two speakers. The total impedance is the impedance of each speaker divided by the number of speakers. Therefore, two 8-ohm speakers wired in parallel deliver a total resistance of four ohms. Those amps that can take extension speakers without modification of the circuit are usually designed to accommodate a parallel system.

Series/Parallel

Four speakers may be connected in a series/parallel system in which speakers 1 and 2 are wired to each

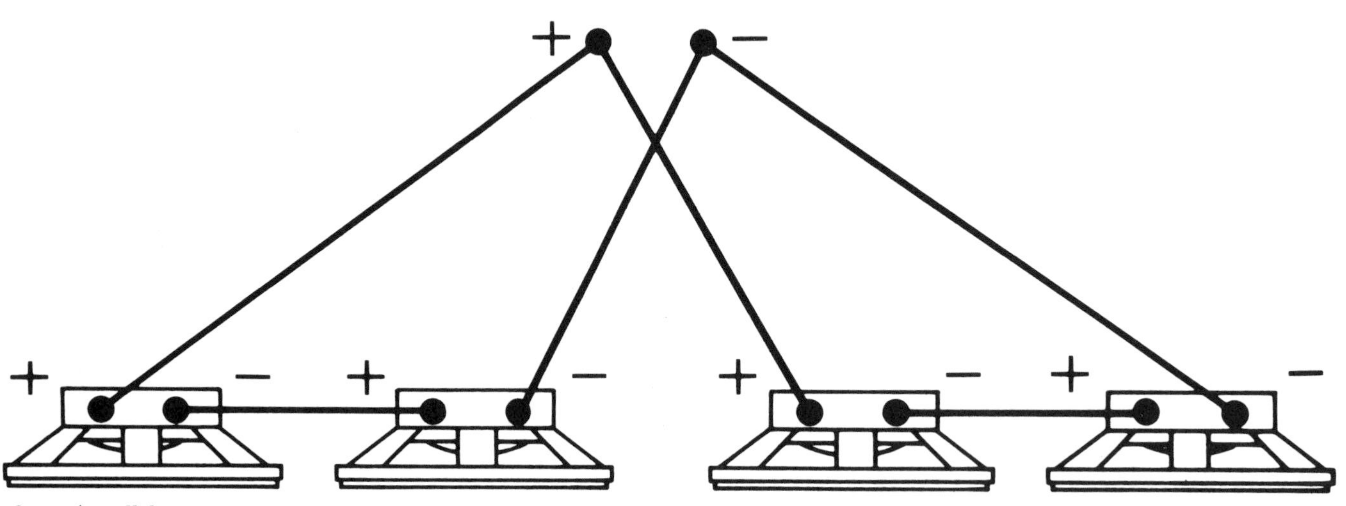

Series/parallel connection

other in series; speakers 3 and 4 are also wired to each other in series. Then the two sets of speakers are wired directly to the source, in parallel. Series/parallel is often used to connect multiple cabinets.

When adding speakers, the parallel connection is recommended, since if one speaker fails, the other will continue to operate, due to both speakers being wired directly to the source. (However, don't run the amp at full power through the remaining speaker.) In the series connection, if one speaker fails, they both fail.

Enclosures with different impedance should not be used together, since the lower impedance device will draw a disproportionately large amount of power.

There is a discussion of the relationship between speaker connections and amplifier volume on page 264.

SPEAKER CABINETS

There is a wonderland of rumors that pervades the various aspects of the electric guitar, but one category that seems to set the record is speaker cabinets. There are several prevailing philosophies, and it's easy to ask the same questions of three experts and receive three apparently conflicting opinions. At any rate, when selecting enclosures, no one else's opinion and no book can substitute for painstaking side-by-side testing.

Cabinets are necessitated by a physical phenomenon of speaker operation. The motion of the cone produces sound waves which emanate both forward and backward. These out-of-phase waves* will meet and cancel each other unless the front and back of the speaker are separated by a panel, or baffle. The design and resonant qualities of the enclosure are as important to the sound as is the speaker itself. There are five basic types of cabinets: open back, infinite baffle, bass reflex, horn projectors, and combination systems.

Open Back (Finite Baffle)

Many compact and some piggyback amps are matched to an open-back cabinet, providing projection from both front and rear. The result is a "live" sound and broad distribution, good for clubs and average-sized rooms. With an open-back enclosure, there will

* See the discussion of phase on page 286.

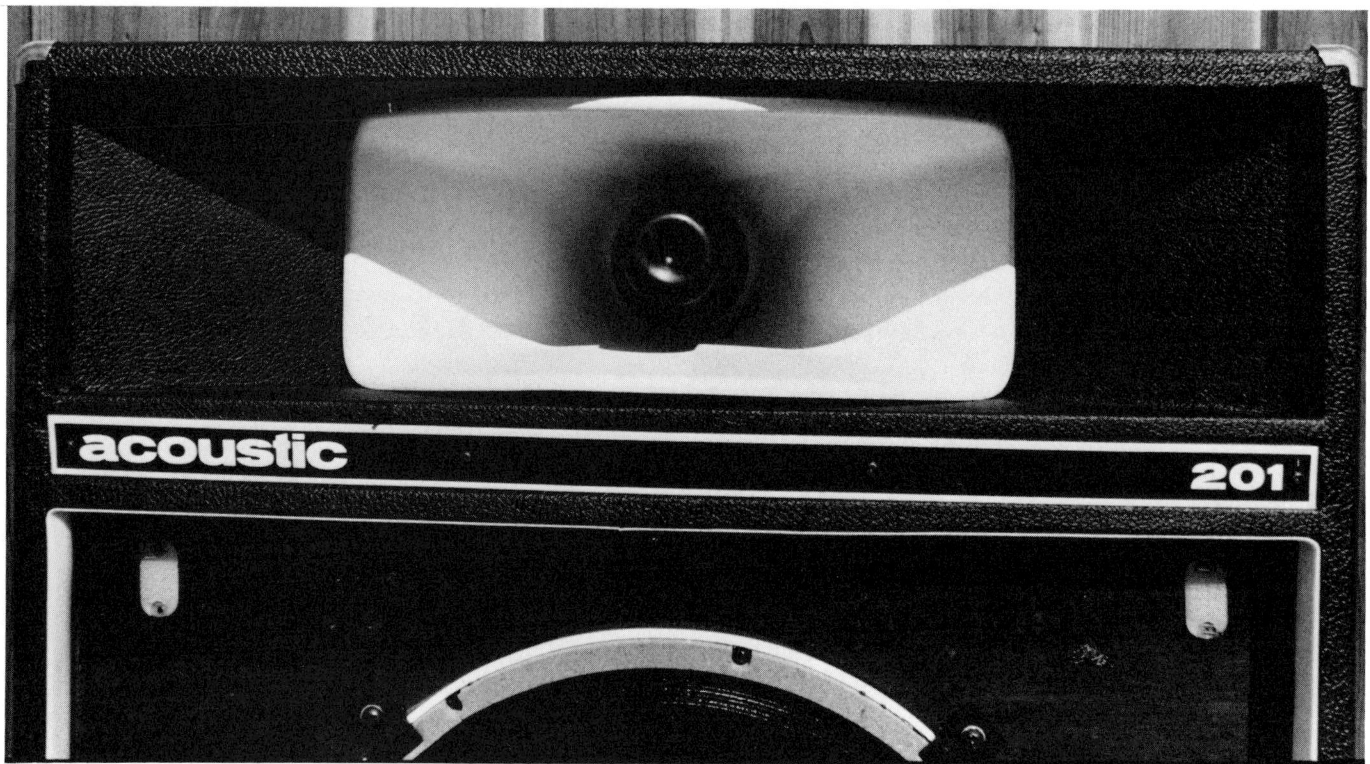

High-frequency radial horn

Rear-loaded horn

be a cancellation of those sound waves that are equal in length to the distance from the front of the speaker around the cabinet to the rear, though this is not considered to be a major drawback. One advantage to the open back is that a performer located behind it will hear the sound waves from the rear of the cone, and is therefore provided with a kind of monitor (p. 303).

Infinite Baffle

Many high-powered guitar amplifiers use an infinite baffle speaker enclosure: a sealed, airtight box, lined with sound-absorbent padding. The amount of midrange brilliance may be varied with the placement of the insulation material.

The loudspeaker will last longer if the forward and backward motions are held to a moderate excursion. Since there is no exchange of air from inside and outside the sealed cabinet, the enclosed volume of air acts as a spring or a stiffening agent, restricting cone movement to a fixed excursion. Removal of the back could strain the speaker.

The infinite baffle avoids the cancellation of some frequencies that occurs in the open-back cabinet. Bass reflex enclosures (p. 261) have greater bass response than the infinite baffle, a fact which may cause the infinite baffle to appear to have a longer, less boomy projection, due to the manner in which certain frequencies are perceived by the ear.

Bass Reflex (Phase-Inversion)

Unlike the sealed infinite baffle, the bass-reflex cabinet has holes of a calculated dimension, called "ports." The size of the ports depends upon the type of transducer and the volume of the enclosure; the larger the enclosure, the larger the ports. Sound waves from the rear of the speaker are reflected and sent out through the ports, where they are added in phase to the front waves. This increase in the percentage of waves leaving the cabinet provides nearly twice the output for each cone movement than the infinite baffle cabinet. In some ranges, the output may be boosted by three to four times. Varying the frequency response with ports or baffles is a process known as "tuning" the cabinet. Among the results of porting: bass response is substantically augmented, fidelity and transient response are improved, and the amount of power that may be handled is increased.

Rear-loaded horn, dual drivers

Front-loaded horn

Horn Enclosures

Megaphones, bull horns, the flared devices attached to the early phonographs, and many sirens and outdoor loudspeakers all operate according to the laws of physics which relate to expanding sound waves. These principles are applied in the design of the front-loaded, rear-loaded, and folding horns, which are commonly employed as acoustical transformers in speaker cabinets. Horns that are coupled to cone-type transducers are used to enhance the reproduction of lower (bass) frequencies, unlike high-frequency radial horns, which are coupled to compression drivers. Correctly designed horn-loaded transducers are exceptionally efficient; that is, they transform a relatively high percentage of the electrical input into acoustical output. Here, the word "load" refers to the part of the speaker connected to the horn, and not to the direction in which the speaker is facing. The projection and dispersion characteristics of any horn depend upon the length, shape, and rate of taper.

Front-loaded horn, dual drivers

Rear-Loaded Horn

The rear-loaded horn takes the waves from the back of the speaker and directs them in a 180° semi-circle out the front. The waves from the front of the cone are radiated directly forward. In most systems now on the market, the rear-loaded horn produces a relatively high percentage of bass (because the shorter high-frequency waves cannot follow the bends in the horn as well), and it is considered to be well suited to rooms where fidelity is the primary consideration. However, it is theoretically possible to design a front-loaded horn with every bit as good bass response as a rear-loaded horn.

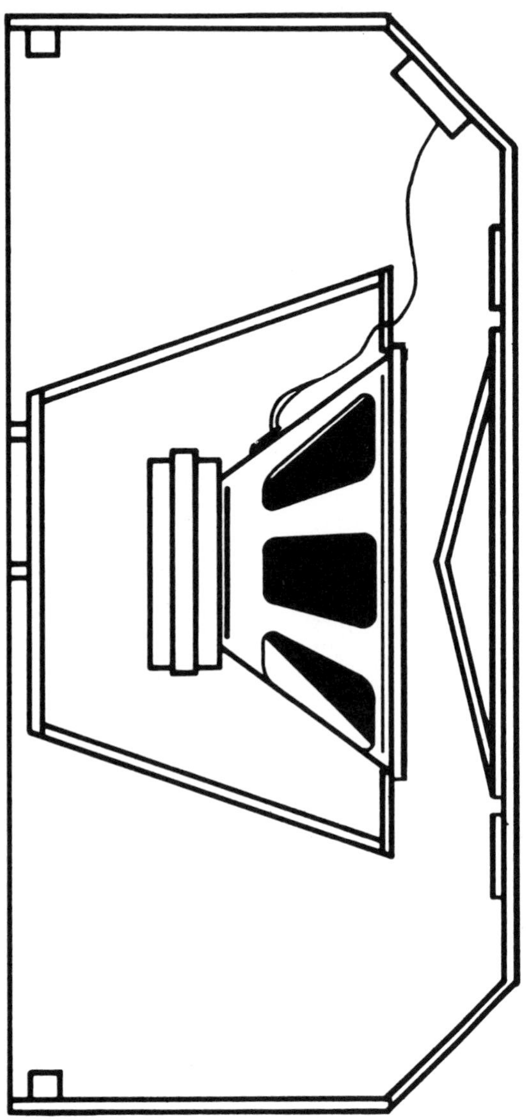

Folded horn enclosure

Front-Loaded Horn

As its name implies, this device extends the waves from the front of the speaker through a fast-taper horn that is much shorter than the slow-taper, rear-loaded horn. Some manufacturers recommend front-loading horns for outdoor concerts or large auditoriums where the bass response below 50 Hz is sometimes sacrificed to get more volume and longer projection.

Folded Horn

Sometimes a horn is folded up in such a way as to fit more conveniently inside the box, a feature permiting extended length. Commercially available folded horns can be about six feet long.

Like the other horns, the folded horn is an acoustic transformer of a gradually expanding cross-sectional area. Its length permits the longer bass waves to be more fully developed before leaving the mouth of the horn, boosting the bass response. There is also an increase in efficiency. Folded horns are particularly suited to systems designed for amplifying the electric bass, since that instrument's lowest frequency—40 Hz at the open E string—produces a wave that is over 28 feet in length. Extremely long waves may require that a folded-horn system be played louder in a small environment than in a large one to obtain a given volume.

Grille Cloth

To guard the cones against damage, a flexible, cloth-covered grille is installed over the face of the cabinet. The grille is a screenlike sheet, and the porous cloth is woven to permit the unimpeded dispersion of the sound waves.

17

Volume Mini-Amps

POWER AND VOLUME*

A standard volume control is a resistor. Its increments do not serve as an arithmetic scale that can be used to measure volume, nor do they indicate maximum power output. The volume knob alters the gain, which is the amount of signal input required to produce a specific output. There is usually a high rate of volume increase over the first third of the control's range; the rate of increase then drops substantially. (On the other hand, a few amps feature a volume control that has a linear rate of increase.) As mentioned earlier, an amp may be driven to its maximum volume at a relatively low setting on a standard, nonlinear control.

Much confusion arises from the fact that sound engineers often attach different meanings to "loudness" and "volume." Due to the sensitivity of the human ear, an increase in perceived loudness is not directly proportional to an increase in power output. To double the loudness (that is, to make the system "sound twice as loud"), it usually requires a 9 or 10 dB intensification. This huge increase could require many times the original power output. For example, if you are pushing a 75-watt source to its limits, delivering a specific Sound Pressure Level, and you wish to double the perceived loudness, you would perhaps require 750 watts to do so, ten times the original power, not merely twice as much. However, doubling

*See decibel table, page 317.

Welding amplifier chassis

Cutting grille cloth

the power increases the volume by 3 dB, still a substantial gain. Doubling the speakers and changing from a 50-watt to a 100-watt source will noticeably increase the loudness, though the level will not be doubled.

Another complicating phenomenon is the fact that the ear responds with more sensitivity to some frequencies (particularly 2,000 to 4,000 Hz) than to others. Notes in certain bands may *appear* to be relatively louder.

MASTER VOLUME CONTROL

Many guitarists like a high-volume sound, not just because it's loud, but because the tone is unique. High-volume distortion ranges from a funky, sassy, guitar tone to a barely recognizable buzz. One of the least desirable methods of causing it is overdriving the speakers, since it may result in temporary or permanent damage. The best stage in which to create internal distortion is the pre-amp, since that is where the character of the tone is primarily determined.

A master volume control is designed for this purpose. Located past the original volume control, in between the pre-amp and the driver stage, it allows you to set the regular volume knob at a high level, overdriving the pre-amp to create the distortion. The actual loudness is regulated by the master volume control, and you can now produce the distorted tone at very low levels.

Some artists prefer the sound of a small, overdriven tube amp, set at a high volume and miked through the sound system or the studio console. Running the instruments through the P.A. facilitates balancing the group's overall volume and tone, though the system must be designed to handle the burden.

SPEAKER CONNECTIONS AND VOLUME

If you increase the power output for more volume, it may be necessary to add speakers. If your amp is using only a part of its total power at the point of maximum safe speaker excursion, you can use more of the available power, boosting the loudness, by adding a second speaker connected either in series or parallel.

Two speakers hooked in series provide a 3 dB loud-

Note: Photos on pages 264, 265 taken at the Music Man factory, Anaheim, California.

ness increase, if the impedance is matched and if the amp has the necessary reserve power.

The parallel connection of two speakers decreases the load to one half its original resistance, with two consequences. First, more power now "gets through" the reduced load, increasing the dangers of clipping (see p. 269). Second, there may or may not be a greater amount of available or usable power output. It depends upon the design of the circuit. Tube amps are high-impedance systems. Speakers respond to a low-impedance signal, so tube amps have a transformer which "transforms" the high-impedance output to low impedance before sending it to the speakers. This fixes a maximum limit on the output. If that limit has already been reached, then the extra speakers cannot use more power. However, the volume will still increase somewhat, due to the larger mass of air being moved by the added cone area. If that limit has not been reached, then extra speakers can take more power, substantially boosting the volume. Some tube models feature an impedance selector, to match the output and load so that the transformer's power limit may be altered when adding supplementary cabinets. The transformer-type amp may have taps for 4-, 8-, or 16-ohm loads, permitting a variety of connections. For example, two 8-ohm speakers connected in series would match the 16-ohm tap, and if connected in parallel, they would match the 4-ohm tap.

Transistor amps are already low-impedance devices, so they are usually "direct coupled" to the speakers, with no intervening transformer stage. Without the fixed output limit, the parallel connection's decrease in resistance will indeed provide more current, substantially increasing the volume. However, *avoid an overload.* If the amp is not designed for the added speakers, the circuits may be blown.

Because of the wide diversity of circuit and cabinet design, rules concerning the addition of speakers are only a starting point. Consult an audio expert about the specific details of your system.

Amplifier assembly

Final electronic check-out

POWER "BOOSTERS"

There are many devices that are advertised to have the ability to boost the amp's power by 10, 50, or even 100 times. Some of the ads are inaccurate. If the amp's maximum power output is fixed, only an additional

A graphic equalizer circuit in a solder bath at the Road factory

power source or circuit modification can increase it. The booster increases the amp's *in*put (output of the guitar). That is, it increases the amp's sensitivity. If the amp requires a certain amount of input in order to reach its maximum output, and your guitar is presently incapable of producing a sufficiently strong signal, then the booster will increase the volume by boosting that input signal. The result is more power out, but in such a case you were not using the amplifier's full potential in the first place.

MINI-AMPS

After the success of the still popular Pignose, several manufacturers joined the subportable amplifier market. Available models now include the Ampeg Sound Cube, Dynamite, Peter Portable, Mitchell, and Dwarf. Though these amps are usually rated at only a few watts RMS or less, they are surprisingly loud. Clearly designed for a limited purpose, they have proved to be most convenient for the mobile guitarist.

Before buying, check to see if the amp offers built-in or optional AC operation. Try to look inside the amp; they vary widely in quality of assembly and construction. Compare wood cabinets to those of particle board. See how loud you can play with and without distortion. A particularly nice feature found on the Pignose: the batteries automatically disconnect when the cord is unplugged.

18

Amplifier and Speaker Maintenance

SAFE VOLUME LEVELS AND SPEAKER EXCURSION

The most common cause of speaker damage is an overload of power, causing excessive heat or mechanical damage to the cone or coil. About 85 percent or more of the electrical signal sent into a high-efficiency transducer produces only heat; the remaining energy is converted to sound waves. In low-efficiency speakers, the percentage of heat generation is even greater. Heat can cause the metal elements to expand, disturbing the balance between the various stages of energy transfer or weakening the connection between the voice coil and cone. The coil itself may even melt if the temperature is high enough. To protect your amplifier and speakers, determine the maximum safe volume level for your system.

Remove the grille cloth and watch the motion of the cone as you play a few notes at a gradually increasing volume level. You will notice a greater movement as you turn up the bass. (If your transducer features an aluminum dome in the center, avoid touching it—it's very delicate.) The distance that the cone can move without damage (its excursion limit) depends upon both its purpose and its workmanship. For example, the excellent JBL musical instrument transducers can move ¼″ with no problems. Their bass-range D-140F has a safe excursion distance of ⅜″. About 3/16″ or ¼″

is considered to be a safe excursion for most speakers, though whether or not a certain excursion is dangerous also depends upon the frequency of the signal that causes it. All other things being equal, the cone will double its excursion each time the frequency is lowered by one octave: if it is ⅛″ at 1,000 Hz, it will be ¼″ at 500 Hz, and ½″ at 250 Hz. Ask your audio specialist about the excursion limits of your speakers, or write to the service department of the manufacturer. Make a note of the volume setting at the point where the excursion reaches its safety limit, and keep the level below that point.

When observing the cone movement, leave your guitar's volume knob all the way up and regulate the loudness with the amplifier's controls. You can then determine a maximum safe level, which takes into consideration both the instrument and the amplifier. Some manufacturers recommend that you permanently set the amp's volume at its safety limit and perform all modifications on the instrument, the advantage being that no further adjustments need ever be made on the amplifier. However, the design of all but a few pickups is such that the tone shifts noticeably with even slight decreases in the instrument's volume setting. As a result, many guitarists perform with the pickups wide open, or close to it, controlling the overall volume with the dials on the amp or with a volume pedal.

SPEAKER DAMAGE AND TONE

Bass frequencies cause greater cone excursion and a resultant increase in wear on the loudspeaker. If you desire a heavy bass tone, adding supplementary transducers will diminish the possibility of overdriving the system at high volumes, provided that the impedance is matched. As previously mentioned, heavy duty speakers are best for low-frequency notes.

When determining your amp's safe maximum volume, leave the bass controls all the way up. If you measure it with a treble setting, you could conceivably exceed that point and overdrive the speakers just by boosting the bass tone.

CHECK-UPS AND EXTERNAL CONNECTIONS

Remove the back panel of the speaker cabinet to see that all wired connections are clean and each cable is properly shielded. A loose wire can interfere with grounding and may even destroy the cone. To maintain the highest standards of performance, test the tubes and circuits periodically—or have the work done by a serviceman—even if they seem to be operating without trouble. A single, inexpensive component can wear out or fail, causing a costly overload.

You have undoubtedly experienced the loud squawk that occurs when you take the loose end of a cord connected to a live amp and plug it into the guitar. That noise is caused by a high-level jolt of energy being forced through the cone. To avoid it, turn the amp's volume all the way down before plugging the cord into the instrument, or better yet, plug the cord into the guitar first, then the amp. During a break in your session, turn the volume all the way down or put the amplifier on standby to avoid the amplification of an accidental bump.

VIBRATION

Excessive vibration fractures solder joints and loosens components, necessitating the majority of amplifier repair work. When transporting an amp by car, keep it on the seat or another padded surface. A dangerous, yet common, cause of damaging vibration is placing the amp top directly on the speaker cabinet. One of the reasons why piggybacks were designed in the first place was to alleviate vibration in high-powered amps. If you place the amp top on a cabinet, you might insert a cushioning piece of foam or other padding. Speaker and chassis bolts should be periodically tightened, but not overtightened.

CLIPPING AND FEEDBACK: CAUSES AND REMEDIES

Overdriving the amp can produce clipping, a disturbing and damaging screech. An amplifier clips when it reaches the point where it can no longer produce the rounded sine wave which it was designed to produce. If charting the output on an oscilloscope, the sine wave begins to square off during clipping, a phenomenon that is interpreted by the ear as distortion. The overloaded amp sends this squared wave to the speaker, placing great acceleration forces on the cone and forcing it to move beyond its intended limits. Excessive heat strain on the coil assembly is also produced, and the speaker may be ruined.

Feedback is caused when the microphone or pickup receives the sound from the speakers and "feeds it back" through the amplifier again and again. The system may have components that are microphonic to particular frequencies. If bombarded by those frequencies, the component may begin to oscillate, resulting in the generation of a tone which, when routed through the amp hundreds or thousands of times, is sufficient to create the screaming "unity gain" or feedback condition.

The musical application of feedback is an art well worth mastering. If you know what you're doing, it can add whole dimensions to your creative adventures. If you don't, it's horrible. Whether you are in control of the feedback or not, it poses a serious danger to your amp and speakers. The voice coil is like a piston in a cylinder. If it doesn't move around enough, it overheats. The many different frequencies that are normally fed into the coil keep it moving, cooling itself as it does so. But the shrill feedback signal will have only one dominant frequency, reducing the motion of the coil. The effect is that the cooling mechanism is thwarted at the same moment the power is overloaded. The result may blow the cone or melt the glues in the coil.

The inherent resonances of hollow-body guitars make them more susceptible to feedback than solid-body guitars. Any one or more of the following precautions will help to alleviate the problem: (1) Do not face in the direction of the amp, and don't stand too close. The possibility of feedback increases as you shift the pickups and speakers nearer to a direct, face-to-face angle; it also increases if the pickups and speakers are moved closer to each other. If you play at high volumes, equip yourself with a long cord (15–25 feet) for stage work, so you can shift the angle of the guitar or move farther away from or to the side of the amp. (2) Pull the connecting cord from the amp between sets or turn the volume all the way down on either the amp or the instrument. (3) *Guitar Player Magazine* has suggested the removal of the pickup covers as a measure to reduce feedback from hollow-body guitars. The cover is magnetic steel, capable of generating a current when vibrated by the top. (4) Covering the f-holes with adhesive cloth tape or stuffing the body of the guitar with cotton, insulation, rags, foam rubber, or other material can reduce feedback, though these interferences with normal resonance may change the tone. If you use tape, minimize the risk of damage to the finish by applying it with as small an overlap as possible onto the face of the guitar body. You can buy guard plates for acoustic guitars made from thin sheets of clear, adhesive-coated plastic. These removable sheets are good for masking f-holes. (When removing, dissolve glue residue with Xylene or a similar solvent, but don't get it on plastic surfaces and follow the directions carefully.) If inserting a sound-deadening material, avoid brushing against the internal wiring. A more permanent damper or mute can be fashioned from flexible plastic or cardboard—cutting it just slightly larger than the f-hole and padding it, snugly, with a thick fabric such as blanket wool. One way to affix it to the inside of the guitar is to staple a couple of looped strings or rubber bands to the outside surface of the mute. Then apply the glue around the edges, which will overlap the f-hole. Insert it at an angle. Center it, and connect the rubber bands or strings to an object over the face of the guitar, to hold the mute in place overnight while the glue dries. The strings may then be snipped off. This is tricky and tedious. Unless you've got steady hands and iron nerves, let a repairman take care of it.

PREVENTION OF ELECTRIC SHOCKS

Proper grounding prevents electric shocks. Buy a volt-ohm meter (VOM) and use it to test for current between two elements in your stage set-up. Put the selector on the appropriate scale and test all combinations—mike and amp, guitar and amp, guitar and mike, and so on, one probe on one piece of equipment and the other probe on another. You might have to flip a few ground switches to make the stage safe; if there's any reading on the meter, then you could get seriously shocked, perhaps electrocuted. Keep flipping ground switches until the reading disappears. If there's no switch on a certain piece of equipment, you can still reverse its ground by pulling its plug, turning it over and plugging it back in, reversing the position of the prongs. Test the grounding of a single amp by inserting one probe into the AC plug receptacle in the back of the amp (*not* in the wall) and touch the other probe to the exposed chassis. Any voltage that appears should be eliminated by reversing the ground switch.

The Interfax Model ST2 is a compact device for testing the level of current leaking from the exposed metal parts of stage gear. It lights up when excess current is too high.

19

Amplifier and Speaker Failure

Your amplifier will perform well if you treat it like your body—take care of it, keep it clean, and exercise it, but don't overwork it or knock it around. Be nice to it. If it gets sick, cure it before it develops into something more serious. A malfunctioning amp will either sound weak, sound strange, or it won't sound at all. It might smoke, stink, or even catch fire. A particularly infuriating amp is the one that performs erratically. You take it to the dealer and it sits there smugly, sounding loud and clear; then on your first gig at the Hollywood Bowl, it makes a noise like a Saturn V and lapses into a coma.

If you don't hear the normal rushing sound or a low hum when the amp is on, test to see if it's still alive. Plug a cord into each input (one at a time), turn the volume up and lightly tap the free end once or twice with your finger. If there is a loud pop, then the amp is hanging in there (keep reading). If not, get out the yellow pages and look under "Musical Instrument—Repairs." Fluorescent or neon lights may cause a buzzing sound, so test the amp in a location free from these disturbances. (Don't keep fooling with the loose input jack—the noise is a strain on the speakers.) If the amplifier smokes or immediately blows out the fuse when you turn it on, the problem is almost surely in the circuitry, another job for the professional electrician or dealer.

TUBES AND CIRCUITS

If the amp malfunctions, test for a short by tapping the tube and listening for static. Many drugstores and hardware shops have simple testing devices. Each tube is filled with gas, and sometimes a leak may develop. The fact that the gas has turned blue or purple is not necessarily indicative of its ability to function. However, if the mirrorlike finish on the surface of the tube has started to take on a rainbowlike coloring, the tube is beginning to fail, due to overheating. See pages 249–253 for more facts about tube performance.

Examine the internal connectors of the input jacks behind the amp's front panel. If they are corroded from nonuse, distortion may result. Simple cleaning will take care of it, and occasional use will keep them polished.

Defects in the transformer, power supply, or components (capacitors, resistors, and so forth) comprise only a fraction of amp failure and malfunction. However, if you have checked the guitar, cord, input jacks, tubes, wires, cabinet fittings, and speakers, and it still won't work, contact a serviceman who will have the necessary testing equipment for making a diagnosis of the circuits. Don't tinker with the circuitry yourself. Tube amps and some transistor components (filter capacitors, for example) can store away a shock of such

Input jacks

a high voltage that anybody on the receiving end would probably swear off the guitar and take up the kazoo.

TROUBLE-SHOOTING FOR SPEAKER DAMAGE

Many electronic components are relatively simple in design, and they rarely break down. The majority of malfunctions occur in only a few areas, one of which is the speakers. Before you decide to perform any exploratory surgery, test the guitar and connecting cord through other equipment to isolate the problem in the amp. Examine the wires leading to the speaker to see if all connections are secure. Then, run the amp through a speaker known to be in good health to determine whether the problem is in the speakers or in the amp itself.

Speaker Distortion

Listen to one speaker at a time for distortion as you play through the amp. If one device is out, the other may be damaged by an overload. A speaker cone, like any piece of paper, can rip or wear through. The result might be an annoying buzz that only occurs when certain notes are played. If the tear is a small one, it can be glued with adhesives specially developed for that purpose. Jack Darr, in *Electric Guitar Amplifier Handbook* (Howard W. Sams, Bobbs-Merrill), suggests the use of rubber-to-metal cement for permanent repairs and surgical adhesive tape for on-the-spot emergency jobs.

If you hear a resonant, droning buzz that sounds almost like a musical tone, it may be caused by a loose fitting in the speaker cabinet. Tighten all screws, hinges, handles, and casters. If the noise persists, an amp repairman can pinpoint the troublesome frequency with an audio signal generator.

Voice Coil

The voice coil is suspended in a magnetic field, but overheating, a sudden jolt, or warping of the cone caused by a change in humidity may force the coil to rub against a surrounding surface. This ailment is called "out of round." Eventually, the coil may short out and cause total speaker failure. Some sources suggest that you test for coil alignment by gently pushing the cone in and out, using both hands to apply equal pressure to the left and right sides. However, in many modern transducers, the clearance between the pole-pieces and the coil is so small that such a test itself may disturb the alignment of the coil, unless performed by an audio expert. If the test uncovers a scraping sound from inside the coil housing, reconing and installation of a new coil is the only solution in almost all cases, though some of the older speakers are constructed to permit a simple realignment. Reconing and a coil-assembly transplant is like getting a new speaker (for less money), since the magnet will last indefinitely and the other parts are virtually trouble-free.

GROUNDING

Sometimes a simple grounding problem is mistaken for a more serious speaker or component defect. A popping sound, a little static, or even a mild electric shock may be produced when touching the strings or one of the metal fittings on the guitar (tailpiece, machine head, and so forth). Try flipping the ground switch on the amp, or (if there is none) take the plug out of the wall socket, turn it over, and reinsert it. Some amps feature the ground control in the form of a power switch with three settings—off, on, and on. The latter two positions comprise the ground selector. The system must be properly grounded to prevent serious electric shocks. (See p. 271.)

NOISY CONTROLS

See the note concerning the control knobs on the guitar; (see p. 231). The same information applies to amplifier dials and knobs.

20

Electronic Special Effects—Guitar Synthesizers

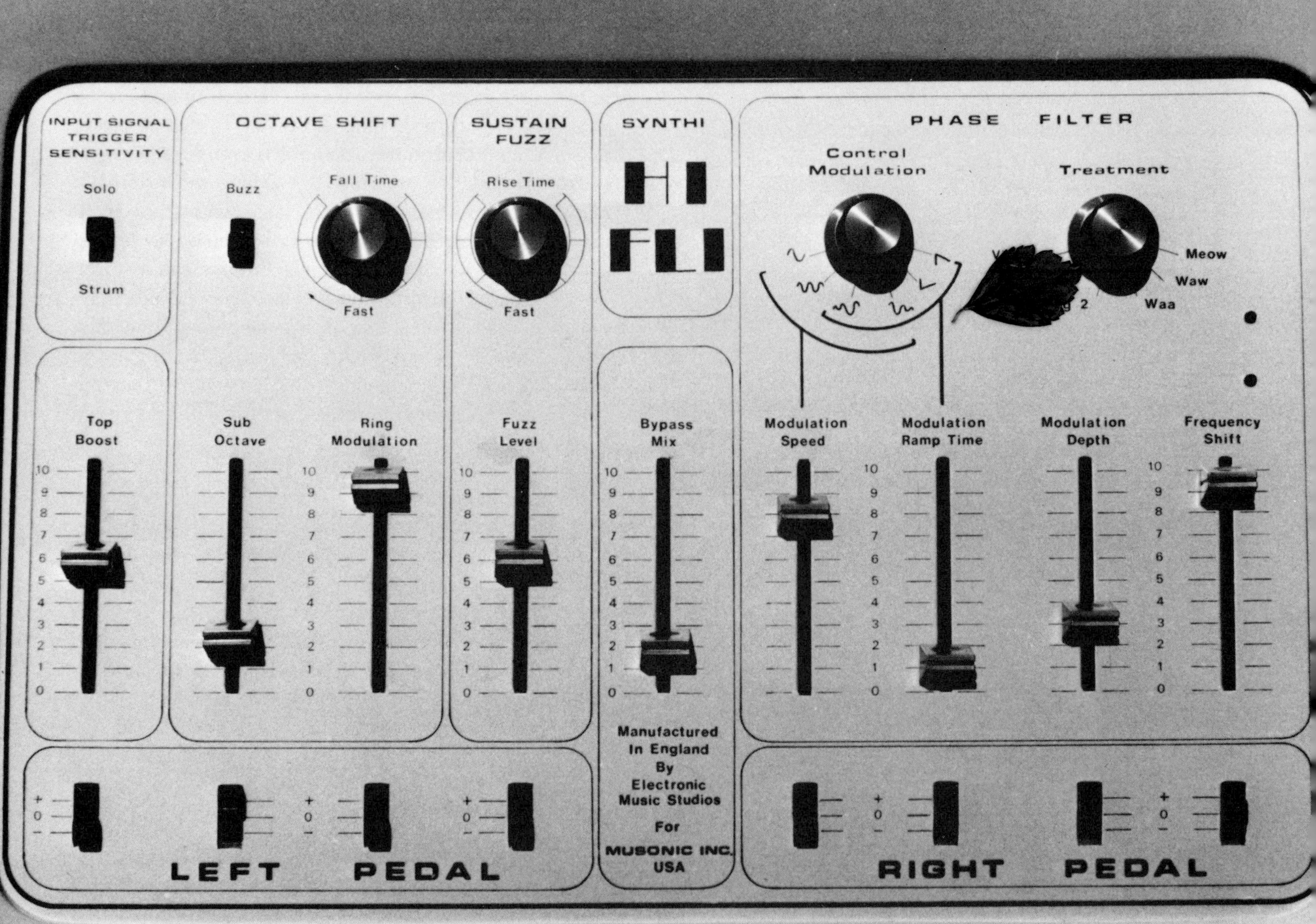

Inside a transistorized device

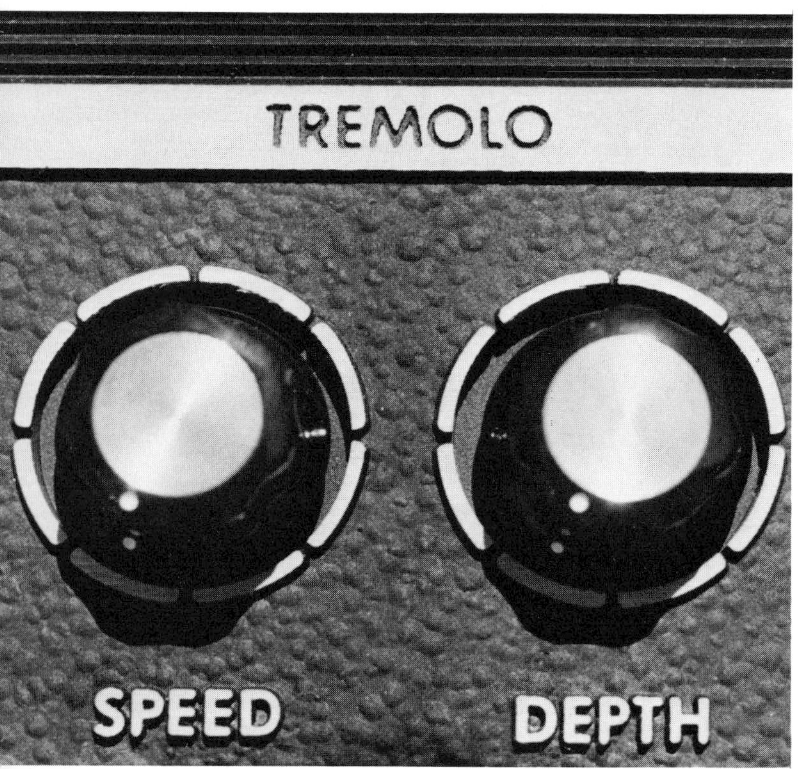

ELECTRONIC SPECIAL EFFECTS

It took long years of painstaking work for America's brightest sound engineers to develop amplification systems which could project a pure, clean signal at high volumes. You can take that signal and mess it up again in about a quarter of a second by stepping on a little metal box. You and your guitar can sound like a bumble bee, a crying baby, a three-car collision, a war, or just about anything else. You can make your instrument sound like a bass, a piano, an organ, a synthesizer, or several other instruments (even a guitar). "Buy Our Product and Rule the World!" However, don't expect sheer magic from your $39.95 investment. Regardless of what some ads may imply, there may be a little more than a fuzztone between you and Jimmy Page.

A special-effects device can make a guitar player sound better only if he knows how to use it. Unfortunately, too many of us take a "turn-it-up-and-cross-your-fingers" attitude, and the result is that it often makes a mediocre guitarist sound horrendous. Take a distortion unit, for example. It can be used to create massive, steady bass lines and soaring leads which are devastatingly powerful and full of emotion. It can also create a pile of boring trash. Forgive the lecture, but remember that although electronic effects may enhance your style, they can't be substituted for talent, practice, or experience. Like the frosting on a cake, just the right amount will really tickle the old tastebuds, but eating a whole bowlful will make you sick.

When choosing a special-effects device, consider serviceability, replacement of parts, and guarantee. If it causes a strain on the amplifier, ask the dealer about how to use it without shortening the life of the rest of your equipment.

If you use two or more pedals in conjunction with each other, connect them with a super-short cord to minimize line noises.

Special Effects Buyer's Checklist

Ask a salesman for tips on how the device is controlled. The finer points of operating even a simple unit are sometimes less obvious than you might think. Then check:

How durable?

The longer life and fewer breakdowns of a heavy, solidly built unit usually outweigh the disadvantage of extra bulk. The steeper purchase price will often be offset by fewer repair bills and a higher resale value.

How noisy?

Just running your signal through the extra stage is bound to cause noise; however, some units are much worse than others. Test for noise with the amp and guitar set at least at fairly high volumes. If you already have other special effects, bring them along to see how they interact with the new device.

How flexible?

Test each control's range of effects. How many different sounds? How easily can you pinpoint the one you want, and how quickly can you change from one effect to another? Observe how each circuit alters the others. For example, test a vibrato's "Depth" at slow, medium, and fast "Speed" settings.

Guarantee—how extensive?

Volume loss?

Except in a booster or preamp, the ability to introduce a special effect without changing your instrument's loudness is a distinct advantage, eliminating the hassle of readjusting a knob every time the box is switched on or off.

Tremolo

A tremolo circuit is an amplitude modulator that produces slight changes in the volume of the signal. The amplitude (amount of fluctuation) is controlled with the depth or intensity dial, providing a range of effects from a gentle waver to an abrupt, echolike repeat. The interval between the peaks of maximum loudness is varied with the speed, frequency, or rate control, from a slow pulse (approximately 2 cps) to a rapid flutter (approximately 8 cps).

Many tremolo units operate with a field-effect transistor (FET). Others use a photoelectric cell known as a light-dependent resistor (LDR), which couples the tremolo-oscillation voltage into the voltage amp circuits. Since tremolo is so similar to vibrato (below), the two are often confused, sometimes resulting in the misnomer "hand tremolo" being applied to the hand vibrato.

Vibrato

A vibrato circuit varies the *pitch* (as opposed to the volume) of the amplified signal. Both the variety of available effects and the controls for selecting them are nearly identical to those mentioned above in the discussion of tremolo. Your repairman can extend the range of slower pulsations by installing a resistor or a potentiometer of higher resistance. A few companies (for example, Kustom) offer both tremolo and vibrato on the same models, though it is much more common to feature one or the other.

Reverberation

Reverb was at its peak of popularity during the days of the surf guitar, when practically every instrumental song incorporated it. Concert and recording artists still use it often for adding depth to guitar and vocals. The basic Hammond-type reverb employs two springs through which the signal is routed. The electrical signal is converted to a mechanical impulse, then sent down the spring and converted back to its electrical state. One spring causes a delay of approximately 29 milliseconds; the other causes a 32- to 37-millisecond delay. Part of the signal is also sent directly to the speakers, by-passing the springs. This direct signal is heard first, and the springs produce the delayed effect. A portion of the signal may be rerouted through the

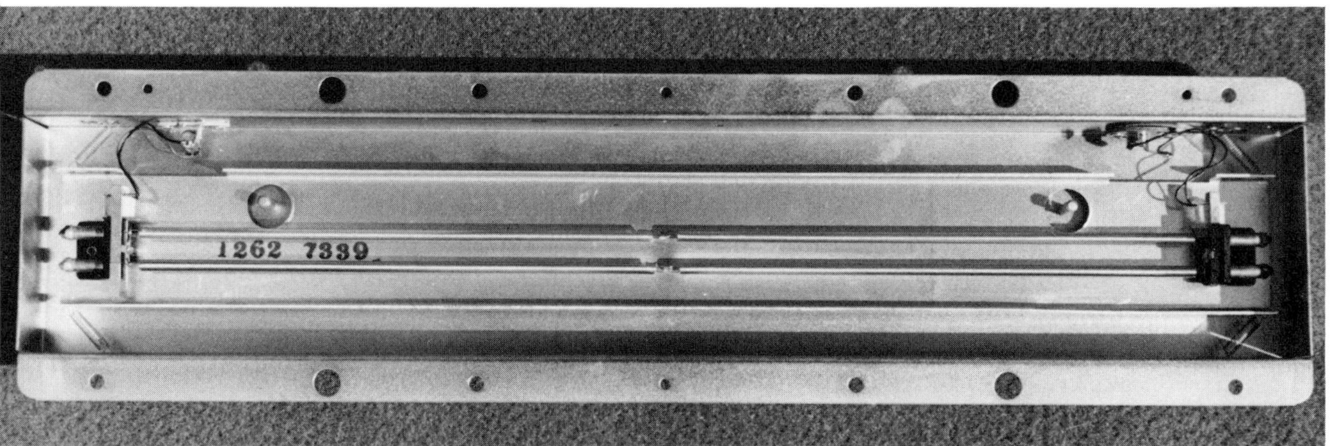

Reverb springs

springs to create a diminishing echo effect. Reverb may be thought of as a series of echoes so close together that the interval between them is imperceptible. The depth of the effect is controlled with a knob which varies the blend between the delayed and straight-through signals.

With a low setting, mild reverb is similar to a concert-hall atmosphere where the listener perceives part of the sound immediately and the rest after it is reflected from the walls and ceiling at different intervals. A high setting provides a haunting sustain, as if the sound were being made at the end of a long tunnel.

If you have ever jarred a reverb unit that was operating at the time, the loud rushing or crash was caused by the springs bouncing against each other. Despite the great noise, it will usually cause no damage to the reverb circuit, though at extreme volumes it could strain the speakers.

Almost all of the major amplifier manufacturers offer reverb on several models. Footswitch-activated external reverb kits are available from Fender, Marshall, Gretsch, and others.

Distortion and Sustain Units

A fuzztone (fuzz box) is a simple, battery-powered, transistorized device that can ideally reproduce effects from the moderate distortion of an overdriven tube amp to a heavy, solid buzz with an almost indefinite sustain. The circuit operates to change the normally smooth wave into a clipped or squared-wave configuration, distorting the signal. A few units plug into the guitar or amp, but most are floor models, activated by a footswitch, leaving the musician's hands free to continue playing.

The fuzz box usually has at least two controls: "volume"—for balancing or boosting the loudness of the distorted signal, and "fuzz"—for adjusting the intensity of the distortion, by changing either the amount of the clipping or the proportion of clipped and normal wave forms. As you will see, there are many variations of these controls.

The fuzz regulator is an important feature which distinguishes a versatile device. Look for a wide range, from light breakup to a super rasp. Even though the knob may be numbered from 1 to 10, it could be little more than an on/off switch. All fuzztones have the ability to sustain, though at least one includes a decay control to abruptly cut off the notes as you play, if desired. A few sustainers can extend the length of a note without substantial distortion.

If your fuzz unit isn't raspy enough, you can increase both its volume and distortion capabilities with the addition of an extra battery. However, you are risking possible damage to the transistors, so experiment with caution.

The many manufacturers include Foxx, Maestro, Fender, Electro-harmonix, Univox, Colorsound, Ampeg, Vox, Guild, Goya, Schaller, Jordan, Kent, Rosac, Musical Inst. Corp. of America, PAIA, and Heath. The do-it-yourself fuzztones and those which attach to the guitar are priced as low as $15 to $20. Most standard floor models cost from $45 to $65.

Another distortion-producing device is the master volume control (see p. 264).

Wah-Wah Pedals

The wah-wah is essentially a floor-model tone control, from treble to bass or vice versa as you depress your foot. Battery-operated and transistorized, a wah-wah can fundamentally alter your playing style. With hard strumming on muted strings, it gives that chunky, tone-changing percussive rhythm—Isaac Hayes' "Shaft". It can approximate a baby's cry—Eric Clapton's "White Room" (*Best of Cream*) and Jimi Hendrix's "Red House" (live version, *Hendrix in the West*). It's also popular in Motown—"Poppa Was a Rolling Stone" (Temptations).

In addition to the usual things such as durability and workmanship, a nice feature in a wah-wah is a broad range of tonality, from bass to treble. You will probably find that the most expressive results are gained with a tight, gradual shift in tone, as opposed to an abrupt jump from mellow to bright. Some of the manufacturers of good wah-wahs are Foxx, Marshall, Morley, Maestro, Colorsound, and the Thomas Organ Company (Cry Baby).

Volume Pedals

The greatest versatility comes from an even, gradual change from low to high volume. Some of the better volume pedals, such as Sho-Bud, Colorsound, Foxx, and Fender, cost around $40 to $60. The Morley photoelectric pedals are exceptionally sensitive, durable, and smooth.

Echo Devices

Echo machines come in a great variety of prices and features, providing that other-worldly repeating signal so often used in the recording studio. One common type uses a continuous tape loop, a recording tape head, and a playback head. The first head picks up the signal and records it on the loop. Then after a slight delay, the second one repeats it, creating the echo effect. Additional playback heads increase the versatility. Furthermore, the delay can be modified by altering the space between the two heads. With a very small interval of delay, a reverb effect is produced.

One way to use echo with the electric guitar is demonstrated during the last half of Jimi Hendrix's typically brilliant solo in "Red House" (studio version, *Smash Hits*). Other tasty examples: "Beck's Bolero" (Jeff Beck) and Robin Trower's "Hannah." You can adjust the rate of the echo to match the tempo of the song (Chet Atkins's "Blue Ocean Echo," *Best Of Chet Atkins*), and with the sound-on-sound option, multitrack recording may be achieved.

Some parts of the echo machine are fragile, and the entire unit should be handled with care. Occasional cleaning of the heads is recommended in order to reduce static. Spare tapes are inexpensive and should be purchased in lots, since the sound quality decreases when the loop wears out. A few of the better tape-echo machines are those by Schaller, Maestro (Sireko, Echoplex), and Guild/Binson (Copicat).

There are nontape electrostatic machines, which usually cost more than the tape-loop models. Operated with an iron oxide-coated magnetic disc or drum with up to six playback heads, they are considered to be both versatile and reliable. Examples are the Echorec models by Guild/Binson and the Tel-Ray Ad-N-Echo.

Computerlike digital delay systems, without tapes, drums, or discs, are capable of spectacular effects including the production of added notes, different from those originally played on the guitar. Digital echo machines are presently distributed by only a very few companies, and they're expensive.

The Morley echo/volume pedal employs a small magnetic disc which passes through an oil bath. Instead of the usual rack-and-pinion potentiometer, the pedal operates with a photoelectric cell.

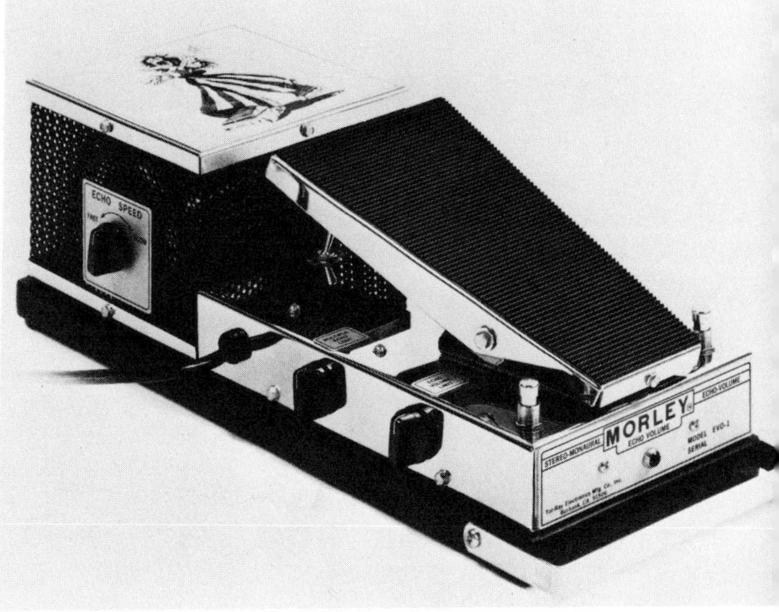

Tone Boosters

These frequency modifiers come in several designs: bass boosters (for example, The Mole, Low Frequency Compressor, and Hog's Foot, all by Electro-harmonix), treble boosters (such as the Screaming Tree and Screaming Bird, also by E-h), and combination low-and-high-frequency boosters, ranging from the $10 Kent EA-2 to Maestro's Full-Range Booster, with controls for each of four frequency bands. Boosters are either peaking or shelving devices. The former ideally boosts only those tones in a relatively narrow band, while the latter boosts *all* frequencies above (or below) the selected point. Graphically, the peaking booster produces a frequency response curve with a single peak, while a shelving booster causes a flat "shelf" of boosted signals extending from the selected frequency to the edge of the graph. (See p. 248, graphic equalizers.)

The Memory Man by Electro-harmonix is an analog delay line, a purely electronic, nonmechanical method of producing echo.

Combination Devices

Most companies offer multi-effect accessories in a broad range. The popular combinations are wah-wah and volume swell, distortion and sustain, wah-wah and fuzz, and there are elaborate models with three or more effects. Test these units to see which effects may be used individually and which combinations are possible.

Some equipment defies categorization. The volume-boosting Pulse Modulator by Electro-harmonix continuously regenerates three pulses of the instrument's sig-ing Pulse Modulator by Electro-harmonix continuously regenerates three pulses of the instrument's signal, each one variable for speed and volume. Since the three beats are controlled individually, you can produce a trio of different signals at the same time for a very strange effect. The versatile Frequency Analyzer (also by E-h) adds notes to those played on the guitar. A filter switch separates two whole categories of sounds, from light, musical overtones to tubby, robotlike electronic signals. You can add endless tones, harmonic or dissonant, varying the blend of original and superimposed sounds. It can be tuned to the guitar by eliminating dissonant pulses (see pp. 193–194). The description of a ring modulator (see p. 287) also fits it.

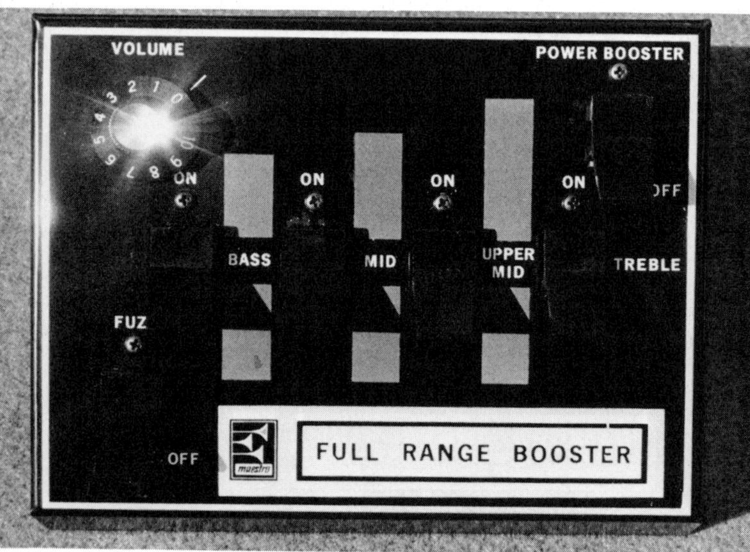

Talk Box

The floor box contains a miniature amplifier and a speaker device that connects to a plastic tube instead of to a speaker cone. The other end of the long, flexible tube goes into your mouth, perhaps held between your teeth. Your mouth is now a speaker "cabinet," which will affect the guitar's sound as you form words (you must keep close to the microphone in order to be heard). With practice, you and your guitar can "talk." Talk boxes are made by Dean Markley, Mitchell, PAIA, Electro-harmonix, and Heil.

Envelope Modifiers

"Envelope" refers to a note's loudness contour, a distinctive portrait that encompasses attack, sustain, and decay. Synthesizer technology has permitted the development of external envelope modifiers (or loudness-to-voltage converters), which alter one or more of these elements to produce special effects. The most common is an electronic wah, in which the guitar's signal is converted to a proportional voltage that in turn activates a filter. The amount of filtering then varies with the intensity of the player's touch, and the effect diminishes as the note decays. It turns your plunks into wahs, wows, quacks, and chirps.

Popular envelope modifiers include Seamoon's Funk Machine and the Mu-tron III, a favorite of Stevie Wonder. Other entries: Doctor Q by Electro-harmonix (E-h), Maestro's Filter Sample & Hold, E-h's Queen-Triggered Wah Pedal, and Systech's Envelope Computer. Also check out Roland's Funny Cat and units by Oberheim and Colorsound.

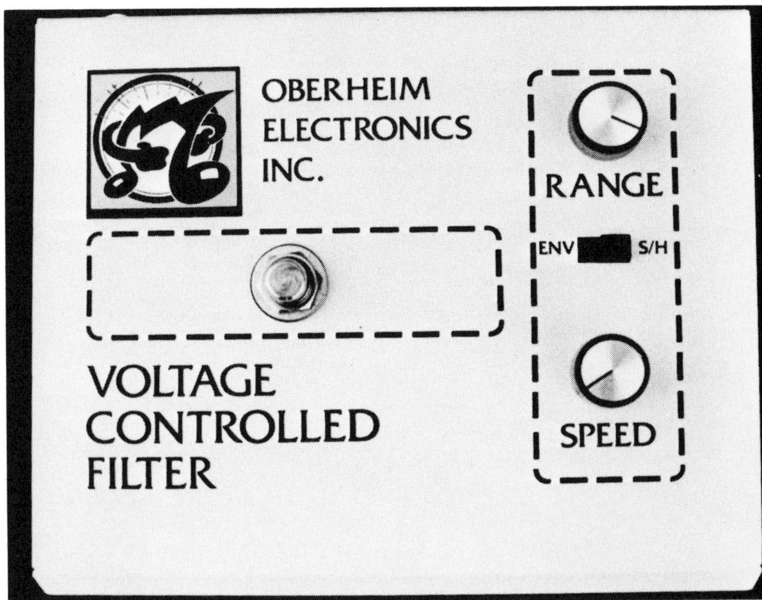

Octave Dividers and Octave Multipliers

The octave divider or splitter ideally adds a tone one or two octaves below the note played, permitting the guitarist to perform duets by himself. However, musicians often have difficulty getting some devices to perform consistently. They are occasionally activated by an overtone of the note played, rather than by the note itself. Furthermore, the added note is sometimes distorted. Some units are particularly touch-sensitive, responding erratically to the slightest fluctuations in pick attack. Finally, chords may "confuse" the octave circuits, causing a jumble of clashing tones. Octave dividers respond much more evenly to pure and consistent signals, such as those produced by

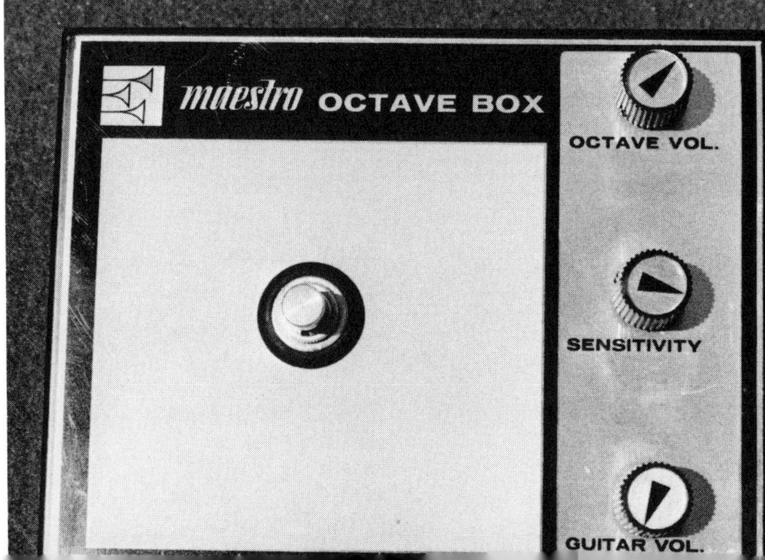

a sax or other horn. Despite the drawbacks, if you work with the device (and with your pick attack), you may control the performance and produce a tolerably clean effect—particularly if the box includes a distortion-reducing filter stage.

An octave multiplier, such as Tycobrahe's Octavia or Dan Armstrong's Green Ringer, is a specialized distortion unit designed to pinpoint the note one octave *above* the note played. The two are combined for a doubling effect.

Compressors

A guitar's wide dynamic range encompasses everything from soft gentle notes to heavily attacked chords, and it poses a problem for the amp. If the amp's sensitivity is set high enough to amplify the soft notes, it may distort the loud ones. On the other hand, if it is set low enough to avoid distorting the loud notes, the soft ones may be completely missed. The dilemma is particularly acute when recording, since the recorder will impose restrictions of its own upon dynamic range.

A compressor is designed to narrow down (compress) the peaks and valleys of output so that the level of signal presented to the amplifier no longer ranges from extreme lows to extreme highs. When it receives a sharply picked note, the device flattens the peak of the initial attack and then gradually increases amplification to offset the note's natural decay. If properly adjusted, this process sustains the note with little or no distortion. By averaging peaks and valleys, a compressor thus changes the signal profile of an intensely picked note from a sharp peak/severe drop-off to a gentle slope. A louder overall signal is possible, and musical sensitivity is increased by amplifying many subtleties which would otherwise be lost. Since sharp attacks are squashed, the compressor's effect on a guitar is particularly noticeable. The unit will likely require some fine adjustment to compress without hissing. There are at least a dozen compressors intended for the guitarist, from about $30 to $100.

Noise Gates

Noise abounds. It comes from instruments, amps, lights, cables, appliances, household wiring, etc. The noise gate is a threshold device, like a compressor, but instead of squashing signals *above* its preset level, it attenuates (diminishes) signals *below* that level. It works on the assumption that all notes played on your guitar, even the softest ones, will still be louder than those unwanted noises. You set the threshold somewhere above the volume of your softest notes, allowing everything you play to pass through the gate. However, signals below that threshold, including unwanted noises, are excluded when the gate "shuts." Set the threshold carefully. If it is too high, some noise will get through the gate; if too low, it will gate off your softest passages or shorten the tail end of decaying notes.

Preamps

When an amp is required to boost a particularly weak guitar signal, it also boosts a lot of noise. An external preamp can boost the signal *before* it reaches the amp, solving most of the problem. It can also be used to overdrive an amp. Since the preamp then produces distortion, it is often compared to a fuzztone. However, the fuzztone itself produces distortion, while a preamp produces a clean signal that is boosted up to a point where it then causes the *amplifier* to distort. Be sure to test preamps when shopping for distortion boxes. Some manufacturers install preamps in their guitars to increase tone control.

Leslie Speakers, Phase Shifters, and Flangers

The Leslie speaker's pulsating vibrato is an example of the Doppler effect, a principle of sound wave theory which states that as a moving source of sound approaches the listener, the perceived pitch rises; as the source recedes, pitch falls. Passing auto horns and train whistles are other examples of this phenomenon. The rise or fall is caused by the changing distances traveled by successive sound waves.

The Leslie speaker rotates inside its cabinet. Pitch is perceived to be at its highest when the speaker is facing the listener and the sound waves are traveling their shortest distance. Pitch appears lowest when the speaker is pointed away. The speaker's circular motion wavers the pitch between these extremes. Since the sound waves travel longer distances from certain points relative to others, an actual or "real time" delay is involved. Unlike a pure tone, a musical note usually includes a complex structure of harmonics (see chap. 11). Since these harmonics vary in wavelength, the Doppler effect is complicated and enriched.

The term "phase" is used in measuring the time synchronization of sound waves or electrical signals. The peaks of two in-phase waves occur at the same time, and the combination reinforces the overall signal. At the other extreme, two waves are perfectly out of phase when the highest peak of one occurs precisely when the other is at its deepest trough. At this maximum of 180° out of phase, every positive wave fragment above the center line is perfectly offset by a corresponding negative fragment below the line. Complete cancellation results—no sound at all. Between these extremes lie many gradations of phase, each producing a distinctive pattern of cancellation and reinforcement. These phase relationships are often plotted on a graph. If the reinforcement peaks are extreme spikes, closely spaced, the graph resembles the teeth of a comb, and the filter used to produce the effect is often called a comb filter.

The phase shifter was originally designed to electronically mimic some of the real-time delay effects of the Leslie. Today it is used more often because of its own celestial sound, a spinning, airy whoosh, often compared to the slowly twisting rush of a distant jet. It uses voltage-controlled filters to alter the phase of incoming signals. By mixing waves of various phase relationships (delayed and nondelayed), cancellation and reinforcement result. Each pair of filters provides a notch of cancellation. The more filter stages, the deeper the effect.

An oscillator sweeps up and down the band width, shifting the point of cancellation. This causes the whooshing noise to rise and fall like the sound of a high-speed wind. The rate of sweep is controlled by either the "Speed" potentiometer, a set of preset switches, or a pedal. Some units include a circuit through which a portion of the signal is rerouted or "regenerated." This feedback adds a harmonic complexity that emphasizes the phasing effect.

"Flanging" is named after a late-Fifties studio technique in which an engineer would press his thumb against the edge (flange) of a tape reel, throwing it slightly out of synch with a second recorder. An electronic flanger uses an analog delay line (a "bucket brigade" series of stages) to shift phase. It is a real-time device, and its points of reinforcement are harmonically related. Whether or not the effect is distinguishable from phasing depends in part upon the harmonic content of the incoming signal; the more complex the signal, the more distinct the flanging effect. Flangers are offered by Tycobrahe (pedal), MXR, Systech, PAIA, Electro-harmonix, and others.

Choosing a phaser

Like any piece of sound equipment, a phase shifter should be checked out for noise, distortion, and ruggedness. Compare units with a regeneration feature to some without. Check the depth of the phasing effect, the range of sweep from low to high, the flexibility of the speed control, how smoothly the sweep occurs, and whether it shifts from upsweep to downsweep evenly or abruptly. Since speed and apparent depth are interrelated, check the depth at each of several speed settings.

Phase shifters are now offered by dozens of manufacturers. In order to appreciate the spectrum of available effects, investigate as many units as possible, certainly those offered by MXR, Morley (photoelectric pedal operation), Electro-harmonix, and Maestro. One of the most flexible units is Mu-tron's elaborate Bi-Phase, with two independent six-stage circuits and a pair of sweep oscillators. The Ibanez Flying Pan incorporates an automatic stereophonic panning function. Other manufacturers include Systech, Seamoon, Foxx, Fender, Colorsound, and Roland.

Ring Modulator

One of the more complex special effects, the ring modulator, produces variable chimelike harmonic tones. As you play a passage on your instrument, the overtones may progress either in the same or opposite direction. You should be able to hear only the fundamentals at one extreme setting, and only the synthesized harmonics at the other, with many variations in between. The ring modulator creates spacy, disjointed and crazy sounds, as well as more subdued, exotic overtones. Available in both console (for example, Maestro) and foot-pedal models (Colorsound).

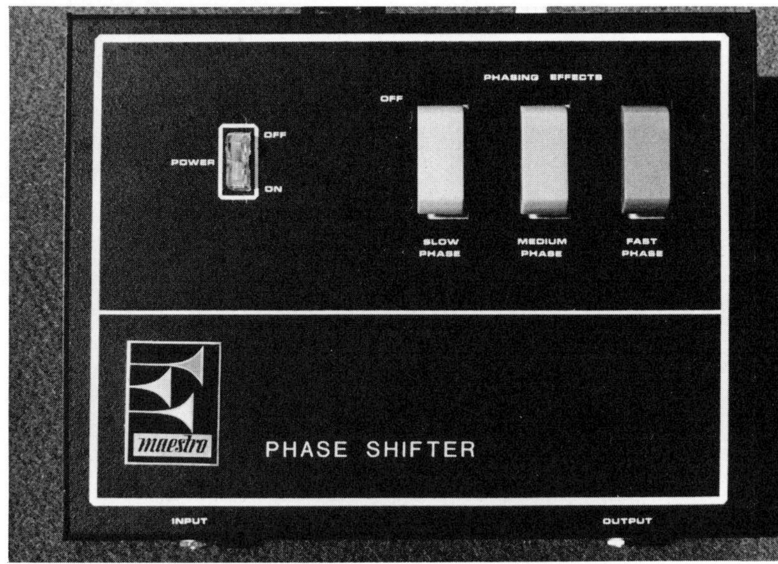

Consoles

With the popularity of electronic music in recent years, compact synthesizers for guitarists were inevitable. England's EMS distributes the Synthi Hi-fli, an elaborate, two-pedal piece of equipment with a dazzling array of available effects, all housed in a portable, futuristic console: fuzz and sustain effects, frequency modulation, phasing, vibrato, wah, and more.

Other versatile units are BCM's Mode Synthesizer, and Maestro's G-2 Guitar System.

Theremin

This is an electronic oscillator/musical instrument named after its inventor, Professor Leon Theremin of Russia. Developed in 1920, it consists of two electrically charged rods attached to high-frequency circuits. The instrument is played by moving the hands closer to the rods or plates, one controlling the pitch and the other the volume. The hands never touch the instrument; rather it is the electrical capacitance of the human body which affects the signal. The theremin produces a smooth, high-pitched sound, capable of imitating woodwinds, violins, and even the human voice. A prominent example: the wobbling wooh-wooh at the end of the Beach Boys' "Good Vibrations."

Special Effects: Order of Connection

There are many possible arrangements for the series connections of several effects; each may have advantages and disadvantages. In the March, 1977, *Guitar Player,* columnist Craig Anderton suggests:

For an increase in level with the least amount of

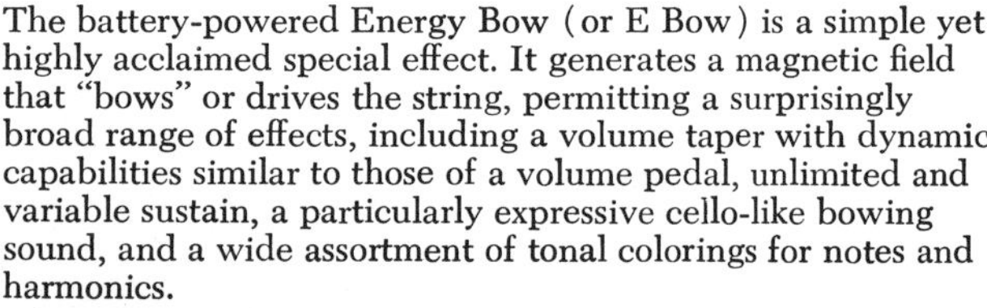

The battery-powered Energy Bow (or E Bow) is a simple yet highly acclaimed special effect. It generates a magnetic field that "bows" or drives the string, permitting a surprisingly broad range of effects, including a volume taper with dynamic capabilities similar to those of a volume pedal, unlimited and variable sustain, a particularly expressive cello-like bowing sound, and a wide assortment of tonal colorings for notes and harmonics.

noise, the preamp should be first in the chain, then the compressor.

A fuzz and ring modulator might come next, in a side-by-side connection which permits selection of one or the other. The fact that an extra link in the chain is omitted—always a plus—outweighs the nominal advantage of being able to use those two particular effects simultaneously.

Next: envelope modifier and wah-wah, again connected in an either/or side-by-side arrangement that eliminates the problems involved in running a signal through a series of two filters at once. Keep in mind that activating the compressor or fuzz will alter the response of the envelope modifier down the line. An option: try positioning the wah-wah ahead of the fuzz. A phase shifter should come toward the end of the chain, since it responds best to harmonically complex input signals.

Finally, the volume pedal and echo. If the pedal precedes the echo, an echo may be sustained after the note has disappeared. If the order is reversed, the pedal can be used to control echo level as well as signal level. Mr. Anderton recommends the use of a volume pedal in order to balance the apparent changes in level caused by the use of several special effects. For details on these and related topics, see his book, *Electronic Projects For Musicians.*

GUITAR SYNTHESIZERS

Until recently, only keyboardists have enjoyed full accessibility to true synthesizers. Early electronic components designed for use with guitars had several drawbacks. One example is the wired-fretboard approach in which an electrical circuit is completed every time the string and fret make contact. An electronic signal that corresponds to the pitch of the selected note is then relayed to a synthesizer. The problem is that such instruments may respond inadequately to bending, sliding, and vibrato, and they may be unable to detect the crucial right-hand changes in dynamics and picking technique.

Several recent products now provide the guitarist with a complete array of synthesized effects without depriving him of the playing techniques that give the guitar its very soul. These include specially wired guitars, interface devices, synthesizers, and complete systems. Current technology limits the use of synthesizers to solid-body guitars due to the resonance

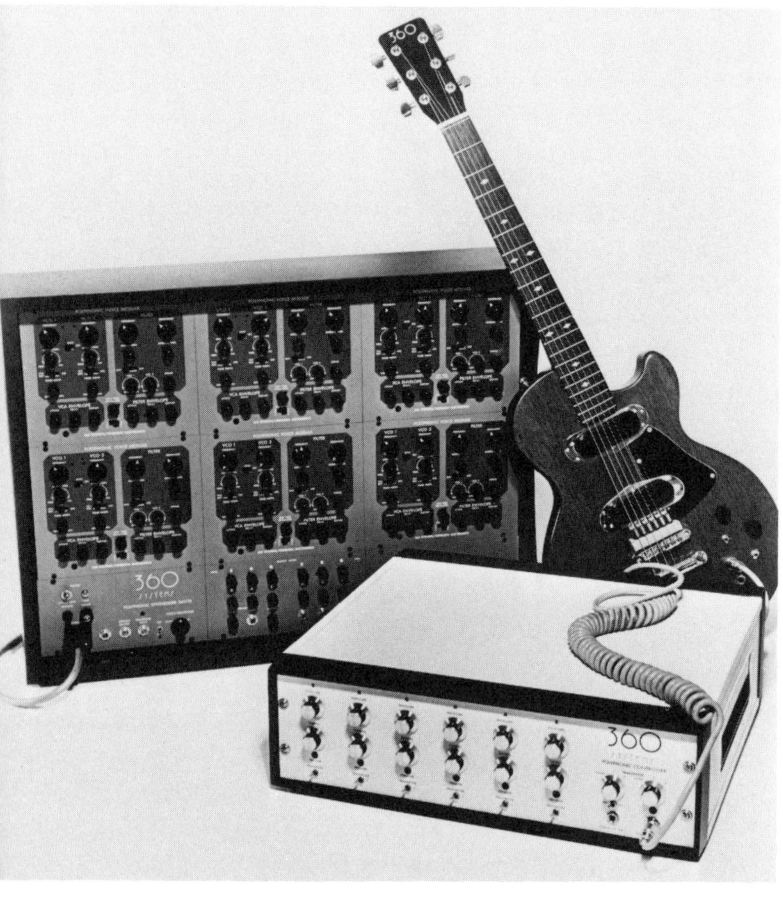

360 Systems Polyphonic Guitar Synthesizer

and harmonic intricacies of acoustic instruments. Furthermore, guitar synthesizers are generally intended for lead work and single-note passages, rather than rhythm strumming. When presented with a chord, properly designed polyphonic units respond correctly, while some monophonic units disintegrate harmonically, and others reproduce only the last note picked. However, sometimes a slight arpeggio technique can provide sufficient isolation of the individual notes to achieve chordal effects without confusing the circuitry.

An interface device is not a synthesizer but rather an intermediate stage located between guitar and synthesizer. Its function is to convert the impulses generated by the instrument into signals which the synthesizer can understand. A good example is the solid-state Slavedriver by 360 Systems. It incorporates a six-channel pickup, a box, and connecting cable. The box houses a pitch-to-voltage converter and a true envelope follower (loudness-to-voltage converter) among other components. The no-hassle front panel includes an octave selector and an interval preset. The pitch of the interval is dialed on the Slavedriver, and the tone and effects are set on the synthesizer itself. 360 Systems also builds synthesizers, including the ones featured on John McLaughlin's *Inner Worlds* album and Lee Ritenour's *Captain Fingers.*

A few years ago, Walter Sear of New York built an extremely expensive polyphonic guitar synthesizer that incorporated a Dan Armstrong plexiglass solidbody, a six-segment pickup, and a synthesizer. The advantage to a polyphonic device is that each string can be programmed to produce a different musical or nonmusical sound to result in a stunning symphonic effect. Sear Sound also builds an interface module which should be compared to the 360 Systems Slavedriver.

ARP Instruments is a major innovator in electronic music, and its beautifully designed Avatar guitar synthesizer offers virtually unlimited effects. The six-channel pickup connects each string to its own gain-adjustable preamp. The synthesizer console is comparable to ARP's popular Odyssey, with a full complement of voltage-controlled oscillators (VCOs), voltage-controlled filters (VCFs), envelope modifiers, and other synthesizer elements. Sophisticated circuitry permits the guitarist to employ all of his fingering technique without confusing the electronics.

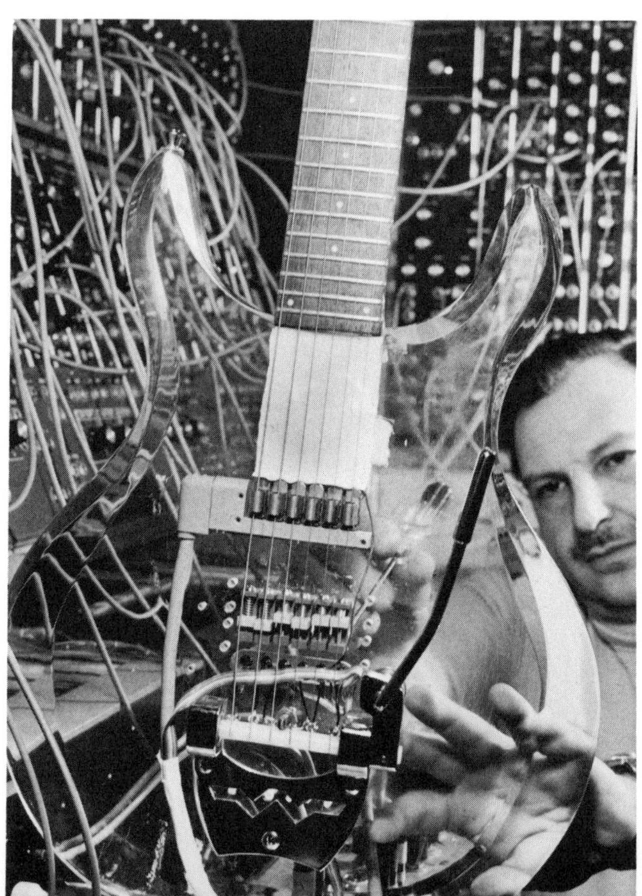

Walter Sear and his Synthesar

Arp Avatar pickup mounted on an Alembic guitar

Ampeg's Patch 2000 is a comparatively low-priced guitar and synthesizer system that incorporates a wired fretboard.

Roland's GR-500 incorporates both a guitar and a versatile synthesizer console. The instrument's strings themselves serve the signal-generating function of the VCO.

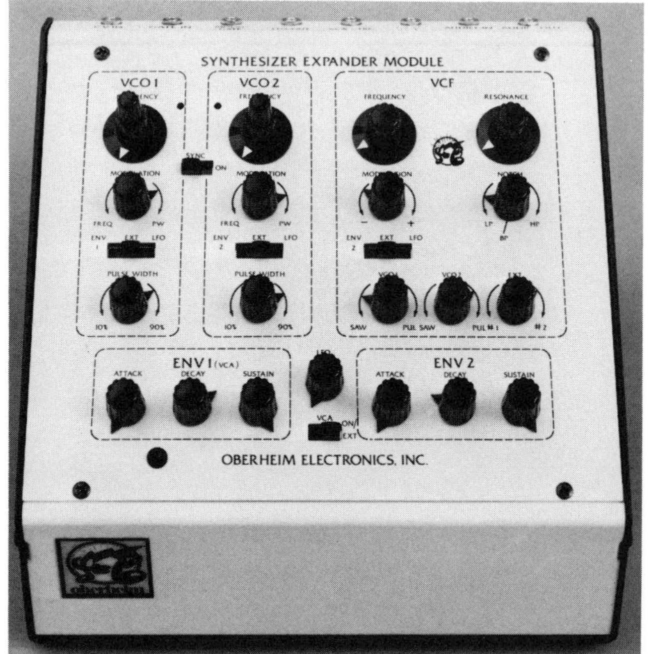

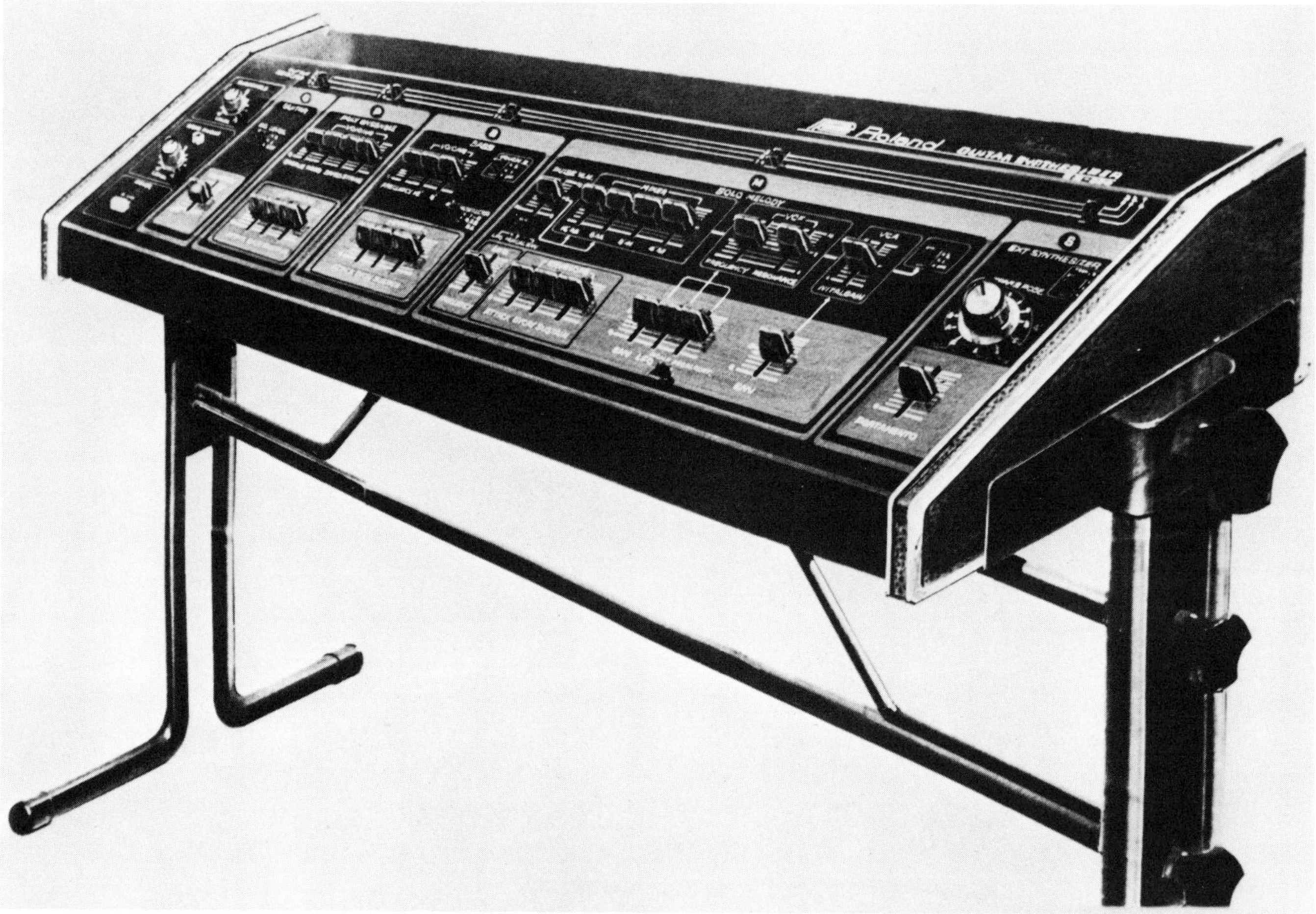

Synthesizer section of the Roland GS-500 Guitar Synthesizer system. The matching guitar is equipped with special pickups and a wide assortment of controls.

21

Sound Systems

AN INTERVIEW WITH TYCOBRAHE SOUND COMPANY

Ralph Morris is Director of Marketing for Tycobrahe, one of the leaders in concert sound reinforcement. He draws on his experience in designing the amplification systems for the Rolling Stones, Faces, Jethro Tull, Fleetwood Mac, Black Sabbath, Ten Years After, and other major groups. He discusses public-address systems, costs, power requirements, room acoustics, speaker devices, crossovers, sound dispersion, line loss, and the miking of guitars.

Costs and Development of Modern Sound Systems

T.W.: What have been the causes for the enormous increases in power requirements?

R.M.: The electric guitar, mainly. If you go back about ten or twelve years, all of the theaters or halls where concerts were being held generally had their own systems, installed by the local established audio contractor, often a music store or an electrical company. These "house systems," as they're called, worked fairly well, until the electric guitar started getting louder. In the early Sixties, Fender built its prototype of the Showman amplifier, featuring a large enclosure and a single JBL 15″ speaker. This was a significant step, and we had much better results. Some of the groups began to take theater components with tube-type amps and construct their own systems, to raise the volume of the voices and drums closer to the guitars. This was about 1963 or 1964. But even the early Beatle concerts were handled with fairly small amps, by today's

VU
-20 -10 -7 -5 -3 -1 0 +1 +2 +3
VU
0 20 40 60 80 100
VU
20 -10 -7 -5 -3 -1
0 20 40 60 80 100
1
2
1 2 3 4 5 6 7
MIX

-10 -7 -5 -3 -1 0 +1 +2 +3 VU
20 40 60 80 100
3
SUB MASTERS
4
MASTER
8

standards, and the effectiveness of the total system was marginal at best.

T.W.: Were the music stores offering any equipment, at that time, which could be used for reinforcement in the larger rooms?

R.M.: Not as a general rule, because the stores had to keep equipment to a competitive cost, and these theater systems were pretty expensive, even in those days. The groups who were assembling their own components were the few who were lucky enough to have a lot of money. Today they try to keep it under $4,000 or $5,000, which isn't expensive at all in relative terms.

T.W.: What are the costs of the hardware that Tycobrahe is using for larger gigs today?

R.M.: The costs are ridiculous. Rock concerts became more commercial, necessitating bigger and bigger rooms, causing more headaches for sound-reinforcement people. Back in the Sixties we used a $10,000 system. When we hit the road today with a high-powered group like the Rolling Stones, we take along at least $60,000 worth of sound equipment. The Stones could easily afford to buy the system, but their accountants tell them that it's just not practical to maintain, operate, and coordinate the equipment, so they arrange a lease for the tour.

T.W.: Can a group ever afford to purchase a system of yours outright?

R.M.: The only groups who have purchased our equipment have been Jethro Tull and Faces. Many groups rent the system for one night, or lease it for a tour. In the early days of 1969 or 1970, groups were still in the tradition of using the house system, or one rented by the local promoter, and it wasn't common for a group to carry its sound equipment with them. You might say that the development was in a transition phase: groups weren't transporting their own, and yet they realized that house systems didn't always make it, so we were called in to erect an adequate P.A. system on a nightly basis.

T.W.: All but a very few groups are limited by the budget. Is there any way that a working band with average resources can get adequate sound for larger rooms?

R.M.: Even the very knowledgeable groups have trouble getting distortion-free sound at high volumes with the present equipment in the medium-price range. It just takes expensive components. There are no big secrets to this business. The people involved in it keep making slight improvements as we go, and it'll be better tomorrow. As of now, costs are still very high. Most of the semi-pro groups with whom I've had contact are using pretty high-powered guitar amps, and if they do go out and buy a commercial sound system from a music store, they're usually forced to remain in the medium-quality category, as far as the mixer is concerned, because a good mixer alone can cost several thousand dollars. There's no way you can get around it. The best switches and potentiometers just cost a lot of money. I'm afraid that groups who spend $2,000 to $5,000 on a system are often disappointed with its performance in larger rooms.

T.W.: We're now talking mainly about the big rooms. Aren't the lower-priced systems sufficient for club work and smaller halls?

R.M.: Yes, I think so, especially if the band is not unreasonably loud. If the group maintains moderate levels on the instruments, then commercially available systems will be adequate for clubs and even rooms such as the type where groups often play at colleges—up to a thousand people or so.

T.W.: When did the trend begin toward self-contained, portable systems?

R.M.: The English groups would have to tour, of course, and other groups tour as well, instead of arranging the weekend type of concert situation. When they discovered a sound system that did the job for them, they didn't want to let it go. The trend really began when groups demanded consistent sound night after night.

T.W.: What are the arrangements for actually transporting the equipment, and who pays for it?

R.M.: On the first tour that we did with the Rolling Stones, they had contracted with a theatrical transfer company that hauls shows around—the really big ones. The Stones had about 40,000 pounds of stage and light equipment. So when we went on tour with them, they just said—oh, we'll put the gear in one of these semis, and you can just come along with us in the airplane. After that we adopted this new concept, and it also worked out fine for groups with smaller budgets than the Stones. We've just encouraged them to rent a bigger truck, so that they can carry our sound system, in addition to their own instruments and amps. That way, we can lease the system to them at a flat rate, for less money than we'd have to charge if we were hauling it around ourselves. We lease it to the group, and the group, in their contracts with the various promoters for the concerts, they pass on the costs, charging so much for the sound system or the lighting or whatever, and the promoter pays for that.

T.W.: Do you also send someone to handle the actual setting up of the equipment on stage?

R.M.: Yes. They take along two of our people, one engineer and one technician. Generally, the engineer is the mixer, and he operates the sound system from the mixer console, which is located out in the auditorium, while the technician remains on stage and makes modifications in the equipment, under the direction of the engineer. They communicate through the intercom. The band or the promoter will provide some roadies or union personnel to help set it up.

Room Acoustics and Power Requirements

T.W.: How much power is needed for the biggest rooms, such as Madison Square Garden in New York?

R.M.: It's about 20,000 seats, and we need 16,000 watts RMS of amplifier power.

T.W.: Isn't that a particularly difficult room to fill?

R.M.: Well, all of the arenas are tough. They aren't very good acoustically, not nearly as good as theater buildings. It's just a matter of physics. In theaters, you have curtains behind the band with an enclosed stage, separated from the area where the audience sits. The room can still sound very live, but the back curtains and side curtains in the wings reduce a lot of the reverb, so the sound doesn't have that tinny characteristic. In an arena, you are out there in the middle of the room on a portable stage; you're in the room environment. The reverberation problem is much greater. Also, when any room is full of people, they absorb the sound, and the noise they make in talking and shuffling around is a factor. The more people, the more power you need.

T.W.: Do you have a calculation for determining power requirements in a given situation?

R.M.: No, we can't really do that. There are just too many variables. We normally take at least ten 500-watt speaker systems for rooms up to 6,000 seats, and this could vary a lot, because one 6,000-seat room will be much quieter than another. That's merely a guide. Now, if we send out twelve 500-watt systems, we know that they'll have enough gear to handle the average room up to 10,000 seats or so. That takes care of most concerts, but if a group is doing an 18,000-seat arena, then naturally we'll need even more power.

T.W.: Do most of the groups you work with perform at fairly constant Sound Pressure Levels?

R.M.: There's quite a bit of variation. For example, when we did Paul Butterfield's new group in concert, they were pretty quiet. A couple of the members were from an acoustic group. There's a lot of difference in dynamics as well. Procol Harum has a vast dynamic range; it's very much like chamber rock music when compared to Ten Years After, a straight-forward, gut-level rock-and-roll band. There are the super-high-powered trios, too.

T.W.: Beginning with Hendrix and Cream?

R.M.: Right—guitar, bass, and drums. The guitar player and bass player would have about twelve amplifiers. We had to cope with that sort of thing when we were doing Grand Funk Railroad, years ago. Their manager liked to turn everything up, until there was just gross distortion, and that's part of a certain style.

T.W.: When did most of the reinforcement companies switch from tubes to solid state?

Speaker columns

R.M.: About 1968 or 1969. Now it's all pretty much solid state. There are a few die-hard people who say that tubes do sound a little better, but that's the funky sound you get when you drive them hard. It's good for certain guitar styles, but not for voices. You want the vocals to be reproduced as clean as possible, without any noticeable distortion. Solid state made for more available power to handle bigger auditoriums.

Speaker Devices And Crossovers

T.W.: At the time when Tycobrahe entered the sound reinforcement industry, had there been many significant improvements in the construction of speakers?

R.M.: Believe it or not, most of the loudspeakers in use at that time were designed about 1932, and the basic elements had not changed very much except for power-handling capabilities. Until recently, columns were very popular for P.A. cabinets. They were originally designed to conserve space and increase distribution, and many rock groups used them. There were problems with the overall efficiency, because the lower portion of the column would often be buried in the audience.

No speaker is perfect for all jobs, so today we use cone-type speakers, compression drivers, direct radiators, and other types, each doing a specific job. In a situation limited to one type of device, because of the budget, cone speakers can be made to reproduce the whole audio spectrum fairly well. But when you get into high levels and you're trying to maintain a flat frequency response, it is necessary to use a large cone speaker for the bass notes, a compression driver to handle mid-range, and an ultra-high-frequency compression driver for frequencies above 6,500 Hz.

A compression driver is a kind of speaker device, connected to a horn, instead of the paper cone. Its diaphragm is coupled very tightly, compressing the air. A horn is another acoustical transformer, its range usually beginning at about 800 cycles, though sometimes it's as low as 500. It's designed for reinforcement in large areas, because its pattern of distribution, or "throw," is narrow and very long. To reach the back of the audience four or five hundred feet away, you wouldn't want a very wide pattern of distribution. You may use other devices to reach the people up front, such as horns with slanted lenses for spreading out the sound. To reach the back, you need to compress the sound waves into a long, powerful band. The main advantage of horns is that they are more efficient; that is, more volume for the same amount of power.

T.W.: Are there any disadvantages?

R.M.: Well, bass horns are big and bulky, and they don't sound quite as pretty as some other systems, but they serve their purpose well.

Note: JBL recommends rear-loaded cabinets and high-frequency radial horns (with lenses) for discotheques, clubs,

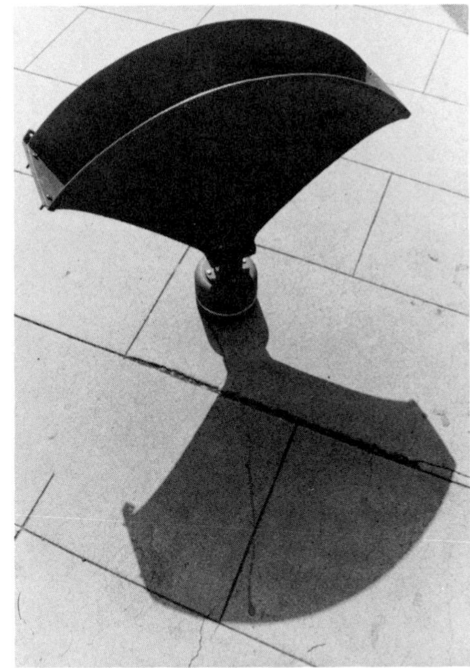

90° Horizontal high-frequency radial horn and driver

Folded plate high-frequency acoustic lens

and small auditoriums, and front-loaded cabinets, each with one or two 15" speakers and single or double high-frequency radial horns (without lenses) for medium and large auditoriums and outdoor stages.

Electronic crossover

T.W.: Have there been many changes in the construction of the electronic components that you use?

R.M.: Oh yes, even the equipment we used in 1968 was very crude compared to the systems we're now using. Aside from the solid-state amplifier, the biggest technical improvement that we've made is the electronic crossover. A crossover divides the various frequencies into two or three different ranges, and then sends them to other components. In the passive type, the frequencies cross over *after* the power-amp stage; that is, one total signal comes from the power amp and the crossover divides it and sends it to the appropriate speaker devices. The newer, active, electronic crossover is quite an improvement. Located on the output of the pre-amp, *before* the power amp stage, it divides the signal into several parts, and then each range of frequencies is fed to its own separate power amp. Each power amp feeds only a specific speaker device. The separate amplification for bass and treble, made possible by the electronic crossover, increases the efficiency, clarity, and control over the sound.

T.W.: This is bi-amping or tri-amping?

R.M.: Exactly. We can have separate amplifiers for bass and treble, eliminating the intermodulation distortion which has been the biggest problem at high levels. If a single amp covers the full spectrum, most of the power is used to handle bass notes, perhaps 90 percent of it. The high notes have to ride on top of the bass wave in the oscilloscope pattern. If the bass wave engulfs them, the highs can't be heard. So we use bi-amping: separate power amps for bass and treble.

Sound Dispersion, Line Loss, and Grounding

T.W.: What are the things you consider in arranging sound dispersion?

R.M.: There are a lot of little things that count. One of the basic considerations has always been to get the speakers up above the heads of the crowd, especially in the larger rooms. If you have them at stage level, it murders the people in the front rows, and the ones in the back still can't hear. So we use risers or platforms on each corner of the stage to accomplish this. If the room is theater-shaped, longer than it is wide, this works out pretty well with speaker systems on either side of the stage. In some large rooms, such as Madison Square Garden and the Los Angeles Forum, we suspend the enclosures from the rafters. A room that is wider than it is long, such as the Hollywood Palladium or the sports arenas with the very deep sides are more difficult to do, because you have to have some speakers out to the side. The wider the dispersion, the less the effect of these speakers all working together, pushing air in a straight line. Again, you really can get a much better sound in a theater-type building than in an arena. Generally, the less volume of air to push, the more you can do with it.

T.W.: How do the power and speaker requirements change when you move outdoors?

R.M.: There are both advantages and disadvantages. For one thing, you don't have the indoor-type reflection from the walls. When the walls are very flat and you don't have any acoustic material, the echo can cause all sorts of difficulties with dispersion and rhythm. The main problem outdoors is the wind. Once the sound leaves the speaker, it's airborne. We did a concert in Texas once where the wind was blowing at 50 miles per hour across the concert field, and the sound came out about ten feet and then blew away. Outdoor jobs require a greater reserve of power.

T.W.: Is the personnel required for an outdoor job about the same as for an indoor concert?

R.M.: Yes, just two, the engineer and the technician can handle it, unless it's a festival with hundreds of thousands of people. There were a number of things we did to the equipment, which allowed it to be operated more easily and with less time involved in loading and setting up. We put wheels on all of the boxes, so we can take it out of the truck and roll it into the auditorium, and all our speaker cables are run through one main line. You don't have to stop and think—well, this is the highs and this is the lows. One cable goes into each box, and they're all the same, and they can only go in one way. We've made it fairly fool-proof so that you don't even have to think. Even after you've been on tour for thirty-six days and you've only gotten three hours sleep most of the time —you can still hook up the system in about forty-five minutes with your eyes half-closed.

T.W.: What is line loss?

R.M.: A piece of wire has a certain amount of resistance, which causes a loss of power. The longer it is, the more resistance it has. So we try to run short speaker cables. Line loss is also affected by the size of the wire and the impedance of the speakers. Theaters tried to overcome it with transformers on the amplifier output to step up the voltage, since line loss is a voltage loss. However, the transformers caused power loss and heavy distortion, particularly at loud levels, so they were not feasible for high-intensity rock concerts. We try to locate the amps as close as possible to the speakers. In fact, we use only 10-foot speaker cables, and the amps sit right behind the speaker enclosures.

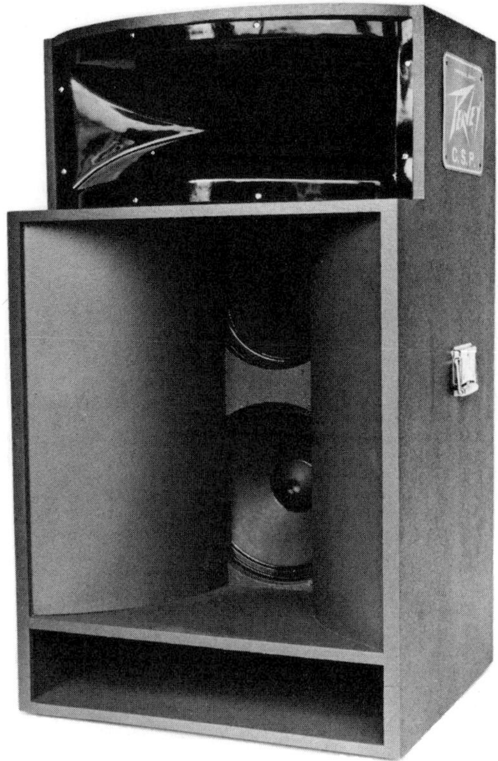

Combination enclosure

Miking Guitars

T.W.: Some rock groups that feature acoustic as well as electric guitars must be hard to balance. Do you have any luck with the Barcus-Berry or the F.R.A.P.-type contact pickup?

R.M.: Acoustic guitars are difficult. You can use contact pickups in concert situations. The problem is to get enough level from the instrument, through the pickup, without causing feedback. You can mike the guitar directly as well, and there's a difference in sound between the two methods. You may even use two or three methods simultaneously. The guitarist will most likely have his preference.

T.W.: Do you find that a lot of groups are miking the guitar amps through the P.A., allowing for smaller amplifiers?

R.M.: Not often, but we do it sometimes. It depends a lot on the group. Some of the bands we work with have very large guitar amplifiers—the Rolling Stones—they use these powerful instrument amps, and they usually don't need to be miked, due to their very high volume. But in extremely large halls, or when we go outdoors, we mike them for added level.

T.W.: What about the artist who prefers the sound of a smaller amp—he's got his little 40-watt Fender and he drives it to get a certain kind of distortion. Can you mike his amp at competitive Sound Pressure Levels, so he'll be heard above his bass player, who's using a 300-watt monster with two cabinets?

R.M.: Yes. On one gig with the Beach Boys, they were using fairly small guitar amps and we boosted them through the P.A. system. It worked well. Actually, it's better to use the P.A. all the way around, I believe, than to use the super-large guitar amps, because you have added flexibility and control through the mixer for adjusting both the level and the equalization.

T.W.: Does it usually help the sound dispersion to place the amp in a tilt-back position or up on a chair?

R.M.: The chair helps to get it over the heads of the crowd. Tilt-back can be undesirable in some cases, creating a reflection problem from a low ceiling. It really depends upon the shape of the room.

T.W.: Who is on your schedule for the coming months?

R.M.: Let's see. We have the Rolling Stones, Ten Years After, Black Sabbath, Deep Purple, Electric Light Orchestra, Robin Trower, Fleetwood Mac, and Savoy Brown. It should keep us pretty busy.

MONITORS AND MIXERS

A monitor is a speaker system that is directed toward the band, so that the members can hear themselves. The bass player, standing two feet in front of his stack of cabinets, might not hear a thing except his own instrument. Perhaps the singer, situated on stage between his P.A. cabinets, is the only person in the room who cannot hear himself sing. The drummer is trying to maintain a steady rhythm, while hearing his beats reflected off of the walls, balconies, and ceiling, all at different intervals. Monitors help solve these problems.

Monitors

In its simplest form, a monitor is merely an extension speaker facing the group. In larger, high-powered systems, the monitors require their own output sources and a separate mix (enabling the group to better hear the vocals) with perhaps a little extra snare or bass drum for rhythm.

A mixer is a centrally located pre-amp and control panel through which the signals from various inputs (instruments and mikes) may be combined, modified, and balanced. The simplest kind is a five-dollar box with two inputs and a single output. Concert public-address systems typically feature mixers with four to twenty-four separate channels, while recording studios usually have equipment with eight, sixteen, or thirty-two channels or "tracks." Each channel may contain many controls, including channel volume, monitor volume, reverb, VU meter, overload indicator, feedback filters, and equalization switches.* Tone controls divide the total spectrum by frequency, covering the bass (roughly below 300 cycles), mid-range (300 to 1,500) and treble (1,500 and up).

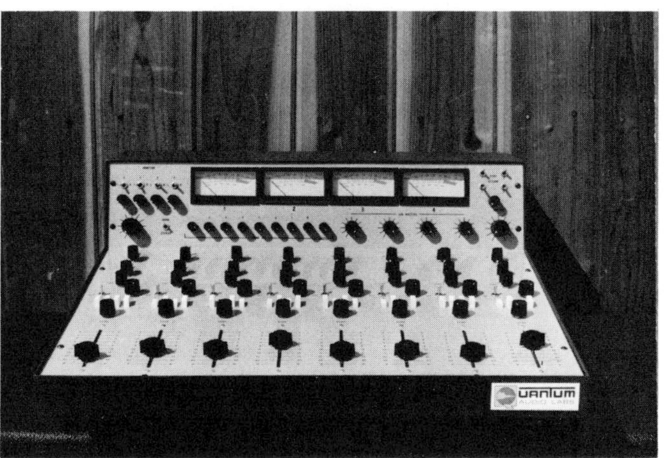

Eight-channel mixer

The master panel includes similar controls, which simultaneously shape the sound of all channels combined. Additional features might be patch jacks for outboard (external) effects, headphones, monitors, or additional power amps (slaves). Providing the flexibility to tailor the P.A. system to the particular acoustics of each room, the mixer is usually controlled by an engineer who positions himself to get the perspective of the audience.

If one instrument were projected exclusively to one side of the arena, while another were projected only to

*For example: high-frequency selector providing a 12 dB cut or boost at 3,000, 5,000, and 10,000 Hz; low-frequency selector providing a 12 dB cut or boost at 100, 300, and 1,000 Hz.

Four-channel mixer

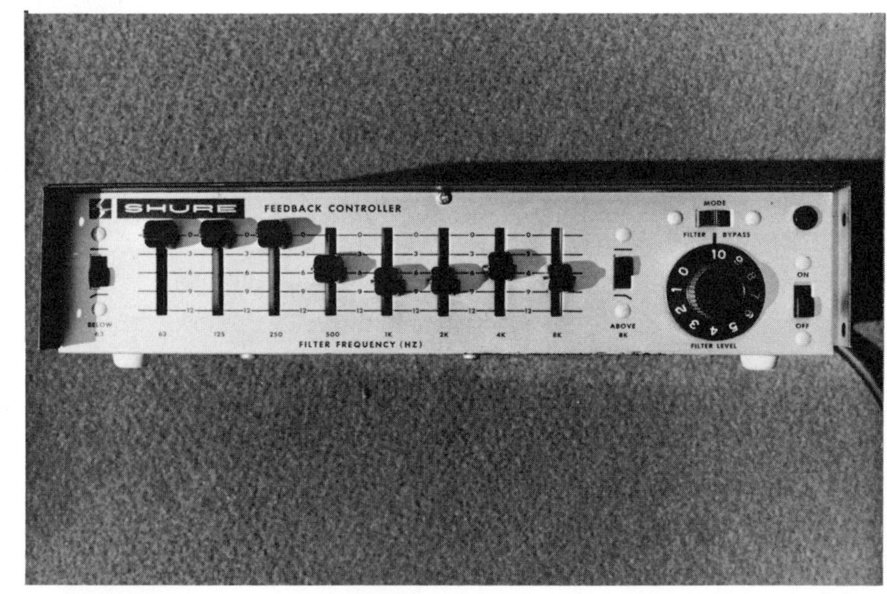

Feedback filter

the other side, the result would be an imbalance of sound at each extreme. Therefore, stereo and quadraphonic approaches to concert reinforcement entail complex equipment. The Stones experimented with stereo mixing during an Australian tour years ago, and the Beach Boys and other groups have had good results with limited separation. Quad systems are sometimes used with overwhelming results by Emerson, Lake and Palmer, The Who, and others, though the nature of the room always affects the equipment's performance. The quality and variety of sound in live concerts is the best it's ever been. However, costs presently confine quad to the biggest budgets.

part III

Appendixes

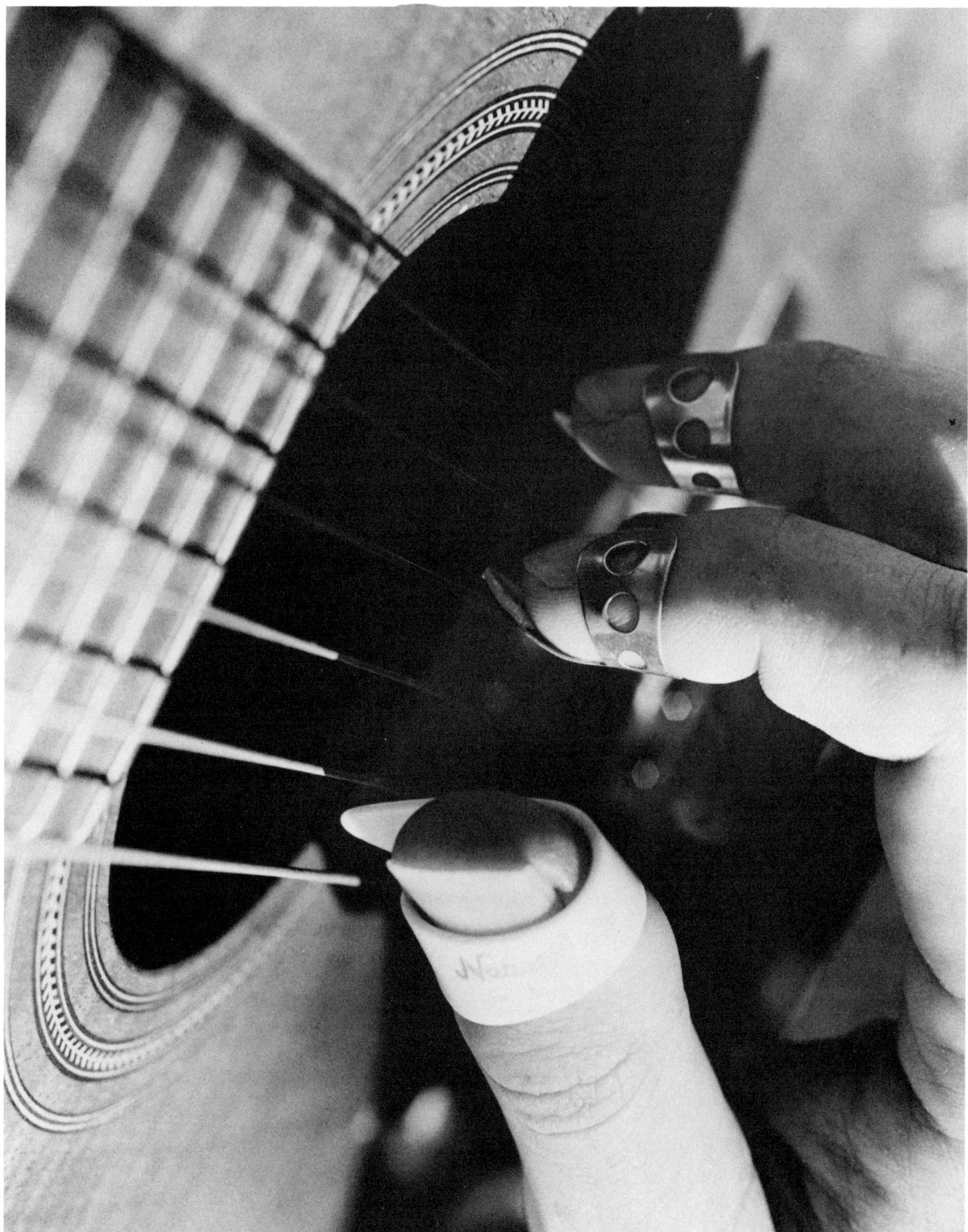

appendix I

Picks and Capos

CHOOSING THE RIGHT GUITAR PICKS

Different picks (plectrums) get different results, so if you have not investigated the available sizes, compositions, thicknesses, and shapes, cruise on over to the music store and select several types. They're made from hard rubber, plastic, tortoise shell, felt, nylon fiber, celluloid, and other materials.

Since any change in picks will require some adjustment, give yourself a little time to get used to the new feel of each one before making a decision. You may decide to use different picks for changing situations.

When it comes to choosing any piece of equipment, sweeping generalizations aren't always helpful. The advice found on the next few pages is based upon the experiences of many guitarists, but after you have read it, try all sizes and thicknesses of picks to find the one best suited to your style.

Rhythm Strumming

The thicker the pick, the less force it takes to produce a note or chord at a given volume, so a medium or large, heavy-gauge pick is often used for rhythm playing, especially on acoustic guitars which are expected to produce that choppy "chunka-chunka" sound. Many rhythm players prefer larger picks, be-

NYLON
LIGHT GAUGE
NYLON
HEAVY GAUGE

cause the greater surface area decreases the chances of dropping the pick during hard strumming.

The artist with an acoustic instrument is more dependent upon the pick for volume, since the electric guitarist needs only to turn up a knob to be louder. The pick also affects the tone. Thick picks sound fuller and are well suited to an aggressive attack; thin picks produce a relatively thin treble tone and cause more of a clicking sound. Pick noises are not necessarily undesirable. The styles of some acoustic guitarists—Cat Stevens, Richie Havens, for example—are readily identifiable *because* of the pick noise, used for a percussive effect. If you try several types with unsatisfactory results, the clicking sound will be alleviated by striking the strings farther away from the bridge and by experimenting with other gauges of strings, a softer strum, and different angles of attack.

Nylon-stringed instruments are almost always played with the fingers, but if you want an even strum with a softer sound than the steel-string, try a classical or flamenco guitar and use a felt pick.

Lead Playing

Lead players use everything from giant hard picks to tiny super-soft picks (and an old BankAmericard will do in a pinch). If there is a valid generalization about lead picks, it is probably that most players use small-to-medium sizes, due to the bulkiness of the larger ones. Long and rapid passages require a particular finesse to which a small pick seems suited, but it's a personal choice.

As far as thickness is concerned, categorization is impossible. Some say that a flexible pick (about 1/64″) is easier to use because it gives with the string. Others prefer a heavy pick (about 1/32″) because it *doesn't* give with the string, allowing for a better connection between hand motion and string response. Seeking the advantages of both thick and thin, many people choose mediums, and a few players couldn't care less (they'll use anything—old tokens, and so on). Anyway, don't choose a pick just because you like the way the psychedelic design moves around as you look at it from different angles.

Dropping the pick. If you have the problem of constantly dropping the pick, buy the kind with a hole or cork ring in the middle or poke a few holes or ridges in the pick with a hot needle. Try a pick of the

same thickness but of a larger size.*

Pick-droppers usually keep a spare stuck between the pickguard and the body, or they suspend one in the strings above the nut or behind the bridge.

Thumbpicks allow you to get a picked sound on the bass strings, leaving the other fingers free to play partial chords and harmony or melody lines in a Chet Atkins or Merle Travis style. They are available in metal, but the celluloid and plastic ones are less raspy. Thumbpicks abound in country, bluegrass, folk, acoustic blues, and to a lesser degree, electric blues and rock.

Fingerpicks also come in plastic or metal; the latter ones are adjustable for size. Both kinds create sounds that are brighter and more crisp than the fingers or fingernails. They are popular among folk players and banjo-pickers-turned-guitarists. Accessory companies offer fingerpicks of different gauges and a choice between rounded or pointed tips.

THE CAPO

A capo (short for capotasto) fits around the neck, pressing the strings to the fingerboard, raising their pitch to a desired fret. It's considered by some to be a crutch, but it serves a practical purpose. Chords with open strings may be raised to suit the range of a singer's voice. For example, a capo at fret 2 raises C to D, D to E, E to F#, and so on.

Sometimes a capo can substitute for bar (barre) chords, and it's only in this sense that a capo becomes a crutch. For instance, chords in the key of G# are G#, C#, and D# (E♭)—all bar chords. With a capo at the first fret, the chords in G (G, C, and D) may be raised to G# without barring the finger. However, if the chords cannot be transposed to a key with all open-string (nonbar) forms, then at least some bar chords must be used, with or without a capo. For example, a chord change of a one-fret interval during a song (A to B♭; C to C#) *must* be accomplished with either a full bar chord or an abbreviated bar chord such as F at fret 1, E♭ at fret 3, or B at fret 2.

A capo is a legitimate accessory because it allows the guitarist to take advantage of open strings at high

*The Band-It pick has a loop which goes around the first finger, preventing dropping and facilitating a change from flat-picking to fingerpicking.

pitches. A song fingerpicked in D (D, G, and A) may be raised to F# with the use of bar chords. However, with a capo at fret 4, it may be played in F# with open-string D, G, and A forms. Open strings are not only easier, they have a musical advantage as well. Two consecutive chords often share a couple of open strings, permitting a smoother flow when changing chords.

In order for any capo to raise the pitch without buzzing, it must fit tightly, just behind the fret. Capos with a curved bar fit the slightly rounded fingerboards on steel-string and electric guitars. Those with a straight bar fit classic and flamenco guitars. Some elastic-covered capos have a plastic core which eventually becomes grooved by the strings. When this happens, just rotate the core to place an ungrooved surface in contact with the fingerboard.

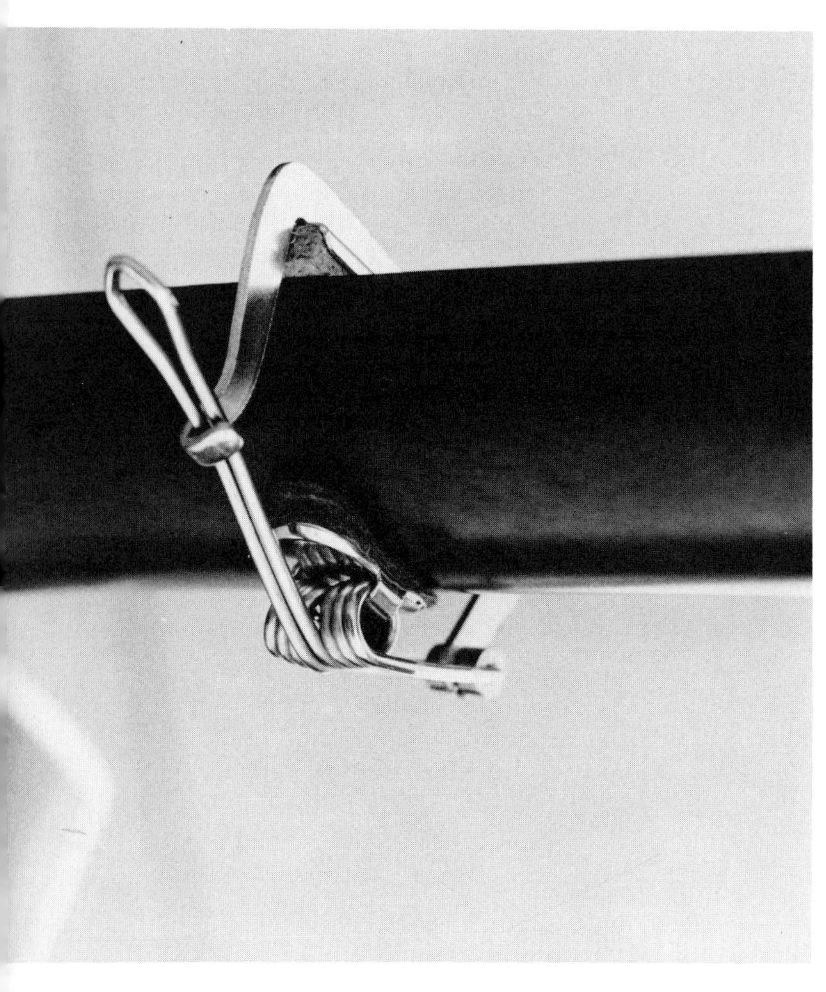

appendix II

Sound Levels and Your Hearing

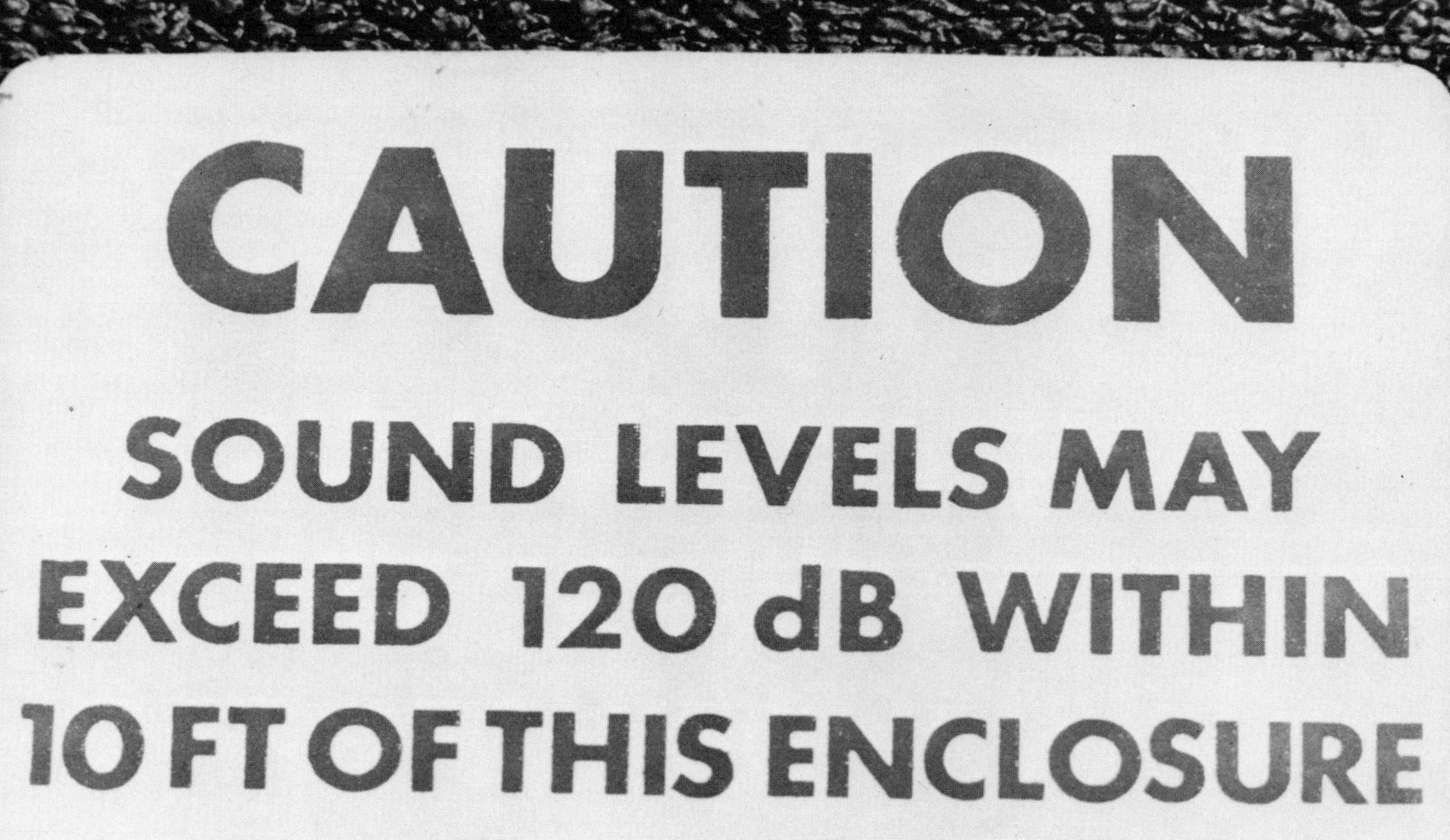

Eric Clapton once reported temporary hearing losses during the high-powered days of Cream. More recently, various champions of public causes have warned that continued exposure to loud rock music can result in permanent damage to the ear. This appendix reviews the scientific studies that have been completed to date, and attempts to describe the situations that are potentially dangerous and those that are not.

Sound waves are alternating rings of compressed, then rarefied (thinned) air, which travel at a constant velocity. Exerting both pushing and pulling motions as they reach an object, sound waves may be strong enough to vibrate a window, or they may even break the glass. The frequency spectrum of audible tones ranges from below 30 Hz (the lowest notes produced on a pipe organ's bass pedals) up to about 18,000 or 20,000 Hz (squeaks and high-pitched whistles).

The intensity or loudness of sound is measured in decibels (dB). The zero point on the scale equals the lowest level that the normal human ear can detect. Because we can hear such a wide range of sounds, the scale must be extraordinarily vast in scope. Unlike linear standards, such as gallons or yards, decibels proceed in a sharply rising logarithmic curve. While 10 dB is ten times louder than 1 dB, 20 dB is one *hundred* (10 x 10) times louder, and 30 dB is a thousand (10 x 10 x 10) times louder, and so on. One hundred dB, then, is 10 billion times the intensity of 1 dB.

The external ear "catches" the sound wave and directs it through a horn-shaped duct to the ear drum, a membrane that moves back and forth in response to vibrations. After passing through the bones of the middle ear, the sound is actually sensed by a spiral, liquid-filled organ called the cochlea, which generates electrochemical impulses with its hundreds of nerve fibers and hair cells. An excessively loud noise can strain these delicate hairs and cells. The ones that appear to be most easily harmed are those which respond to high frequencies. If the damage occurs to the auditory nerve or to the cochlea itself, the result is incurable deafness.

Loss of hearing is either temporary or permanent. Brief or sporadic exposure to intense Sound Pressure Levels may cause temporary loss, while exposure to a constant high-level noise is more likely to induce permanent damage. While the evidence is insufficient

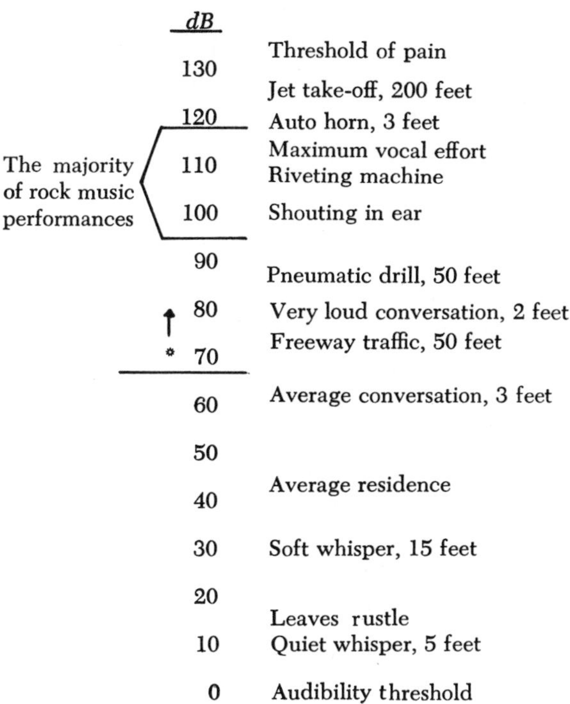

*In constant (as opposed to intermittent) exposure situations, contribution to hearing impairment begins at about 70 dB.

at present, and while studies which employed different testing procedures have arrived at conflicting conclusions, everyone nevertheless seems to agree that potential hazards exist in typical rock listening environments (105–114 dB). Additionally, scientific research indicates that a *permanent* hearing impairment is possible, though not necessarily likely.

In 1970, teams of audiologists and otolaryngologists (sound experts and medical specialists) from all over the country performed Sound Pressure Level measurements on rock groups and hearing tests on scores of musicians. These studies revealed that the actual loudness of most bands (104–111 dB) is considerably less than the 130 dB levels which were reported to be typical in a number of less-scientific articles in the general press. In fact, only three of the thirty-six rock groups tested produced an average Sound Pressure Level higher than 115 dB, though the ultra-high-power rock bands, such as the Stones and Grand Funk Railroad, have exceeded the 130 dB mark in the stage area. The Grateful Dead has performed at 127 dB, and Deep Purple at 117 dB.

There are plenty of reasons for caution. Evidence

of inner-ear damage was discovered in experimental animals after long exposure to a level of 122 or 123 dB, an SPL that is reached by a few rock groups. Signs of TTS, or Temporary Threshold Shift (temporary hearing impairment) in humans were discovered after tests were performed during single 1–4 hour sessions, but the significance of these findings is in doubt because of the lack of substantial scientific correlation between temporary and permanent losses. Some studies suggest that high-school-age rock musicians consistently have poorer hearing in the high frequency range (over 10,000 Hz) than their contemporaries.

The Rintelmann and Borus studies (1968) found that when forty-two rock musicians were exposed to an average of 105 dB for approximately 11½ hours a week over a three-year period, 95 percent of them had normal hearing, when tested under both the pure-tone air-conduction threshold and bone-conduction threshold methods. The results (which surprised some people) may be due to a characteristic of the human hearing system. The ear gets a chance to rest during periods of silence (between songs and sets), decreasing the risk of damage. This fact is suggested by some experts as a reason why exposure to the intermittent (on, then off) sound waves of loud music may be less harmful than exposure to noises of a consistently high SPL (in industrial surroundings, for example), even though the music may actually be louder at its peak. Music is only one cause, but together with other high noise levels, it can contribute to hearing losses. In 1968, Dr. D. M. Lipscomb, author of *Noise—the Unwanted Sounds*, found that a third of nearly 3,000 freshmen at the University of Tennessee failed to respond normally to high-frequency hearing tests. In 1969, well over half failed the test.

The only intelligent thing to do is play it safe. Even the very scientists who proved that some of the earlier alarming claims were unfounded have stressed that the potential for damage clearly exists. The louder the music, the higher the frequency, and the longer the exposure—the greater the risks. One difficulty is that while it is known that some people are much more susceptible to ear damage than others, no reliable testing procedures have as yet been developed that can determine just who these sensitive people are. Another problem concerns the reliability of routine hearing tests. Dr. Lipscomb discovered substantial cell destruction in animal ear tissue, even though it had not been revealed in hearing tests. He lists the following signals that warn of possible ear damage: ringing ears, a plugged sensation, or a decrease in hearing sensitivity.

The experts recommend that people who are often exposed to high SPL's, including rock musicians, should save their hearing from possible impairment by wearing ear plugs. They come in a broad range of design (and effectiveness). A wad of cotton is not recommended; even though it may conceivably offer some protection to the ear, it will prevent an accurate reception of the sound. Plastic swimming and diving plugs, available in drugstores, and special-design ear muffs (resembling headphones) are usually effective but often uncomfortable. If you often play at extremely loud volumes call your doctor or pharmacist and ask him about the protectors made of spun glass or the liquid silicone or rubber type. Anyone associated with a high-noise-level industry may offer some advice, or you could try to obtain information from a sporting goods dealer who furnishes equipment to hunters and marksmen.

Norton's Sonic II Noise Filter

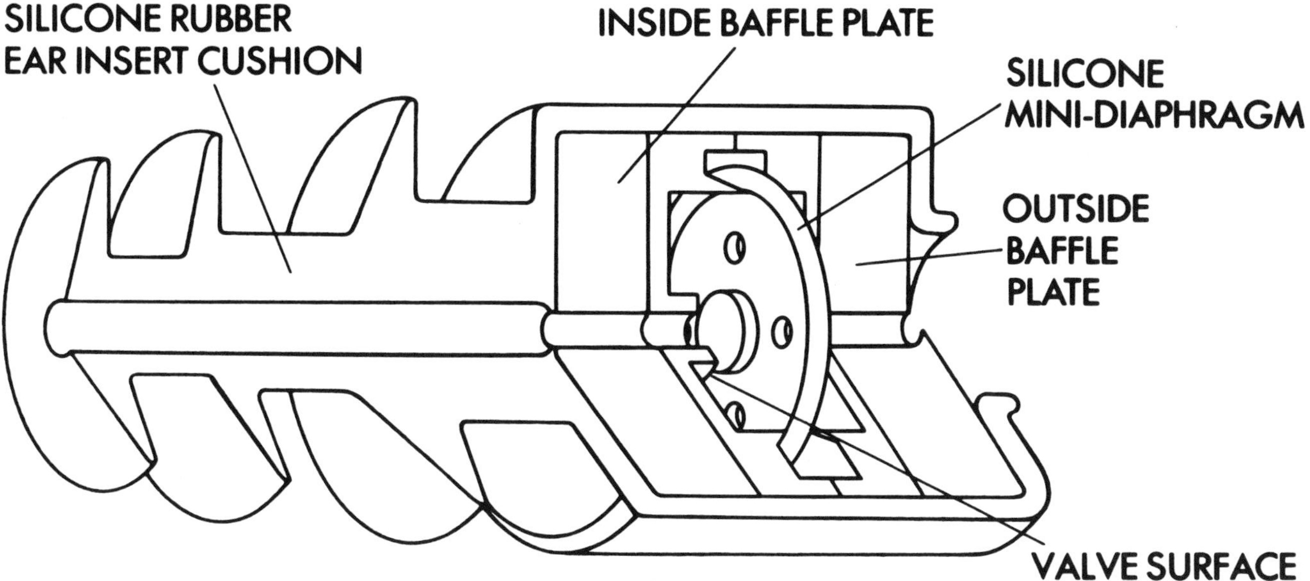

appendix III

Chord Charts and Chord Builder

Basic Chords

The numbers refer to the fingers of the left hand. The small circle above a string means the open string is included in the chord. If a string is unfretted, and does not have the circle designation, it is not strummed.

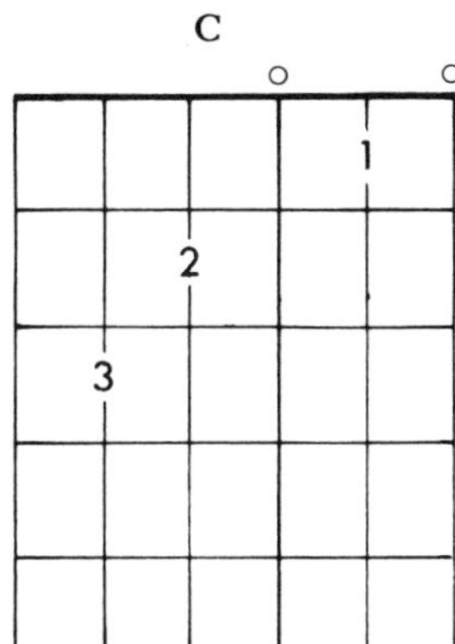

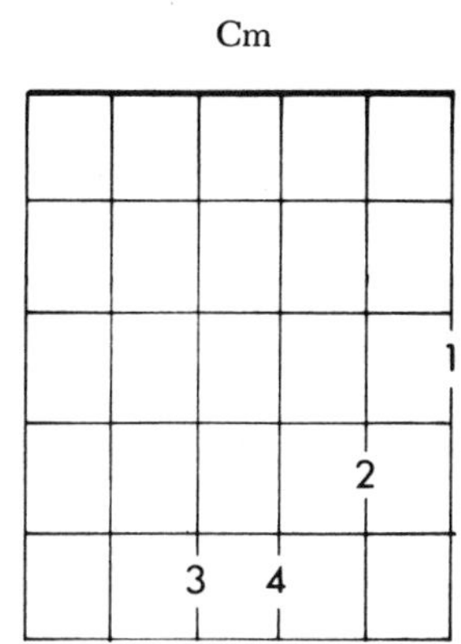

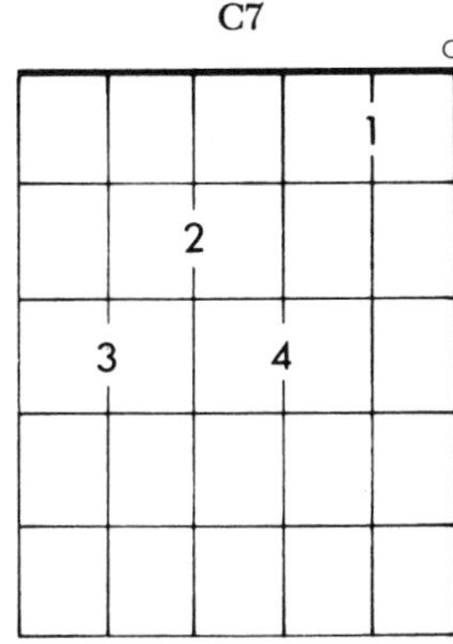

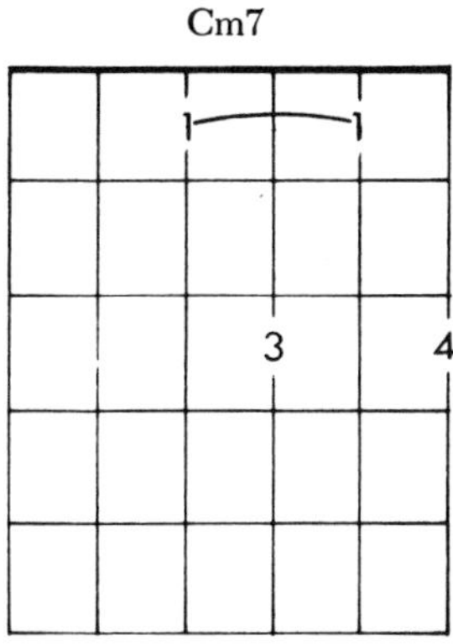

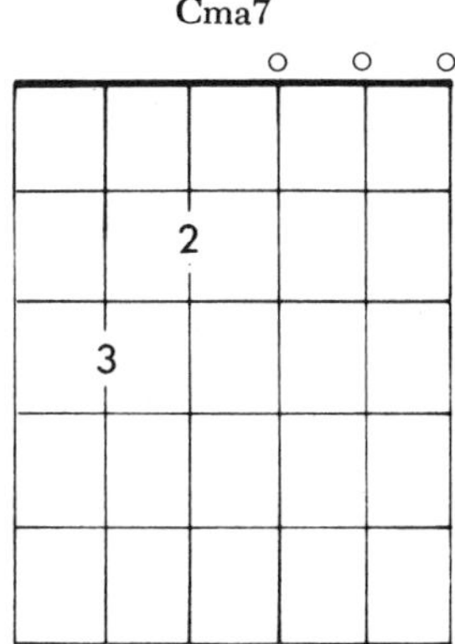

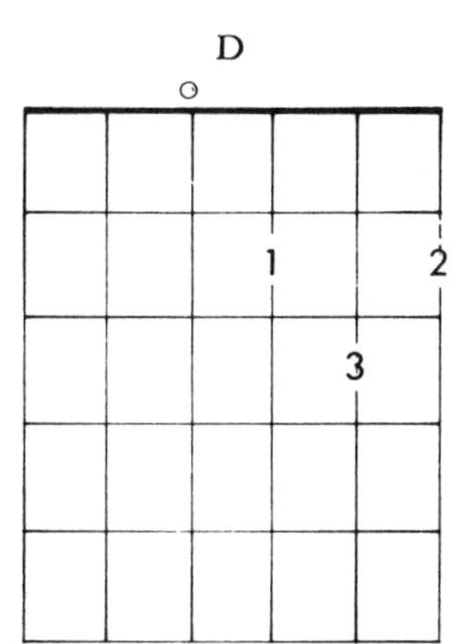

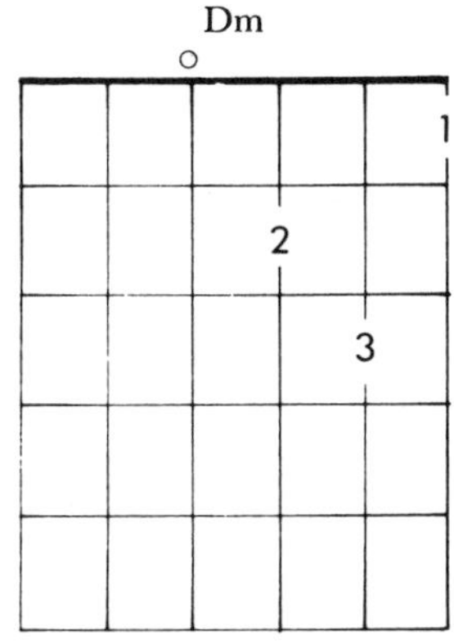

D7

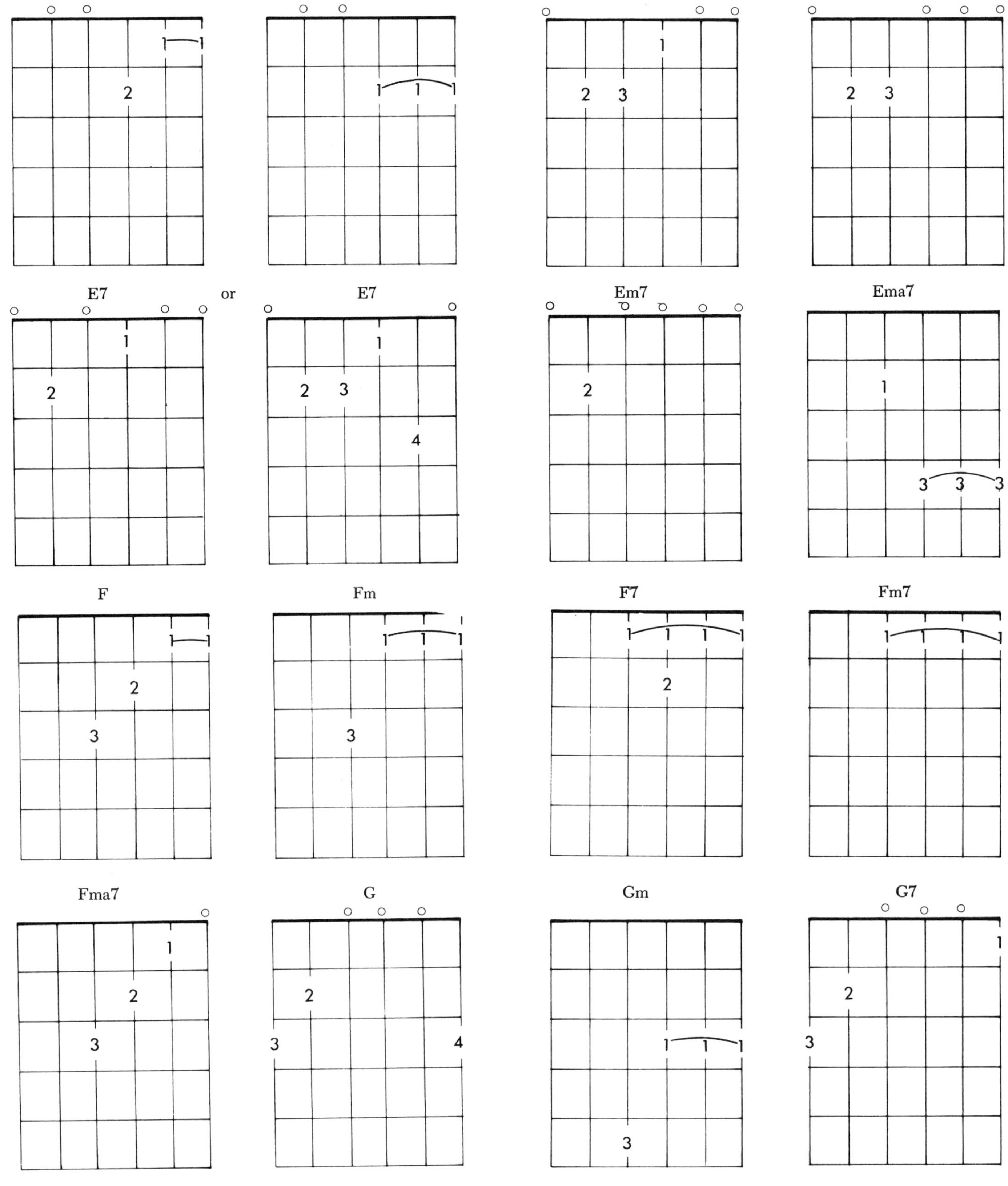
Dm7
Dma7
E
Em
E7
or
E7
Em7
Ema7
F
Fm
F7
Fm7
Fma7
G
Gm
G7

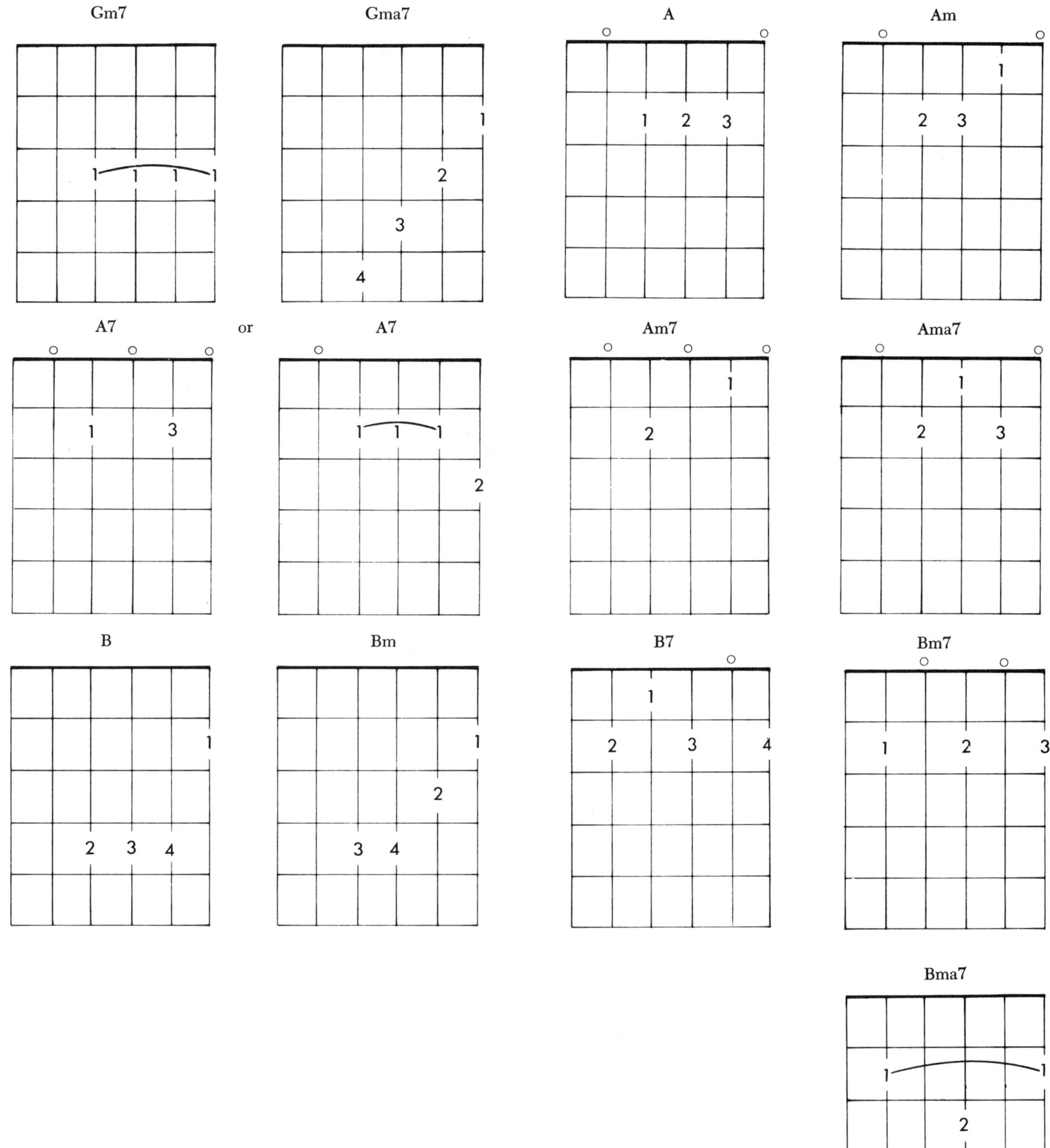
Gm7
Gma7
A
Am
A7
or
A7
Am7
Ama7
B
Bm
B7
Bm7
Bma7

Bar Chords

Form I

The curved line represents the first finger covering several strings. These forms are movable. The circled note names the chord.

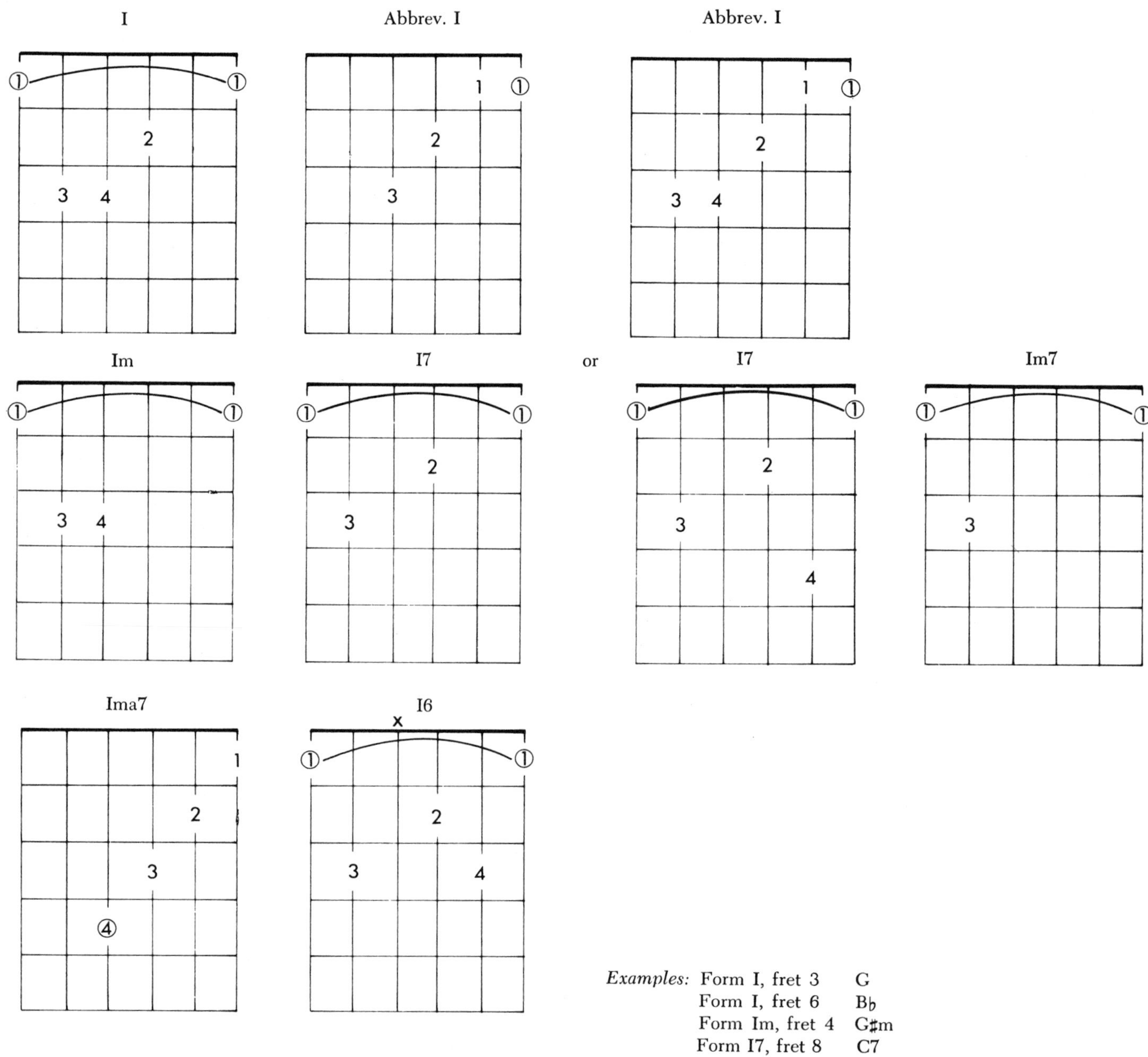

Examples: Form I, fret 3 G
Form I, fret 6 B♭
Form Im, fret 4 G♯m
Form I7, fret 8 C7

A X represents a deadened, or muted, string.

Form II

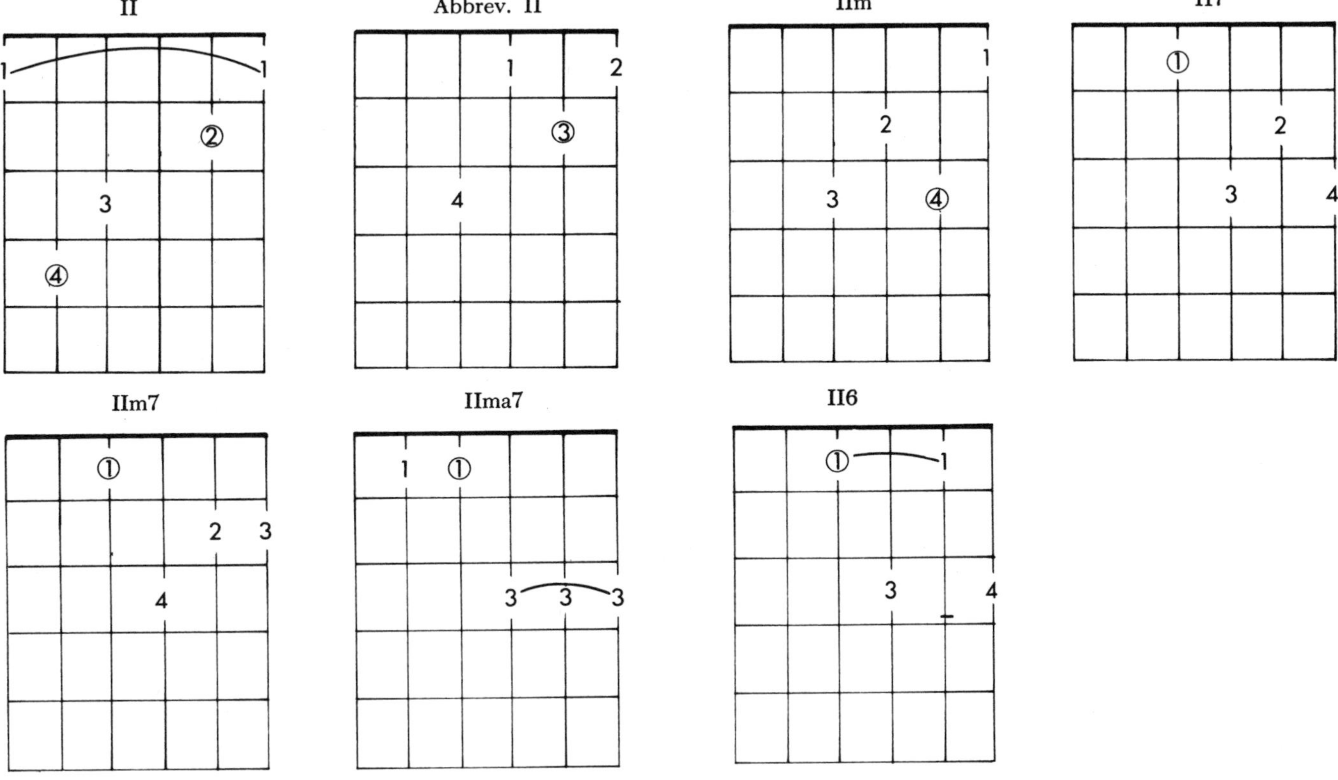

Examples: Form II, fret 3: E♭
Form IIma7, fret 5: Gma7

Form III

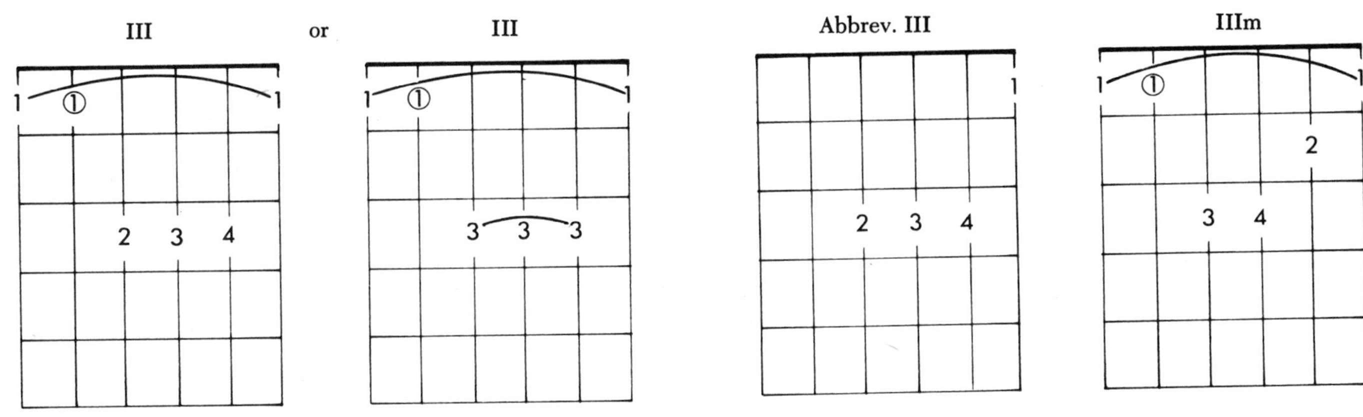

III7 or

III7

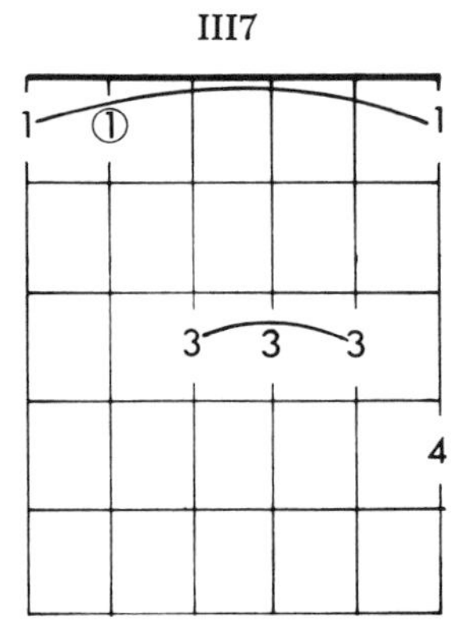

IIIm7

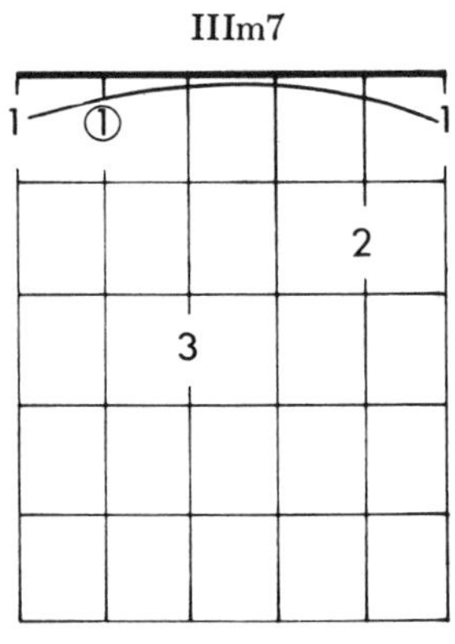

IIIma7

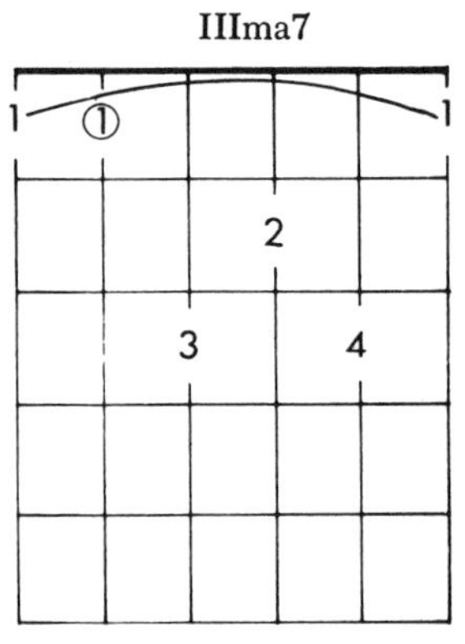

III6

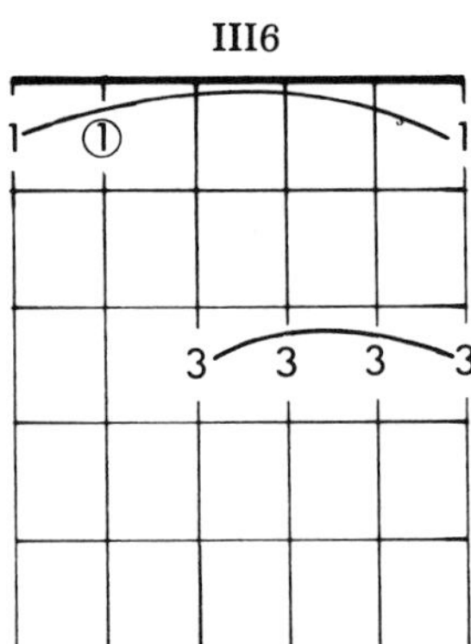

Examples: Form III, fret 3: C
Form IIIm, fret 7: Em
Form IIIma7, fret 4: C♯ma7

Naming Bar Chords

The note that names a chord is called the root. In certain chord forms, the root is located in several places. For example, in the Form I major, there are roots on strings 1, 4, and 6 (counting from right to left or treble to bass). As previously stated, at least one root is circled in each diagram.

In Form I full-bar forms, the 6th string is used to name the chord, as is the 1st. Abbreviated Form Is are usually named by string 1.

In Form IIs, notice that the location of the root varies more than the others.

Full-bar Form IIIs are most conveniently named by string 5.

Any chord may be played in several forms, or *inversions*. In other words, you can rearrange the order or pattern of the notes to achieve a certain sound or to make the chord convenient to play.

In this table, the numbered fret refers to the position of the first (barring) finger.

Fret No.:	open	1	2	3	4	5	6	7	8	9	10	11	12	13	14	15
Form I	E	F	F♯	G	G♯	A	B♭	B	C	C♯	D	E♭	E	F	F♯	G
Form II	C	C♯	D	E♭	E	F	F♯	G	G♯	A	B♭	B	C	C♯	D	E♭
Form III	A	B♭	B	C	C♯	D	E♭	E	F	F♯	G	G♯	A	B♭	B	C

Other Movable Forms

9th

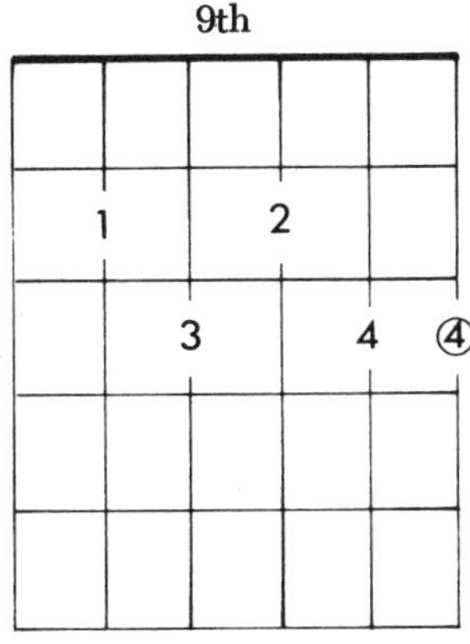

A9 on frets 4 and 5. If you move it up one fret at a time: B♭9, B9, C9, etc.

9th

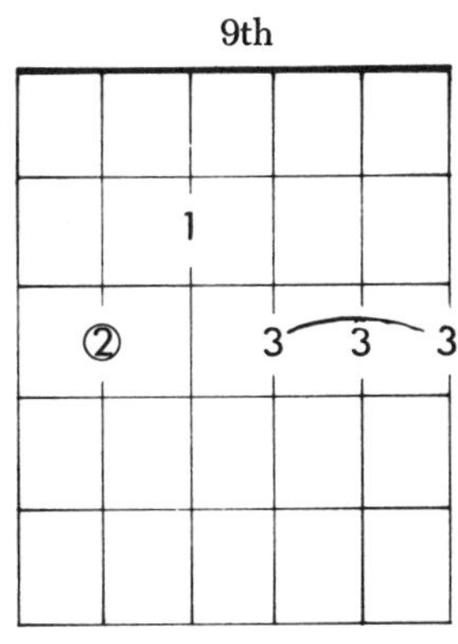

C9 with 2d finger on fret 3. One fret higher, it's C♯9; then D9, E♭9, E9, etc.

6th

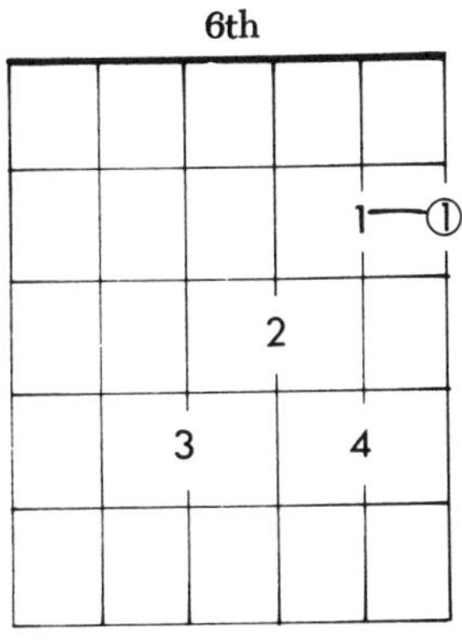

G6 on fret 3
F6 on fret 1
C6 on fret 8
E6 on fret 12, etc.

Aug. (+)

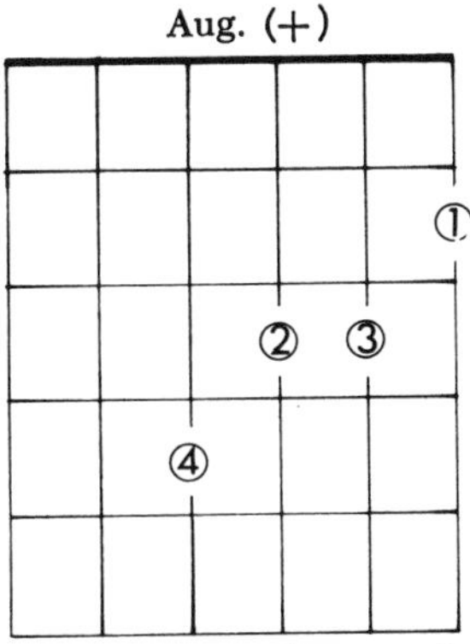

The augmented is named by every note in the chord.
Example: With 1st finger at fret 2, it's the augmented form for F♯, B♭ and D.

Dim. (°, —)

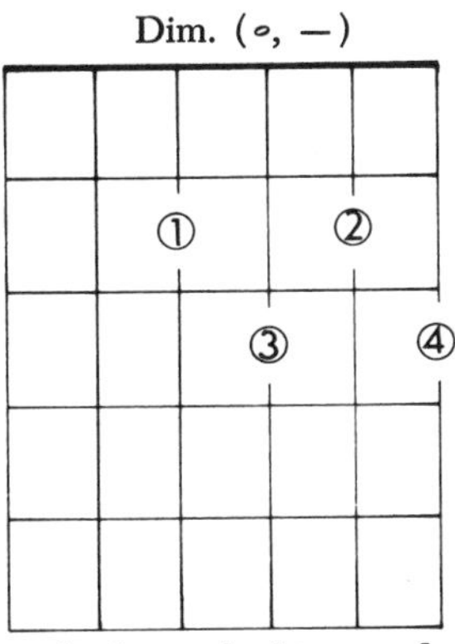

The diminished is named by every note in the chord.
Example: at fret 2 it's the diminished for E, B♭, C♯ and G.

Major add 9

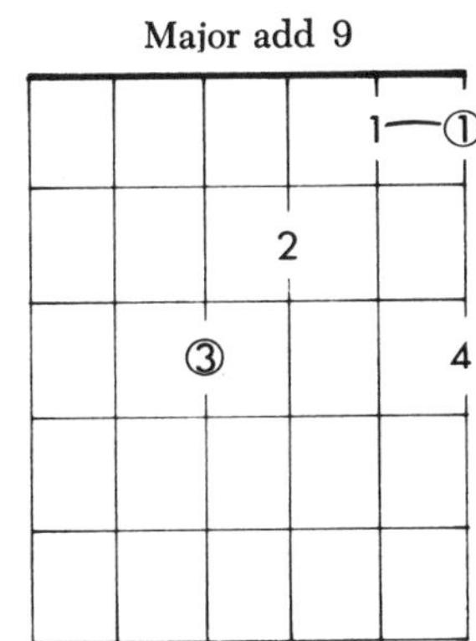

Example: With finger 1 at fret 4 it's G♯ +9.
fret 7: B +9
fret 10: D +9

m6

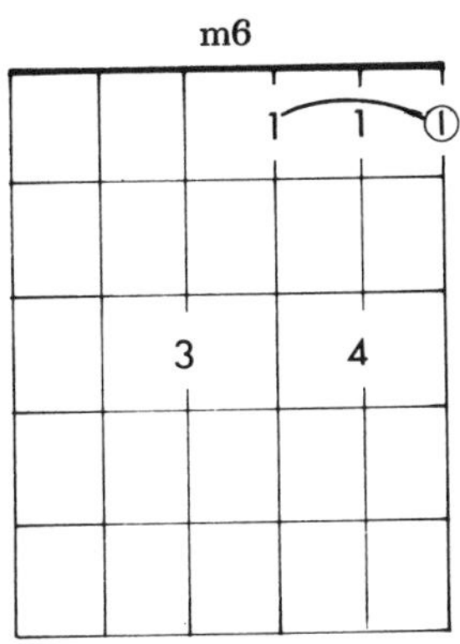

Example: at fret 6 it's B♭m6.
fret 2: F♯m6
fret 5: Am6

The Guitar Book Chord Builder

The purpose of this section is to enable you to find any chord you need or to correctly name any chords you may discover on your own. In general, each step depends upon your understanding of the previous steps. However, if you should get stuck, read ahead to the end of the section and then go back.

Chords are built from scales. A scale is a series of tones (ascending or descending) with fixed intervals between them. Each scale spans an octave.

ASCENDING →

(intervals)		2		2		1	2		2		2		1
I Diatonic Scale, Familiar Names	doh		re		mi	fa		so		la		ti	doh
II Diatonic Scale, Numbers	1(8)		2		3	4		5		6		7	8(1)
III Diatonic C Scale	C		D		E	F		G		A		B	C
IV Chromatic C Scale	C	C♯ D♭	D	D♯ E♭	E	F	F♯ G♭	G	G♯ A♭	A	A♯ B♭	B	C
V Chromatic Scale, Numbers	1(8)	♭9	2(9)	♭3	3	4(11)	♭5	5	♯5	6(13)	♭7	7	8(1)
VI Diatonic E Scale	E		F♯ G♭		G♯ A♭	A		B		C♯ D♭		D♯ E♭	E
VII Chromatic G Scale	G	G♯ A♭	A	A♯ B♭	B	C	C♯ D♭	D	D♯ E♭	E	F	F♯ G♭	G
VIII Diatonic A Scale	A		B		C♯	D		E		F♯		G♯	A

Don't be intimidated by all of the sharps, flats, notes, and numbers. It is not necessary that you learn all the notes in all the scales. It's much easier than that. Since all of the scales are based on the same arrangement, a solid grasp of chord theory requires that you understand the intervals in *one scale.* That information is found in columns II and V and will only take a few minutes to learn. The other columns are mere examples, and there is really very little in them that you need to memorize. For example, you need not know offhand that a 6th in a G scale is an E note, etc. The numbers and symbols look formidable, but if you can hum doh, re, mi, etc., you won't have much trouble with this stuff once you get into it. Take a couple of hours or so, and go through the next few pages one step at a time. You will be able to construct any chord in several positions, not because you've memorized them all (which is far too much effort), but because you understand how your guitar works.

Column I lists the common names for the familiar *diatonic* scale (doh, re, mi, etc.). These same tones are given numbers in Column II.

Check the intervals: notes 3 and 4 are always 1 fret (½ step) apart; 7 and 8(1) are also 1 fret apart. The other consecutive tones are 2 frets (whole step) apart.

Note 1 (doh) and note 8 (also doh, an octave higher) bear the same name. This note, called the root, names both the scale and the chords derived from the scale.

Column III is an example of the diatonic scale, in C. A C scale starts and ends with C; a B♭ scale starts and ends with B♭, and so on.

A note in between two consecutive alphabetical notes is called *either* a sharp or a flat. A sharp (♯) raises the named note one fret; a flat (♭) lowers it one fret. Examples: the note between D and E could be called either D♯ or E♭; the note between A and B could be called A♯ or B♭.

In Column IV, the notes in between the diatonic notes are filled in with sharps and flats. The result is the *chromatic* scale: every tone in the octave. These notes are numbered in Column V.

Several tones are sometimes designated by the corresponding number in the next highest octave. Thus: 2=9, 4=11, 6=13.

Columns VI, VII and VIII are other examples: a diatonic E scale, a chromatic G scale, and a diatonic A scale.

Chords are derived from Columns II and V, the numbered scales.

This chart arranges the scales on the fingerboard. For convenience, some of the notes are left out. The entire chromatic scale appears on string 1 (including the diatonic in bold print), and the diatonic appears on the other strings.

The frets are unnumbered, so that the following discussion can be applied to *any* scale and chord. To work with a B scale or any of the B chords (B, B minor, B7, and so on), begin the scale with note #1 (doh) at B. For the A scale or A chords, begin with note #1 (doh) at A, and so on. Try playing a few scales, up and down one string and across the fingerboard.

A chord is a certain combination of tones, selected from a scale. Each type of chord (major, 9th, ma7 and so on) has its own formula.

Here is a list of chords & formulas:

Major	1	3	5*			
Minor (m)	1	♭3	5			
Dominant 7th or 7th (7)	1	3	5	♭7		
Major 7th (ma7)	1	3	5	7		
Minor 7th (m7)	1	♭3	5	♭7		
Augmented (Aug., or +)	1	3	#5			
Diminished 7th (°)	1	♭3	♭5	♭♭7(6)		
Major 6th (6)	1	3	5	6		
9th (9)	1	3	5	♭7	9	
11th (11)	1	3	5	♭7	9	11
13th (13)	1	3	5	♭7	9	13
Suspended or Suspended 4th (Sus., 4, or Sus. 4)	1	4	5			
Major add 9 (+9)	1	3	5	9		

Many other chords reveal their formulas in the names. Examples:

Minor 9th (m9)	1	♭3	5	♭7	9	
Major 6/9th (6/9)	1	3	5	6	9	
Minor 11th (m11)	1	♭3	5	♭7	9	11

According to the scale in Column V, several notes have two names:

2(9); 4(11); 6(13)

In constructing a chord, either of the two names may be used. Thus,

1 3 5 ♭7 13 = 1 3 5 6 ♭7

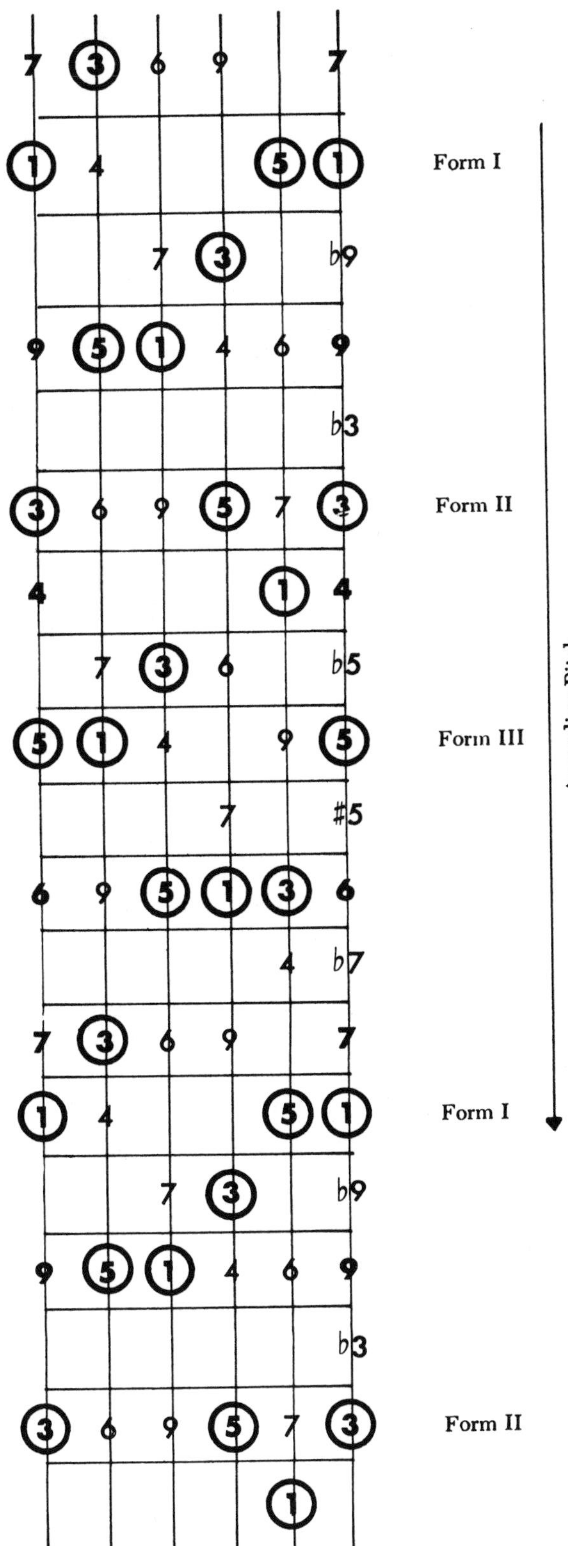

Fingerboard Diagram: Scale Tones

*The circled 1s, 3s and 5s on the fingerboard diagram comprise the various forms for playing a major chord.

To get your bearings, notice the F shape of the Form I (near the top of the page), and the triangular arrangement of the open D shape a few frets above that. (If you're lost, the "Ascending Pitch" arrow at the far right will remind you which way is up.) Further up, observe the three notes lined up in a row (5, 1, 3) on the same fret, as in an open A chord. Can you locate other familiar chord shapes? They are all there. A couple of hints: the E shape is part of the Form I; to find C, locate note 1 on strings 2 and 5, counting from right to left.

Note: in order to keep the diagram on p. 329 from becoming cluttered, many of the frets are left blank. It's easy to figure out the number of any position on the fingerboard. *All* of the numbers along string 1 are given, and the other strings work the same way. For example, a ♭5 is always found between notes 4 and 5; ♭7 is between 6 and 7 and so on.

Using the formulas in conjunction with the diagram sometimes requires that you determine and locate the note that names the chord, or *root*. Avoid a common mistake: if a chord has a sharp or a flat in its name, then *the root of that chord MUST include that sharp or flat*. Examples: the root of an E chord is an E note. The root of an E7 is also E. But the root of an E♭ chord is E♭ (not E). The root of C♯m7 is C♯ (not C). The root of F♯9 is F♯ (not F), etc.

1 5 1
3
5 1

The notes within a formula may be played in any order. Each pattern or arrangement is called an *inversion* of the chord. Example: compare the various inversions for a major chord—Forms I, II and III. They're circled on the fingerboard diagram.

How to Read the Formulas:

Major = 1 3 5

The C chord consists of the 1st (doh), 3rd (mi) and 5th (so) tones in the C Scale:

Diatonic C Scale:

(C)	D	(E)	F	(G)	A	B	C
(1)	2(9)	(3)	4(11)	(5)	6(13)	7	8

Therefore, a C chord consists of the notes C, E and G. Likewise, an F♯ chord consists of the 1st, 3rd and 5th tones in the F♯ scale (F♯, B♭, C♯).

The 7th chord = 1 3 5 ♭7

The D7 chord = 1, 3, 5 and ♭7 in the D scale:

Chromatic D Scale:

(D)	D♯ E♭	E	F	(F♯ G♭)	G	G♯ A♭	(A)	A♯ B♭	B	(C)	C♯ D♭	D
(1)	♭9	2(9)	♭3	(3)	4(11)	♭5	(5)	♯5	6(13)	(♭7)	7	8(1)

Therefore, the D7 chord = D, F♯, A, and C.

The G7 chord = 1, 3, 5, ♭7 in the G scale: G, B, D, and F.

How to Apply the Formulas to the Fingerboard:

Chord theory often seems a lot harder than it really is. To keep from getting bogged down, *work with numbers* and with doh, re, mi, etc., not with alphabetical names (A, B♭, etc.). The numbers may be instantly applied to any scale or chord, while the letter names change from scale to scale or chord to chord. Understanding chord theory does not require memorizing the entire fingerboard—far from it. About the only things you need to memorize are the intervals in the diatonic scale and the arrangement of scale tones in a couple of major bar-chord forms. When constructing chords, you'll make things much easier on yourself (and develop your ear) if you hum or think of the appropriate notes in the scale. Remember, the note that names the chord is your starting point: doh. Example: to construct Am7, the scale begins with doh at A.

Here is the arrangement of scale tones in a Form I major bar chord. Pick a starting point, then hum the scale (doh, re, mi, etc.), matching the 1s (doh), 3s (mi) and 5s (so) to the diagram.

Find each of these chords on the diagram on p. 329. *Important:* observe the location of *every* note in each chord diagram, *including open strings.* For example, the C chord has five notes, not just three.

The C is a Form II that overlaps into the Form III area. The A and the Am are Form IIIs. The E7 is a Form I.

C (1 3 5)

A (1 3 5)

Am (1 ♭3 5)

E7 (1 3 5 ♭7)

In these pairs of diagrams, compare the fingering (*left*) to the form or arrangement of the scale tones (*right*); note the scale numbers of the open strings:

Fingering

Scale Tones

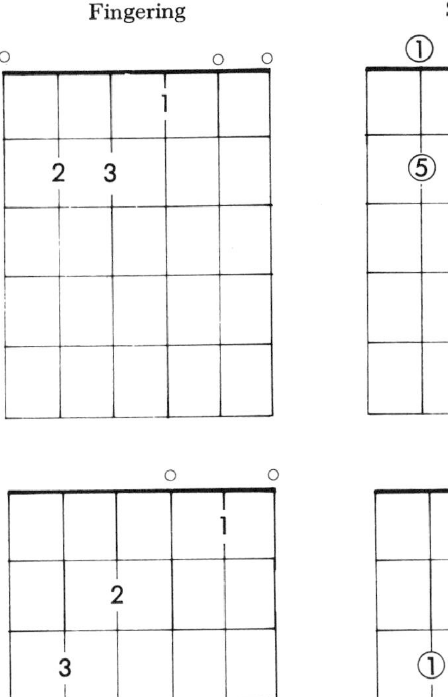

compare forms

More complex examples:

According to the chord diagram on p. 327, an A9 chord may be played on frets 4 and 5 in this form: According to the formula, A9 = 1 3 5 ♭7 9 of the A scale. By checking the scale number of each of these notes on the fingerboard diagram, you'll see that the formula is matched. In getting started, the best reference is always the root of the chord: note 1. Notice that in this case, note 1 (A) is on the 1st string.

Fingers

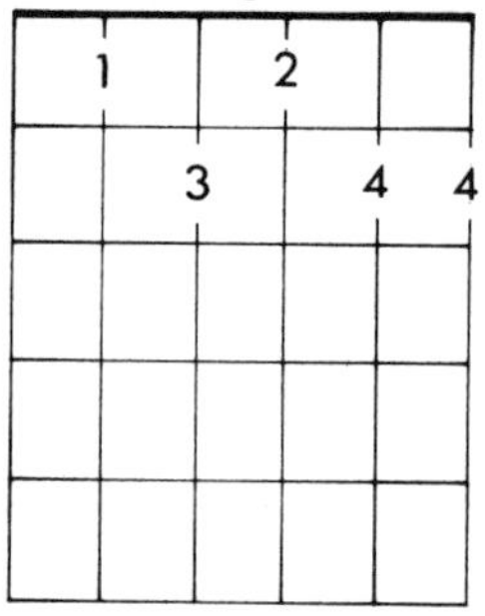

1 2
3 4 4

Scale Numbers

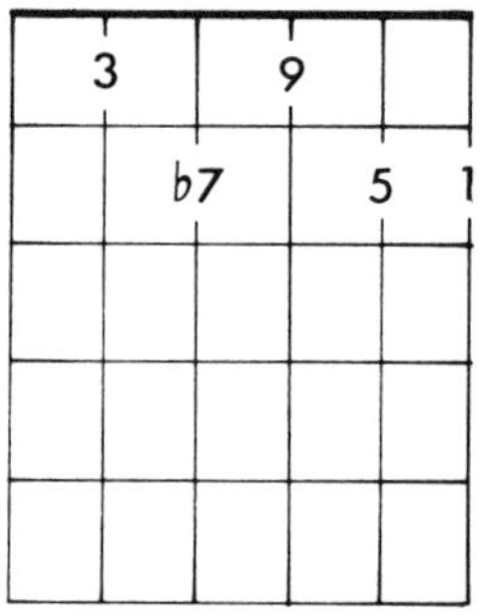

3 9
♭7 5 1

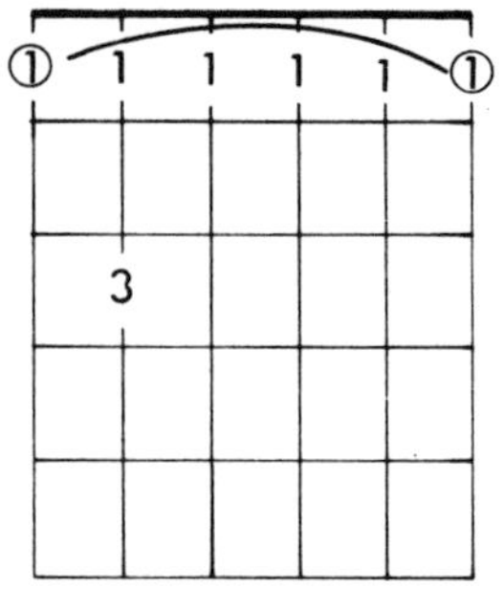

① 1 1 1 1 ①
3

Fingers

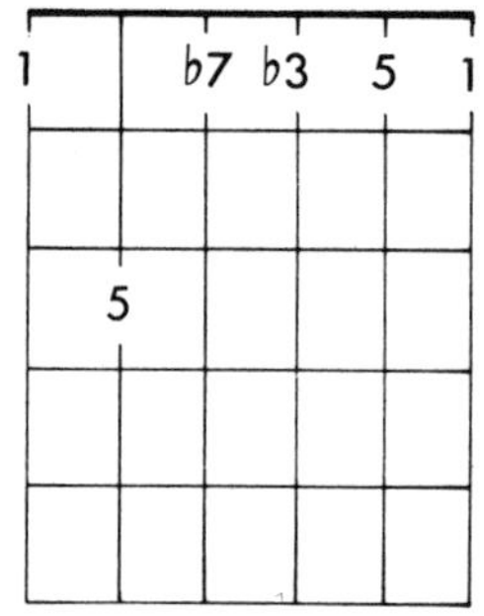

1 ♭7 ♭3 5 1
5

Scale Numbers

By superimposing the unnamed chord (*far left*) on the fingerboard diagram, the scale numbers are revealed (*left*).

In ascending order, this formula is 1 ♭3 5 ♭7. Look up the formula; it's a minor 7th chord, named by the root, note #1. (For instance, at fret 9, it's C♯m7; at fret 5, it's Am7; at fret 2, it's F♯m7.)

The formulas and fingerboard diagram may be used together to solve several kinds of problems, including: (1) you are given the name of a chord and need to figure out how to play it; or (2) you discover a chord on your guitar and you want to determine its correct name.

The first problem is often solved by starting with a familiar chord that closely resembles the chord you need, and then modifying it to match the formula. Example: Suppose you needed an A6. Look at the formula for a major 6 and compare it to the major. They are identical except for the 6. So you need not construct a chord from the ground up—just play an A chord in any form (you know that it will take care of the 1, 3, and 5), and use the fingerboard diagram to locate a convenient 6. Add the 6.

Another example: Cma7. Compare the formulas for a major and a major 7. Any plain C chord will take care of most of the notes (1, 3, 5); all you need to do is add a 7. Try an open C chord. Find it on the fingerboard diagram. Notice that your first finger is on a 1, and that you can drop it to the 7 merely by lifting that finger. (There is another note 1 on the 5th string, so the chord still has a root.) Now change a Form I C and a Form III C into Cma7s.

A handy rule: *Find the chord which you already know that most closely resembles the chord you are looking for.* Use the formulas if necessary. Another example: Suppose you need an m9. If you already know how to play either a 9 or a m7, you only need to worry about one note. Compare those formulas to the m9. Play the m9 either by modifying a convenient 9 or m7.

Notice that in solving this type of problem, you consult the *formulas* first to determine which scale notes you need, then the fingerboard diagram, to locate those notes.

Suppose you make up a chord on the guitar and you wish to name it. The same principles apply. First, determine the chord you already know that *most closely resembles* the new one and go from there. Example:

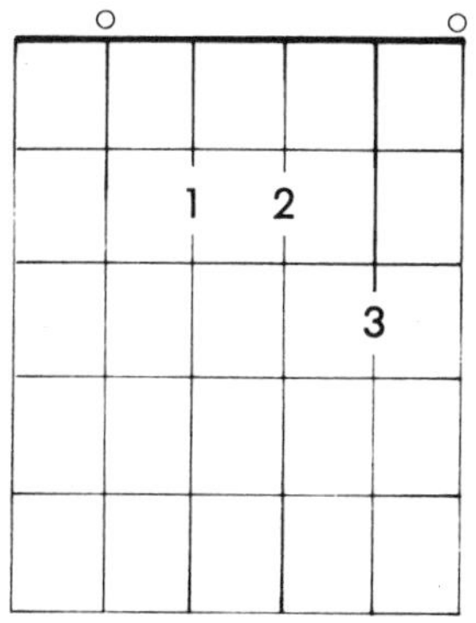

This chord most closely resembles an open A. The fingerboard diagram tells you that the odd note is a 4 in the scale. The formulas tell you that the chord is called a "suspended 4th."

Notice the difference between solving this type of problem and the previous ones. Here, you are consulting the fingerboard *diagram* first, to see what group of numbers you are playing, then the formulas in order to name that group.

Many basic chords and bar chords appear in previous pages. You could gain a thorough understanding of the fingerboard by matching *them* to the fingerboard diagram. Since there are only a few basic forms, each one of which accounts for dozens of chords, your task is simpler than it may first appear. (If you have trouble, remember that the note that names the chord —the root—will always be a 1 on the fingerboard. *Locate the 1, and the others will fall into place.*)

Index

Illustration credits are listed by page numbers; all other illustrations courtesy of J. Richard Forbes for the original edition, the author for the revised edition.

vii The Metropolitan Museum of Art, The Crosby Brown Collection of Musical Instruments, 1889
xvi ABC/Dunhill Records. Photo by Kriegsmann
1 The Metropolitan Museum of Art, Bequest of Benjamin Altman, 1913
3 The Metropolitan Museum of Art, The Crosby Brown Collection of Musical Instruments, 1889
4 *Top:* The Metropolitan Museum of Art, The Crosby Brown Collection of Musical Instruments, 1889
4 *Bottom:* The Metropolitan Museum of Art, Gift of Alice E. Getty, 1946
5 The Metropolitan Museum of Art, The Crosby Brown Collection of Musical Instruments, 1889
6 The Metropolitan Museum of Art, Gift of the Estate of Mary Flagler Cary, 1969
7 *Top:* The Metropolitan Museum of Art, The Crosby Brown Collection of Musical Instruments, 1889
7 *Bottom:* Walecki Collection
8 The Metropolitan Museum of Art, Gift of Miss Alice Getty, 1946
9 The Metropolitan Museum of Art, The Crosby Brown Collection of Musical Instruments, 1889
10 Sol Hurok Concerts, Inc.
11 Courtesy Les Paul
12 *Top:* Courtesy Marjorie Guthrie
13 Photos this page courtesy of Country Music Foundation, Nashville
14 *Bottom:* RCA Records
15 Culver Pictures, Inc.
16 *Bottom:* RCA Records
20 *Bottom:* ABC/Dunhill Records
22 RSO Records and Tapes
23 Jeffrey Okun
24 *Top:* Capricorn/Warner Bros.
Bottom: CBS
25 *Top:* Photo courtesy Mildred White
26 Adapted by Gerry Kano from a drawing by Petruccelli; projected by Chico Taylor; Courtesy *Guitar Review*
46-50 Bret Lopez
51 *Top left:* Bret Lopez
Bottom right: Bret Lopez
54 Paul Stull
53 *Bottom:* Fred Walecki
55 *Top left:* Paul Stull
Bottom left: Paul Stull
56 *Right:* Paul Stull
57 *Left:* Paul Stull
59 Paul Stull
60-61 C. F. Martin & Co.
62 CBS Musical Instruments
67 Jeffrey Okun
70 *Bottom:* Ward C. Morgan Studio
93 *Bottom:* Leo Fender
94 Photo by Leo Fender
96 *Top:* Fender Musical Instruments
Bottom: Photo by Robert Perine
98 Fender Musical Instruments
107 *Bottom left:* Fender Musical Instruments
114 *Upper right:* Viellette-Citron Guitars
116 *Lower left:* Photography by Jim R. Hall
121 *Bottom:* Drawing by Gerry Kano
122 Drawing by Mike McDonald
143 *Lower right:* Courtesy Jol Dantzig
161 *Bottom:* Harold A. Jacobs Company, Inc./Advertising
162 *Top:* Chrysalis. Photo by Robert Ellis
163 *Top left:* Jeffrey Okun
Bottom left: John Tutora
Top right: Capricorn Records
Bottom right: Atlantic Records
166 *Top:* Stax Records
Bottom: Chess Records
186 Drawing by Gerry Kano
195 *Top:* Capitol Records
Bottom: Warner Brothers
200-202 Drawings by Gerry Kano
209 *Top:* Fender Musical Instruments
213 *Top:* Fender Musical Instruments
Extreme Bottom: Drawings by Gerry Kano
218 *Top:* Ward C. Morgan Studio
221 Robert C. Cleveland
236 Howard Reinlieb
240 Adapted by Gerry Kano from *Electric Guitar Amplifier Handbook* (Howard W. Sams & Co., Inc., The Bobbs-Merrill Co., Inc.) by Jack Darr
241 *Bottom:* Photograph by George E. Ernst
242 *Bottom:* Harlan A. Bourdon & Assoc.
246 *Top left:* Dallas Music Industries
255 Drawing by Gerry Kano
258 Drawings by Gerry Kano
260 *Bottom:* James B. Lansing Sound, Inc.
261 James B. Lansing Sound, Inc.
262 Drawing by Gerry Kano
290 *Bottom:* Dan J. McCoy
301 Peavey Electronics
303 *Top:* Peavey Electronics